Memory, Migration and Travel

Migration and forcible displacement are growing and impactful dynamics of the current global age. These processes generate mobility flows, travel patterns and touristic behaviour driven by personal and collective memories. The chapters in this book highlight the importance of travel and tourism for enabling such memories and memory-based identity practices to unfold.

This book investigates how diasporic communities, transnational migrants, refugees and the internally displaced recreate home in their host place of residence through material culture, performativity and social relations; and how involuntary tangible and intangible stimuli evoke memories of home. It explores an array of diverse geographical contexts, balancing ethnographic vignettes of contemporary migrant societies with archival research providing historical accounts that reach back more than a century.

Memory, Migration and Travel makes an original contribution by linking the emergent field of memory studies to the disciplines of tourism and migration/diaspora studies, and will be of interest to students and researchers in the fields of tourism, geography, migration/diaspora studies, anthropology and sociology.

Sabine Marschall is Professor of Cultural and Heritage Tourism (School of Social Sciences) at the University of KwaZulu-Natal, Durban, South Africa.

Contemporary Geographies of Leisure, Tourism and Mobility
Series Editor: C. Michael Hall, Professor at the Department of Management, College of Business and Economics, University of Canterbury, Christchurch, New Zealand

The aim of this series is to explore and communicate the intersections and relationships between leisure, tourism and human mobility within the social sciences.

It will incorporate both traditional and new perspectives on leisure and tourism from contemporary geography, e.g. notions of identity, representation and culture, while also providing for perspectives from cognate areas such as anthropology, cultural studies, gastronomy and food studies, marketing, policy studies and political economy, regional and urban planning, and sociology, within the development of an integrated field of leisure and tourism studies.

Also, increasingly, tourism and leisure are regarded as steps in a continuum of human mobility. Inclusion of mobility in the series offers the prospect to examine the relationship between tourism and migration, the sojourner, educational travel, and second home and retirement travel phenomena.

The series comprises two strands:

Contemporary Geographies of Leisure, Tourism and Mobility aims to address the needs of students and academics, and the titles will be published in hardback and paperback. Titles include:

Co-Creating Tourism Research
Towards Collaborative Ways of Knowing
Edited by Carina Ren, Gunnar Thór Jóhannesson and René van der Duim

Routledge Studies in Contemporary Geographies of Leisure, Tourism and Mobility is a forum for innovative new research intended for research students and academics, and the titles will be available in hardback only. Titles include:

Negotiating Hospitality
Ethics of Tourism Development in the Nicaraguan Highlands
Emily Höckert

For more information about this series, please visit: www.routledge.com/ Contemporary-Geographies-of-Leisure-Tourism-and-Mobility/book-series/ SE0522.

Memory, Migration and Travel

Edited by Sabine Marschall

Routledge
Taylor & Francis Group

LONDON AND NEW YORK

First published 2018 by Routledge

2 Park Square, Milton Park, Abingdon, Oxon OX14 4RN
605 Third Avenue, New York, NY 10017

Routledge is an imprint of the Taylor & Francis Group, an informa business

First issued in paperback 2022

Publisher's Note

The publisher has gone to great lengths to ensure the quality of this reprint but points out that some imperfections in the original copies may be apparent.

British Library Cataloguing-in-Publication Data
A catalogue record for this book is available from the British Library

Library of Congress Cataloging-in-Publication Data
A catalog record has been requested for this book

ISBN: 978-1-138-74644-2 (hbk)
ISBN: 978-1-03-233909-2 (pbk)
DOI: 10.4324/9781315180465

Typeset in Times New Roman
by Swales & Willis Ltd, Exeter, Devon, UK

Contents

List of figures   vii
Notes on contributors   viii
Acknowledgements   xii

1 Memory, migration and travel: introduction   1
SABINE MARSCHALL

2 'Travelling memories': the homemaking practices of skilled
mobile settlers   24
ROSIE ROBERTS

3 Material culture, memory and commemoration: family and
community celebrations and connections to 'home' among
Asian Indian immigrants   45
CAROLINE B. BRETTELL

4 Remembrance, cultural performance and travel: the Greek migrants
of Brasilia and the *panigiri* festival   66
STYLIANOS KOSTAS

5 Gallipoli revisited: transnational and transgenerational memory
among Turkish and Sikh communities in Australia   85
BURCU CEVIK-COMPIEGNE AND JOSEF PLONER

6 'To live in France': the confluence of tourism, memory, migration
and war   104
BERTRAM M. GORDON

7 Pajouste Forest, 23 August 1941: memory, migration and massacre   125
ARON MAZEL

8 Old homes made new: American Jews travelling to Eastern Europe
   from 1920 to the present   146
   OSKAR CZENDZE AND JASON FRANCISCO

9 The Macanese *Encontros*: remembrance in diaspora 'homecomings'   170
   MARIANA PINTO LEITÃO PEREIRA

10 Dinner in the homeland: memory, food and the Armenian diaspora   189
   CAREL BERTRAM

11 Memoryscapes of the homeland by two generations of
   British Bangladeshis   213
   MD FARID MIAH AND RUSSELL KING

12 Translocal narratives of memory, place and belonging:
   second-generation Turkish-Germans' home-making upon
   'return' to Turkey   234
   NILAY KILINÇ AND RUSSELL KING

13 Conclusion   256
   SABINE MARSCHALL

   Index   267

Figures

3.1   Statue of Ganesh, Indian wedding   51

3.2   Gandhi Memorial Plaza, Irving, Texas   57

7.1   A single page from the 'Report on mass murder of 1 December 1941 by the Commander-in-Chief of the SS Security Police and the Security Service in Kovno, SS-Standartenführer (SS-Colonel) Dr. Karl Jäger'   128

7.2   The author's father and grandparents in Dvinsk, in 1937   130

7.3   The author and his daughter, Nicola, at the Pajouste Forest murder site on 23 August 2011   135

7.4   Road sign to the Pajouste Forest massacre site   138

7.5   Pajouste Forest massacre site   139

8.1   Julius Blackman during his visit to Petroverovka (Zhovten) in the Soviet Union, 1932   151

10.1   Sona eats 'hatz', the bread of her grandmother's village   190

10.2   The Gözüküçükyan House, Antep   194

10.3   Pilgrims eating 'Armenian food' at a Turkish restaurant   203

12.1   Jewellery shop in Antalya owned by a Turkish-German returnee   241

Contributors

Carel Bertram is faculty in Middle East and Islamic Studies and an Associate Professor of Humanities at San Francisco State University. Her interest in the connections between memory and place led to *Imagining the Turkish House: Collective Visions of Home* (University of Texas, 2008), a book on how the Ottoman half-timbered house became an icon of a disappearing Ottoman past in an emerging Republic of Turkey. Her current work returns to the end of the Ottoman period to uncover the nature of the memories of houses lost by Armenians and Assyrians and other minorities during that tumultuous era.

Caroline B. Brettell is University Distinguished Professor of Anthropology and Ruth Collins Altshuler Director of the Dedman College Interdisciplinary Institute at Southern Methodist University. She has spent her career studying immigration in Europe, Canada and the United States. Her particular interests are in gender and migration, identity and citizenship, and immigrants in cities. In addition to numerous journal articles and book chapters, she is the author, co-author or editor/co-editor of 17 books. Her most recent books are *Gender and Migration* (2016) and *Identity and the Second Generation* (co-edited with Faith Nibbs) (2016). She has recently been elected to the American Academy of Arts and Sciences.

Burcu Cevik-Compiegne completed her first BA in English Language, Literature and Civilisation and then in History at Aix-Marseille University, France. She undertook Master's Research on the commemoration of Gallipoli in Australia, New Zealand and Turkey from a comparative perspective before moving to Australia where she obtained her PhD at the University of Technology Sydney. She is currently a Research Associate at UTS, working on a monograph based on her thesis entitled 'Empire and War: Indian and Turkish Experiences and Remembrance of the First World War'.

Oskar Czendze is a PhD student in the History Department and at the Carolina Center for Jewish Studies at the University of North Carolina, Chapel Hill. He received his MA (History) and his BEd (German, History) from the University of Augsburg, Germany. In 2015–16, he spent a graduate exchange year in the

History Department at Emory University. His research interests include modern Jewish history, Central and Eastern European history, transnationalism, and cultural and memory studies.

Jason Francisco is an acclaimed artist, essayist, curator and educator. Widely exhibited nationally and internationally, he is the author of *Far from Zion: Jews, Diaspora, Memory* (Stanford University Press, 2006), *The Steerage and Alfred Stieglitz*, co-authored with Anne McCauley (University of California Press, 2012), *An Unfinished Memory* (Galicia Jewish Museum, Kraków, 2014), as well as numerous photoworks, articles, reviews and artist's books. At Emory University, Francisco is Associate Professor in Photography Studies in the Department of Film and Media Studies.

Bertram M. Gordon, Professor of European History at Mills College in Oakland, California, is General Secretary of the International Commission for the History of Travel and Tourism. He serves on the *Journal of Tourism History* editorial board and as H-Travel Internet co-editor. He was Chercheur associé étranger at the Institut d'Histoire du Temps Présent, CNRS, in France and is currently a core member of the University of California Berkeley Tourism Studies Working Group. A specialist in modern French history, he has written on French collaboration with Germany during World War II, the 1968 French student revolt and French food history. His book, *War Tourism: Second World War France from Defeat and Occupation to the Creation of Heritage*, will be published by Cornell University Press in 2018.

Nilay Kılınç has recently completed her PhD at the University of Surrey, working on the return migration of the Turkish-German second generation to the tourist regions of southern Turkey. Following her Master's degree in European Studies at Lund University, she worked as a research assistant for Malmö University, Erasmus University Rotterdam and the University of Surrey. Kılınç currently holds a Pontica Magna Fellow position at New Europe College Bucharest and is researching the deportation of the Turkish second generation from Germany to Turkey and their social reintegration through tourism-related careers.

Russell King is Professor of Geography at the University of Sussex and Visiting Professor of Migration Studies at Malmö University. He has wideranging interests in migration, mobility and diaspora studies. His recent book, joint with Anastasia Christou, is entitled *Counter-Diaspora: The Greek Second Generation Returns 'Home'* (Harvard University Press, 2014). He has directed several large-scale projects on migration, including research on diasporic return migration, international student migration, international retirement migration, migration and development, and intra-European youth migration. From 2000 to 2012 he was Editor of the *Journal of Ethnic and Migration Studies*.

Stylianos Kostas is a political scientist from Greece, specializing in the fields of migration, asylum, security and border management, who presently works for the UNHCR in Kinshasa, DRC. He holds a Master's in Democratic Governance, Democracy and Human Rights in the MENA Region, from the European Inter-University Centre for Human Rights and Democratisation (EIUC) in Venice, Italy, and a Master's in European Studies from the LUISS Guido Carli University in Rome, Italy. He previously worked for the Greek Ministry of Interior, the Greek Diplomatic Mission in Tehran, Iran and as researcher-advisor at the Brazilian National Committee for Refugees. His publications include 'The Development of a Common European Immigration Policy' (*Journal of Identity and Migration Studies*, 2017) and *Morocco's Triple Role in the Euro-African Migration System* (Middle East Institute, 2017).

Sabine Marschall is Professor of Cultural and Heritage Tourism (School of Social Sciences) at the University of KwaZulu-Natal, Durban (South Africa). She holds a PhD from the Eberhardt-Karls-University in Tübingen (Germany) and has published widely in the fields of South African art and architecture; commemoration and cultural heritage; and tourism and migrant return journeys with a particular emphasis on issues of memory. Her last book, *Tourism and Memories of Home* (Channel View), was published in 2017.

Aron Mazel is a Reader in Heritage Studies in Media, Culture, Heritage (MCH) at Newcastle University and a Research Associate in the School of Geography, Archaeology and Environmental Sciences (GAES) at the University of the Witwatersrand. Mazel had a 25-year career in archaeological research and heritage and museum management in South Africa before moving to the United Kingdom in 2002. Posts he held in SA and the UK have included Assistant Director of the Natal Museum (1994–7), Director of the South African Cultural History Museum (1998–2002) and Director of the International Centre for Cultural and Heritage Studies, Newcastle University (2012–15). His research and publication career in SA and the UK has included archaeological investigations, museum and archaeology histories, digital heritage, and the safeguarding and interpretation of tangible and intangible cultural heritage.

Md Farid Miah is a PhD candidate in Human Geography at the University of Sussex. He did his Bachelor studies at the University of Dhaka, followed by an MBA from Cardiff Metropolitan University and an MSc in Tourism from the University of Sunderland. Currently he is researching his PhD in Migration Studies at the University of Sussex, on VFR (visiting friends and relatives) mobilities within the Bangladeshi diaspora, based on fieldwork in London and Bangladesh. On a broader research front, he is interested in exploring relationships between migration and tourism.

Mariana Pinto Leitão Pereira was born and raised in Macau (China). After graduating with a Bachelor's and a Master's Degree in Archaeology (Porto, Portugal), and with a second Master's in World Heritage Studies (Cottbus, Germany), Pereira worked as an archaeologist and heritage expert for the Cultural Affairs Bureau of the Government of Macau (SAR) between 2014 and 2016. She is currently undertaking an MPhil in Archaeology – Heritage Studies and Museums at the University of Cambridge, and preparing her way to a PhD. Among her various projects, she has presented and published on safeguarding and transmitting endangered languages in the diaspora context, as well as on the challenges and opportunities surrounding heritage preservation and interpretation.

Josef Ploner is Lecturer in International Education at the Faculty of Arts, Cultures and Education (FACE) at the University of Hull, UK. Interdisciplinary in scope, Ploner's academic portfolio features an MA in Cultural Anthropology (University of Vienna) and a PhD in Tourism and Heritage Studies (Leeds Beckett University). Ploner's research focuses on international educational mobilities and discourses around diversity, inclusion and transformation in inter- and transnational higher education. His other main area of expertise encompasses travel, tourism and heritage as forms of learning, ideological contest and memory formation. Ploner is Co-Editor of the *Journal of Tourism and Cultural Change*.

Rosie Roberts is Lecturer in Cultural Studies at the University of South Australia. Using processes of narrative inquiry, her work focuses on the intersections of culture, identity, mobility and belonging. Her research expands upon labour-centred constructions of skilled migration to explore the complex mobility pathways, connections and stories that reflect the continuum of migration experiences over time and through space.

Acknowledgements

My greatest thanks is owed to all the contributors of this volume, many of whom I have only met virtually. Not only has their scholarly expertise shaped the content of this book, but most of them also wrote from a position of personal experience as (frequently travelling) members of diasporic communities. I deeply appreciate the effort, patience and excellent cooperation on behalf of all the contributors, but most especially I want to highlight the enthusiasm displayed by several 'young' academics, who tirelessly worked on improving their chapters. Sincere gratitude is also due to all those, near and far, who contributed their time and expertise to the double-blind peer review of all the individual chapters in this volume. They have been a source of sharp scrutiny and healthy scepticism, constructive criticism and useful suggestions that have shaped the authors' revisions. Institutional support for this project came from the University of KwaZulu-Natal, notably the School of Social Sciences. I am especially grateful for having been granted a sabbatical during the second semester of 2016 which enabled me to spend time on the conceptualization and exploration phase of this book. Lastly, I am indebted to the production team at Routledge and most notably, the editorial assistant, Carlotta Fanton.

1 Memory, migration and travel

Introduction

Sabine Marschall

But can anyone ever truly return to the land of one's memory?

Or is remembering the only form that such return can be actualized?

(Um, 2012: 845)

'Migrants' has become a buzz word of our current global age, often dominating the news; changing societies, economies and the nation state; affecting the familiar look of our urban environments and social worlds. Compared to the highly visible and contentious dynamic of forced displacement and economic migration – refugees and asylum-seekers fleeing war and persecution; natural and human-made disaster; poverty and lack of economic opportunities – the equally prominent phenomenon of life-style or 'elite' migration draws far less media attention. Well-educated professionals emanating from privileged spaces in the Global North pursue career opportunities abroad; second home-owners divide their time between home and their dream place of leisure; retirees relocate to more comfortable climates or the 'pleasure periphery', sometimes following family members already established there. All over the world, people who have the means move temporarily or permanently to the destination of their choice for health reasons; on religious missions or spiritual quests; to marry, study or spend a 'gap year'; to pursue personal goals and eccentric passions. Neat divisions between forced and voluntary forms of resettlement are blurred where a complex combination of push and pull factors, compulsion and choice influences migrants in their decision to move ('mixed migration'; see Van Hear, 2010).

Clear distinction between asylum-seekers, diasporic communities, displaced people, emigrants, evacuees, exiles, expatriates, expellees, foreign students, guest workers, immigrants, migrants, refugees, settlers, sojourners and transnationals is rendered more complex by the subjective meanings attached to these terms. We frequently note disjuncture between self-identification and official classification, emic and etic perspectives (see Roberts in this volume). From the viewpoint of host nations, for instance, 'economic migrants' have largely chosen to come in search of economic betterment, while they may see themselves as refugees fleeing poverty. Those emigrating in response to dramatic political changes in their home country (e.g. the end of colonialism) may identify themselves as refugees, exiles or self-exiles, but be classified in less victim-centred terms by the new government in the origin country or even host nations. Prevailing societal discourses and official terminology (e.g. 'guest worker') within the host countries determine the legal status and societal positioning of migrants, the perceived durability of their stay and – through official documentation – their capacity for cross-border mobility. Such differences in perception and subjective experiences stress the importance of ethnography and other qualitative empirical research that aims to delve deep into the psychosocial worlds of migrants and bring first-person accounts to the fore.

Whether they have relocated voluntarily or forcibly, legally or illegally, temporarily or permanently, these migrants and members of diaspora engage in local and international travel; they generate distinct mobility flows that deserve closer examination. Most of them return to their origin country at varying frequencies – some almost never, others regularly and many essentially commuting between two homes. Most also travel within their host country for recreational, business, health, religious, educational or other reasons, some to third-country destinations. Older adults embark on touristic journeys to revisit the places where they once spent a gap year; where they were stationed during a war (see Gordon in this volume); where they worked and lived for a formative period of their life. Many migrants and refugees return permanently to their place of origin someday. For their descendants and members of later generations of diasporic communities, the old homeland remains an aspect of their identity and consciousness, albeit of varying degrees of significance. Some travel there, either regularly or on a singular exploratory journey; a few even move there, bringing their family's migration experience full circle, but maintaining the link with the country of their birth through temporary visits of friends and family.

The relationships, interdependencies and intersections between migration, travel, tourism and return migration have only recently become a subject of scholarly interest and investigation (e.g. Coles & Timothy, 2004; Feng & Page, 2000; Hall & Williams, 2002). The new 'mobilities paradigm' (Sheller & Urry, 2006; Urry, 2007) advocates shifting focus from narrowly defined categories of mobility such as tourism to the complex interrelationships between diverse dynamics of movement – of persons, goods and ideas. Migration is now recognized as generating tourism, notably Visiting Friends and Relatives (VFR) tourism or what Duval (2003, 2004) calls migrant 'return visits', but also tourism for recreational, educational, religious, health and other purposes within the host country and to other destinations (Dwyer *et al.*, 2014). Tourism in turn leads to further migration, encouraged by migrants hosting visiting friends and relatives and establishing new social and economic ties and routes between home and host countries (Coles & Timothy, 2004). Singular and periodic home visits, 'provisional returns' (Long & Oxfeld, 2004), entice some migrants to return permanently and descendants of migrants to 're-migrate' to real or imagined ancestral places of origin.

This book examines the diverse mobility flows, travel patterns and touristic behaviour generated through migration, displacement and diaspora. It advocates a closer integration of research around migrant return visits, diasporic roots tourism and related forms of travel with migration studies and diaspora theory. Conversely, extant scholarship in the latter fields may benefit from more in-depth investigation of the role of travel. More specifically, this volume examines the intersection of travel and migration through the analytical lens of memory. Personal and collective forms of memory drive return trips 'home' and many other types of touristic mobility by migrants and members of diaspora. Such journeys are themselves vehicles for remembrance, as they provide occasion for voluntary and spontaneous recall; for the deliberate refreshing, preserving and sharing of memories; but also the critical interrogation of memories, discovery of memory distortions and dispelling of nostalgic myths. Post-trip narration and recall of the memorable journey in different situations in turn contextualize the experience, and induce comparisons, reflection and new insights that can lead to a shift in consciousness.

Memory as frame of analysis

As memory is the basis of all human experience and social interaction, it constitutes the foundation of individual and group identity, as well as a person's consciousness and sense of self. Perhaps it is precisely because of this all-pervasiveness that memory is largely taken for granted and rarely subjected to intense scholarly scrutiny in the social sciences and humanities. Only recently has the emergent interdisciplinary field of Memory Studies become a focal point for academic research that describes and investigates personal and collective forms of memory in different societal and geographic contexts and fosters the theoretical advancement of our understanding of memory. Increasing institutionalization – not without contestation – manifests itself, among others, in the introduction of dedicated scientific journals and book series, academic degree programmes and the recent foundation of the International Memory Studies Association.

Since the late 1970s, this academic engagement with memory has gone hand in glove with a broader societal interest in memory and commemoration. Internationally, a vast array of private and public endeavours geared towards remembrance fuelled scholarly research on commemorative festivals, events, museums, public monuments and many other types of *lieux de mémoires*, or 'sites of memory' (Nora, 1989). Many of these commemorative endeavours were presented as sites of national importance and cultural and heritage tourist attractions. This prompted scholarly studies within the field of travel and tourism to investigate issues of collective, social, cultural or public memory linked to discourses of national, ethnic and local group identity. Much less research attention has been paid to the significance of personal memory in the experiences, emotions, perceptions and motivations of individuals, especially tourists themselves. Memory features to some extent in the literature on different forms of diasporic return tourism, usually embedded in discussions of identity and belonging. Ultimately, memory remains neglected in the field of tourism studies (Marschall, 2017a).

While memory is frequently referenced or obliquely explored in many empirical studies on migration and diaspora, it is rarely explicitly discussed in diaspora theory (exceptions include Stock, 2010) or made the primary focus of investigation. Perhaps the most significant exception is Kleist and Glynn's (2012) pioneering collection *History, Memory and Migration*, which systematically brings together the fields of Memory Studies and Migration Studies. Chapters in the book explore how migrants negotiate their identities through remembrance practices, how memory is employed to construct social cohesion in host societies and how it informs migration policies by the state. None of the contributions in Kleist and Glynn's (2012) collection, however, investigates migrant return journeys and the role of travel more generally as vehicles of remembrance.

Diaspora

The difficulty, if not impossibility, of precisely defining the term diaspora is widely acknowledged and much of the theoretical literature in the field focuses on the identification and critical revision of core characteristics of diaspora, and the conceptualization of typologies, taxonomies and meaningful analytical schemes (e.g. Butler, 2001; Clifford, 1994; Cohen, 2008; Safran, 1991; Shuval, 2000). Without attempting to present a comprehensive review, the following aims to focus on the always implied yet rarely explicitly explored dimension of memory in diaspora theory, before discussing the role of travel and tourism in diaspora.

From its original reference to the Jewish and other prototypical diasporas (Armenians, Greeks), usage of the term diaspora has been dramatically extended in recent decades, including through self-identification by ethnic minority groups who embrace diaspora as an empowering frame of belonging in a context of marginalization. Cohen's (2008) five-fold typology of victim, labour, imperial and trade, cultural and global deterritorialized diaspora is perhaps the most frequently cited model of classification. Pursuing a different approach, Bauböck and Faist (2010) distinguish older and newer uses of the term diaspora, pointing out their partial incompatibility. Most scholars, however, agree on three broad characteristics defining diaspora, namely attachment to an original homeland; dispersal to more than one place; and self-awareness or maintenance of a diasporic consciousness (e.g. Butler, 2001; Cohen, 2008). Closely related, the following dimensions (among others) feature prominently in theorizations of diaspora: the causes and circumstances of the original dispersal; relationship with homeland and hostland; connection with members of the diaspora located elsewhere; the salience of return; citizenship and the nation state; and assimilation, hybridity and formations of diasporic identity.

'[D]iaspora members have lost their material relationship to the territory of origin, but they can still preserve their cultural or spiritual relationship through memory' (Bruneau, 2010: 48). 'At the core of the concept of diaspora lies the image of a remembered home' (Stock, 2010: 24). Whether articulated as explicitly as in these quotations, or implied in discourses around home, identity and belonging, memory plays a central role in all conceptualizations of diaspora. Identification with a collective historical and cultural memory of the displacement from an original homeland or 'centre' (Safran, 1991) have been widely described as a defining feature of diaspora. The connection with (or construction, invention, revival of) a prior homeland to which one longs to return is the constitutive basis of collective diasporic identity, distinguishing it from other ethnic minority groups. It is so strongly felt that it resists erasure through forgetting, assimilation and active suppression by the host society (Butler, 2001; Clifford, 1994: 310; Cohen, 2008; Shuval, 2000; Stock, 2010). Even without actual social ties to an origin country, individuals can have a profound sense of connection through memory, nostalgia, cultural competency or imagination, constituting *ways of belonging* as opposed to *ways of being* (Levitt & Glick Schiller, 2004). Bolstered by real or perceived isolation in their country of residence, the notion of return to the homeland in reality remains mostly a myth, but may inspire temporary visits and other types of travel, as will be shown below.

The influence of constructionism and postmodernism has diminished the salience of the homeland as a defining characteristic of diaspora and discredited essentialist notions of diasporic identity. Attention has shifted from 'the community' to the transnational practices and activities of specific groups and individuals, including the ways in which they foster ties with other diasporic groups. Several scholars have drawn attention to the dynamic, temporal and historical dimensions of diaspora and its existence over several generations; fluid processes of diasporization and identity formation; and histories of onward or re-migration and the emergence of secondary diasporas that render the notion of homeland more complex (Bauböck & Faist, 2010; Butler, 2001; Cohen, 2008; Shuval, 2000).

Such conceptual developments notwithstanding, the significance of memory and historical consciousness as a foundation of group identity and the construction of an 'imagined community' remains indisputable. Diasporic consciousness and identity require active maintenance through social memory embedded and embodied in everyday practices and through organized forms of public commemoration. For victim diasporas in particular, the collective memory of trauma – a mutual history of persecution, the Holocaust, slavery or disaster – binds members across time and space. Personal levels of identification with the shared past may differ considerably or change over time, hence allowing for the fluidity and dynamic emergence of diasporic identity, as well as the coexistence of multiple identities within the same diaspora (Butler, 2001; see also Roberts in this volume). Remembering always occurs within social 'frames of memory' (Halbwachs, 1992). A successful sense of belonging is not solely based on one's own nurturing of diasporic memory and home attachment, but also on the role of others (e.g. homeland residents, public opinion, life partners, etc.) and their approval, acceptance and support for inclusion in collective memories and notions of home (Stock, 2010).

Where members of diaspora deploy memory in minority politics of identity or where immigrants try to resist absorption into the dominant culture, the fostering of difference requires strategies of gaining public visibility. Fortier (2000) illustrates a wide range of performative acts and 'displays of presence' – from religious rituals and commemorative processions to card games and beauty contests – which produce notions of migrant belonging and unique diasporic culture. As the author aptly observes, it is through the practice of remembrance and commemoration, not through recourse to some primordial homeland culture, that diaspora identity is maintained (2000: 146). Commitment to the preservation and cross-generational transfer of memory requires both family-based remembrance and public forms of commemoration that facilitate connection with the larger diasporic community, ideally across borders.

Diasporas have an exceptional symbolic and 'iconographic' capital, writes Bruneau (2010: 47–8), that lives on in shared memory and enables them to reproduce their identity in exile and dispersion. They need 'places for periodic gatherings' and 'places of memory' such as monuments, religious structures and community premises, but also restaurants, grocery shops and other functional arenas, in which core symbols of identity are visible or palpably present (ibid: 38). Importantly for the purpose of this book, people travel to 'places of memory'; they embark on journeys, sometimes transnationally, to attend commemorative days, festivals, events and other types of diasporic gatherings. The creation of territorial markers and places of memory compensates diasporic communities for the loss of the original home and expresses their strong anchoring in the host country. Bruneau (2010: 49) views this relationship to places and territories as the basis of distinction between diasporism and transnationalism.

Diaspora, migration and transnationalism

Compared to the durability and the long-term sedimentation of diaspora, migration is of a fleeting nature (Bruneau, 2010; Butler, 2001; Van Hear, 2010). Apart from forced displacement – large groups of people fleeing conflict zones and catastrophe to places of safety near and far for varying lengths of time – the voluntary migration of skilled and unskilled individuals has been facilitated by improvements in the transportation sector and advances in information and communication technology (ICT). It includes short and medium-term stays for work, health, religious or study purposes; seasonal migration in search of employment and other opportunities; and to some extent periodic long-term holidays by retirees and those owning second homes ('snow-birds'). Existing diasporas are drivers of migration through family reunification and other forms of chain migration, but not all migrants cohere into communities, develop a homeland consciousness or are able and willing to connect with co-ethnics in their new country of residence (Knott & McLoughlin, 2010; Cohen, 2008). The host society's perception of ethnic homogeneity and common roots may be juxtaposed by nuanced forms of self-identification based on sharp recognition of cultural differences between newcomers and established members of the local diaspora.

When migrants settle permanently and become immigrants, their children and grandchildren either retain the collective memory of their homeland and foster a diasporic identity, or assimilate into the host society (although diasporic consciousness is sometimes revived many generations later). Since the 1990s, this dichotomous notion of diaspora versus integration; home versus host country; indeed, assimilation as a corner stone of migration theory has been rendered more complex by the concept of transnationalism. The term is used either in a broad sense to refer to all sorts of social formations, organizations and multinational corporations that operate transnationally, or more narrowly to migrants and members of diaspora who maintain durable ties across countries and organize their lives across multiple borders (Bauböck & Faist, 2010: 9; Brettell, 2006; Levitt, 2010; Van Hear, 2010). Transnationalism should not necessarily be conceived of in opposition to assimilation, as elements of both are prevalent in the experience of many migrants. One may also distinguish between economic and cultural assimilation; private transnationalism versus public localism (Boccagni, 2010); or exterior assimilation versus the private fostering of group memories of ethnic identity and homeland culture.

Although the utility, valence and even novelty of transnationalism are disputed (e.g. Foner, 1997), there can be no doubt that political and economic changes associated with neo-liberalism and globalization; technological developments; and not least advances in the travel and tourism industry (e.g. the availability of low-cost airlines and consumer online booking systems) facilitate transnational forms of living. Regular contact through phone, Skype and social media can both reduce the need for face-to-face contact and create new demand for personal visits (Griffin, 2015). 'It is the very immateriality of the virtual landscape that compels the return to the actual . . . place itself', maintain Hirsch and Miller (2011: 12). While periodic home visits; bi-directional VFR; family reunions; and travel for the maintenance of economic, health and other purposes are seen as characteristics of transnationalism, O'Flaherty *et al.* (2007) question what quantity and rate of frequency of such home visits and phone/Skype calls defines someone as a transnational. Koppenfels *et al.* (2015) critically examine the tendency to conceptualize visits home by migrants from the Global North as tourism and those from the Global South as transnational engagement, but found that there is no clear distinction between tourism and transnationalism and indeed advocate a more integrated conceptualization of the two terms. For the purposes of this volume, the concept of transnationalism is useful for its attention to micro-level activities of migrants, notably their cross-border mobility. It is argued here that the physical transnational engagement with social relations and places promotes the preservation, refreshing and exchanging of memories, which in turn enables the social and material reproduction of home atmosphere and home culture, but also the emergence of new identities in the host country.

Migration and memories of home

Discussing the differences and commonalities between diaspora and transnational approaches, Bauböck and Faist (2010) point out that issues of collective identity are usually associated with diaspora, yet they also matter from a transnational perspective. The migration context leads to cultural 'translation', mélange, hybridity or a 'third space' (Bhabha, 1994), but seen through the transnational lens (and in synch with the new mobilities paradigm) such identity changes are considered the result of cross-border mobility of persons and other flows of goods and ideas (Bauböck & Faist, 2010: 21–2). Memories of home are equally salient for refugees, transnational migrants and diasporas, but in fundamentally different ways. As opposed to members of diaspora removed from their place of origin by several generations, migrants have personal memory based on lived experience. They can draw on episodic and autobiographical memories of concrete places and social relations in their home country, where in most cases material and social bonds continue to exist, prompting many to visit periodically.

Migrants and especially those forcibly displaced experience loss and nostalgia; they feel 'homesick' and attempt to recreate elements of the remembered home environment in their country of settlement. Some literally take a piece of their home along in the form of furniture and home decorations, which acquire new meaning in the host country context; others engage in specific domestic homemaking practices. Photographs and small mementoes of important social relations, reminders of momentous episodes in their life or sentimental objects symbolic of the home country may be kept in special places or displayed in a quasi-sacred manner (Boym, 2001; Philipp & Ho, 2010; Tolia-Kelly, 2004; Turan, 2010; Uusihakala, 2008). Refugees fleeing conflict or disaster often keep 'transitional objects' (Winnicott, 1953), small items of a practical or sentimental nature that they took along in a hurry. These modest belongings encapsulate episodic memories and become symbols of home; they fulfil an important psychological role in linking the displaced with their past life and re-establish personhood in a new context (Parkin, 1999).

Connerton's (1989) seminal work on social memory, stressing the importance of performativity, habit, bodily automatisms and repetition in conveying and sustaining memory in social setting, takes on new importance in the context of migration and displacement. Much empirical research has been conducted on the multifarious ways in which migrants nurture and transfer memories of home and homeland culture through language, food, music, performances, sport, visual and material culture, story-telling, domestic homemaking, healing and childrearing practices (e.g. Alpers, 2000; Crang, 2010; Hage, 2010; Iain MacDonald, 2006; Joseph, 2011; Ricatti & Klugman, 2013; Stone *et al.*, 2005; Thomas, 1996; Tolia-Kelly, 2004; Whitehouse, 2009; Wolff, 2013). Multisensory ephemeral stimuli such as smells, sounds, tastes and tactile experiences are equally important in precipitating memories of home among migrants and refugees. The availability and affordability of local resources necessitate compromises and adaptions, resulting in cultural invention and 'mixities' (Bruneau, 2010). Once settled in the host country, many migrants begin to create family traditions and customs; small private rituals and routines geared towards remembrance; and communal icons and physical, artistic or metaphorical spaces of memory and identity (Bhandari, 2017; Blunt & Bonnerjee, 2013; D'Alisera, 2002; Um, 2012).

Children and grandchildren of immigrants have their own relationship with the family's place of origin and it is important not to generalize cross-generationally.

Some were born in the homeland (the so-called 1.5 generation); others have child-hood memories of family trips back home, yet they may not necessarily share the older generation's nostalgia. Some descendants have no personal experience of the place, but they have absorbed memories of parents and grandparents through story-telling and material culture in the home, constituting what Tolia-Kelly (2004) (drawing on Toni Morrison) calls 're-memory'. Hirsch (2001) similarly developed the concept of 'postmemory' with specific reference to the transgen-erational transmission of trauma memory. Remembered narratives and images of collective trauma that children of survivors grew up with can be 'so powerful, so monumental, as to constitute memories in their own right' (Hirsch, 2001: 9). Postmemory (like re-memory) is inherited secondary or second-generation mem-ory that is different in temporal and qualitative terms from survivor memory, yet can be extremely vivid and even produce a 'déjà vu' effect when descendants 'return' to the home they have never seen before (Marschall, 2015; Basu, 2001).

In the transgenerational transfer of memory, 'old' mnemonic forms (narratives, images) can be used to make sense of related, yet different, experiences of the younger generation (Erll, 2011a: 14). Dhupelia-Mesthrie (2016) shows how the older generation's memories of home and displacement can become a foil against which a more recent generation's experience of forced relocation is narrated and understood. Such intertwined transnational narratives in turn influence the experi-ence of diasporic 'return' journeys undertaken by the current generation.

The salience of return

The notion of return – permanent or temporary, real or imagined – is an integral aspect of migration and the diasporic experience (Long & Oxfeld, 2004). A per-manent return to the original homeland is often illusory, impossible, non-feasible or undesirable for pragmatic and emotional reasons. It is not so much the real desire for return but rather the *issue* or the idea of return, and claims to the 'right to return', that are intrinsic to the diasporan experience (Butler, 2001; Safran, 1991; Shuval, 2000). For transnational migrants, notions of circular mobility and exchange across borders, and the maintenance of two or more domestic bases, have to some extent replaced the emphasis on return (Bauböck & Faist, 2010: 13), but for most, home will always serve as a 'pole of attraction' via memory (Bruneau, 2010: 36). Even for those who do not desire to return, even temporarily, the old home(land) is never completely forgotten and memories of the past invariably sur-face and overlay experiences in the present.

'Return' includes the repatriation of refugees and displaced people; return migration to the country of family origin; counter-diasporic migration of later generations of diaspora; the permanent return of migrants and transnationals to their home country; 'provisional returns' of migrants and displaced people; tem-porary migrant return visits home; and a host of roots tourism-related journeys to ancestral homelands. It includes return journeys to refugee camps and other meaningful places once associated with home or formative periods of one's life

(West, 2014; Pearce, 2012). Return may also be carried out symbolically, through ritualized forms of mobility (Kuusisto-Arponen, 2009), or entail virtual, meta-phorical and imaginary journeys played out in the mind, in one's dreams or in creative spaces and artistic forms of expression (Hirsch & Miller, 2011).

Although this book focuses on physical mobility, such imaginary returns are important because they always precede the actual resettlement. Return migration entails many processes of planning and preparation, including usually at least one temporary visit, provisional return or exploratory journey (e.g. King & Christou, 2010; Reynolds, 2010; Wessendorf, 2007). Refugees and exiles may first have to con-struct new narratives about their earlier lives, confronting or overcoming memories of trauma and horror, before a return to the homeland can be considered. Provisional return trips may reveal the impossibility or undesirability of repatriation (Long & Oxfeld, 2004: 6–8). For those who have grown up abroad, memories of childhood trips to the homeland (King, Christou, & Teerling, 2011), postmemory and parental nostalgia absorbed since childhood (Wessendorf, 2007) can be influential in the deci-sion to relocate and in the experience of settled returnees. Resettlement in the homeland is never easy. Disappointments, exposition of myths and challenges encountered in their relationship with homeland society can foster renewed attachment to the coun-try of birth or result in a redefinition of 'exile' into homeland (Muggeridge & Doná, 2006; Newbury, 2005; Shuval, 2000; Silbereisen *et al.*, 2016). Even in cases of suc-cessful resettlement, returnees may embark on 'return trips' in the opposite direction to maintain ties with remaining friends, families and economic interests in the country of their birth. Return hence produces its own types of return mobility.

Return is not a universal category but is always situated in particular events and experiences, and our understanding of return is contingent on how we con-ceptualize 'home' (Long & Oxfeld, 2004: 3; Newbury, 2005). Some scholars have questioned the relevance of home as an analytical category, given the diversity and all-encompassing nature of extant conceptualizations, but home (like return) remains important because it is an emic term, highly salient for diasporic subjects themselves (Stock, 2010: 27). The return home is both a spatial journey to a specific geographical locale and a temporal journey into the autobiographical or mythical past, a place frozen in memory or the imagination. Return after only a short period of absence will already reveal changes in political, social or physical terms, requir-ing adjustment, re-evaluation and active re-engagement (Newbury, 2005; Long & Oxfeld, 2004). Memory mediates between past and present, home and hostland, as those who return – provisionally or permanently – systematically search for what is familiar and traces of their remembered past, and compare what they see with what they recall. The re-encounter of home and its accustomed places and social rela-tions can be a profoundly significant experience for migrants, resulting in shifts of consciousness and their sense of identity and belonging (Marschall, 2017b).

Touristic return of the diaspora

'Diaspora cultures thus mediate, in a lived tension, the experiences of separa-tion and entanglement, of living here and remembering/desiring another place'

(Clifford, 1994: 311). The trope of loss, longing and belonging, return to the homeland and reconnecting with other times, and places and members of diaspora inspires many types of journeys. Of these, the 'return' visits to real or imagined homelands have drawn by far the most attention from academic researchers, government authorities and the tourism industry. The increased interest in roots and origins in recent decades, a manifestation of the search for identity and belonging, is itself a result of globalization and marks perhaps a different phase of the historical phenomena of migration and diaspora. Various types of diasporic 'roots tourism' have been distinguished in the literature and the observation of patterns in motivation, activities and emotional responses among the increased volume of travellers has facilitated a certain extent of institutionalization, commercialization and the emergence of specialized tour operators and entrepreneurs.

This is especially true for the phenomenon of African American and, more generally, African diasporic roots tourism, ethnic reunion and 'homecomings' along the West African coast, which has spawned a thriving niche touristic industry and much scholarly interest (e.g. Bruner, 1996; Ebron, 1999; Forte, 2007; Fourie & Santana-Gallego, 2013; Schramm, 2010). Lacking historical knowledge about precise places of origin leaves diasporic Africans little choice but to visit largely symbolic homelands and gather at emotive sites of memory as metonyms of ancestral life-worlds. Many of these locales have been carefully restored by heritage authorities; developed into tourist attractions; and surrounded by commercial products and services, targeted at both diasporic and more general visitors. While diasporic Africans are inspired by collective and cultural memories, many members of the Scottish, Irish and select other diasporas are able to draw on family memories supported by archival documentation. They can visit more idiosyncratic personal sites of memory; trace specific named ancestors and extended family members; or participate in clan gatherings and related events. Based on motivation and behavioural patterns, scholars have defined a range of different niche area types of tourism, including genealogy tourism (Meethan, 2004; Higginbotham, 2012); legacy tourism (McCain & Ray, 2003); and emigrant homecomings (Harper, 2005; Basu, 2004, 2005).

There are a number of more specialized forms of diasporic returns to the homeland, such as Israeli birthright tourism (Kelner, 2010). As scholarly research tends to track emergent mobility trends, much literature has recently been produced on the return visits of the Chinese diaspora (e.g. Tie *et al.*, 2015; Hung *et al.*, 2013; Huang *et al.*, 2016), although most of these studies focus on the second and third generation. The same applies to the rapidly increasing range of case studies from many different social and geo-political contexts (e.g. Garrido, 2011; Hughes & Allen, 2010; Iorio & Corsale, 2013; Nguyen & King, 2004).

As opposed to poor economic migrants and many first or second-generation exiles on home visits, members of diaspora on roots trips are generally prosperous leisure tourists. They have the discretionary income and time to embark on journeys in search of self-actualization, identity and belonging. They tend to stay in hotels, eat in restaurants, purchase souvenirs and engage in many touristic activities that blur their distinction from 'ordinary' non-diasporic tourists, certainly from the destination society perspective. It is perhaps precisely for this reason that roots tourists tend to distance themselves vehemently from being regarded as tourists. The perceived negative connotations of tourism, especially its association with escapism and commercialization, threaten to trivialize the seriousness of their purpose, their existential quest and the quasi-sacred character of their 'pilgrimage'. In some places, souvenir sellers and clever local entrepreneurs have developed sensitivity towards and learnt to negotiate these attitudinal ambivalences in their interaction with roots tourists as customers (Powers, 2017).

Migrant return visits

Of course, many tourists throughout the world reject the tourist label, preferring to see themselves as a 'travellers', 'adventurers' or 'explorers' (McCabe, 2005). Many first and second-generation transnational migrants also do not see themselves as tourists, because they narrowly associate tourism with prosperous holidaymakers while they themselves are 'just going home' (Marschall, 2017b). Other diasporic return travellers feel like a local, but act like a tourist and are easily unmasked as outsiders because they lack familiarity with subtle cultural codes in mundane activities such as shopping (Wagner, 2015). Conversely, Eritrean migrants in Arnone's (2011) research precisely want to be regarded as tourists. They prefer staying in hotels rather than with family and deliberately perform touristic identities on home visits to enhance their 'otherness' as an indicator of migratory success. Other migrants are proud to combine family visits with sightseeing and ostentatiously leisure-based explorations of their home country, in emulation of the touristic behaviour observed among friends and colleagues in the host country (Bhandari, 2017).

Duval's (2003) study of Toronto-based migrants from the Caribbean, influenced by Baldassar's (1997, 2001) pioneering work on Italian migrants in Australia, shows how the relationship between the visiting migrant and the hosting home community becomes a stage for the negotiation of identities. The return travel of migrants is about memory, nostalgia and longing for home as a specific localized place of belonging, but also, more generally, as an environment of cultural familiarity and significant social relations (see also Duval, 2004). Various scholars (e.g. Scheyvens, 2007) agree that migrant 'return visits' are related to but conceptually distinct from their common association with VFR tourism, especially on the basis of the cultural differences between the home and the host society. The need to maintain social and other ties with the homeland; to immerse oneself in the familiar environment of traditional cultural and religious values; and to 'top up' one's own cultural capital underpins many international case studies (e.g. Hung *et al.*, 2013; Koppenfels *et al.*, 2015; Nguyen & King, 2004; Stephenson, 2002). Return visits are an important means of cultural transmission to children (Koppenfels *et al.*, 2015); some transnational migrant parents even send their children back to their home countries for long periods to be raised by relatives and acculturated into homeland norms and values (Whitehouse, 2009).

Echoing Newbury's (2005: 283) caution against homogenizing conceptualizations of migrant groups, migrant return visits equally defy simplistic generalization. The expanding literature on case studies from different geopolitical contexts illustrates much diversity and nuance in motivations for and experiences of such journeys home. They are contingent on subjective perceptions and personal histories of individuals, starting with the erstwhile reason for migration and the relationship to home and hostland, as well as larger societal specificities around issues of race, gender, class, religion and socio-economic status, as well as socio-cultural norms and values.

The monthly home trip of a transnational professional life-style migrant, for instance, has almost nothing in common with the first-time return visit of a forcibly displaced person. For many refugees, return visits may be impossible or very difficult. Some are adamant about never wanting to return, because the emotional pain and the outrage over the injustice of the loss are unbearable. Yet, for others, the pull of the homeland, the quest to see the old home again, even if in ruins or erased from the map, drives them to undertake the journey against all odds. They may have to travel clandestinely or under the guide of leisure tourism; some cross borders illegally or enter forbidden territory. The home visit may pose potential danger to their health, or expose them to the risk of persecution in the homeland or loss of refugee status in the host country (Abu-Lughod, 2011; Kadman & Kabha, 2017; Muggeridge & Doná, 2006; Thomas, 1996; Hannam & Yankovska, 2017).

The victim status of some displaced people and the legitimacy of their return may be a matter of perception and contestation, as in the case of German 'homesick tourists' (Marschall, 2015). The conceptual boundaries between forced and voluntary forms of migration become extremely complex when considering the case of transnational adoptees and the increasingly popular trend towards return visits of adolescent and adult adoptees is equally difficult to classify. Such journeys do not fit the mould of Duval's 'return visit', because these individuals lack personal and even family memories of their country of origin; they are culturally different from the homeland population and ethnically from their adoptive parents' society (Homans, 2011; Powers, 2017).

Other forms of travel in the context of migration and diaspora

Some types of touristic mobility – e.g. Visiting Home and Familiar Places (VHFP) tourism (Pearce, 2012); Personal Memory tourism (Marschall, 2012); Personal Heritage tourism (Timothy, 1997); and Memory tourism (Sturken, 2011) – involve returns to former homes and other significant places or 'memory sites', but are not exclusively undertaken by migrants or members of diaspora. Conversely, as this section aims to demonstrate, some forms of domestic and cross-border travel involve no returns to homelands, but are undertaken specifically by migrant communities and diaspora. The touristic experiences and behaviour of migrants and the wider role of travel and tourism in processes of migration, diaporization and maintaining diaspora consciousness remain neglected areas of research.

The fostering of interrelationships with other members of diaspora precipitates much travel and tourism, both within the host country and across borders. This includes ethnic homecomings organized outside the homeland, i.e. in the host country or third locations (e.g. Bieter *et al.*, 2017); attendance of conventions, festivals and events; and travel to religious gatherings or for the purpose of political advocacy. Such gatherings may involve group participation in performances, activities and visits to sites that testify to collective memories. The staged remembrance of a mutual past, and the sharing of mutual experiences, including that of marginalization, can be invoked to strengthen connections with total strangers in foreign countries, as well as nurture and initiate the younger generation into diasporic consciousness.

Diasporic memories of home evolve in constant dialogue with new memories of other places, experiences and changing circumstances (Stock, 2010: 25). Memories of other journeys and destinations fuel the imagination and filter into the ways the original homeland is 'remembered' or imagined. Some members of diaspora suddenly discover emotional resonances, a deeply felt affinity with particular places that they have never seen before, but in which they believe their ancestral roots run deep. They describe feelings and memories they cannot explain, linked in one way or another to their ancestors' lives – a phenomenon referred to as 'genetic memory' or 'gene memory' (Leite, 2005: 275).

Similarly, when first and second-generation migrants travel locally or abroad, multisensory stimuli, such as the smell of food or the sound of rain on particular surfaces, can spontaneously evoke memories of home and imaginatively transport the person 'back' for an instant (Marschall, 2017b). Some deliberately travel to places that 'feel like home' or spend their holidays in 'surrogate homelands'. They seek out landscapes that evoke the familiar look of the remembered home environment and are attracted to sites filled with the smells, sounds and tactile qualities associated with memories of home (Stephenson, 2004). Some might travel to 'ethnic spaces' within their host country, developed as tourist attractions for the dominant host country culture and international tourists (Thomas, 1996). Apart from migrants hosting friends and family (bi-directional VFR), transnational family reunions among migrants dispersed within the host country and across borders may be organized in independent locations conveniently accessible to all or combined into a string of journeys, a family reunion route. Sharing memories and recreating home(land) atmosphere by indulging in customary food and cultural traditions will inevitably be an important part of such events. Ramirez *et al.* (2007) examine the emotional dynamics of such reunions: how the family members commit the reunion itself to memory and memorialize the family's presence.

Compared to the extensive scholarly attention paid to migrant VFR tourism and home visits, far less is known about other types of travel conducted by first and second-generation migrants within the host country and across borders. Among the exceptions is Dwyer *et al.*'s (2014) study, which found that Vietnamese migrants in Australia also embark on sightseeing and recreational holidays within the host country. As migrants settle in, they begin visiting tourist attractions in their new place of residence as a means of establishing a sense of belonging and developing a better understanding of the local culture and dominant society (Feng & Page, 2000: 253). Conversely, their own group culture and heritage, national pride, and political memory and advocacy are equally important travel motivators, as migrants participate in commemorative celebrations and politically motivated gatherings within the host country (Thomas, 1996). Migrant travel behaviour for the purpose of leisure, business, education, health or religious worship warrants research because migrant identity (issues of race, ethnicity, legal status, etc.) can constitute an important factor in touristic experience (Stephenson, 2004). In some cases, special industry provisions and government interventions might be required to target the needs of these 'migrant tourists' (Marschall, 2017b).

Beyond obvious interest to tourism studies, investigating the touristic behaviour of migrants and diasporas can open up new perspectives on our conceptualization of diaspora itself. Joseph's (2011) study on sports tourism of Caribbean-Canadians illustrates that diaspora is not necessarily defined by relationship to the original homeland and the desire to return, but (drawing on Gilroy, 1993) 'as a social process, the result of circulating people and cultural forms' between several geographic nodes outside the ancestral homeland (2011: 148). For the Caribbean-Canadian cricket fans of her study, travel was an essential element of memory making. Sports-related trips to the Caribbean to play cricket, watch tournaments and visit empty stadia evoke nostalgia for old times and reminiscence about sporting heroes; they generate collective memories through socializing and a broad sense of community and belonging.

Organization of this book

Most of the contributors in this volume are themselves migrants, transnationals or members of diasporic communities who write from a perspective of deep personal understanding. The reader may notice that the chapters have a higher word count than the average article in scientific journals, allowing the authors to quote more extensively from their rich ethnographic material and provide them ample space for discussion and analysis.

The chapters in this book are arranged in two broad sections, although there is much overlap and implicit cross-reference between individual contributions. The first section foregrounds memory practices focused on former homes, ancestral homelands and distant places of personal significance. The collection opens with Roberts' exploration of memory and attachment to home in the daily routines and embodied homemaking practices of 'mobile settlers' in Australia, highly skilled migrants with multiple transnational points of reference. Brettell's research of Asian Indian immigrants in Dallas-Fort Worth, Texas extends the discussion beyond the private/personal realm by examining three specific sites at different scales of embodied engagement with the homeland and cultural memory, ranging from the level of the personal/familial (wedding), to the local community (festival), to the international diasporic community and beyond (public commemorative statue). Virtually all of these celebrations involve some kind of travel, local or international, and in some cases 'return' visits to India. Kostas' investigation of the *panigiri* festival among Greek migrants in Brasilia directly connects with the previous chapter, but introduces an important generational differentiation. First-generation migrants base the celebration of this important cultural identity performance on their pre-migration memories; descendants – partly inspired by touristic journeys to Greece – re-organize and reinterpret the festival to negotiate their own cultural identity and relationship with the parental place of origin.

The two final chapters of this section discuss the linkage between memory, migration and travel in relation to the legacy of the First and Second World Wars. Cevik-Compiegne and Ploner interrogate how annual ANZAC celebrations help members of Sikh and Turkish communities in Australia attain a sense of national belonging based on their ancestors' contribution to the battle of Gallipoli during WWI. Some descendants of Sikh veterans travel to Turkey in pursuit of their forefathers' memory, while Turkish migrants may combine home visits with family research around Gallipoli. Gordon's chapter then explores the confluence of tourism, migration and the memory of war in relation to German and Allied combatants in France during WWII, where especially officers combined military service with touristic exploration when off-duty. After the war, some veterans travelled to France to revisit memorable tourist sites and significant places where they had been stationed or imprisoned in what has been called 'veteran tourism', an emergent niche area in its own right.

This leads us to the second section of this book, which explores different types and experiences of return to places of ancestral, parental or personal origin by migrants, exiles and members of diaspora. The section opens with Aron Mazel's deeply personal narrative of his and his daughter's journey to Panevėžys and Pajouste Forest, Lithuania, from where his parents had fled, while his grandparents perished during the Holocaust. Partly based on personal interviews with his parents, Mazel's account underscores the difficulty of classifying such emotional, subjective and idiosyncratic travel experiences in prevailing schemata and tourism typologies. Czendze and Francisco's chapter helps us understand personal accounts like Mazel's within a wider historical and geographic context through their focus on American Jewish tourists in Eastern Europe from the 1920s to the present. The authors examine the remembrance practices of these immigrants, their return travel to former homes and sites of traumatic memory, and shifting notions of home and diasporic homeland. The authors' detailed examination of Jewish hometown associations (*landsmanshaftn*), notably their increasingly mnemonic function, connects with Pereira's discussion of the role of migrant community organizations (*Casas*) in diasporic gatherings staged in the formerly Portuguese enclave of Macau, now part of China. While roots tourism and diasporic homecomings are usually organized 'from below' and promoted by the tourism industry, the Macanese case represents an interesting variant on account of being partly organized with government support. Issues of memory, identity and belonging unfold during the week-long programme of activities, ritualistic performances and visits, which place language, gastronomy and selected other cultural traits at the core of 'Macaneseness'.

Linking with the first section, Bertram's contribution highlights the role of food and food-ways in diasporic memory, but investigates these in the specific context of the return journey. American members of the Armenian exilic diaspora embark on visits to their ancestral homeland in Anatolia, a place associated with persecution, trauma and the enemy, with a sense of fear, but attain a sense of belonging and identification through food and food-induced remembrance. Miah and King discuss the 'memoryscapes' associated with the migration and the visits back and forth of British Bangladeshis in London. Comparing the first and second generation, the experiences and practices of these migrants' mobilities demonstrate that the transnational social field linking London and Bangladesh is highly interactive and performative. Bringing the migration cycle full circle, Kılınç and King write about the 'return' migration of second-generation Turkish-Germans, who opt not to settle in their parents' hometown, but in the cosmopolitan tourist hub of Antalyia. Not only is this a place associated with happy childhood memories of family holidays for the young returnees, but it is also a socially liberal space replete with job opportunities in the tourism sector, allowing for new lifestyles and identities to unfold. Lastly, the Conclusion will summarize key findings, highlight common themes and offer some insights in relation to the intersection of memory, migration and travel.

Conclusion

Long before the current age of globalization and transnationalism, immigrants to the 'New World' embarked on occasional return voyages; colonial settlers went on extended trips to the 'mother country'; and adolescent children would be sent back home to get an education (Harper, 2005, 2017). Why are return journeys home generating so much scholarly interest only now? One answer lies in the sheer growth in volume of such travel. The current age of accelerated globalization and technological advancement has given rise to unparalleled mobility and new modes of transnational living and working. In addition, increasing flows of migrants and forcibly displaced people result in unprecedented demand for homebound travel of various descriptions. More importantly, as this book illustrates, we are only now beginning to understand the subjective meanings and significance of such journeys, their cultural, economic and psychosocial impacts on migrants themselves, and the people they interact with in home- and hostland environments.

The recent scholarly attention to home trips has eclipsed the multifarious other types of touristic journeys and travel activities undertaken by migrants, exiles and diaspora. In fact, the notion of migrants as tourists still rings unfamiliar. Neither tourism authorities nor academic scholars have paid enough attention to the volume, types, distinct characteristics and effects of migrant and diaspora travel (apart from home visits) and especially the ways in which their touristic experiences might differ from those of other tourists. This book makes a small contribution to addressing this lacuna and illuminating the interrelationships between migration and travel more generally, hence bringing the fields of tourism and migration/diaspora studies closer together.

What can the analytical focus on memory add to our current understanding of travel undertaken by migrants and diaspora? Conversely, what can an investigation of migrant (travel) memories contribute to the emergent field of Memory Studies? As mentioned earlier, in the past three decades, much scholarship has focused on investigating different types of *lieux de mémoires* in various national and socio-political contexts. Erll (2011a) argues that it is time for Memory Studies to change gear, to move into a new phase that can add fresh intellectual stimulus and broaden our understanding of memory, especially cultural memory, beyond the confines of the nation state and bounded social formations or 'cultures'. Drawing on Rigney (2005), she advocates a shift from 'sites of memory' to 'dynamics of memory', or what she calls 'travelling memory', to draw attention to the movement of people, objects and media in the activation and preservation of memory (Erll, 2011a, 2011b). Memory relies on activation and circulation, not only within the defined territorial and societal boundaries, but also across time, space and cultures, prompting the author to speak of 'transcultural' rather than cultural memory.

The chapters in this book illustrate that the realm of tourism and migration, two separate yet interrelated facets of human mobility, provides fertile ground for the exploration of memory in transcultural and transnational contexts. Importantly, this is evidenced not only in relation to collective forms of memory (e.g. cultural memory), but also personal and family memory. Migrants are carriers of memory that literally take remembered personal and collective pasts across borders and cultures. Such recollections are shared, disseminated and transferred to the younger generation, but always dynamically modified, adjusted, re-assembled, contextualized, and infused with other people's memories and the memories of personal journeys, literal and metaphorical. If the arena of travel hence provides a rich field of exploration for the study of memory, this volume conversely generates new insights, perspectives and approaches to tourism and migration.

References

Abu-Lughod, L. (2011). Return to half-ruins: fathers and daughters, memory and history in Palestine. In: M. Hirsch & N.K. Miller (eds.), *Rites of return: diaspora poetics and the politics of memory*. New York and Chichester: Columbia University Press, pp. 124–136.

Alpers, E.A. (2000). Recollecting Africa: diasporic memory in the Indian Ocean world. *African Studies Review*, 43(1), 83–99.

Arnone, A. (2011). Tourism and the Eritrean diaspora. *Journal of Contemporary African Studies*, 29(4), 441–454.

Baldassar, L. (1997). Home and away: migration, the return visit and 'transnational' identity. *Communal/Plural*, 5, 69–94.

Baldassar, L. (2001). *Visits home: migration experiences between Italy and Australia*. Melbourne: Melbourne University Press.

Basu, P. (2001). Hunting down home: reflections on homeland and the search for identity in the Scottish diaspora. In: B. Bender & M. Winer (eds.), *Contested landscapes: movement, exile, and place*. Oxford: Berg, pp. 333–348.

Basu, P. (2004). My own island home: the Orkney homecoming. *Journal of Material Culture*, 9(1), 27–42.

Basu, P. (2005). Roots-tourism as return movement: semantics and the Scottish diaspora. In: M. Harper (ed.), *Emigrant homecomings: the return movement of emigrants, 1600–2000*. Manchester: Manchester University Press, pp. 131–150.

Bauböck, R., & Faist, T. (eds.). (2010). *Diaspora and transnationalism: concepts, theories and methods*. Amsterdam: Amsterdam University Press.

Bhabha, H.K. (1994). *The location of culture*. London and New York: Routledge.

Bhandari, K. (2017). Travelling at special times: the Nepali diaspora's yearning for belongingness. In: S. Marschall (ed.), *Tourism and memories of home, migrants, displaced people, exiles and diasporic communities*. Bristol: Channel View, pp. 113–131.

Bieter, J., Ireland, P.R., & Ray, N.M. (2017). Ongi Etorri Etxera (welcome home): a gathering of homecomings: personal and ancestral memory. In: S. Marschall (ed.), *Tourism and memories of home, migrants, displaced people, exiles and diasporic communities*. Bristol: Channel View, pp. 246–268.

Blunt, A., & Bonnerjee, J. (2013). Home, city and diaspora: Anglo-Indian and Chinese attachments to Calcutta. *Global Networks*, 13(2), 220–240.

Boccagni, P. (2010). Private, public or both? On the scope and impact of transnationalism in immigrants' everyday lives. In: R. Bauböck & T. Faist (eds.), *Diaspora and transnationalism: concepts, theories and methods*. Amsterdam: Amsterdam University Press, pp. 185–203.

Boym, S. (2001). *The future of nostalgia*. New York: Basic Books.

Brettell, C.B. (2006). Introduction: global spaces/local places: transnationalism, diaspora, and the meaning of home. *Identities*, 13(3), 327–333.

Bruneau, M. (2010). Diasporas, transnational spaces and communities. In: R. Bauböck & T. Faist (eds.), *Diaspora and transnationalism: concepts, theories and methods*. Amsterdam: Amsterdam University Press, pp. 35–50.

Bruner, E.M. (1996). Tourism in Ghana: the representation of the slave trade and the return of the black diaspora. *American Anthropologist*, 98(2), 290–304.

Butler, K.D. (2001). Defining diaspora, refining a discourse. *Diaspora: A Journal of Transnational Studies*, 10(2), 189–219.

Clifford, J. (1994). Diasporas. *Cultural Anthropology*, 9(3), 302–338.

Cohen, R. (2008). *Global diasporas: an introduction* (2nd ed.). London and New York: Routledge.

Coles, T., & Timothy, D.J. (eds.). (2004). *Tourism, diasporas and space*. London and New York: Routledge.

Connerton, P. (1989). *How societies remember*. Cambridge: Cambridge University Press.

Crang, P. (2010). Diasporas and material culture. In: K. Knott & S. McLoughlin (eds.), *Diasporas: concepts, intersections, identities*. New York: Zed Books, pp. 139–144.

D'Alisera, J. (2002). Icons of longing: homeland and memory in the Sierra Leonean diaspora. *PoLAR: Political and Legal Anthropology Review*, 25(2), 73–89.

Dhupelia-Mesthrie, U. (2016). Re-locating memories: transnational and local narratives of Indian South Africans in Cape Town. *Journal of Asian and African Studies*, 1–5, DOI: 10.1177/0021909616642793.

Duval, D.T. (2003). When hosts become guests: return visits and diasporic identities in a Commonwealth Eastern Caribbean community. *Current Issues in Tourism*, 6(4), 267–308.

Duval, D.T. (2004). Conceptualising return visits: a transnational perspective. In: T. Coles & D.J. Timothy (eds.), *Tourism diasporas and space*. London: Routledge, pp. 50–61.

Dwyer, L., Seetaram, N., Forsyth, P., & King, B. (2014). Is the migration-tourism relationship only about VFR? *Annals of Tourism Research*, 46, 130–143.

Ebron, P. (1999). Tourists as pilgrims: commercial fashioning of transatlantic politics. *American Ethnologist*, 26(4), 910–932.

Erll, A. (2011a). Travelling memory. *Parallax*, 17(4), 4–18.

Erll, A. (2011b). *Memory in culture*. London and New York: Palgrave.

Feng, K., & Page, S.J. (2000). An exploratory study of the tourism, migration-immigration nexus: travel experiences of Chinese residents in New Zealand. *Current Issues in Tourism*, 3(3), 246–281.

Foner, N. (1997). What's new about transnationalism?: New York immigrants today and at the turn of the century. *Diaspora: A Journal of Transnational Studies*, 6(3), 355–375.

Forte, J. R. (2007). 'Ways of remembering': transatlantic connections and African diaspora's homecoming in the Republic of Benin. *Social Dynamics*, 33(2), 123–143.

Fortier, A.M.F. (2000). *Migrant belongings: memory, space, identity*. Oxford: Berg.

Fourie, J., & Santana-Gallego, M. (2013). Ethnic reunion and cultural affinity. *Tourism Management*, 36, 411–420.

Garrido, M. (2011). Home is another country: ethnic identification in Philippine homeland tours. *Qualitative Sociology*, 34(1), 177–199.

Gilroy, P. (1993). *The black Atlantic: modernity and double consciousness*. Cambridge, MA: Harvard University Press.

Griffin, T. (2015). The experience and implications of immigrant hosts. In: E. Backer & B. King (eds.), *VFR travel research: international perspectives*. Bristol: Channel View, pp. 73–86.

Hage, G. (2010). Migration, food, memory, and home-building. In: S. Radstone & B. Schwarz (eds.), *Memory: histories, theories, debates*. New York: Fordham University Press, pp. 416–427.

Halbwachs, M. (1992). *On collective memory*. Chicago, IL: University of Chicago Press.

Hall, C.M., & Williams, A. (eds.). (2002). *Tourism and migration: new relationships between production and consumption*. Dordrecht, The Netherlands: Kluwer Academic Publishers.

Hannam, K., & Yankovska, G. (2017). You can't go home again – only visit: memory, trauma and tourism at Chernobyl. In: S. Marschall (ed.), *Tourism and memories of home, migrants, displaced people, exiles and diasporic communities*. Bristol: Channel View, pp. 53–68.

Harper, M. (2005). *Emigrant homecomings: the return movements of emigrants, 1600–2000*. Manchester: Manchester University Press.

Harper, M. (2017). Homecoming emigrants as tourists: reconnecting the Scottish diaspora. In: S. Marschall (ed.), *Tourism and memories of home, migrants, displaced people, exiles and diasporic communities*. Bristol: Channel View, pp. 32–52.

Higginbotham, G. (2012). Seeking roots and tracing lineages: constructing a framework of reference for roots and genealogical tourism. *Journal of Heritage Tourism*, 7(3), 189–203.

Hirsch, M. (2001). Surviving images: Holocaust photographs and the work of postmemory. *The Yale Journal of Criticism*, 14(1), 5–37.

Hirsch, M. (2012). *The generation of postmemory: writing and visual culture after the Holocaust*. New York: Columbia University Press.

Hirsch, M., & Miller, N.K. (eds.). (2011). *Rites of return: diaspora poetics and the politics of memory*. New York and Chichester: Columbia University Press.

Homans, M. (2011). Adoption and return: transnational genealogies, maternal legacies. In: M. Hirsch & N.K. Miller (eds.), *Rites of return: diaspora poetics and the politics of memory*. New York and Chichester: Columbia University Press, pp. 185–199.

Hughes, H., & Allen, D. (2010). Holidays of the Irish diaspora: the pull of the 'homeland'?. *Current Issues in Tourism*, 13(1), 1–19.

Huang, W.-J, Ramshaw, G., & Norman, W.C. (2016). Homecoming or tourism? Diaspora tourism experience of second-generation immigrants. *Tourism Geographies*, 18(1), 59–79.

Hung, K., Xiao, H., & Yang, X. (2013). Why immigrants travel to their home places: social capital and acculturation perspective. *Tourism Management*, 36, 304–313.

Iain MacDonald, K. (2006). Memories of Tibet: transnationalism, transculturation and the production of cultural identity in Northern Pakistan. *India Review*, 5(2), 190–219.

Iorio, M., & Corsale, A. (2013). Diaspora and tourism: Transylvanian Saxons visiting the homeland. *Tourism Geographies*, 15(2), 198–232.

Joseph, J. (2011). A diaspora approach to sport tourism. *Journal of Sport & Social Issues*, 35(2), 146–167.

Kadman, N., & Kabha, M. (2017). 'Home tourism' within a conflict: Palestinian visits to houses and villages depopulated in 1948. In: S. Marschall (ed.), *Tourism and memories of home, migrants, displaced people, exiles and diasporic communities*. Bristol: Channel View, pp. 88–112.

Kelner, S. (2010). *Tours that bind: diaspora, pilgrimage, and Israeli birthright tourism*. New York: New York University Press.

King, R., & Christou, A. (2010). Cultural geographies of counter-diasporic migration: perspectives from the study of second-generation 'returnees' to Greece. *Population, Space and Place*, 16(2), 103–119.

King, R., Christou, A., & Teerling, J. 2011. 'We took a bath with the chickens': memories of childhood visits to the homeland by second-generation Greek and Greek Cypriot returnees. *Global Networks*, 11(1), 1–23.

Kleist, J.O., & Glynn, I. (eds.). (2012). *History, memory and migration*. London: Palgrave Macmillan UK, pp. 3–29.

Knott, K., & McLoughlin, S. (2010). *Diasporas: concepts, intersections, identities*. New York: Zed Books.

Koppenfels, A.K., Mulholland, J., & Ryan, L. (2015). 'Gotta go visit family': reconsidering the relationship between tourism and transnationalism. *Population, Space and Place*, 21(7), 612–624.

Kuusisto-Arponen, A.-K. (2009). The mobilities of forced displacement: commemorating Karelian evacuation in Finland. *Social & Cultural Geography*, 10(5), 545–563.

Leite, N. (2005). Travels to an ancestral past: on diasporic tourism, embodied memory, and identity. *Anthropologicas*, 9, 273–302.

Levitt, P. (2010). Transnationalism. In: K. Knott & S. McLoughlin (eds.), *Diasporas: concepts, intersections, identities*. New York: Zed Books, pp. 39–44.

Levitt, P., & Glick Schiller, N. (2004). Conceptualizing simultaneity: a transnational social field perspective on society. *International Migration Review*, 38(3), 1002–1039.

Long, L.D., & Oxfeld, E. (eds.). (2004). *Coming home? Refugees, migrants, and those who stayed behind*. Philadelphia, PA: University of Pennsylvania Press.

Marschall, S. (2012). 'Personal memory tourism' and a wider exploration of the tourism–memory nexus. *Journal of Tourism and Cultural Change*, 10(4), 321–335.

Marschall, S. (2015). 'Homesick tourism': memory, identity and (be)longing. *Current Issues in Tourism*, 18(9), 876–892.

Marschall, S. (2017a). *Tourism and memories of home: migrants, displaced people, exiles and diasporic communities*. Bristol: Channel View.

Marschall, S. (2017b). Transnational migrant home visits as identity practice: the case of African migrants in South Africa. *Annals of Tourism Research*, 63(4), 140–150.

McCabe, S. (2005). 'Who is a tourist?' A critical review. *Tourist Studies*, 5(1), 85–106.

McCain, G., & Ray, N.M. (2003). Legacy tourism: the search for personal meaning in heritage travel. *Tourism Management*, 24(6), 713–717.

Meethan, K. (2004). 'To stand in the shoes of my ancestors': tourism and genealogy. In: T. Coles & J.D. Timothy (eds.), *Tourism, diasporas and space*. London and New York: Routledge, pp. 139–150.

Muggeridge, H., & Doná, G. (2006). Back home? Refugees' experiences of their first visit back to their country of origin. *Journal of Refugee Studies*, 19(4), 415–432.

Newbury, D. (2005). Returning refugees: four historical patterns of 'coming home' to Rwanda. *Comparative Studies in Society and History*, 47(2), 252–285.

Nguyen, T.-H., & King, B. (2004). The culture of tourism in the diaspora: the case of the Vietnamese community in Australia. In: T. Coles & D.J. Timothy (eds.), *Tourism, diasporas and space*. London and New York: Routledge, pp. 172–187.

Nora, P. (1989). Between memory and history: *les lieux de mémoire*. *Representations*, 26(Spring), 7–25.

O'Flaherty, M., Skrbis, Z., & Tranter, B. (2007). Home visits: transnationalism among Australian migrants. *Ethnic and Racial Studies*, 30(5), 817–844.

Parkin, D.J. (1999). Mementoes as transitional objects in human displacement. *Journal of Material Culture*, 4(3), 303–320.

Pearce, P.L. (2012). The experience of visiting home and familiar places. *Annals of Tourism Research*, 39(2), 1024–1047.

Philipp, A., & Ho, E. (2010). Migration, home and belonging: South African migrant women in Hamilton, New Zealand. *New Zealand Population Review*, 36, 81–101.

Powers, J.L. (2017). Collecting kinship and crafting home: the souveniring of self and other in diaspora homeland tourism. In: S. Marschall (ed.), *Tourism and memories of home, migrants, displaced people, exiles and diasporic communities*. Bristol: Channel View, pp. 132–156.

Ramirez, M., Skrbis, Z., & Emmison, M. (2007). Transnational family reunions as lived experience: narrating a Salvadoran auto-ethnography. *Global Studies in Culture and Power*, 14(4), 411–431.

Reynolds, T. (2010). Transnational family relationships, social networks and return migration among British-Caribbean young people. *Ethnic and Racial Studies*, 33(5), 797–815.

Ricatti, F., & Klugman, M. (2013). 'Connected to something': soccer and the transnational passions, memories and communities of Sydney's Italian migrants. *The International Journal of the History of Sport*, 30(5), 469–483.

Rigney, A. (2005). Plenitude, scarcity and the circulation of cultural memory. *Journal of European Studies*, 35(1), 11–28.

Safran, W. (1991). Diasporas in modern societies: myths of homeland and return. *Diaspora*, 1(1), 83–99.

Scheyvens, R. (2007). Poor cousins no more valuing the development potential of domestic and diaspora tourism. *Progress in Development Studies*, 7(4), 307–325.

Schramm, K. (2010). *African homecoming: pan-African ideology and contested heritage*. Walnut Creek, CA: Left Coast Press.

Sheller, M., & Urry, J. (2006). The new mobilities paradigm. *Environment and Planning A*, 38, 207–226.

Shuval, J.T. (2000). Diaspora migration: definitional ambiguities and a theoretical paradigm. *International Migration*, 38(5), 41–56.

Silbereisen, R.K., Titzmann, P.F., & Shavit, Y. (2016). *The challenges of diaspora migration: interdisciplinary perspectives on Israel and Germany*. London: Routledge.

Stephenson, M.L. (2002). Travelling to the ancestral homelands: the aspirations and experiences of a UK Caribbean community. *Current Issues in Tourism*, 5(5), 378–425.

Stephenson, M.L. (2004). Tourism, racism and the UK Afro-Carribbean diaspora. In: T. Coles & D.J. Timothy (eds.), *Tourism, diasporas and space*. London and New York: Routledge, pp. 62–77.

Stock, F. (2010). Home and memory. In: K. Knott & S. McLoughlin (eds.), *Diasporas: concepts, intersections, identities*. New York: Zed Books, pp. 24–28.

Stone, E., Gomez, E., Hotzoglou, D., & Lipnitsky, J.Y. (2005). Transnationalism as a motif in family stories. *Family Process*, 44(4), 381–398.

Sturken, M. (2011). Pilgrimages, reenactment and souvenirs: modes of memory tourism. In: M. Hirsch & N.K. Miller (eds.), *Rites of return: diaspora poetics and the politics of memory*. New York and Chichester: Columbia University Press, pp. 280–293.

Thomas, M. (1996). *Place, memory, and identity in the Vietnamese diaspora*. A thesis submitted for the degree of Doctor of Philosophy of the Australian National University.

Tie, C., Holden, A., & Yu Park, H. (2015). A 'reality of return': the case of the Sarawakian-Chinese visiting China. *Tourism Management*, 47, 206–212.

Timothy, D.J. (1997). Tourism and the personal heritage experience. *Annals of Tourism Research*, 24 (3), 751–754.

Tolia-Kelly, D.P. (2004). Locating processes of identification: studying the precipitates of re-memory through artefacts in the British Asian home. *Transactions of the Institute of British Geographers*, 29(3), 314–329.

Turan, Z. (2010). Material objects as facilitating environments: the Palestinian Diaspora. *Home Cultures*, 7(1), 43–56.

Um, K. (2012). Exiled memory: history, identity, and remembering in Southeast Asia and Southeast Asian diaspora. *Positions*, 20(3), 831–850.

Urry, J. (2007). *Mobilities*. Cambridge and Malden, MA: Polity.

Uusihakala, K. (2008). *Memory meanders: place, home and commemoration in an ex-Rhodesian diaspora community*. Academic Dissertation. Research Series in Anthropology University of Helsinki, Finland.

Van Hear, N. 2010. Migration. In: K. Knott & S. McLoughlin (eds.), *Diasporas: concepts, intersections, identities*. New York: Zed Books, pp. 34–38.

Wagner, L. (2015). Shopping for diasporic belonging: being 'local' or being 'mobile' as a VFR visitor in the ancestral homeland. *Population, Space and Place*, 21(7), 654–668.

Wessendorf, S. (2007). 'Roots migrants': transnationalism and 'return' among second-generation Italians in Switzerland. *Journal of Ethnic and Migration Studies*, 33(7), 1083–1102.

West, T. (2014). Remembering displacement: photography and the interactive spaces of memory. *Memory Studies*, 7(2), 176–190.

Whitehouse, B. (2009). Transnational childrearing and the preservation of transnational identity in Brazzaville, Congo. *Global Networks*, 9(1), 82–99.

Winnicott, D.W. (1953). Transitional objects and transitional phenomena. *International Journal of Psycho-Analysis*, 34, 89–97.

Wolff, F. (2013). Revolutionary identity and migration: the commemorative transnationalism of Bundist culture. *East European Jewish Affairs*, 43(3), 314–331.

2 'Travelling memories'

The homemaking practices of skilled mobile settlers

Rosie Roberts

Introduction

This chapter is informed by research that examined the diverse pathways, practices and identities of skilled migrants over time and through space. All of the participants were tertiary educated, skilled and had lived in Australia at some point in their lives, although not necessarily on a skilled visa. Australia is viewed as a single site within a range of transnational connections, recognising contemporary mobility as a complex system of interactions rather than one-way permanent relocation. The phrase educated and skilled 'mobile settlers' is introduced to capture the diversity of experiences amongst migrants and to describe the practices of people whose life histories have been punctuated by a range of visa classifications and 'multiple moorings' of 'various durations' (Cohen, Duncan & Thulemark, 2015: 162).

By examining participants' everyday and embodied homemaking practices, this chapter reveals some of the ways people come to inhabit homes and communities near and far through performative, narrativised and multisensory ways of knowing, connecting and remembering. Their experiences show a fluidity between traditional demarcations of travel and migration, home and away, foreign and familiar where temporary mobility often turns into longer-term migration and produces multiple spaces of belonging, both lived and imagined. Some individuals regularly travelled to familiar-looking landscapes in their migration country as a way of connecting back to past homes while others experienced in-betweenness on an ongoing basis through successive return migrations. The participants' narratives show how every relocation carries with it traces of previous local, national and transnational memories that embed themselves in new contexts (Kennedy & Nugent, 2016; Kennedy & Radstone, 2013: 242).

In recent years a more agent-centred approach to global mobility and transnationalism research has emerged, which recognises the individualised, local and lived experiences of migration processes. However, this body of work has often focused on single sites, linear links between origin and destination countries, distinct groups of people, or an isolated migrant classificatory scheme such as humanitarian, low-end labour, lifestyle or skilled migrant (Benson & O'Reilly, 2016; Conradson & Latham, 2007; Ho, E., 2011; Ryan & Mulholland, 2014). It has rarely been considered how these categories can shift over time for an individual and involve multiple origins and destinations. As such, there is less recognition of the mobility practices of people who are not typified by rigid national, religious, ethnic or government-defined visa categories (see Clark & Withers, 2008; Kofman & Raghuram, 2005; Nagel, 2005; Rutten & Verstappen, 2014 for some exceptions). The research informing this chapter shifts the focus from migrant categories to the dynamism of migration pathways, practices, identities and stories over an individual's life course.

To be included in this research participants needed to be tertiary educated, have worked in professional positions and lived in Australia at some point in their lives. The aim of this selection was to explore the diversity of skilled migration experiences into and out of Australia that may include people outside of official government-defined working visa categories. This resulted in a diverse group in relation to age, profession, gender, religion, ethnicity and country of origin as well as mobility pathways and motivations for relocation. Participants were identified for inclusion in the study through migrant community groups and respondent-driven sampling techniques (Noy, 2008), accessing informants through contact information provided by other informants. This approach used the dynamic character of organic social networks, complementary to the study of mobility.

Narrative interviews were conducted in person, via Skype and email and collected over a period of three years with thirty participants. With many of the participants I had ongoing conversations over this period, capturing the ways their identities shifted over their life course and during the data collection time frame (i.e. resident, tourist, guest, migrant, student, local, visitor and traveller). In parallel to this life course approach, I draw upon the perspectives of Erll (2011: 5) who, within the field of Memory Studies, contends that we need to understand the differing ways people 'handle time' by 'working through the past', the present and 'visions for the future'. Erll (2011) criticises, as have many, the idea of cultures as being discrete entities, instead emphasising the need for a transcultural approach to memory that examines how phenomena stretch across and beyond cultures, through processes of globalisation. Erll (2011: 11) describes this understanding of memory as 'travelling memory', which sustains itself in and through movement and changing 'social, temporal and local contexts'. Migration and diaspora, whether forced, voluntary or a combination of the two, are fundamental ways in which individual and collective memories become mobilised. As people and their imaginations travel across the globe, their memories are transformed through local contexts and interactions.

Processes of narrative inquiry (Bruner, 2003; Riessman, 2008) are used because this approach permits the layering of time and space and provided a more contingent view of skilled migration that often unfolded, through their stories, as a series of serendipitous encounters rather than pre-determined routes. By reconceptualising skilled migration as a biographical and temporal project, and tracing people's diverse pathways towards becoming skilled, bureaucratic and static conceptualisations of skilled migration are expanded and contextualised to include multiple and intersecting personal, cultural and professional identities and sites of belonging.

From migrants to movers

Debates around citizenship, belonging, transnationalism and mobility have been circulating for several decades (Ehrkamp & Leitner, 2006; Ho, 2009; Werbner & Yuval-Davis, 1999; Yuval-Davis, 2006), each with a range of contributions that are relevant for examining the mobile pathways of individuals in this research. From national and transnational belonging to the most local and intimate spheres of our daily lives, there has been an increasing focus on people's attachments to diverse sites and the ways such attachments, and people's social locations, intersect with notions of identity. Emotional subjectivities are central to such discussions because people's mobility in terms of whether they belong or don't belong in a new location, whether they stay temporarily or are able to become permanent residents, is affected as much by their emotional experiences as it is by the legal constraints which govern the length of their stay (Boccagni & Baldassar, 2015; Skrbis, 2008; Svasek, 2010). As Boccagni and Baldassar (2015: 74) suggest in a recent special issue on migration and emotion, when people move away or between homes, their emotions are also 'on the move'.

Migration research increasingly conceptualises mobility in fluid terms, breaking down singular categorisations such as traveller, migrant, tourist and resident, and instead focusing on their intersections (Cohen, Duncan & Thulemark, 2015; Hannam, 2008; Williams & Hall, 2000). Cohen *et al.* (2015: 160), for example, use the phrase 'lifestyle mobilities' to examine people's ongoing semi-permanent relocations of varying durations, with multiple sites of attachment, that may involve many return journeys to home/s. Cohen *et al.* (2015) prefer lifestyle mobilities to lifestyle migration (see work of Benson & O'Reilly, 2016) because this conceptualisation allows for periods of immobility and mobility, rather than a perceived singular movement from one place to the next as lifestyle migration appears to infer.

Mobility research has examined a range of areas including transnational networks and flows of people and capital within global cities (e.g. in the work of Castells, 2000; Sassen, 2001; Taylor, 2004) as well as more agent-centred approaches to global mobility that recognise the local experience of global processes (Gardner, 2006; Gilmartin & Migge, 2016). The field has also explored the experiences of people who have been forced to migrate either for humanitarian reasons or who are low-end labour migrants (May, Wills, Datta, Evans, Herbert & McIlwaine, 2007; McDowell, Batnitzky & Dyer, 2008), in addition to those defined as the global elite (Beaverstock, 2005; Fan, 2002). However, there has been less research investigating the mobility practices of people who move within and between categories of low-end labour and elite labour. One notable exception that explores mobility between these groups is found in the work of Conradson and Latham (2005: 229), who acknowledge that transnationalism has become the practice of many more people than just the elite and developing world migrants. They argue for a space in between that captures 'middling' forms of transnationalism. However, while their conceptualisation of middling transnationals usefully deconstructs binaries between low and high-end labour mobility, it remains focused on discrete categories (i.e. the middle) rather than the mobile practices that migrants engage with, which may challenge such classifications. By contrast, this research builds on work that captures people's movements between typologies of developing world migrants, middling transnationals and elite labour sectors throughout their lives as well as recognising the diversity of migratory experiences that exist within 'the middle' (Kofman & Raghuram, 2005; Nagel, 2005; Rutten & Verstappen, 2014; Ryan, Klekowski Von Koppenfels & Mulholland, 2015). This is as much about how migrants perceive themselves as it is about how they are constructed through official immigration discourses.

Consequently, in addition to the blurring between types of mobility that Duncan, Cohen and Thulemark (2013) observe (e.g. travel, leisure and migration), there is also blurring between the categories used to define mobile people over their life course (e.g. skilled migrant, international student, tourist, family-sponsored migrant, refugee, working holiday maker). Furthermore, while people may personally identify with a category or identity, it may not be recognised by the legal system. For instance, an individual might see themselves as a skilled migrant even when they relocated under a spousal or tourist visa, tactically subverting the immigration system to initiate relocation and extend their stay. A life-cycle approach takes account not only of the diversity of movements (e.g. travel, leisure, migration, escape) but also the diversity of movers, private and public identities and sites of attachment over a person's life course. This conceptualisation also acknowledges that those who engage in 'lifestyle mobility' (Duncan *et al.*, 2013), for example, may not have always been so privileged, as people negotiate a range of shifting socio-cultural, political, economic and personal conditions that constrain and enable movement over their lives.

As an alternative framing to skilled migrant, I describe participants' practices of 'mobile settlement' or as 'mobile settlers'. The aim of this conceptualisation is to articulate the practices of people whose life histories have been punctuated by relatively frequent relocations, either repeatedly going away and coming back or moving incrementally from point to point. Braidotti (2002) talks about becoming in the Deleuzian sense, where we view people as 'in-process', affirming 'fluid boundaries' rather than fixed categories. Participants did not always identify as skilled migrants but often identified themselves as 'being mobile'. This framing unsettles traditional categories of immigration that are seen to be static, in order to show that in many cases migrants become movers (Recchi, 2006). The term settler is included in this framing to ground participants' mobility because even though their lives often involved frequent relocations of varying durations, they also developed strong localised connections to particular places and people, even if those connections change and disperse.

What refugees, migrants, temporary residents and tourists have in common is that they are all humans 'on the move' seeking a better life in the short or long term. Where they differ is in their freedom and level of choice. By examining the mobility of people in broad terms, intersections between identities of tourist, traveller, worker, resident, refugee and student become visible. This chapter will show that throughout their lives, participants travel in a range of ways. They travel across national borders to flee persecution, to find temporary and longer-term work, to seek new experiences and lifestyles, to engage in tourism and recreation, to visit friends and family. They travel in more localised spaces, inhabiting their homes, streets and communities through their repetitive homemaking practices. They also travel through their imaginations as threads of memory at multiple scales (local, national, transnational) are woven into their lives in new contexts (Erll, 2011; Kennedy & Nugent, 2016). Finally, they sometimes occupy the official category of traveller or tourist when they are actually engaged in practices that contravene this label. The purpose of this chapter is to examine some of these different forms of travel through two lenses. I first provide examples of the ways participants traverse multiple physical locations across the globe, disrupting categories of migrant, resident, tourist and traveller over their lives. I then consider some of the ways places and mobilities co-exist in creative tension through participants' daily practices in more localised spaces, which involved both physical and imagined journeys. In this way we may then understand, in a more complex manner, the experiences and journeys of contemporary skilled mobile settlers.

Migrant, resident, tourist, traveller: undoing home and away, foreign and familiar

In a mobile world, the locations of home and belonging are becoming more complex and multi-sited. Often participants' connections were not tied to a particular country but were expressed as being 'in between' a range of loyalties. Staying, leaving, visiting and returning were bound up in notions of home and belonging. For many their lives in a new country were always lived in relation to the question of return, whether a realistic option or an imaginative desire. Nilaya, who was born in India and had lived and worked in Europe, the US and now resides in Australia, commented on the way perspectives on home can change over time. Nilaya describes how her whole family has now become accustomed to a different way of life and India no longer feels like the primary location of home. While the country may have changed since they lived there, they have also changed. Paradoxically, each visit home brings them closer to a home in Australia, and this was a common experience for many participants. The visit home might instead be read as a way of moving forward in their foreign lives rather than of homecoming (Baldassar, 2001). Nilaya states:

> The first time we went back to India it was fantastic and that was still home. The second time we started feeling a bit like Australia is home, and we went in December this year and the first thing, within the first day when we went there it was OK. By night both my kids were in tears and said 'We miss Australia, we want to go back home'. And slowly I think we've all realised this is home now, the bond, and it's a bit sad as well because the only thing that pulls me back there is my mum and my sisters and brothers, my immediate family, for both of us, but other than that, no.

It is the space from which Nilaya and her children originated – in a sense, the 'real' home – which is now the most unfamiliar to them. It is the place to which they return every few years to visit family members, but they are now returning as guests rather than residents (Dhingra, 1993: 99). Ahmed (1999: 330) suggests that there are often too many homes to secure the 'roots and routes of one's destination'. Nilaya's relationship to home has been altered through her mobility. She has multiple sites of home, although some provide a more powerful sense of belonging than others, and she experiences these homes from shifting subject positions (e.g. as resident, guest, traveller, visitor and migrant).

Emily moved from Zimbabwe to Australia, accompanying her husband on a spousal visa even though she is highly educated (i.e. has a Master's and Doctoral degree) and skilled, having worked in professional positions in the education and healthcare sector. C. Ho's (2006) research has challenged the 'success story' narrative of skilled migrants entering Australia to suggest that this kind of government rhetoric disguises a more complex reality. Her research shows the difficulties that women, in particular, face when settling into a new country. Migration often leads to a 'feminisation' of their roles, as women are often forced to take up more traditional gender roles as wives and mothers to support their male partners who often arrive as the 'lead' migrant. Women are precluded from working in some instances due to visa restrictions associated with migrating as a spouse, or simply because they are unable to find work commensurate to their skills and experience (Ho, C., 2006: 498). When Emily did secure employment in Australia, she recounted multiple experiences of sexism and racism where several clients who visited the healthcare agency that she worked for refused to be served by her. As a skilled migrant, Emily is rendered invisible, yet she is made visible through her skin colour, as someone who is assumed not to speak English and is most likely perceived as unskilled and uneducated.

> Everyone I speak to, I have to let them know that I'm a skilled migrant if they start questioning my identity . . . I think the image of the African woman out there is the one who is uneducated, you know, oppressed and all that kind of stuff, so that's the picture that you're put into, even before you open your mouth.
>
> (Emily)

Ironically, Emily has a distinctive formal English accent through her colonial schooling in Zimbabwe, and most likely sounded more 'British' than the 'Anglo-Australians' who refused to be served by her. Emily also talked about experiencing reverse culture shock when she had returned to Zimbabwe to visit family several times over the past decade. In her memory, her country of origin had been frozen in time, but the return visit reminded her that not only had past homes and the people who inhabited them changed, but so had she.

> I don't know if I really call Australia home. I know I'm here, like on a practical level. I've been here for a long time, but part of me still tells me, the home that I associate Zimbabwe with, is kind of a fantasy now really because

the Zimbabwe that I knew when I've gone back to visit is five or ten years older than when I left. So my idea of home, it's like a myth, because it really doesn't exist in that state anymore because it is changing while I'm not there.

(Emily)

Marschall's (2017) research on the temporary home visits of African transnational migrants living in South Africa similarly found that the return journey, and the memories and narratives this evokes, fosters a sense of self-reflection that can profoundly shift a person's identities and attachments. While Emily still feels like an outsider living in Australia, she also now feels that she no longer belongs in her country of birth, a sentiment expressed by many participants, and echoed in numerous other studies that examine how migrants often crystallise a sense of place after their departure (e.g. Al-Ali & Koser, 2002; Madison, 2009). Emily reflected on a recent visit that 'things had gone bad, people's attitudes were different, the language had changed'. She was frustrated that as a consequence of trying to fit into Australian society, she did not realise 'how much further away from your own culture you're getting as well'. As Massey (2003: 230) states, 'Journeys "home" are, in the imagination, often travels in time as well as space – journeys to the past. But places go on without you'. Thus, returning to past homes may not be about returning to a fixed location (if a place can ever be 'fixed') but returning to an in-between place – between proximity and distance, self and other. While participants' subjectivities changed over time as a result of their experiences in new locations, their previous homes did not remain 'still' either.

Similarly, other participants commented:

All of my points of reference are no one else's points of reference when I go home. It feels like they have continued their life there, which of course they should, and when I go back, the life that I want to continue leading isn't available to me anymore. It's like it's not really my place anymore, it's theirs, but if that's not my place and this isn't my place, where is my place?

(Jen)

I returned home about two times a year, but gradually over the years nomination of 'home' lost its clear boundaries. So it was common when I visited Australia to talk of Nagoya or my apartment there as 'back home'. I started looking at Australia through new eyes, perhaps those of a visitor.

(James)

In these excerpts the location of home is lived as an enduring tension. There is a kind of melancholic recognition in their reflections where they suggest that they will always occupy an in-between state, and may never find a place above all others that feels like home, and when they talk of multiple homes, this is often a vague and ambiguous sense of attachment. The experience of leaving home/s is always related to the inability of our memory to fully understand the new places one comes to occupy (Ahmed, 1999: 343). Furthermore, the process of returning to a home is similarly related to the inability to fully inhabit spaces that were once familiar.

Lan was born in what she refers to as Saigon, what we now know as Ho Chi Minh City, during the Vietnam War. She came to Australia with her father as a refugee in 1980. Lan's father was imprisoned for three years following the Vietnam War, and she says that while in prison, he learned that those on the 'losing side' would be oppressed for three generations, meaning his children would be the second generation and would be 'unable to reach their full potential' (Lan). Lan talks about the outcomes of migration on her career and professional context while also narrating personal and emotional memories of the leaking boat on which she and her father escaped Vietnam. After being rescued by people on a passing yacht, she recalled how she felt watching the escape vessel disappear towards the horizon: 'That night our boat drifted away in the ocean; it was like a paper boat that I would make at home in Vietnam when it rained a lot and the water rose up to my little knees.' Once in Australia, Lan went on to complete her schooling, undergraduate and doctoral degree in Adelaide. After completing her PhD, Lan and her British-born, Australian-raised husband, Scott, moved to Seattle where she has since completed a postdoctoral research position. Lan originally thought they would stay for three years, but they have now been living in the US for five years and have no intention of returning to Australia in the near future.

When Lan first relocated to the US, she went on an exchange-scholar visa and her partner accompanied her on a spousal visa. When her postdoctoral employment came to an end, her husband's employer sponsored him to have temporary-employment status. Lan then spent time on several tourist visas before gaining a dependent visa for a short-term appointment in Canada. Her authorisation to work is currently dependent on her husband's continued employment in the US, but she hopes that her new position will result in work sponsorship so that she does not have to rely on his employment status. Although on different scales of necessity, a sense of uncertainty in relation to Lan's mobility has been a persistent theme, from her escape from Vietnam to her skilled migration experiences in the US. However, Lan and Scott do exercise a degree of agency amidst this uncertainty, tactically subverting structures of power – as de Certeau (1984: 9) would claim – that manage migrant flows, using different categories of visa to extend their overseas stay. They use tactics so that while they may be 'caught in the nets of discipline' (de Certeau, 1984: xiv–xv), they also use the visa system to extend their stay in the US by taking out successive tourist visas or spousal visas while they build up a case for long-term residency. While the strategy of governmental migration departments is to administer and institutionalise closure and control, migrants often subvert these disciplined spaces to their own ends. These tactics are not merely reactionary but active processes that expose the limits of institutional structures of control. This perspective also shows that while there are intersections between travel, tourism and migration in the literal sense (e.g. migrants travel to previous homes and visit potential new homes as tourists), people also inhabit official categories of 'tourist' that do not necessarily match up with what they are actually doing in a place or how they perceive themselves (i.e. seeking longer-term settlement, work options and residency).

Lan also experiences 'return' in both a physical and imagined sense with the location of the return occupying multiple sites. Since living in the US, she has returned to one of her former homes (Adelaide, Australia) to visit friends and family. Lan, during these visits, could be seen as a skilled migrant returning home. However, she has also contemplated a return to Vietnam, the original home from which she and her father escaped as political refugees. When I asked Lan if they had ever returned to her place of birth in Vietnam she replied, 'Neither of us has returned to Vietnam. My heart wants to visit though I am still wondering if it will be safe to do so since we escaped from the country.' Lan refers to a fear, whether real or imagined, that state policies in Vietnam would preclude her from returning to her original homeland. Even though this is extremely unlikely, the fear associated with her escape from Vietnam overlays the possibility of a return in the present. In this example, the idea of return is experienced through multiple identities and differing emotions depending on the location of home. Returning to Australia is experienced as a migrant professional and imagining a return to Vietnam is experienced through the lens of being forcibly displaced as a refugee. This return could also be seen as a diasporic journey home, whereas her return to Australia would not.

Two final examples show the complexity of defining home and away and the relative subject positions of resident, traveller and migrant, illustrating the ways in which people can move through a series of intersecting mobility categories over their life course. When I first interviewed Hannah and Pete, Hannah (born in Australia) had recently met Pete (born in Germany) while travelling home to Australia after her two-year working holiday in the UK. Pete had relocated to Australia with Hannah and although he was having difficulty securing adequate employment in his field, Australia was seen then as a relatively permanent move. At this point, his migration may have been viewed as relatively linear. Hannah was a returned working holiday migrant and Pete a spousal migrant turned Australian resident. Six months later, after continued employment frustration for Pete as well as wanting to 'give both countries a try' (Hannah), they returned to Germany. For Pete this might categorise him as a returning settler. For Hannah it was another settlement in her expanding history of mobility. After a year and a half living in Germany they felt that they needed to decide on a place to settle and raise a family and chose to return to Australia via a six-month tour by motorbike through Africa.

There is an added complexity in living between homes for this transnational couple because they each experience in-betweenness on an ongoing basis. When Hannah is at home in Australia, Pete is not, and when Pete is at home in Germany, Hannah is not. Furthermore, when one was at home in their country of origin the other felt that they were migrating/travelling/visiting, resulting in the development of multilocational living arrangements and identifications. They have spent considerable amounts of time 'trying to fit into both contexts' (Hannah) as citizens of each nation and they feel they are now somewhere in the middle – no longer at home in their country of origin or their partner's. Notions of home and away as well as short-term versus permanent settlement have become sites of continual negotiation throughout their relationship.

James, a participant who was born in Scotland, grew up in Australia, went to university in the US and worked in Australia for a decade before moving to Japan for fifteen years, similarly describes a sense of being between homes. He describes how he feels much less connected to a nation than to particular people and groups of friends in disparate locations around the world. Privileging identification with other nationals is problematic because it assumes that sharing formal state-based membership is stronger than connections through alternative affiliative ties (Bosniak, 2001: 248). His attachments to smaller, translocal (Anthias, 2002) support groups in multiple countries allow for a particular global disposition and identity, although this is a relatively privileged positioning that may not be realistic for many people. During the time he lived and worked in Japan, Japan became a prominent site of 'home' and Australia became 'away'. However, when he visited Australia, he would sometimes refer to it as home, but once in Australia he would refer to Japan as home. Equally, when he was a child and moved to Australia, Scotland was still home for many years, although now Scotland does not figure prominently as a site of home or citizenship but rather a place of beginning. Australia is now home, James having recently returned from Japan to 'put down roots' (James) and retire. Interestingly, regardless of his highly mobile life and connections, he still seeks one place, above all others, to return to. Thus while James constructs himself as de-nationalised, he simultaneously and contradictorily finds home in its strongest sense in Australia.

> I am more at home in Australia than anywhere else, though to a certain extent I am more an observer here than a participant. This is something to do with living in several other countries – I have been de-nationalised. This is not anything approaching alienation or angst, merely a broader base of identity.
>
> (James)

However, the contradictions and ambivalences of migration continue as migrants' lives unfold. While James moved back to Australia with the intention that this move would be permanent, he has recently moved again, this time to Macau. This was supposed to be for a one-year posting but has now been extended for another twelve months. This example reinforces the need to take a life-course approach to the study of migrant lives in order to understand the complex mobility pathways, practices and circumstances that people engage with over time and space.

This section has described some of the ways participants negotiate mobility across national borders, which has produced a range of official categorisations to describe them as well as shifting personal identifications including refugee, tourist, temporary migrant, resident, traveller, visitor, guest and citizen. Home and belonging are complicated ideas that are subject to influences of time, space and identity shifts. Thus, migrant categories tend to be too limiting to understand the complexities of migrant journeys, their experiences and dispersed connections.

The next section focuses on mobility within more local, everyday spaces. While these movements within homes are physically localised, they are also highly transnational at the level of the imagination. Current homes are constructed through multiple translocal connections and memories.

Travelling memories and rituals

There is a growing body of theoretical and empirical literature on embodiment and the senses within migration studies and geography (Chau, 2008; Classen, 1997; Conradson & Latham, 2007; Howes, 2006; Hsu, 2008; Low, 2012; Tolia-Kelly, 2006, 2007). Dunn (2010: 7) has argued that if the scale of analysis for researching migrants is at the level of bodies, it keeps studies from moving too far away from 'place' and too far towards mobility. Massey (1992: 14) notes that 'a large component of the identity of that place called home derived precisely from the fact that it had always in one way or another been open; constructed out of movement, communication, social relations which always stretched beyond it'. Homes are never cut off from the exterior worlds that surround and circulate through such spaces. The physical journey back is always an emotional and imaginative journey through memory (Marschall, 2012, 2015). While homesickness refers to a particular longing for a spatial and geographical location, nostalgia appeals to a temporal location. As Emily's and Nilaya's experience highlighted in the previous section, even when someone returns to the place where they grew up, they can never truly return to the 'original home of childhood, since it exists mostly as a place in the imagination' (Rubenstein, 2001: 4). Reflecting further on the meaning of home, Jen, who relocated from Canada to Australia, remarked:

> It resonates with you. You feel like everything's kind of right in a way, because that's your place, you're comfortable. And so it becomes home because you walk down a street [in Nova Scotia, Canada] that I remember falling on when I was a kid and skinning my knee; or it's home because I meet up with a friend and I remember twenty years ago we walked down the same road; or I drive past my high school and I remember every day going in there.
>
> (Jen)

As Jen highlights, homes hold strong social and emotional attachments and they are also understood to be open places that are developed through social relations that stretch beyond their walls. Her home in Halifax, Nova Scotia resonates with her via her imagination because the place is imbued with memories of familiar and well-worn pavements on which particular events, like falling and skinning her knee, occurred. The 'long poem of walking' those spaces builds up a narrative of someone's life and inserts its countless references and orientations into them, such as 'social models, cultural mores, [and] personal factors' (de Certeau, 1984: 101). The roads Jen describes are not just physical markers of the home and community in which she once lived, but sensory markers that hold memories and reconnect her to that location. For Jen, her present home in Australia never quite feels like the home of her childhood, yet the home, place and relationships of her childhood no longer exist outside of her imagination. Home is not just the physical structure or geographical location of Adelaide or Halifax but also an emotional and imagined/remembered space.

The use of the word 'resonate' in Jen's excerpt featured in many participants' descriptions of home and belonging. This word is an interesting choice because part of the difficulty of describing feelings of home and belonging is that these concepts are not just thought and imagined in the mind as a cognitive process but thought and felt through the body, and they are therefore difficult to articulate through language alone. The concepts have physical, emotional, imaginative and spiritual connotations. The word 'resonate' gives voice, within the limits of language, to the embodied character of these concepts, where repeated practices in a location build up over time to produce a sense of belonging and home. The places in which we live (physically and imaginatively) continue to ring out or echo with signs of ourselves, our practices in space and our relations to other people. Belonging is an embodied process and is therefore thought *through* the body, 'not in a flight away from it' (Braidotti, 2002: 5).

Sharon, having lived in several European countries as a journalist, moved from the UK to Australia ten years ago. Describing her motivation for moving, she said:

> We came partly due to economics. We also came in search of the fabled better life. But to be honest, we came for the same reason that most things happen in life, serendipity met determination to do something more with our lives.
>
> (Sharon)

Like Jen, she feels like she belongs in Australia but it does not feel like home because her history in Australia is relatively short.

> Belonging and home are different to me. I feel I now belong here, in Adelaide – particularly at the swimming pool, at my surf club and with my Pommy friends. Home is something else. It's a feeling of relief, safety, refuge and feeling totally at one with your surroundings and their history. I used to feel that in one room at my parents' house in the UK. I have never felt it since. Sadly, my parents sold that house to their local airport (Stansted) last year. I've just found out that plans for the airport's expansion – hotly debated since I was seven years old – have now been approved. My room, my refuge, is about to be bulldozed and buried under a runway.
>
> (Sharon)

While the act of migration forces people to learn how to adapt in a new environment, it also forces them to question and reflect upon where they have come from. Even though people may develop multiple sites of belonging throughout their lives, these sites may never replace their homes of childhood, the separation from which caused them to reflect upon and search for a renewed sense of belonging. In Probyn's (1996) words, home is a 'suspended beginning'. For Sharon, home can no longer be physically returned to and her reflections and memories of past homes reinstate and revise her memories of home in the present. Fortier (2001) describes how homes can be a destination and an origin, in that the homes we move towards always relate to those left behind. Movement towards some homes requires the imaginative 'fixing' of others.

Sharon's statement that home is 'feeling totally at one with your surroundings' underscores the impossibility of returning to a place once conceived of as home, precisely because home 'is not exterior to a self, but implicated in it' (Ahmed, 1999: 343). The emotional connotations projected onto Sharon's previous home, through the repetitive homemaking practices of her childhood, are problematised in a metaphorical and physical sense through the destruction caused by the bulldozer. Until now, Sharon was able to return to this space in her memory, particularly because it still existed as a physical site, which provided a sense of home at a distance and which she could always visit if she desired. While it was unlikely that Sharon would ever return there permanently, there was a sense of comfort in knowing it was there. What she longed for is a spatial and geographical location that has been destroyed in a physical sense, which in turn has interrupted her imaginative nostalgia for this temporal childhood location. The destruction of the site of such longing disrupts and transforms her narrative of home. Ultimately, Jen's and Sharon's examples demonstrate how their mobility has produced, by a sort of reversal, an exploration of the abandoned places of their memory.

Sharon also narrated how she found characteristics in new homes that reminded her of a previous home. However, she continues to feel in between homes because neither the UK nor Australia fulfil the role of 'home' in an uninterrupted sense:

The landscape, where we live [in Australia], looks very similar to the rolling green hills where I grew up in the UK. Sometimes when I drive up Alexander Road there's a connection that's made in my brain, and I suddenly have a sensation of 'home' – the kind of feeling I had as a child when I'd been at school all day and then I would head home. But it doesn't last. My brain fights with itself and reminds me that this isn't my home and that I've only been here five years. It's like a switch goes on and then it's cut off. I find that hard. I so desperately want to feel at home here or somewhere. When I go back to the UK now, I don't feel at home there either.

(Sharon)

Travelling memories are always lived locally. The sensory experience of driving up this road connects Sharon to a previous home through a complex intertwining of emotion, meaning and memory. It is both a physical and embodied journey as well as a symbolic and imaginative one. As she says, driving up this road, she is momentarily transplanted to another time and place, though this never lasts long. Low and Kalekin-Fishman's (2010: 198) concept of 'sensorial transnationalism' is relevant to Sharon's experience. While she is visually sensing a localised space in

Adelaide, Australia, she consumes it through her memory of transnational sense-scapes and previous homes. How she responds to the sensory pull of previous homes in different cultural contexts may change depending on how long she lives in Australia. Sharon tries to reconcile a sensory interface between the familiar landscapes of her homeland and her new 'surrogate' (Leite, 2005: 283) surroundings in Australia. Staeheli and Nagel (2006: 1599) suggest that 'in leaving home, immigrants must make a new home, and they must negotiate the contradictions of both homes, even as they may feel they belong to neither'. Expressed in a slightly different way, Ahmed (1999: 330–331) suggests that 'home becomes the impossibility and necessity of the subject's future (one never gets there, but is always getting there), rather than the past which binds the self to a given place'. Sharon visually consumes landscapes in Australia that remind her of home in Britain. However, recognition of this British countryside aesthetic is fleeting and often leaves her more emotionally bereft of a home in either place. Neither place, here or there, fulfils the expectation of a home in its fullest sense.

With terms like 'flows' (Favell, Feldblum & Smith, 2007; Sassen, 2001), 'liquid modernity' (Bauman, 2000) and 'tipping points' (Urry, 2005), the past two decades have produced a range of metaphors to capture the increasing global movement of people, ideas, information and capital. However, even if identities are becoming more flexible and 'privatised', as Bauman (2000) suggests, people often continue to desire a sense of belonging and attachment to a grounded community. Eva was born in Poland and migrated to Australia with her mother when she was a child. Her current profession as a university researcher involves many overseas visits of various durations and has incorporated multiple trips back to her homeland. She describes how she did not feel as though Australia was her home for about fifteen years. She did not feel she had been 'part of the landscape' long enough and that this could only be attained 'through the passing of time' and the creation of 'new memories' in Australia. In the following excerpt, Eva talks about how she came to 're-articulate' her new surroundings in Adelaide as 'home':

> I started walking some of the familiar streets as an adult rather than a child, and having that sense of history. 'Once upon a time I was here as a child and now I am here as an adult'. I remember walking outside and I thought 'I could really stay here for the next twenty years and not move anywhere', and I found that striking because we moved thirteen times in the first two years in Australia, so not to be on the move, not to be living in boxes, I had this realisation, 'I could stay here' and I thought 'Why? Is it because it's my home?' And part of it was because something familiar from Poland happened to me on Hunter Rd [in Adelaide], the trees, the leafage. And so I think I re-identified it and re-articulated it back into a new landscape.

> (Eva)

Several ideas thread through this passage. First, the act of walking itself can be a practice that intensifies a person's relationship between self and landscape (Cresswell & Merriman, 2011: 6; Lorimer, 2011: 24). In the line 'once upon a time I was here as a child and now I am here as an adult', Eva invokes the genre of the archetypal fairy-tale, which accomplishes a sense of inevitability that this is how life should be, and until she had lived these experiences in Australia, she could not identify with the normalcy of this narrative. She was outside of that archetypal linear narrative until she realised the sense of history here that had not previously been available to her. Eva also describes how she 're-identified and re-articulated' her previous Polish home 'back into a new landscape', expressing a particularly creative way of negotiating foreign surroundings. Like Sharon, she also finds familiar aspects of the European scenery that she remembers as a child and either recreates them in her garden at home or searches for them in public spaces in order to insert former connections and identities into new homes.

Eva discusses the labour she has put into creating a space of belonging in her garden at home. By actively working the earth, she feels as though she is creating a connection and attachment to that place. Many scholars have explored the ways dwellings are transformed into homes in the context of everyday and habitual activities (e.g. Blunt & Dowling, 2006; Pink, 2004). This might include cyclical events, such as birthdays and religious gatherings, as well as routine activities. We embed our 'selves' in places through routine activities such as walking, or in this case, gardening, creating spaces for the enunciation and expression of a self in space:

You often associate home with a building, a street, so that's one layer. Then another layer, at home with my chickens in my garden, where I can smell familiar smells, my cooking smells, I'm walking around and I know this is my space and my place . . . I was walking home from a bus recently and I saw my house in the distance, and I went 'This is my home', and I thought 'Oh, why did I think that?' and it's because it's as a result of the labour of my hands, because I garden in it, I've made it look the way it looks, it's that claiming, that sense of having a home because I have worked on the land.

(Eva)

In Eva's garden she plants vegetables from her childhood in Poland (e.g. potatoes, beetroots, radishes and parsley) and uses these to make dishes that her mother used to cook for her. Bergson's concept of 'habit memory' is relevant here, which describes the way memory 'accumulates in the body' through repetitive activities that invoke the past to be re-lived in the present (Whitehead, 2009: 133). Eva's narrative once again highlights the sensory geographies of home through smell, sight and repetitive activity within a space – a 'domestic entanglement of nature and culture' (Blunt, 2005: 512). Eva talks about her 'intimate relationship' with the soil, a garden she has created, and how she 'feeds, nurtures and works' with it. She is able to develop a sense of knowing about her place through her homemaking and gardening experiences, which perform an embodied claiming of space as a form of belonging (Tilley, 2006; Wise & Chapman, 2005).

Other participants also found ways to creatively bring together the past and the present. Nilaya reconciles her traditional Indian culture with an Australian sense of identity in a form of creative 'reappropriation' (Nilaya). For example, for the past five years Nilaya's family have spent ANZAC Day (national day of remembrance to commemorate Australians and New Zealanders who served in war) with a group of their Australian friends, and she always brings Indian food to share with them on this occasion. Aussie lamb is creatively altered using Indian spices:

> As for ANZAC Day – we do go for the march to see 'our Uncle Bob' march and then gather at our friends. I do Aussie lamb with Indian spices and our friends (local extended family) cook it in the Weber with coals and wood chips!! Potatoes too I do with Indian spices – they do not last very long! Through all this process, the smells, sounds (grinding, pounding etc.) do bring back childhood memories – interestingly my girls find this noise in the 'early morning' too disturbing! They also say, I do agree on this one, the house 'stinks' of Indian spices – I am trying to find a way to overcome this.
>
> (Nilaya)

De Certeau (1984: xvii) would liken Nilaya's appropriation to 'poach[ing]' a particular understanding of the ANZAC celebration. Nilaya states that it is about creating 'familial' ties and 'doing things together'. She also remarks how 'you don't see the resemblance at first' but then local and national understandings of belonging can be taken and inflected with their own personal meanings and interpretation. The ritual of ANZAC Day becomes an opportunity for performing solidarity amongst diversity. It is a particular occasion for coming together and solidifying or renewing national identity – even when inflected with cross-cultural 'spices'. Nilaya's participation includes their heritage in this national occasion, connecting them to a (white settler) narrative of Australia and part of its relatively recent history. Tastes of her past are inserted into English-Australian dishes through making, sharing and eating together (Demossier, 2000; Duruz, 2011; Karaosmanoglu, 2009; Sutton, 2010). De Certeau (1985: 158) has said that we cannot 'reduce to assimilation the adaptability of a foreign body to the host country', but rather this adaptability involves 'a whole panoply of tactics to reuse parts of the culture for one's own purposes'. In the ANZAC Day example, Nilaya and her family creatively inhabit different cultural configurations as acts of both assimilation and reappropriation. Insinuating themselves into the place of another by dwelling, cooking and reappropriating (de Certeau, 1984: 117) becomes a form of creative bricolage linking old homes to new ones.

Conclusion

This chapter has shown how participants were often caught between multiple homes, personal ties, shifting subject positions and insider/outsider identities such as tourist, resident, migrant, traveller, guest and citizen. The reality is that they were all of these and more at different times and in different places. However, they continued to make and re-make home, despite feelings of 'in-betweenness', through their homemaking practices and a rearticulation of sensory geographies in new contexts. Participants' embodied practices of socialising, speaking, gardening, cooking, walking and interpreting have the purpose of 'carv[ing] out life chances' from spaces that at first appeared too foreign (Deleuze, 1997: 3). They sought to make strange places familiar through repetitive practices that echoed former selves and homes. While memories travel along with these mobile settlers, they are still practised, rehearsed and invoked in local contexts. Participants' memories function far more than simply 'remembrances' but involve complex and intertwining stories, scripts (Erll, 2011: 14) and embodied knowledge that are continually reinforced as well as revised in new locations.

While the mobility of participants meant that home had become multi-sited, these participants still desired strong, embedded connections. They put down roots and dwell in locations rather than simply passing through them. For example, participants' sense of belonging was developed through multiple grounded practices such as gardening and Eva's tactile interaction with the soil; visual practices such as Sharon's search for familiar landscapes in Australia; and the sharing of different tastes when Nilaya cooked 'Aussie lamb' in 'Indian spices'. Importantly, participants' homemaking practices highlight that working with everyday home spaces involves making connections between past, present and future homes. The multiple sites of home are experienced as 'material and immaterial, lived and imagined, localized and (trans)national space[s]' of belonging (Walsh, 2006: 123). Remembering becomes an active process and constitutes a motion of attachment that journeys back and forth between homes and involves a 'continual reprocessing of what home is/was/might have been' (Fortier, 2003). In this way, their everyday worlds are not bounded zones of activity but are produced through movements and entanglements within and beyond them.

As this chapter has shown, sensory experiences are often the site of uneasy tensions between surrender and resistance, between 'fitting in' by 'borrowing' the practices of another and actively 're-interpreting' local habits with personal inflections. Their sense of belonging involved tangible resources, everyday embodied practices, as well as memory and emotion, and was represented by the participants as both an imagined and actual geography. It was also a fluid and temporal process where people sometimes feel they belong and sometimes do not, at different times and in different places (as well as the same places). Their relations to mobility and dwelling, migration and travel, home and belonging are understood as mutually constitutive processes.

References

Ahmed, S. (1999). Home and away: Narratives of migration and estrangement. *International Journal of Cultural Studies*, 2(3), 329–347.

Al-Ali, N. & Koser, K. (2002). *New approaches to migration? Transnational communities and the transformation of home*. London, New York: Routledge.

Anthias, F. (2002). Where do I belong: Narrating collective identity and translocational positionality. *Ethnicities*, 2(4), 491–514.

Baldassar, L. (2001). *Visits Home: Migration Experiences Between Italy and Australia.* Carlton Victoria: Melbourne University Press.

Bauman, Z. (2000). *Liquid Modernity.* Cambridge: Polity Press.

Beaverstock, J. (2005). Transnational elites in the city: British highly-skilled inter-company transferees in New York city's financial district. *Journal of Ethnic and Migration Studies,* 31(2), 245–268.

Benson, M. & O'Reilly K. (2016). *Lifestyle Migration: Expectations, Aspirations and Experiences.* Farnham: Ashgate.

Blunt, A. (2005). Cultural geography: Cultural geographies of home. *Progress in Human Geography,* 29(4), 505–515.

Blunt, A. & Dowling, R. (2006). *Home.* London: Routledge.

Boccagni, P. & Baldassar, L. (2015). Emotions on the move: Mapping the emergent field of emotion and migration. *Emotion, Space and Society,* 16, 73–80.

Bosniak, L. (2001). Denationalising citizenship. In: T. Aleinikoff & D. Klumeyer, eds., *Citizenship Today: Global Perspectives and Practices.* Washington DC: Brookings Inst./Carnegie Endow. Int. Peace, pp. 237–252.

Braidotti, R. (2002). *Metamorphoses: Towards a Materialist Theory of Becoming.* Cambridge: Polity.

Bruner, J. (2003). *Making Stories: Law, Literature and Life.* Cambridge, MA: Harvard University Press.

Castells, M. (2000). Towards a sociology of the network society. *Contemporary Sociology,* 29(5), 693–699.

Chau, A. (2008). The sensorial production of the social. *Ethnos: Journal of Anthropology,* 73, 485–504.

Clark, W. & Withers, S. (2008). Family migration and mobility sequences in the United States: Spatial mobility in the context of the life course. *Demographic Research,* 17(20), 591–615.

Classen, C. (1997). Foundations for an anthropology of the senses. *International Social Science Journal,* 153, 401–412.

Cohen, S., Duncan, T. & Thulemark, M. (2015). Lifestyle mobilities: The crossroads of travel, leisure and migration. *Mobilities,* 10(1), 155–172.

Conradson, D. & Latham, A. (2005). Friendship, networks and transnationality in a world city: Antipodean transmigrants in London. *Journal of Ethnic and Migration Studies,* 31(2), 287–305.

Conradson, D. & Latham, A. (2007). The affective possibilities of London: Antipodean transnationals and the overseas experience. *Mobilities,* 2(2), 231–254.

Cresswell, T. & Merriman, P. (2011). Introduction. In: T. Cresswell & P. Merriman, eds., *Geographies and Mobilities: Practices, Space, Subjects.* Farnham: Ashgate, pp. 1–15.

de Certeau, M. (1984). *The Practice of Everyday Life.* Berkeley, CA: University of California Press.

de Certeau, M. (1985). L'actif et le passif des appurtenances. *Esprit,* June, 155–171.

Deleuze, G. (1997). *Essays Critical and Clinical.* Minneapolis, MN: University of Minnesota Press.

Demossier, M. (2000). Culinary heritage and *produits of terroir* in France: Food for thought. In: S. Blowen, M. Demossier & J. Picard, eds., *Recollections of France: Memories, Identities and Heritage in Contemporary France.* Oxford: Berghahn, pp. 141–153.

Dhingra, L. (1993). La vie en rose. In: K. Pullinger, ed., *Border Lines: Stories of Exile and Home.* New York: Serpent's Tail, pp. 97–118.

Duncan, T., Cohen, S. & Thulemark, M. (2013). *Lifestyle Mobilities: Intersections of Travel, Leisure and Migration.* New York: Routledge.

Dunn, K. (2010). Embodied transnationalism: Bodies in transnational spaces. *Population, Space and Place*, 16(1), 1–9.

Duruz, J. (2011). Quesadillas with Chinese black bean puree: Eating together in 'ethnic' neighbourhoods. *New Formations*, 74, winter, 46–64.

Ehrkamp, P. & Leitner, H. (2006). Rethinking immigration and citizenship: New spaces of migrant transnationalism and belonging. *Environment & Planning A*, 38, 1591–1597.

Erll, A. (2011). Travelling memory. *Parallax*, 17(4), 4–18.

Fan, C. (2002). The elite, the natives, and the outsiders: Migration and labor market segmentation in urban China. *Annals of the Association of American Geographers*, 92(1), 103–124.

Favell, A., Feldblum, M. & Smith, M. (2007). The human face of global mobility: A research agenda. *Transaction Social Science and Modern Society*, 44(2), 15–25.

Fortier, A. (2001). 'Coming home': Queer migrations and multiple evocations of home. *European Journal of Cultural Studies*, 4(4), 405–424.

Fortier, A. (2003). Making home: Queer migrations and motions of attachments In: S. Ahmed, C. Castaneda, A. Fortier & M. Sheller, eds., *Uprootings/Regroundings: Questions of Home and Migration.* Oxford: Berg, pp. 115–136.

Gardner, K. (2006). The transnational work of kinship and caring: Bengali-British marriages in historical perspective. *Global Networks*, 6(4), 373–387.

Gilmartin, M. & Migge, B. (2016). Migrant mothers and the geographies of belonging. *Gender, Place and Culture*, 23(2), 147–161.

Hannam, K. (2008). Tourism geographies, tourist studies and the turn towards mobilities. *Geography Compass*, 2(1), 127–139.

Ho, C. (2006). Migration as feminisation? Chinese women's experiences of work and family in Australia. *Journal of Ethnic and Migration Studies*, 23(3), 497–514.

Ho, E. (2009). Constituting citizenship through the emotions: Singaporean transmigrants in London. *Annals of the Association of American Geographers*, 99(4), 788–804.

Ho, E. (2011). Migration trajectories of 'highly skilled' middling transnationals: Singaporean transmigrants in London. *Population, Space and Place*, 17(1), 116–129.

Howes, D. (2006). Cross-talk between the senses. *Senses and Society*, 1(3), 381–390.

Hsu, E. (2008). The senses and the social: An introduction. *Ethnos: Journal of Anthropology*, 73(4), 433–443.

Karaosmanoglu, D. (2009). Eating the past: Multiple spaces, multiple times – Performing 'Ottomanness' in Istanbul. *International Journal of Cultural Studies*, 12, 339–358.

Kennedy, R. & Nugent, M. (2016). Scales of memory: Reflections on an emerging concept. *Australian Humanities Review*, April/May, 61–76.

Kennedy, R. & Radstone, S. (2013). Memory up close: Memory studies in Australia. *Memory Studies*, 6(3), 237–244.

Kofman, E. & Raghuram, P. (2005). Gender and skilled migrations: Into and beyond the work place. *GeoForum*, 36(2), 149–154.

Leite, N. (2005). Travels to an ancestral past: On diasporic tourism, embodied memory, and identity. *Antropológicas*, 9, 273–302.

Lorimer, H. (2011). Walking: New forms and spaces for studies of pedestrianism. In: T. Cresswell & P. Merriman, eds., *Geographies and Mobilities: Practices, Space, Subjects.* Farnham: Ashgate, pp. 19–34.

Low, K. (2012). The social life of the senses: Charting directions. *Sociology Compass*, 6(3), 271–282.

Low, K. & Kalekin-Fishman, D. (2010). Afterword: Towards transnational sensescapes. In: D. Kalekin-Fishman and K. Low, eds., *Everyday Life in Asia: Social Perspectives on the Senses*. Farnham: Ashgate, pp. 195–203.

Madison, G. (2009). *The End of Belonging: Untold Stories of Leaving Home and the Psychology of Global Relocation*. London: Greg A. Madison.

Marschall, S. (2012). 'Personal memory tourism' and a wider exploration of the tourism-memory nexus. *Journal of Tourism and Cultural Change*, 10(4), 321–335.

Marschall, S. (2015). 'Travelling down memory lane': Personal memory as a generator of tourism. *Tourism Geographies*, 17(1), 36–53.

Marschall, S. (2017). Migrants on home visits: Memory, identity and a shifting sense of self. *International Journal of Tourism Research*, 19(2), 214–222.

Massey, D. (1992). A place called home. *New Formations*, 7, 3–15.

Massey, D. (2003). Some times of space. In: S. May, ed., *Olafur Eliassen: The Weather Project*. Exhibition Catalogue. London: Tate Publishing, pp. 107–118.

May, J., Wills, J., Datta, K., Evans, Y., Herbert, J. & McIlwaine, C. (2007). Keeping London working: Global cities, the British state and London's new migrant division of labour. *Transactions of the Institute of British Geographers*, 32(2), 151–167.

McDowell, L., Batnitzky, A. & Dyer, S. (2008). Internationalization and the spaces of temporary labour: The global assembly of local workforce. *British Journal of Industrial Relations*, 46(4), 750–770.

Nagel, C. (2005). Skilled migration in global cities from 'Other' perspectives: British Arabs, identity politics, and local embededdness. *GeoForum*, 36, 197–210.

Noy, C. (2008). Sampling knowledge: The hermeneutics of snowball sampling in qualitative research. *International Journal of Social Research Methodology*, 11(4), 327–344.

Pink, S. (2004). *Home Truths: Gender, Domestic Objects and Everyday Life*. Oxford: Berg.

Probyn, E. (1996). *Outside Belongings*. New York: Routledge.

Recchi, E. (2006). From migrants to movers: Citizenship and mobility in the European Union. *The Human Face of Global Mobility*, 53–77.

Riessman C. (2008). *Narrative Methods for the Human Sciences*. London: Sage.

Rubenstein, R. (2001). *Home Matters: Longing and Belonging, Nostalgia and Mourning in Women's Fiction*. New York: Palgrave.

Rutten, M. & Verstappen, S. (2014). Middling migration: Contradictory experiences of Indian youth in London. *Journal of Ethnic and Migration Studies*, 40(8), 1217–1235.

Ryan, L., Klekowski Von Koppenfels, A. & Mulholland, J. (2015). 'The distance between us': A comparative examination of the technical, spatial and temporal dimensions of the transnational social relationships of highly skilled migrants. *Global Networks*, 15, 198–216.

Ryan, L. & Mulholland, J. (2014). Trading places: French highly skilled migrants negotiating mobility and emplacement in London. *Journal of Ethnic and Migration Studies*, 40(4), 584–600.

Sassen, S. (2001). *Global Networks, Linked Cities*. New York: Routledge.

Skrbis, Z. (2008). Transnational families: Theorising migration, emotions and belonging. *Journal of Intercultural Studies*, 29(3), 231–246.

Staeheli, L. & Nagel, C. (2006). Topographies of home and citizenship: Arab American activists. *Environment and Planning A*, 38(9), 1599–1614.

Sutton, D. (2010). Food and the senses. *Annual Review of Anthropology*, 39, 209–223.

Svasek, M. (2010). On the move: Emotions and human mobility. *Journal of Ethnic and Migration Studies*, 36(6), 865–880.

Taylor, P. (2004). *World City Network: A Global Urban Analysis*. New York: Routledge.

Tilley, C. (2006). The sensory dimensions of gardening. *Senses and Society*, 1(3), 311–330.

Tolia-Kelly, D. (2006). Affect – an ethnocentric encounter? Exploring the 'universalist' imperative of emotional/affectual geographies. *Area*, 38(2), 213–217.

Tolia-Kelly, D. (2007). Fear in paradise: The affective registers of the English Lake District landscape re-visited. *Senses and Society*, 2(3), 329–352.

Urry, J. (2005). The complexities of the global. *Theory, Culture & Society*, 22(5), 235–254.

Walsh, K. (2006). British expatriate belongings: Mobile homes and transnational homing. *Home Cultures*, 3(2), 123–144.

Werbner, P. & Yuval-Davis, N. (1999). Women and the new discourse of citizenship. In: N. Yuval-Davis & P. Werbner, eds., *Women, Citizenship and Difference*. London: Zed Books, pp. 1–38.

Whitehead, A. (2009). *Memory*. London: Routledge.

Williams, A. & Hall, C. (2000). Tourism and migration: New relationships between production and consumption. *Tourism Geographies: An International Journal of Tourism Space, Place and Environment*, 2(1), 5–27.

Wise, A. & Chapman, A. (2005). Introduction: Migration, affect and the senses. *Journal of Intercultural Studies*, 26(1–2), 1–3.

Yuval-Davis, N. (2006). Belonging and the politics of belonging. *Patterns of Prejudice*, 40(3), 197–214.

3 Material culture, memory and commemoration

Family and community celebrations and connections to 'home' among Asian Indian immigrants

Caroline B. Brettell

Introduction

In her novel *Umbertina*, Helen Barolini (1979) organizes her story of several generations of an Italian-American family around a material artefact that evokes memory. This artefact, a matrimonial bedspread that the title character Umbertina brings with her to America, symbolizes hopes and dreams, a lost past, the passing on of tradition, a sense of belonging, a family history. The bedspread embodies cultural memory and hence alleviates the distress of displacement. At the end of the novel, Umbertina's great-granddaughter Tina, who is not aware of the story of the bedspread, sees it in an exhibit of immigrant life at Ellis Island, labelled as 'owner unknown' and acquired by a social worker named Anna Giordani in 1886 – when it was sold by a heartbroken and poor Umbertina so that she could start life anew in upstate New York. Tina exclaims (the reader understands the irony):

> Look at that . . . isn't it gorgeous? Calabria – that's where my grandmother's people were from. In fact I'm named for the immigrant named Umbertina. She should have brought such a spread with her – isn't it gorgeous! Then it would have been passed down to me, maybe.

Barolini describes Tina standing before the vitrine

> drinking in the beauty and warmth of the old spread. Its colors irradiated her spirit; the woven designs of grapes and tendrils and fig leaves and flowers and spreading acanthus spoke to her of Italy and the past and keeping it all together for the future. It was as if her old ancestor, the Umbertina she had fruitlessly sought in Castagna, had suddenly become manifest in the New World and spoken to her.
>
> (Barolini, 1979: 407–408)

While Umbertina is a fictional character, Ana Bogart is not. She was born in Poland and was a teenager when Germany invaded her country in 1939. She escaped Nazi Germany into Siberia, eventually married and made her way to America with a prized possession, a thimble. In the United States she fulfilled her ambition to become a professional fashion designer. Writing her story, Ron Siebler (2017: 4P) observes that the thimble, 'a childhood gift, was among the few things that survived the war alongside her. Ultimately, it would serve her as a poignant reminder, one that connected her new life with the one destroyed by war'. He saw it perched on a stand next to her bed when he visited her as she was dying – 'as a symbol of persistence, endurance, resilience, strength, tenacity, and of life well-lived'.

During the last decade, inspired by the essays in Arjun Appadurai's (1986) edited volume on the social life of things as well as by a renewed emphasis on commodities, consumption and materiality within cultural anthropology more broadly (Miller, 2005, 2010; Tilley *et al.*, 2006), anthropologists and other social scientists have begun to explore the associations between migration and material culture (Basu & Coleman, 2008; Svašek, 2012a; Wang, 2016). They have described the items that migrants (like the fictional Umbertina and the real-life Ana Bogart) carry with them (Burrell, 2012); they have documented domestic spaces that are replete with objects and foodstuffs from native countries that invoke emotions, memories and a sense of belonging (Attan, 2006; Gronseth, 2012; Parrott, 2012; Rosales, 2010; Sutton, 2001; Tolia-Kelly, 2004, 2006); they have described videos and artistic artefacts (such as Hmong story cloths) that serve to sustain traditions and customs (Koltyk, 1998); and they have analysed the commodities that flow across the global landscape to support religious and other activities within immigrant diasporic communities (Abranches, 2014; Burrell, 2012; Norris, 2008; Plasquy, 2012). Material objects clearly travel within transnational social fields connecting migrants to their home societies as they also root them in the place to which they have migrated. David Parkin (1999: 315), who writes primarily about the things that refugees take with them with minimal time to decide, has argued that people on the move 'store their precluded social personhood within mementoes of mind and matter, including cherished small objects, songs, dances and rituals, which can, under favourable circumstances, be re-articulated (even recreated) as bases of social activity'. Thus, migration is not only about 'migrants' relationships with migrant or non-migrant people, but also about their relationships with migrant objects'. These objects materialize memory.

Many of these objects function in relationship to ritual practices that operate in transnational space, a relatively under-researched phenomenon, according to Gardner and Grillo (2002), by comparison with transnational economic and political practices. Among these are lifecycle rituals such as weddings and funerals which in their performance yield important understandings of how mobile populations conceptualize space and belonging (Fortier, 2000; Gardner, 1998; Kaiser, 2008; Olwig, 2002). The transnational practice of some of these rituals can highlight dimensions of status and hierarchy, and particularly success abroad (Mand, 2002; Salih, 2002). Scholars have called attention to the vast resources – social, symbolic and material – that are mustered to carry out transnational rituals, particularly wedding rituals. They also emphasize how the study of the performance of such lifecycle events can open up understanding about how ritual is connected to 'memory and the construction of personhood under conditions of transnationalism' (Gardner & Grillo, 2002: 188). As Svašek (2012b: 6, 19, 27) has suggested, through ritual practices (as a form of 'embodied engagement'), and with the aid of religious artefacts, diasporic identities are enacted and ties to the homeland are sustained. Cultural or collective memory is thus encoded in rituals and celebrations as well as in the objects and monuments with which they are related.

This chapter offers an analysis of the intersections of migration, cultural memory, commemoration and material culture at three sites of embodied engagement that link Asian Indian immigrants who have settled in the Dallas-Fort Worth (henceforth, DFW) metropolitan area with their homeland.[1] One of these sites is more personal and familial; the second involves the broader immigrant community of Indian national origin who live in the DFW area; and the third carries not only local but also international and diasporic dimensions. The central question here is how rituals and community celebrations and gatherings, as well as the material culture with which they are associated, play a role in the formation of identity and the maintenance of a presence in and hence connection to the country of birth or heritage both in memory and in practice. The chapter begins with a brief discussion of the growth of the Asian Indian immigrant population in DFW. It then turns to a discussion of the varied sensory and material dimensions of transnational wedding rituals. This is followed by a discussion of one community festival that serves as an arena of collective memory and commemoration and that is equally replete with the material objects of home that foster belonging and identity. The next section focuses on the creation, by the DFW Indian-American community, of a memorial plaza dedicated to Mahatma Gandhi. Here a single monumental object that materially embodies the idea of India has become a gathering place for the local population, a place of pilgrimage for distinguished Indian visitors from abroad, and ultimately, a site of political memory. Each of the sites of engagement discussed in this chapter involves travel, real or virtual, of people and/or things.

The data introduced in this chapter are drawn from a broader research project on processes of immigrant political, social and economic incorporation in a new urban gateway (Brettell, 2005a, 2008a; Brettell & Reed-Danahay, 2012). While the aims of this project were not expressly to study family and community rituals, through participant observation fieldwork I inevitably found myself attending numerous public and private events, including weddings and community festivals. This chapter is based largely on these fieldwork data.

Asian Indians in the Dallas metropolitan area

During the first two decades of the twenty-first century, Asian Indians were one of the fastest-growing immigrant populations in the United States. Although individuals from the Indian subcontinent have been in the country since the nineteenth century (Leonard, 1997), they were generally few in number by comparison with other immigrant populations. It was not until 1980 that the US Census officially categorized them as a separate group, counting 387,223 nationwide. By 2000, the number of foreign-born from India rose to just over 1 million, representing 3.3 percent of the total foreign-born population in the United States. A decade later, the census counted just over 3 million. While the largest areas of settlement for Asian Indians are in the states of California, New York, New Jersey and Illinois, Asian Indians can also be found in significant numbers in Greater Washington, DC, Atlanta, Houston, Phoenix and Dallas. In DFW, a small number of Indians arrived in the early 1960s to take up employment in scientific and technical fields at local universities and with companies such as Texas Instruments. With the expansion of hi-tech industries, the growth of the city, including the growth in the health sector, the number of Asian Indians also increased, especially after 1980. As some of them became citizens, they began to sponsor relatives, some of whom did not have the same level of education. The second-wave immigrants found employment as small-business owners, providing a range of services from restaurants, to motels, to grocery and convenience stores, to jewellery and sari shops. The new boom in technology in the 1990s, coupled with the expansion of the H1B highly skilled worker visa category, resulted in a new wave of young and well-educated Indians, many of them software engineers. The significant growth in the health sector was another draw. Thus, despite some class diversity, the DFW area has attracted a large number of new economy professionals who are extremely prosperous. Given their employment patterns and high levels of education (in 2010, 40 percent of Asian Indians in Dallas had graduate or professional degrees), it is no surprise that Asian Indians in DFW, according to the 2010 US Census, had the highest median household income of all Asian groups. At $85,000, this income was also well above the overall median income of $69,000 for non-Hispanic whites.[2]

In Dallas County, Indians first settled in the inner-ring suburb of Richardson where the public school system was strong and where some of the early hi-tech companies set up offices. The population doubled during each decade and with this growth expanded north into the suburban communities of Collin County, especially Plano, west into the community of Irving, and most recently northwest into communities such as Carrollton and Lewisville in Denton County. Between 2000 and 2010, the foreign-born Asian Indian population in Collin, Dallas, Denton, Rockwall and Tarrant Counties (the core counties of the DFW metroplex) rose from 49,181 to 106,964. If their US-born children are added to these numbers, this community has a significant presence in the area.

Over the years an economic, social and religious infrastructure has emerged to accommodate this growing community, beginning with the DFW Hindu Temple in Irving, an inner suburb adjacent to and west of the city of Dallas and the Taj Mahal Grocery Store located in a strip mall in Richardson, a suburb adjacent to and just north of the city of Dallas (Brettell, 2005b, 2008b). Today, however, this infrastructure (or cultural landscape [Brettell & Reed-Danahay, 2012]) includes other temples, churches, mosques and grocery stores, as well as restaurants, clothing stores, radio stations, an entertainment facility called 'FunAsia' and a broad range of community organizations. In relation to material culture, the grocery stores are certainly important as they are the marketplace for finding familiar items that form the basis for family meals and ritual activities as well as, occasionally, public rituals. The Taj Mahal store, for example, at the appropriate time of year, sells coloured powders to celebrate Holi, a Hindu spring festival marking the triumph of good over evil that involves people throwing these powders or coloured water at one another – referred to as 'playing holi'. Other objects, *diya* lamps, coloured powders with which to make 'Rangoli' paintings, *puja* (prayer) objects such as sandalwood, betel leaves and coconut, small statues of Lakshmi (Goddess of wealth) and Lord Ganesh, and all kinds of sweets, are sold in the fall for the celebration of Diwali, the Hindu festival of lights.

Marriage in Asian Indian immigrant communities

On December 25, 2016, the *New York Times* reported on the wedding of Smriti Keshari and Matthew Danzico (Kurutz, 2016). The reporter described the groom, mounted on a white horse, leading a parade of guests who 'danced their way to the site of an Indian tradition known as Baraat. A Hindu priest lit a fire to symbolize the illumination of the mind, knowledge and happiness'. The story goes on to mention that two days after the wedding, which took place in Hudson, New York, the couple flew to India to hold another ceremony witnessed by the bride's extended family. These elaborate two-part transnational weddings are common within Indian immigrant communities in the United States.

Social scientists have certainly recognized the significance of marriage within Asian Indian diasporic communities. They have described the process of searching for a 'suitable boy' in the context of 'arranged' marriages (Raj, 2002: 105ff; Ramdya, 2010), an activity that sometimes includes matrimonial events where the primary purpose is to bring eligible boys and girls together (Rangaswamy, 2000). Host-country-based Indian newspapers (for example, *India Abroad*) carry ads posted by families looking for matches for their children (Khandelwal, 2002) and in recent years marriage websites such as Shaadii.com have been developed. Rangaswamy (2000: 181) has pointed to a California-based matchmaking service boasting a database of 6,000 candidates that is continuously updated. She suggests that while young Indian teenagers prefer to date non-Indians, when they consider marriage they prefer Indians. Maira (2002: 123) describes some second-generation youth who worry about marrying a non-Indian, an act that would 'sully' the ethnic purity of their children and move them further away from India as a site of 'cultural authenticity'. But overall scholars identify cases of young people who go along with their parents' choices and others who are more conflicted (Dhingra, 2007; Shankar, 2008), or of marriages that are more 'assisted' than arranged (Gopalkrishnan & Babacan, 2007).

While marriage negotiations are richly treated, the weddings themselves are not as well documented (see, however, Sutherland, 2003), even though South Asian weddings are well known for their elaborate, if not ostentatious, dimensions as domestic rituals that reify social hierarchies, revitalize cultural practices, and affirm or reaffirm social relations (Werbner, 1986: 230). Further, little attention has been paid to the material and transnational dimensions of these weddings.

Leonard (1997: 164) has noted that several decades ago the preferred locations for marriage, for South Asians in the US, was in South Asia itself, not only because it was the major source for brides, but also because supplies were available and the costs were much less. However, by the 1990s South Asian weddings have increasingly been occurring in the United States or in both places. As the *New York Times* story cited above suggests, Indian diasporic marriages are often celebrated twice, once in the home country and once in the city of immigrant settlement. Immigrants and their children thus travel back (almost as a form of return tourism) during what has now become an important phase in the time-extended traditional wedding. But the transnational spaces within which people move are also arenas within which objects move – invitations, wedding clothing and jewellery, wedding decorations, and even filmed documentations. While providers of goods and services are now increasingly available in the United States, many items still come from India. A discussion of one Hindu wedding reception that I attended will illustrate these dimensions as well as the embodied sensory experiences that evoke memories of 'home'. What I describe here I witnessed at several other weddings and while this one did not include a white horse, I have certainly seen the *baraat* as part of another wedding I attended.

The wedding was that of a daughter of one of my research participants. The actual marriage had taken place in India three months earlier at 3am (the auspicious time), while what occurred in the United States was a reception for approximately 750 people at a resort area on Lake Grapevine – to the northwest of the city of Dallas. In the foyer of the area that was rented for this reception was a large Ganesh (the elephant God) altar – a 'sighted' sensory experience that immediately marked this event as a Hindu wedding (see Figure 3.1). It was there that 'cocktails' were served, beginning at 5:30. These consisted of non-alcoholic drinks, punch bowls of mango *lassi* (an Indian yogurt-based drink), and lavishly decorated tables full of Indian hors d'oeuvre – the tastes and smells of the Indian homeland on US soil. At the end of one of the tables was a large gift box where people dropped in envelopes with monetary gifts – the invitation had expressly stated 'no boxed gifts'. This practice is visually and starkly different from the tables where beautifully wrapped packages are placed at 'mainstream' American wedding receptions.

At 7 o'clock the doors to a big ballroom opened. Guests entered under a large flowered arbour which marked the room as an Indian space for the evening. They had their pictures taken, and found their table. On the tables there were Indian party favours – small picture frames used as place cards and little gold bags with cashews (a major Indian export commodity) and Indian sweets (*mithai*) in them. While guests were being seated, large screens at the front of the room showed a film of the wedding that had taken place in India including the multiple rituals that are part of the ceremony and that occur across several days – all of these telescoped into the film we were watching that transported us across oceans as virtual tourists to a place familiar to some but foreign to others. One of the other guests seated at my table observed that while Indian wedding rituals do vary by region, generally they include the henna painting of the hands and feet, the foot-washing

Figure 3.1 Statue of Ganesh, Indian wedding

Author's photograph, September 5, 2015

ceremony, the various blessings by parents, the exchange of floral garlands (*var-mala*), and the seven perambulations around a fire (*sapta-padi*) with bride and groom 'tied' to one another, and bride following groom. Ramdya (2010: 77) has explained that solemn wedding vows are encoded in these steps – with the first, the couple vows to live through happiness and sorrow together; with the third step they promise 'to speak with kindness and patience'; and with the fourth 'to remain together through good times and bad'. The fifth and sixth steps pledge absolute monogamy and honesty.

My table partner commented on the importance of celebrating these weddings in both places (India and the US) so that young people would hold on to traditions. The film shown at this wedding also included footage of a visit to the home town of the groom, thus connecting both 'home places' with one another and with the DFW area. Further, family members in India, through the film made there, were connected with the broader 'diasporic family' (the friends of the parents of the bride and groom as well as the friends of the bride and groom) that had been created in the United States. Many Indian immigrants talk about their biological kin in India and their social 'family' in the country to which they have immigrated. The wedding film is a critical form of memory-material culture, a memento of personal memory that will be kept by the married couple throughout their lives.

Once everyone was seated, a young woman, a friend of the bride, introduced herself as the emcee and then proceeded to introduce the wedding party, each entering the ballroom in turn – first, the brother of the bride, then the brother and sister of the groom, then the groom's parents, then the bride's parents, and then the bride and groom who proceeded to the stage and sat in chairs. Many of these individuals, but interestingly not the mothers of the bride and groom, came up to address the guests. Siblings joked about their brother or sister but also extended a welcome to a new family member. In this diasporic context and at this particular wedding mention was also made of the fact that the bride and groom were from different regional backgrounds with distinct languages – Tamil and Telugu. This was considered to be a hurdle in what was a 'love' marriage between a young woman who is a medical doctor and a young man who is an engineer. Indeed, the father of the groom told the assembled guests that they had been trying to find a bride for their son in India without success and had never thought to look in the Dallas area. The bride described how she met her groom at a Hindu religious centre. They hardly spoke until one day, when she was having a problem with her digital device, a friend sent a young man (her future groom) to fix it. An uncle of the groom told the story of how his nephew, whom he viewed as almost a son, had the courage to come on his own to the United States to study. These narratives of relationships and journeys are a form of oral material culture integral to the celebration of the ritual.

While most of the speeches were in English, the father of the bride, when it was his turn at the microphone, spoke initially in his native language (Telugu) (an auditory invocation of home) and then later translated his remarks into English. He thanked everyone for coming to help celebrate his daughter's wedding; he thanked all the women who had gathered to help make the wedding sweets; and he thanked those who had travelled a long distance for the event. His speech was followed by another piece of visual material culture, an amusing film made by the groom about his adjustment to married life. He used a 'before and after' approach that indicated his new duties in the household; in one segment he was shown reading a magazine in Telugu and then one in Tamil; in another he juxtaposed the movies they watched – the action films he likes and the romances she likes. Friends of the groom then performed two traditional pieces of music on a sitar and tabla, creating another auditory memory of home in the space of this very American hotel ballroom. Finally, in a concession to western weddings, the bride and groom shared a dance together and then cut the wedding cake and fed one another a bite. And then, in deference to Indian tradition, and after each had spoken to the other about their love for one another, the groom kissed his bride's hand and they embraced. It was at this point that the guests were invited to approach the buffet tables, replete with hot Indian food, vegetarian and non-vegetarian, for their meal – the tastes of home. The evening continued into the later hours with a band and dancing; much of the music consisted of familiar songs from Bollywood movies – another indication of a very Indian-style wedding reception held in the United States. As Ramdya (2010: 84) has observed, 'rather than see Bollywood's movies as a conglomeration of eastern and western cultures, second-generation Indian-American Hindus view it as an authentic source of Indian culture from which to draw in staging an ethnic Indian wedding and reception'. Music is clearly another important material dimension of 'home'.

Indian weddings are multisensory embodied experiences (Wang, 2016) where cultural memory is evoked alongside presence in the United States through sight, sound, smell and taste. Following Olwig (2002: 216), home in these weddings is first a site of social relations and obligations that connects not only families in the United States with those in India, but also the second generation to the culture and traditions of the immigrant generation. But home is also an 'entity of belonging' that marries an Indian identity with an American identity. As Salih (2002: 223) has argued, in her case for Moroccan migrants in Europe, rituals such as weddings are 'fertile and creative terrains in which ideas of traditional or modern, westernization or authentic, are molded, subverted, and reformulated'. Indian-American weddings not only involve the travel of people home to celebrate the ritual in the society of origin, but also the travel of material culture (and sometimes also of people) to the United States to recreate and reformulate the ritual in the society of immigration.

The Anand Bazaar: a public community festival

Wedding rituals and celebrations occur within transnational family spaces. Immigrant communities in the United States are also involved in broader community festivals; that is, cultural spectacles 'in which a group represents itself both to its own members and to non-members' (Bramadat, 2001: 79; see also Shukla, 1997). These events are not only sites of 'civic engagement in an expressive context' (Stepick, Stepick & Labissiere, 2002), but also occasions for commemoration and the celebration of cultural memory and heritage. As Dallen and Pena (2016: 153) argue, ethnic festivals, in their appeal to first-generation immigrants and their second-generation offspring, 'are fundamental in helping immigrant groups to maintain connection with their homeland'.

The Asian Indian community in DFW celebrates two important community-wide events annually, both of which commemorate major Indian national holidays and both of which are organized by the primary umbrella association in the area – the India Association of North Texas.[3] These festivals offer the same multisensory embodied experiences of home as weddings but in a more public arena. One of these festivals is the Anand Bazaar, celebrated every August to recognize Indian Independence Day (August 15) – hence reminding Indians in the United States of an important event in their collective national past that reshaped their global identity. The Anand Bazaar takes place at Lone Star Park, a horseracing track located in Grand Prairie, a town located between the cities of Dallas and Fort Worth. The park is decorated for the day with rows of both Indian and American flags and balloons in the colours of the Indian flag. These help to remake the place into a space of material (food, clothing, jewellery) and performative culture that reinforces cultural memory as it simultaneously establishes the presence of Indian immigrants in the United States.

The Anand Bazaar generally gets underway in the later afternoon, but people continue to arrive well into the evening hours.[4] The event is very much a family affair, with children of all ages, as well as extended family members. One year I met a woman who said that her mother was visiting from India and was very excited to be in town at the time of the Anand Bazaar and to see so many Indians in the DFW area gathered together. She felt 'at home', as if India had travelled with her. Most adult women are dressed in Indian clothing but young people and men are generally in American dress. Later in the evening, groups of teenagers and young adults arrive together, mostly to take in the food and music. One year, at the entrance to the park, there was a petting zoo where lots of parents with younger children gathered. There was also a trampoline room which was a big attraction, as well as a tall Uncle Sam on stilts who was making balloon toys for children. These were clearly an assembly of material objects that indicate, as in Indian weddings, the incorporation of elements of American festival culture into an otherwise Indian gathering to commemorate an important political holiday in India.

However, the centrepiece of the event is the bazaar, a space carved out for vendors selling clothing, rugs, handbags, jewellery, DVDs and other objects of home. Some of these vendors travel to the DFW area from other cities in Texas. One woman, who had brought her goods from Houston, said she had been in the United States for twenty-one years, first in the Boston area and then in Houston when her husband got a job there. She sold Indian clothing, all of it made in India, out of her home but also attended these bazaars when she had the opportunity. She moreover worked selling real estate in the Houston area. Another female clothing vendor, who said she had designed clothing in India, arrived in the United States three months earlier and like the first woman was now selling Indian-made clothing that she imported out of her home to make some money while raising her family. In her booth she was also selling her own artwork – Indian-style paintings.

Equally present were booths sponsored by various local businesses, particularly travel agencies who promote deals on trips back to India. One year,

American Airlines had a booth to advertise a route to India via Zurich. As Indians 'travel' virtually back to India within a recreated Indian space for a day, they are confronted with the opportunities to think about, if not plan, real travel home. Mortgage lenders, insurance companies, and even physicians and immigration attorneys sometimes take booths to promote their activities, thus offering avenues for setting down secure roots in the country of immigration. Also included might be radio stations and cell-phone vendors. New businesses use this bazaar as an opportunity to announce their presence, handing out promotional materials. Some religious organizations also sponsor booths – for example, one year a Caribbean Hindu temple took a spot, as did a Methodist Church, the Hare Krishna organization and the Swaminarayan temple. Various locally based Indian charities, such as ASHA and Pratham (both organizations raise money for the education of children in India), also pay for booths to raise awareness and ask for donations. But equally present sometimes are international organizations such as the Salvation Army and the Lion's Club, albeit the latter through local Indian chapters such as the Indian Lion's Club of DFW. Finally, several community organizations (for example, the Telugu Association, the Caribbean Hindu Association of North Texas, the Kerala Association) are often participants in the bazaar. All these entities disseminate literature about their causes as well as invite people to attend their events. Finally, the local Indo-American Chamber of Commerce has sponsored a booth that distributes materials to promote its mission – that of supporting business contacts both locally and with India, as well as promoting trade with India.

During election years, at the local, state or national levels, there are booths for particular campaigns, as well as a voter registration booth. Those running for office hand out material, and one year I saw someone handing out copies of the US Constitution. That year there was an Asian man running for a local office campaigning next to a white Anglo running for judge. Other years the campaign for democratic US Senator was present, as was the campaign for Mayor of Dallas. Clearly, politicians have discovered that the Anand Bazaar is a good place to reach an important segment of the DFW population.

As the evening progresses it is the food booths, located in another area of the park, that attract the most attention and in the air are the aromatic smells of spices and curries. Most are sponsored by local-area Indian restaurants. Lines at the booths, by the height of the evening, are long. Banners advertise kebabs, mango lassi, fruit ices, hot naan and various *chaat* dishes (Indian savoury snacks). While there is an area with park benches and tables where people can sit down, most people eat standing up, gathered in small groups in the middle of the main square that is surrounding by the tastes of India.

The bazaar space also includes a stage and throughout the afternoon and into the evening there is live entertainment – various groups of singers and dancers performing both traditional Indian dances and songs as well as Bollywood fare. Their performances are projected onto a large video screen for all to see no matter where they are in the park. Various sponsors of the Anand Bazaar are also promoted on these screens during lulls in the entertainment. Not all the music that permeates the atmosphere through massive racetrack speakers is

Indian, especially as the night goes on and more and more young people make up the crowd. A variety of international artists are played and there is a concert that is introduced by invited dignitaries who make opening remarks. One year, in light of terrorist incidents in different parts of Europe, the speaker (a Texas Congressman) claimed that his top priority was to make sure that Indians in the United States could travel safely back and forth to India. He talked of the important relationship and 'friendship' America has with India, and indicated his interest in working with the community to address concerns and foster economic growth. During the concert, there is often a raffle drawing with several prizes awarded, including such items as airline tickets to India. The evening usually ends with a fireworks display and one year there was a laser show.

Paul Connerton (1989: 7) has argued that recollection works through commemorative ceremonies and bodily practices. The Anand Bazaar reinforces recollections of home for Indian immigrants in DFW not only by annually commemorating Indian independence but also by creating an Indian space of sights, sounds and smells in a park that for much of the rest of the year gathers people to bet on winning horses racing along an oval track. For a single night one is hardly aware of this other purpose because the place temporarily transports those who attend back to India as it stimulates facets of embodied cultural memory. In DFW, there is another site of cultural/political memory and commemoration that is more permanent. This site has been constructed around a significant monumental object that not only brings together immigrants of Indian national origin who reside in the region, but also links them to a broader Indian international diaspora.

The Mahatma Gandhi Memorial Plaza

At the heart of the suburban community of Irving, Texas, a town located between the cities of Dallas and Fort Worth that is home to many local and multinational companies (including the global headquarters of six Fortune 500 companies), is a neighbourhood park with several trails, ponds and recreation facilities. At one end of the park is a statue of Thomas Jefferson, for whom the park is named; at the other end is a statue of Mahatma Gandhi. The juxtaposition of these two statues could not be more significant – the third President of the United States and the principal author of the US Declaration of Independence paired with the leader of the Indian Independence movement in British-ruled India. The heritage of the world's oldest democracy and the world's largest democracy are symbolically and materially represented and conjoined by these two monuments at a site of engagement that has assumed increasing importance for the Indian immigrant community in DFW.

The Mahatma Gandhi Memorial Plaza (see Figure 3.2) resulted from several years of negotiation between officials of the city of Irving and members of the Indian community in the DFW area, under the direction of a management team composed of prominent leaders in the community (many of whom have held the position of President of the India Association of North Texas). Positioned on a six-foot-tall pedestal, the larger-than-life-size bronze of Gandhi, dressed in his

Figure 3.2 Gandhi Memorial Plaza, Irving, Texas

Author's photograph, October 18, 2014

traditional dhoti with a shawl covering his shoulders, strides forward. He carries a book and a walking stick. On the wall behind the statue are quotations from Gandhi himself, from Reverend Martin Luther King and from Nelson Mandela.

This statue, made in India and shipped to the United States, is the artistic work of Burra Sai Varprasad, an award-winning Indian sculptor.

The construction of the plaza, for which money was raised largely within the DFW-based Indian-American community, began with a ground-breaking ceremony on May 3, 2014. Among the dignitaries who travelled to DFW for this ceremony was Nikki Randhawa Haley, an Indian-American who at the time was serving as Governor of South Carolina and who, as of 2017, is serving as the U.S. Ambassador to the United Nations. Joining her was Parvathaneni Harish, the Consulate General of India from Houston. About 200 people, including the mayor of Irving and other local city officials, gathered to celebrate the realization of a long-held dream for Indian immigrants in DFW. Everyone was given a shovel and a hard hat as mementoes of the day.

The statue was unveiled and dedicated on October 2 (Gandhi's birthday), 2014 with even more elaborate ceremonies and a host of distinguished guests present. These included Satish Dhupelia, a great-grandson of Gandhi and Ndaba Mandela, a grandson of Nelson Mandela, both of whom travelled from South Africa; Reverend Jerome G. LeDoux, representing the family of Martin Luther King Jr.; and Prasad Gollanapalli, Managing Trustee of the Gandhi King foundation in India. Joining them were Congresswoman Eddie Bernice Johns, Irving Mayor Beth Van Duyne, and the Consul General of India Mr P. Harish. Two days after the unveiling the Indian community scheduled a Gandhi Peace walk at the plaza and has organized these repeatedly in succeeding years.

Mahatma Gandhi Memorial Plaza is a project of civic engagement and political presence. It not only commemorates the work of Gandhi, but has quickly become a gathering place for various activities and prayer ceremonies in the DFW-area Indian community. Annual events are scheduled on the anniversary of Gandhi's birth and death (January 30), but also on the International Day of Peace (September 21), India Independence Day (August 15), and India Republic Day (January 26). In the spring of 2017, for example, a flag-hoisting followed by tea and snacks took place on January 26 and a tribute to 'Gandhiji', in the form of a moment of silence and an offering of flowers, took place at 5pm on January 30. But the plaza does not just draw to it those who are part of the DFW-area Indian community. In the fall of 2016 members of a delegation from Mumbai who were visiting Dallas for business meetings made a special excursion to Irving to see the Gandhi memorial. In the spring of 2017, the Indian community welcomed the Chief Minister Chandra Babu Naidu of Andhra Pradesh to the memorial. He called it an 'outstanding and inspirational monument for future generations' and praised the DFW Indian community for their fundraising efforts to erect the largest Gandhi memorial in the United States. Ela Gandhi, the seventy-six-year-old granddaughter of Mahatma Gandhi, also visited the site in the spring of 2017 and made a floral tribute. Mrs Gandhi is an activist for peace and a former Member of Parliament for South Africa. The presence of these Indian officials at this new Indian space within the DFW metropolitan area, as well as that of other dignitaries who have visited since the site was inaugurated, reinforces transnational connections to the homeland and to the Indian diaspora more broadly. The Gandhi Memorial Plaza is a place or destination for Indians who come to visit the DFW area that balances the return travel that many Indian immigrants in America engage in every year or two to visit family at home. Thus, the Gandhi Memorial Plaza supports connections to home as well as acts of commemoration embodied in a material object of monumental stature.

Beckstead *et al.* (2011: 194) have argued that memorials and monuments 'anchor memories'; they are 'physical and social products that shape and inform individual and collective identities'. The Gandhi Memorial Plaza has quickly become a focal point for commemorative rituals and activities that forge feelings of community and togetherness for an Indian community that is heterolocally dispersed throughout the DFW area. Divisions within the community, by region, by religion and by social class, are bridged in the process. But these commemorative activities also link immigrants in the United States, in this case Indian immigrants, to their homeland and to significant events in the history of their country of origin – chiefly when it gained its independence from Great Britain and became an autonomous, self-directed democracy. The material, sensorial and ritual dimensions of such commemorations are of utmost importance. Finally, the Gandhi Plaza has become a place of pilgrimage for individuals throughout the global Indian diaspora who find themselves travelling to the United States. Such visits are 'essential to imbuing memorials with personal meaning' (Beckstead *et al.*, 2011: 198).

Discussion and conclusion

Cangbai Wang (2016: 2) has argued that the 'material turn' in migration studies focuses on 'how people and things interact on different scales and in various contexts in the making of "migrant worlds"'. These interactions are often the stuff of memory that links migrants with their homelands in complex and differentiated ways. In this chapter I have discussed three distinct sites of engagement that involve different scales of interaction from the personal/ family (in the form of weddings), to the immigrant community (in the form of a local community event), to the international (in the form of a statue that evokes a national and world leader). These sites can be interpreted in many ways but I have chosen to read them in relation to the materiality by which they are characterized, the personal, experiential and cultural memories that they invoke, and the travel and displacement, whether real or virtual, whether of people or of objects, that they foster. Each of these sites of engagement and interaction has rich material dimensions from food, clothing and small objects, to monumental statuary and architecture. As Beckstead *et al.* (2011: 195) have suggested, memory is 'not only "stored in brains" but rather distributed through social artifacts and cultural tools . . . it is through the objectification of memory in memorials, monuments, and other material objects that social and individual memories meet', as they do in the context of Indian-American weddings, festivals and monumental memorials discussed here.

Many scholars have noted that transnational migrants often return to their place of origin to perform traditional rituals, such as weddings, that are associated with turning points in their lives. Salih (2002), for example, argues that when Moroccan migrants are in their home country for summer holidays, they engage in these rituals as a way to symbolically reintegrate themselves and claim their place as members of the home community. Other scholars focus on the life-cycle rituals and practices that are transported to and celebrated in the country of immigration (Gardner, 1998; Werbner, 1986). What is most significant about the wedding rituals discussed in this chapter is that they are bi-national, observed in both places and important to identity, social status and belonging in both places. The ability (including the resources) to travel makes this possible – to celebrate, as the case I have discussed indicates, the elaborate multi-day wedding rituals at home in India, but also to bring the material culture of home (including the film of the actual wedding) to US terrain so that the wedding (in the form of a single evening reception) can be recreated and reformulated as an embodied and sensory social experience that is both Indian and American. Cultural memory, heritage and tradition are perpetuated, but new practices are also introduced.

Cultural memory and heritage are also central to ethnic festivals which are displays of the economic, social, political and symbolic life of a community, 'organized and presented to members of the community by members of the community' (Farber, 1983: 33). Such festivals are equally replete with material culture that evokes the senses and reminds people of home.

In the history of American immigrant communities, ethnic festivals are often recreations of patron saint festivals that were celebrated at home (Leal, 2005, 2016; Moss, 1995; Orsi, 1985), albeit with some adaptations for the new world context. What is intriguing about the Anand Bazaar discussed here is that it is a new and invented 'tradition', but one where attendees are virtually transported for a single day back to their home country. They find themselves among the thousands of other individuals of Indian origin or heritage who have settled in the DFW area, all of whom have come together in a temporarily reformulated Indian space not only to commemorate an important date in the history of their country, but also to share a sense of unity, togetherness and belonging through their shared memories of and perhaps even nostalgia for the country for their birth or heritage.

The third memory site, the Gandhi Memorial Plaza, speaks even more forcefully to this shared or collective identity and to the cultural/political memory of the founding of an independent Indian post-colonial nation. As Assmann (2006: 215) has argued, monuments are 'vessels for social and embodied memories' and offer 'repeated occasions for collective participation'. The Gandhi Memorial Plaza certainly fulfils these roles. It is a place imbued with ideas of peace, non-violence and human rights and it establishes the civic presence of the Indian community in the greater DFW area. It is a site that illustrates well how diasporic groups use material culture to establish 'sites of affective engagement that create and emphasize shared identities and highlight ongoing connections with the homeland' (Svašek, 2012a: 19). The Gandhi Memorial Plaza achieves this purpose not only through the power of Mahatma Gandhi himself, a figure who is both Indian and transcends

India, but also because it draws a population dispersed throughout the DFW area to it for commemorative observances that reinforce their identity as Indian. But it has equally, as noted earlier, become a place of pilgrimage for international visitors of Indian heritage.

To conclude, the varied sites of material and cultural engagement I have discussed in this chapter involve different forms of memory, whether individual or collective, different forms of travel, and various dimensions of belonging and identity. They bring processes of place-making and home-making together. As writer and critic John Berger (1984) has suggested, ideas about home are embedded in the rituals and routines of daily life and in the material objects, including food and clothing, which are associated with them. Through the material dimensions of life, people 'reconstruct and remember synesthetically, [they] return to that whole world of home, which is subjectively experienced both locally and nationally, if not at other levels as well' (Sutton, 2001: 86). Synesthesia occurs when the stimulation of one sensory or cognitive pathway invokes another (dictionary.com). I have particularly emphasized the importance of embodied sensory experiences (sights, smells, sounds, tastes and objects of various forms) in the sites of engagement and memory-making discussed here – participants are reminded of (and hence virtually transported to) their homeland.

But these sites also involve, variously, real travel back to India, travel within India, the travel of Indians to Dallas and the travel of a dispersed population within the DFW area to important local sites of commemoration that they have built for themselves. Clearly, the objects of home, in whatever form, are particularly important for mobile/migratory populations. And if these objects evoke the senses, they can be very powerful dimensions of what Abranches (2014) refers to as the 'travel of the land' from one place to another. This is then another dimension of movement that should be considered within the broader field of mobility studies, memory-making and materiality.

Notes

1 The data were gathered as part of almost a decade of field research first by the National Science Foundation (BCS 0003938 – 'Immigrants, Rights and Incorporation in a Suburban Metropolis) and subsequently by the Russell Sage Foundation ('Civic Engagement of Indian and Vietnamese Immigrants in DFW'). Other investigators on the NSF project were James F. Hollifield, Dennis Cordell and Manuel Garcia y Griego. The co-investigator for the Russell Sage Project was Deborah Reed-Danahay. Any opinions, findings and conclusions or recommendations expressed in this chapter are those of the author alone and do not necessarily reflect the views of co-investigators, the National Science Foundation or the Russell Sage Foundation. In both projects, Brettell was responsible for the field research with Asian Indians. Both projects included additional immigrant populations.
2 This economic status is important to the story being told here. It facilitates lavish weddings and important civic projects. Indicative of its impact is the fact that late in 2016 it was announced that the Tamil community in DFW raised $500,000 to help establish a chair in Tamil literature at Harvard University (Holly Haber, D-FW Give Big for Harvard Tamil Chair, *Dallas Morning News*, December 30, 2016, p. 5D).

3 For further discussion of the India Association of North Texas see Brettell (2005b) and for discussion of India Nite, one of these community celebrations, see Brettell and Reed-Danahay (2012).
4 My discussion here is based on a compilation of repeated annual visits to the Anand Bazaar over several years.

References

Abranches, M. (2014). Remitting Wealth, Reciprocating Health? The 'Travel' of the Land from Guinea-Bissau to Portugal. *American Ethnologist*, 41(2), 261–275.
Appadurai, A. (ed.) (1986). *The Social Life of Things: Commodities in Cultural Perspective*. Cambridge: Cambridge University Press.
Assmann, A. (2006). Memory, Individual and Collective. In: R. Goodin & C. Tilly, eds., *The Oxford Handbook of Contextual Political Analysis*. Oxford: Oxford University Press, pp. 210–224.
Attan, C. (2006). Hidden Objects in the World of Cultural Migrants: Significant Objects used by European Migrants to Layer Thoughts and Memories. In: K. Burrell & P. Panayi, eds., *Histories and Memories: Migrants and their History in Britain*. London: Auris Academic Studies, pp. 171–188.
Barolini, H. (1979). *Umbertina*. New York: Seaview Books.
Basu, P. & Coleman, S. (2008). Introduction: Migrant Worlds, Material Cultures. *Mobilities*, 3(3): 313–330.
Beckstead, Z., Twose, G., Levesque-Gottlieb, E. & Rizzo, J. (2011). Collective Remembering through the Materiality and Organization of War Memorials. *Journal of Material Culture*, 16(2): 193–213.
Berger, J. (1984). *And Our Faces, My Heart, Brief as Photos*. New York: Vintage Books.
Bramadat, P. A. (2001). Shows, Selves, and Solidarity: Ethnic Identity and Cultural Spectacles in Canada. *Canadian Ethnic Studies Journal*, 33, 78–100.
Brettell, C. B. (2005a). The Spatial, Social, and Political Incorporation of Asian Indian Immigrants in Dallas. *Urban Anthropology*, 34, 247–280.
Brettell, C. B. (2005b). Voluntary Organizations, Social Capital, and the Social Incorporation of Asian Indian Immigrants in the Dallas-Fort Worth Metroplex. *Anthropological Quarterly*, 78, 821–851.
Brettell, C. B. (2008a). 'Big D': Incorporating New Immigrants in a Sunbelt Suburban Metropolis. In: A. Singer, S. Hardwick & C. Brettell, eds., *Twenty-First Century Gateways: Immigrant Incorporation in Suburbia*. Washington, DC: Brookings Institution Press, pp. 53–86.
Brettell, C. B. (2008b). Meet Me at the Chat Corner: The Cultural Embeddedness of Immigrant Entrepreneurs. In: E. Barkan, H. Diner & A. Kraut, eds., *From Arrival to Incorporation: Migrants to the U.S. in a Global Era*. New York: New York University Press, pp. 121–142.
Brettell, C. B. & Reed-Danahay, D. (2012). *Civic Engagements: The Citizenship Practices of Indian and Vietnamese Immigrants*. Stanford, CA: Stanford University Press.
Burrell, K. (2012). The Objects of Christmas: The Politics of Festive Materiality in the Lives of Polish Immigrants. In: M. Svašek, ed., *Moving Subjects Moving Objects: Transnationalism, Cultural Production and Emotions*. Oxford: Berghahn Books, pp. 55–74.
Connerton, P. (1989). *How Societies Remember*. Cambridge: Cambridge University Press.

Dallen, J. T. & Pena, M. (2016). Celebrating Heritage Foods: Culinary Festivals, Tourism and Food Production. In: J. T. Dallen, ed., *Heritage Cuisines: Traditions, Identities and Tourism*. New York: Routledge, pp. 149–165.

Dhingra, P. (2007). *Managing Multicultural Lives: Asian American Professionals and the Challenge of Multiple Identities*. Stanford, CA: Stanford University Press.

Farber, C. (1983). High, Healthy, and Happy: Ontario Mythology on Parade. In: F.E. Manning, ed., *The Celebration of Society: Perspectives on Contemporary Performance*. Bowling Green, OH: Bowling Green State University Popular Press, pp. 33–50.

Fortier, A.-M. (2000). *Migrant Belongings: Memory, Space, Identity*. Oxford: Berg Publishers.

Gardner, K. (1998). Deaths, Burial and Bereavement amongst Bengali Muslims in Tower Hamlets, East London. *Journal of Ethnic and Migration Studies*, 24, 507–523.

Gardner, K. & Grillo, R. (2002). Transnational Households and Ritual: An Overview. *Global Networks*, 2(3), 179–190.

Gopalkrishnan, N. & Babacan, H. (2007). Ties that Bind: Marriage and Partner Choice in the Indian Community in Australia in a Transnational Context. *Identities: Global Studies in Culture and Power*, 14(4), 507–526.

Gronseth, A. S. (2012). Moving Tamils, Moving Amulets: Creating Self-Identity, Belonging and Emotional Well-being. In: M. Svašek, ed., *Moving Subjects Moving Objects: Transnationalism, Cultural Production and Emotions*. Oxford: Berghahn Books, pp. 117–136.

Hui, A. (2015). Networks of Home, Travel and Use during Hong Kong Return Migration: Thinking Topologically about the Spaces of Human-Material Practices. *Global Networks*, 5(4), 536–552.

Kaiser, T. (2008). Social and Ritual Activity In and Out of Place: The 'Negotiation of Locality' in a Sudanese Refugee Settlement. *Mobilities*, 3(3), 375–395.

Kelly, E. (1990). Transcontinental Families: Gujarat and Lancashire: A Comparative Study. In: C. Clarke, C. Peach & S. Vertovec, eds., *South Asians Overseas: Migration and Ethnicity*. Cambridge: Cambridge University Press, pp. 251–268.

Khandelwal, M. S. (2002). *Becoming American, Being Indian: An Immigrant Community in New York City*. Ithaca, NY: Cornell University Press.

Koltyk, J. A. (1998). *New Pioneers in the Heartland: Hmong Life in Wisconsin*. Boston, MA: Allyn and Bacon.

Kopytoff, I. (1986). The Cultural Biography of Things: Commoditization as Process. In: A. Appadurai, ed., *The Social Life of Things: Commodities in Cultural Perspective*. Cambridge: Cambridge University Press, pp. 64–91.

Kurutz, S. (2016). Instant Chemistry, Caught on Video. *The New York Times*, Sunday, December 25, Sunday Styles, p. 10.

Leal, J. (2005). Travelling Rituals: Azorean Holy Ghost Festivals in the United States. *Croatian Journal of Ethnology and Folklore Research*, 42(1), 101–124.

Leal, J. (2016). Festivals, Group Making, Remaking and Unmaking. *Ethnos*, 81(4), 584–599.

Leonard, K. I. (1997). *The South Asian Americans*. Westport, CT: Greenwood Press.

Maira, S. M. (2002). *Desis in the House: Indian American Youth Culture in New York City*. Philadelphia, PA: Temple University Press.

Mand, K. (2002). Place, Gender and Power in Transnational Sikh Marriages. *Global Networks*, 2(3), 233–248.

Miller, D. (ed.) (2005). *Materiality*. Durham, NC: Duke University Press.

Miller, D. (2010). *Stuff*. Cambridge: Polity Press.

Moss, K. (1995). St. Patrick's Day Celebrations and the Formation of Irish American Identity, 1845–1875. *Journal of Social History*, 29, 125–148.

Norris, L. (2008). Recycling and Reincarnation: The Journeys of Indian Saris. *Mobilities*, 3(3), 415–436.

Olwig, K. F. (2002). A Wedding in the Family: Home Making in a Global Kin Network. *Global Networks*, 2(3), 205–218.

Onken, E.-C. (2007). The Baltic States and Moscow's 9 May Commemoration: Analysing Memory Politics in Europe. *Europe-Asia Studies*, 59(1), 23–46.

Orsi, R. A. (1985). *The Madonna of 115th Street: Faith and Community in Italian Harlem, 1880–1950*. New Haven, CT: Yale University Press.

Parkin, D. (1999). Mementoes as Transnational Objects in Human Displacement. *Journal of Material Culture*, 4(3), 303–332.

Parrott, F. R. (2012). Materiality, Memories and Emotions: A View on Migration from a Street in South London. In: M. Svašek, ed., *Moving Subjects Moving Objects: Transnationalism, Cultural Production and Emotions*. Oxford: Berghahn Books, pp. 41–74.

Plasquy, E. (2012). From Shop to Chapel: The Changing Emotional Efficacy of the Statue of the Virgin Mary of El Rocio within a Spanish Community in Belgium. In: M. Svašek, ed., *Moving Subjects Moving Objects: Transnationalism, Cultural Production and Emotions*. Oxford: Berghahn Books, pp. 75–95.

Raj, D. S. (2002). *Where Are You From? Middle-Class Migrants in the Modern World*. Berkeley, CA: University of California Press.

Ramdya, K. (2010). *Bollywood Weddings: Dating, Engagement, and Marriage in Hindu America*. Lanham, MD: Lexington Books.

Rangaswamy, P. (2000). *Namaste America: Indian Immigrants in an American Metropolis*. University Park, PA: Pennsylvania State University Press.

Rosales, M. V. (2010). The Domestic Work of Consumption: Materiality, Migration and Home-Making. *Etnográfica*, 14(3), 507–525.

Salih, R. (2002). Reformulating Tradition and Modernity: Moroccan Migrant Women and the Transnational Division of Ritual Space. *Global Networks*, 2(3), 219–231.

Shankar, S. (2008). *Desi Land: Teen Culture, Class, and Success in Silicon Valley*. Durham, NC: Duke University Press.

Shukla, S. (1997). Building Diaspora and Nation: The 1991 'Cultural Festival of India'. *Cultural Studies*, 11(2), 296–315.

Siebler, R. (2017). How a Thimble Became a Symbol of Survival. *The Dallas Morning News*, Sunday, February 5, p. 4P.

Stepick, A., Stepick, C. D. & Labissiere, Y. (2002). Becoming American, Constructing Ethnicity: Immigrant Youth and Civic Engagement. *Applied Developmental Science*, 6, 247–257.

Sutherland, G. H. (2003). The Wedding Pavilion: Performing, Recreating, and Regendering Hindu Identity in Houston. *International Journal of Hindu Studies*, 7, 117–146.

Sutton, D. E. (2001). *Remembrance of Repasts: An Anthropology of Food and Memory*. Oxford: Berg.

Svašek, M. (ed.) (2012a). *Moving Subjects Moving Objects: Transnationalism, Cultural Production and Emotions*. Oxford: Berghahn Books.

Svašek, M. (2012b). Introduction: Affective Moves: Transit, Transition and Transformation. In: M. Svašek, ed., *Moving Subjects Moving Objects: Transnationalism, Cultural Production and Emotions*. Oxford: Berghahn Books, pp. 1–40.

Tilley, C., Keane, W., Kuchler, S., Rowlands, M. & Spyer, P. (eds.) (2006). *Handbook of Material Culture*. Thousand Oaks, CA: Sage Publications.

Tolia-Kelly, D. (2004). Materializing Post-Colonial Geographies: Examining the Textural Landscapes of Migration in the South Asian Home. *Geoforum*, 35(6), 675–688.

Tolia-Kelly, D. (2006). A Journey through the Material Geographies of Diaspora Cultures: Four Modes of Environmental Memory. In: K. Burrell & P. Panayi, eds., *Histories and Memories: Migrants and their History in Britain*. London: Auris Academic Studies, pp. 149–170.

Wang, C. (2016). Introduction: The 'Material Turn' in Migration Studies. *Modern Languages Open*, doi: http://doi.org/10.3828/mlo.voio.88.

Werbner, P. (1986). The Virgin and the Clown: Ritual Elaboration in Pakistani Migrants' Weddings. *Man*, 21(2), 227–250.

4 Remembrance, cultural performance and travel

The Greek migrants of Brasilia and the *panigiri* festival

Stylianos Kostas

Introduction

'All of my parents' memories and my experiences from the community's events revived then as my own experiences while travelling in Greece', states a second-generation Greek immigrant in Brazil's capital Brasilia. This declaration indicates how memories of older generations shape new experiences in the lives of diasporic migrants, reinforced through travel to the 'motherland', which in turn provides opportunities for verification and the formation of new memories. 'Prior to any single experience, our mind is always already predisposed with a framework of outlines, of typical shapes of experienced objects', states Connerton (1989: 6) in his seminal book *How Societies Remember*. Social groups, he explains, are endeavouring to create a starting point with regard to their belonging in a society which refers inexorably to a pattern of social memories, foreseen to be present in commemorative ceremonies and bodily automatisms (ibid: 5, 13). Moreover, he draws attention to the fact that performances, regardless of their degree of rituality, deliver through time and endorse images and recollected knowledge of the past (ibid: 40). Social memory can be understood as a 'social-habit memory', the functioning of which is an indispensable component in performing codes and cultural rules both effectively and accurately (ibid: 36).

Following Connerton's (1989) conceptualization and focusing on the role of the traditional Greek *panigiri* festival in promoting 'belonging' and the meaning of 'homeland', this chapter explores memories and experiences of Greek immigrants in Brasilia and their perceived need for travel back to their country of origin. Social habits and cultural memories are often found in festivals, which 'as sites of cultural practice and experience are complex, multiple and dynamic' (Frost, 2015: 569), and even more so in 'feasts linked to seasonal cycles or held in honour of a local saint', as exemplified by the religiously underpinned *panigiri* (Panopoulou, 2008: 437).

This chapter is based on research into the lives and community functions of Greek immigrants in Brasilia, one of the newly established communities in the Greek diaspora, and in particular in Brazil, through the mass immigration flows from Greece in the mid-20th century. Previous scholarly work in this field has explored such aspects as the reconstruction of identity of returnee Greek-Brazilian migrants (Bryant, 2016), or the international interpersonal friendships of Greek immigrants in Brazil, evaluating their engagement with the host culture (Garcia, Costa & de Oliveira, 2016). Rich photographic and narrative material documenting the Greek immigrants' lives has been published by Constantinidou – in 2009 with respect to Brazil more generally and in 2016 specifically focused on the community in Brasilia (Constantinidou, 2009, 2016) – in an attempt to capture immigrant memories and preserve them for the next generation. The current research draws on this material and extends it through systematic scholarly investigation.

The chapter is based on semi-structured interviews, with a focus on narratives and observations of behaviour among members of the Greek community of Brasilia, conducted between July 2016 and May 2017. Notably, 10 participants of the first generation and six second-generation immigrants were interviewed. Anonymity has been retained for all participants. The selected testimonies represented in this chapter were translated from Greek by the author and reflect the majority of the responses, based on immigrants' personal beliefs and common cultural experiences within the community. Largely ignored for the purposes of this research were individual divergent views based on family rivalries and tensions related to social inequalities.

The chapter starts with a brief description of the community before discussing the meaning of migrating cultural experiences. It then focuses on the organization of the community's feasts as vehicles to reinforcing the first generation's memories and attachment to home, as well as their transfer to the second generation along with and embedded in more general cultural knowledge. Finally, the last part of this chapter draws attention to memory preservation in relation to the immigrants' travel to Greece and in particular the consequences, for both generations, of evaluating old and newly created memories and experiences.

The Greek-Orthodox community of Brasilia

The decision by the Brazilian government to create the city of Brasilia as the country's new capital in the 1950s prompted the need for a workforce specialized in technical occupations; construction work thus offered an employment opportunity for Greek immigrants scattered throughout the country. The presence of the Greeks in Brasilia has significantly increased since the beginning of 1957, initially attracting young men without families to move in search of a better life. According to Constantinidou (2016), there is no record as to how many Greeks arrived during the period of building the new capital, but it is estimated that eventually around 250 families settled in the town throughout its recent history.

The election of the first board of the 'Greek-Orthodox Community of Brasilia' on 17 June 1965 formally established the immigrant community and provided an exclusive space in which families could gather, preserve their memories of Greece and maintain their cultural identity centred on the Orthodox Faith. While for these men, the permanent or even temporary return home may not have been a reality, the cultural construction of identity within diasporic communities is usually based on what the migrants nostalgically keep to believe in, namely their potential return one day back to their home country (Silva, 2009: 695). Trying to preserve cultural, social and religious components associated with their origin assists with survival far from the motherland.

From the beginning of their migratory journey, the first Greek immigrants created a bridge between the motherland and the destination country. Essential cultural values and practices experienced during their youth in Greece were transferred into their new environment and forged into a unique migrant culture in what they perceived as the 'culturally empty' environment of Brasilia. An inevitable consequence of migration is usually seen in the establishment of contacts between diverse groups, notably migrants and the local population pre-existing in the host country (Gailey, 1989: 14). However, the new city of Brasilia, which was literally created in the midst of the tropical savannah, did not have a rooted cultural identity; neither did the first Brazilian residents of the city constitute a homogeneous entity, as they emanated from culturally diverse regions throughout Brazil. This assisted the first immigrants' initiatives in shaping their community's cultural identity towards a more exclusive Greek ethnic dimension. This isolation and culturally protected space could, however, not guarantee the long-term maintenance of Greek family tradition and prevent the younger generation from being influenced 'by the mores of the dominant group' (Smolicz, 2010: 24).

While reinforcing attachment to the home environment, such preservation of culture also strengthens the harmony and homogeneity of the ethnic group in their new surroundings. Hirschman (2004: 1207) indicates that 'the idea of community, of shared values and enduring association' motivates its members to strive towards trustful relationships, helping each other, even if they are not used to such long-established personal relationships. Among the Greek immigrants in Brasilia, priority was given to the construction of the church, as a key element of the community's cohesion, even though the depth and extent of religiosity among the new immigrants were somewhat questionable (Hirschman, 2004: 1218). Its foundation stone was laid on 9 January 1966 in the midst of what was decided to be the future location of the Greek community. The church quickly became the centre of community remembrance not only in relation to its religious role, but also its embedded social contribution. Over time, the first wooden church was replaced by a bigger building as the gradual increase of Greek immigrants in the city required more functional premises for the fulfilment of the community's religious needs and a space for cultural activities. As Hirschman (2004: 1208) observed, 'immigrants tend to be drawn to the fellowship of ethnic churches and temples', which are seen as the spiritual places of both delivering material assistance with traditional foods and keeping alive customs and cultural traditions, hence creating and strengthening the relationships among the devotees.

Migrating cultural experiences

The first Greeks of Brasilia were part of the migration flows from Greece between the mid-1940s and the early 1950s. From the 50s onwards, Greeks were numerous and present in almost all regions of Brazil and especially in the city of Sao Paulo, where the largest number of immigrants had gathered. They carried little, according to Constantinidou (2016), but had ambitious dreams and many memories from their life prior to immigration. These memories of personal and collective experiences were influenced by the particular conditions following the aftermath of both the Second World War (1939–1945) and the Greek Civil War (1946–1949). Moreover, deep religiosity and traditionalism shaped the character of the family and its members. The respect towards other family members, and in particular to the older ones, and the obligations arising from that familial frame were values strongly internalized and often related to the ethnic culture (Evergeti, 2006: 351). In short, the immigrants carried with them a piece of their cultural identity, formed by their experiences of daily life in Greece and preserved in their memories after migration. Keeping in mind that 'cultures and identities are dynamic sets that change over time and adapt to circumstances' (Bitsani, 2016: 3), we see also that culture migrates alongside its carriers, while at the same time migrants' personal belongings 'are manifestations of their past cultural performance' (Gailey, 1989: 5). A first-generation immigrant remembers:

> During my last year at school and while most of the young Greeks of my generation were migrating, our teacher who knew that many of his students would go abroad gave us an advice. He said that from the moment of our departure from Greece, all of us as immigrants would automatically become ambassadors of the Greek civilization. That would be the most effective indicator of our identity and everybody else could understand at that time what it means to be a Greek. His words were wise, but most of us lagged to understand the importance and the value of what he was trying to explain.

With immigration to Brazil and the consequent melancholic feeling of absence from the motherland, even unpleasant memories related to the war period were transformed into invaluable supporting material, which was able to connect the immigrants selectively with loved ones and fondly remembered situations back in Greece. Memories thus supported individuals in forging their identity, both social and personal; this was important considering the 'fragmented and fractured' nature of their subjectivity in their new social environment (Marcu, 2014: 334). Thus, these immigrants could remain well connected with their life prior to immigration until, hopefully, their ultimate return to Greece or at least the possibility of a visit emerged. However, it is only relatively recently and especially in the mid-1990s that the majority of the Greek families of Brasilia have begun to visit Greece frequently. For most of the first-generation immigrants, there was limited opportunity for return trips home prior to this period, for financial reasons and because the distance between Brazil and Greece seemed insurmountable in relation to available transport options. Exceptions pertained only to the journeys of the wealthiest or spontaneous travel in the case of family emergencies.

Although immigrants might have a 'collective identity' with regard to their origin from the same country or because they share common religious, national or ethnic characteristics, 'home is not always remembered in the same way' (Marcu, 2014: 333). The first immigrants to Brasilia came from almost all regions of Greece, a country that is geographically small, but characterized by a pluralism of local cultural traditions. Prior to their immigration, culture was experienced in the Greek home context through different commemorative performances, customs and a variety of local folklore and religious traditions. Participation in those cultural manifestations has to be seen as an expression of individual or collective needs to be engaged in activities that strengthen national identity, religiosity or other cultural values. Moreover, such performances were crucially influenced both by the participants' social environment, i.e. the family and/or local community, and the place or location of engagement. In short, the specific place where somebody is growing up plays an important role in the way in which s/he will participate in expressions of culture. We thus need to foreground 'the agents' behaviour' (Connerton, 1989: 21), i.e. the immigrants in relation to significant places and social conditions that characterized their pre-migration life.

It is important to note that the cultural diversity present in the immigrants' place of origin was to some extent forged into a unique culture through the strong concept of 'Greekness' formulated under the influence of the Greek-Orthodox doctrine. This 'connection between the notions of "Greekness" and the Greek-Orthodox Church' had an influential impact on the Greek diaspora, as other studies have indicated (Panagakos, 2003, cited in Evergeti, 2006: 361). As a second-generation immigrant confirms,

> Our parents grew up at a time when religion was the main aspect of their social lives and of being a Greek. For them, it was self-evident that they should bring to us the idea of the association of religion with national identity and it was inevitably a life course for all the second-generation immigrants.

The complex connection between religious and cultural aspects of Greek identity favoured Christianity over the ancient Greek paradigm, which had passed into folkloric tradition over time. The second generation of the Greek immigrants of Brasilia hence grew up following the conception of the inseparable co-existence of the religious alongside the national principles, which had always dominated the collective memory and shaped their own lives in the community's functioning.

First-generation immigrants' memories of the *panigiri* festival

After the family groups were established, the first Greek immigrants in Brasilia started to organize small feasts in order to maintain a symbolic channel of communication with their motherland based on their experience of living in Greece. Connerton (1989: 45) observed that such commemorative ceremonies 'do not simply imply continuity with the past but explicitly claim such continuity'. Following the traditions of the Greek-Orthodox Christian faith, the *panigiri* is organized on the occasion of a local saint's remembrance day. Over time, this became the most popular public cultural engagement of the Greek immigrants in Brasilia, and the most typical example of the strong relationship between religion and tradition.

The first cultural celebrations of the community were small family festivals, rather than a traditional big *panigiri*, since the events lacked the scale and typical organizational pattern of their corresponding model in Greece. The first immigrants were initially in a financially weak position, trying to improve their livelihoods. However, since their common aim was to strengthen the social links among the community's members, they were all generous within their limited means to contribute to organizing those first festive engagements. It is worth noting that Greek life at the time was characterized both by strong relationships among family members and 'the spirit of solidarity and collectivism' within the local communities (Smolicz, 2010: 20). A first-generation immigrant, who was among the organizers of the pioneer gatherings in the community, remembers:

> Our first small *panigiri* festivals in the community were more family-friendly and were organized at the minimum cost. Most of the immigrants at the beginning were still not economically stable to contribute with big donations for the community fund. However, through the voluntary involvement of the community's families, our celebrations were reflecting the collective efforts among immigrants.

Given that in the 1950s, society in Greece was culturally steered towards national homogeneity and unity, the immigrant community followed traditions in the motherland by periodically organizing their first gatherings on the occasion of the most important national feasts: the Assumption of the Virgin Mary on 15 August; the Orthodox Easter; and the two Greek National Days on 25 March and 28 October. The latter were in commemoration of the Greek independence from the Ottomans in 1821, and the so-called 'Day of No', the denial of Greek participation in the Italian military claims and the start of the Greek–Italian war in 1940. However as Hirschman (2004: 1211) observes, customary religious and national practices often take on new meanings after migration, especially when performed in the new cultural environment of the host country.

For the young Greek immigrants, organizing the first *panigiri* festivals was synonymous with individual and collective efforts to strengthen their Greek pride. This was important for their survival as migrants in a new urban environment with extremely different characteristics. Because of the unique identity of Brasilia as an exceptionally modernist city, with big avenues that necessitated mobility by car, there was an absence of the kind of crowding that migrants were highly used to from their life in Greece. In their small villages, one could easily meet people on streets and in public squares. While they had previously complained about public crowding, especially Greek migrants already previously settled in cities like Rio de Janeiro, they now missed the kind of social life which a city was supposed to offer to its citizens, especially in public places (Holston, 1989: 105). Feeling rather isolated in their spacious new city, the Greek immigrants sought to set up a mirror image of their previous social space through the organization of small banquets and participation in gatherings prior to the pioneer *panigiri* festival. These engagements offered them the pleasure of socializing and especially the sense of remembering similar events that took place back in Greece, at familiar places and with beloved people.

Given that in the past, most of the villages in Greece had no other kind of entertainment, the social life provided by the *panigiri* festivals was critical for locals and visitors. To that extent, the festival provides an opportunity for the members of a community 'to periodically reaffirm group sentiments' (Håland, 2014: 34). A female first-generation Greek immigrant of Brasilia remembers her childhood in the 1940s:

> In my village, we used to commemorate St. Constantine's day and to organize a beautiful and very big festival. Everyone was involved and everyone was happy to be part of that. Relatives and friends had the opportunity to escape from their daily routine and to visit us. There was a nice atmosphere and we were all united. That was our *panigiri* that time and was held for a week.

The *panigiri* performances essentially represent a unique expression of nationalistic, traditional and religious beliefs and customs based on the transition from the past pagan and mythological conceptions of the Greeks to the conservatism of the Greek-Orthodox Christian religion. That expression was further interpreted and conceptualized by the conservative Greek governments in the aftermath of the Greek Civil War in 1949, which tried to enforce among the Greeks an 'official culture based on a nationalist identity, the religious credo and ancient Greek heritage' (Zorba, 2009: 246). This could condone excesses in people's public behaviour during the festivities as an attempt to preserve traditions and customs integral to national cultural identity. A first-generation immigrant states:

> I left Greece as a teenager in the late 40s. In our village, we used to celebrate the Assumption of Virgin Mary on 15 August. People who were attending the *panigiri* were involved in such a pagan celebration, drinking and dancing. The *panigiri* became part of our tradition, both the religious and the national one, and gave us all a great opportunity for gathering and socializing. That is why the Church does not criticize the concept of the *panigiri* festival, although it is considered that many people are beyond the limits of an ethical social life.

The cultivation of traditions along with the conservative religiosity expressed through cultural performances have been important factors for immigrants in relation to the preservation of their memories of home. Immigrants' experiences from the corresponding context that characterized Greek society between the 1940s and 1950s up to the time of their departure were hence expressed and transferred through cultural activities, rather than simply remaining memories from a previous life. The concepts of collegiality and collectivism were of particular importance to the first immigrants in order to ensure the cohesion of the community and to maintain its continuity, acting as their parents used to do, especially in the small villages of the Greek countryside. One of the first Greek immigrants of Brasilia remembers:

> In the 1950s, the *panigiri* festival in Greece became an opportunity to reunite the population of the village, to bring harmony to the village, which was particularly important after the Civil War, and to lead to the conciliation and making of common decisions in local communities, working towards the benefit of all.

Thus the first *panigiri* festivals of the immigrant community in Brasilia were distinguished by their collective character and family atmosphere. Participation was an expression of the immigrants' longing for the homeland and linked to their personal beliefs about what it means to be Greek. Motivated by nostalgia, they worked on a 'trans-historical reconstruction' of the home they lost because of their migration and ended up developing symbols and rituals that signify both home and the motherland 'in an attempt to conquer and spatialize time' (Marcu, 2014: 333).

Transfer of memory and cultural knowledge to the second generation

Organizing small feasts compliant with the standards of the *panigiri* festivities was also a moral obligation in terms of providing the second generation of immigrants with the chance to entrench knowledge of Greek culture. Moreover, it sparked an interest in potential travel to Greece to experience the parents' place of origin and memories. Cultural festivals generally play an important role in creating opportunities for the expression and celebration of local culture, building 'a sense of pride in heritage and preserving it' (Cudny, 2014: 134). Those cultural festivities gave the second generation an important glimpse into their national and cultural origin, somewhat different from the perspective offered from inside their families' daily life, and created a desire to know their parental homeland better. A second-generation immigrant explains:

> I remember when I was little that our mothers and grandmothers were preparing the food for the feast of the community. The *panigiri* was a collective celebration. Over time, the *panigiri* started losing its familiar concept and gained more commercial characteristics. However, you could still see the nostalgic feeling among the older people and the need for all of us, the younger generations, to work again to strengthen our identity and discover Greece by ourselves.

Particularly through the powerful role of the Greek family, the second generation of immigrants could acquire their first impressions of the values that govern the microcosm of Greek society. The families in the immigrant community undertook the responsibility of informally teaching their children the *panigiri* rituals, thus transferring knowledge and skills, including among other religious and cultural habits, as well as the ability to follow the older generation on the dance floor, as a basic element of participation. Images of young children dancing alongside their parents perfectly illustrate the festival rituals in Greece, hence fulfilling the first immigrants' ambitions for sharing a sense of their memories of home with the new generation in Brasilia.

Moreover, maintaining customs from daily life in Greece in the 1950s, such as matchmaking, could achieve the continuity of Greek identity among the members of the community. The extended network of the Greek family contributed essentially to this process, as well as the various national and religious community celebrations (Evergeti, 2006: 351). For members of the first generation, a mixed-descendant family was not seen as capable of safeguarding 'Greekness'. In fact, such developments resulted in disappointment among the first immigrants. Interestingly, the Greek immigrants who had spent most of their lives as 'foreigners' and 'guests' in a country outside their place of origin readily referred to the Brazilian spouses of their children as 'foreigners'. This is a strong indicator of their sense of 'Greekness' and at the same time shows that many of the first-generation immigrants lived in a kind of time capsule, keeping alive perceptions of older times based on their life back in Greece. As mothers and grandmothers, three of the first-generation female immigrants, commented:

> Most of our children are married to 'foreigners'. And the foreigners keep our children close to their own side and culturally affiliate more with the Brazilian society. In the beginning, they [the Brazilian spouses] may come to the community, in respect to us, but after a while no one comes, nor our children.
>
> The boys got 'foreigner' wives and the girls got 'foreigner' husbands. We tried to introduce them to other Greek-origin immigrants of their age but finally they got married into the Brazilian society.
>
> Even [those] married to 'foreigners' may organize the wedding ceremony in our church and baptize their children according to the Greek-Orthodox faith. But this is done by our children out of habit rather than because of a religious feeling. Our children are introducing their spouses to our religion and customs but from the moment they get married, their foreigner spouses are moving them away from our church and traditions.

For the first Greek immigrants, memory was of particular significance in the formation of new experiences. Preserving Greek values was important and modern approaches were not easily accepted, even if the traditions had changed in Greece itself. Indeed, migrants' children are often aware of the possibility that their parents' beliefs and perspectives on different issues might no longer be held by the population of their motherland (Rosenthal *et al.*, 1989: 59).

Travelling to Greece: first and second generation

As was shown above, the traditional *panigiri* feasts became one of the community's main efforts to preserve its past and cultural identity. In particular, because of their connection with those who have a similar sense of dislocation (Silva, 2009: 701), the feasts have a strong impact on the community, both for the first and second generation, albeit it in different ways. What makes festivals and performative events particularly effective systems of mnemonics is their reliance on physical, bodily practices, manifestations of embodied memory. Connerton (1989: 102) argues that social groups are anxiously concerned to maintain particular principles and customs which they finally 'entrust to bodily automatisms'. With regard to immigrants, however, each generation might over time develop their own variation of customary practices in relation to differing conceptualizations of the motherland's cultural heritage and perceptions of its relation to national identity. Similarly, each generation develops its own emotional relationship towards the country of origin and fosters different perceptions of the need to travel there.

The first immigrants were ambassadors and messengers of 'authentic' performativity, based on their personal experiences of cultural practices and arrangements in Greece, which at that time were naturally flowing from tradition and the habits of social life. In the migratory context, however, such cultural practices are dependent on the active efforts and expediency of the immigrants to maintain a cultural identity – based on their own experiences regenerated through memory. A first-generation Greek immigrant woman comments:

> Organizing the community festivals, our celebrations, it was an opportunity to gather all of us. It was the reason, in fact, to keep alive our traditions and customs, our dances. With our way of remembering Greece, the most important of what we succeeded is that we passed our tradition to our children. And that made our children to have a passion about Greece and a strong will to find out more about our country.

Indeed, both practising and expressing culture assist in developing a sense of understanding, hence constituting an integral component 'of an evolving spatial imaginary and cultural space' (McCabe, 1998: 232). The immigrant community's cultural identity was shaped both through the 'moving' of their traditions with their migration from Greece and continuously thereafter through the development of new traditions after their arrival in Brasilia. This process of cultural evolution continued and slowly created, over time, a new backdrop of cultural experiences and memories – this time relevant to the life in diaspora. The newly developed traits co-exist and alternate with those dating back to the time prior to the immigration; this situation creates incentives for preserving Greek identity, sometimes manifested in the desire for a short visit to Greece.

The first immigrants were nostalgic and could never forget their time in Greece. Travelling home frequently can relieve the nostalgic desire for the motherland, but such travel can never be a 'straightforward, unreflective movement between two locations', as Skrbiš (2007: 314) puts it. For the first immigrants, the temporary trip to Greece was an expression of their continued efforts to keep alive the feelings associated with their experiences before immigration. A first-generation immigrant explains:

> I lived my whole life in Brasilia as a Greek immigrant. However, I always look forward to travel back to Greece for vacations. Back there I am simply Greek, one more Greek among the others. I follow my memories and try to relive the same experiences, and then return back to Brasilia with renewed memories and new experiences, which will keep me alive and motivated.

For the members of the Greek community of Brasilia, every single journey to Greece meant that their return to Brazil would result in the creation of opportunities for renewing and maintaining the 'Greekness' of their migratory identity. Some scholars argue that past memories and experiences shape homeland visitors' travel motivation and identity quests as well as the need for connection with the place in which visitors formed their early personal and historical biographies (Pearce, 2012; Marschall, 2012). Home, as a 'tangible place and an intangible set of perceptions', although a complex concept encapsulating different meanings and dichotomous elements, is able to define the meaning of space with regard to the individual, the family or the community (Rosbrook & Schweitzer, 2010: 160). Perspectives of home may differ over time and are invariably influenced by the experiences immigrants have as travellers to Greece. While visiting their country of origin, immigrants are initially expected to recall and verify their homeland's memories and furthermore to eventually combine these experiences 'into a memorable tourist experience' (Io, 2014: 192).

The interpretation of these travel experiences and the memories they engender are expressed in new activities that demonstrate the ongoing cultural production cycle referred to above. Immigrants are always negotiating their identity based on new experiences linked with their visits to the motherland. At the same time, and especially for the younger generation, there is a constant need for understanding new concepts and situations they encounter during those visits, which can result in a more conscious adoption of their self-determination as Greeks. This continuous process of experiences and memories provides opportunities for new cultural expressions and the evolution of migrant identities, who paradoxically make great efforts at maintaining their cultural and national identity. A second-generation immigrant describes his own experience:

> When I first visited Greece after school, I understood the value of music for the Greeks. I realized how music influences the modern Greek life while at the same time it keeps alive traditions and customs. All of my parents' memories and my experiences from the community's events revived then as my own experiences while travelling in Greece. When I returned to Brasilia, I decided to have a more active participation in the community's cultural festivities, trying to offer new experiences to the rest of the community based on my own memories from Greece.

For descendants who started to accompany their parents while travelling to Greece, the journey had a completely different character compared with that of simply returning to their parental motherland. Of course, the way an individual understands the meaning of home depends on how that notion is 'socially and culturally constructed' (Lewin, 2001: 356). The children of the first immigrants had been born and raised in what their parents might have perceived as an 'ideal' Greek environment. Through the experience of being Greek within the Greek community, these descendants developed a deep sense of belonging. However, the environment in which they grew up was created according to their parents' criteria, which were in turn based on experiences prior to their immigration, i.e. following established moral values that reflected the society in which they had grown up. Meanwhile, and especially since their parents' migration, Greece has developed following the globalization of the economy and culture and modernized due to the consequences of European Union integration and the advent of mass tourism; this had profound effects on the traditional character of the countryside, along with internal migration to urban centres (King, Christou & Teerling, 2010: 21). Moreover, as mentioned earlier, the first-generation immigrants had a strong sense of nationalism and conservatism in their understanding of 'Greekness', enhanced by their migration, and tried to develop in their children the idea of belonging to a strictly defined concept of Greek identity. A female first-generation Greek immigrant explains:

> When we first arrived here, out of nostalgia for Greece, out of mood and love we did everything to preserve our tradition and our religion. The new generation now does not have the same passion like us. Our children do not even speak Greek to our grandchildren. However, they are anxious about visiting Greece and discovering for themselves the country of their origin.

Without personal experiences of the Greek reality, the second generation of immigrants in Brasilia were introduced to Greece and the prevailing concept of national identity through their parents' memories as they had developed pre-migration. These 'old memories' became the subject-matter which the second and following generations used naturally in developing their own understanding of what it means to be Greek. The descendants lacked the opportunity at the early stages of their life to be engaged in aspects of their national tradition in Greece as their parents had during their childhood. Therefore, when travelling to Greece for the first time, descendants were guided by the memories – and followed in the footsteps – of their parents. As Marcu (2014: 334) observes, 'memory looks back in order to move forward and transform disabling fictions to enabling fictions, altering our relation to the present and the future'. While travelling to Greece, the descendants had an opportunity to interpret for themselves the feelings shared by their parents about previous engagement in activities in their natural environment in the motherland. Moreover, the descendant travellers' own participation in cultural activities during their visits to Greece would provide new perspectives on strengthening their sense of national heritage. An immigrant of the first generation says:

A few years ago, I decided to go to Greece on holiday. At that time I asked my grandson to follow me. It was summer and as usual, my village was to hold the traditional *panigiri* festival. He had experienced the *panigiri* in the community before, but he understood that the one in Greece was the original and the unique one. After that visit, he decided to participate in the community's dance group. He went back to Brasilia full of new experiences and a motivation to keep a link with his motherland. He feels when he is dancing that he participates once again in the celebration of my village and he tries to share that with all of us.

The second generation has, in a sense, taken responsibility for maintaining memories and creating new community experiences, which emphasize the importance of participating in the collective cultural activities and give further impetus to the need for more journeys to Greece. Moreover, these visits allow the travellers to recognize those constituents of their cultural identity that can only be achieved through personal travel to the place of origin. The connection between the consequences of a journey and the remembrance of events then allows second-generation immigrants to create new understandings of what they have absorbed from their parents, hence opening up novel perspectives on their sense of identity.

The new *panigiri* festival: tourism, secularism and cultural diversity

McCabe (1998: 233) observes that tourism nowadays is essentially influencing the shaping of critical representations within society and in particular those 'of cultural landscape, identity, and heritage'. This will eventually have an effect on diasporic communities, as is evident from the testimony of a second-generation immigrant:

When I began to visit Greece, I always preferred to spend more time on my father's island and not so much in Athens. There, in the island's villages, was always a *panigiri* festival to attend. I felt that I knew exactly what was happening, as we had similar festivals in the community. This made me spend more time in the villages of the island every time, as I did not feel like a stranger among the locals. From that experience, I took many lessons that shaped my feelings about Greek culture. When I took over a more responsible role on the community's board, among the first things I suggested to work on was to organize a big *panigiri* festival, open to all the members of the community and to the Brazilians, creating a new promoting channel for Greece and our cultural identity.

On the occasion of the 50th anniversary of the Greek-Orthodox community of Brasilia in 2015, a special two-day cultural event was planned for the first time, on 2 and 3 October. It was the first edition of a big *panigiri* festival that had little to do with the celebrations organized by the community in the past. With an appropriate layout of community space, a big stage, lights and professional services, always under the supervision of the members of the board, the organization was completely different from any previous staging of the festival.

Perhaps the most significant divergence was the new *panigiri*'s disconnection from the religious functions of the community; it was a cultural event without any association with religious celebrations or national anniversaries. It was a unique festival where participants were entertained by live Greek music and dancing performances by members of the younger generations, who eventually created a great atmosphere, inviting everybody to dance. Moreover, for the first time, an open invitation to attend the *panigiri* was extended beyond the Greek-born members of the community to their Brazilian fellows. Over time, because of the mixed marriages, most of the immigrants' Brazilian spouses and on some occasions their relatives and local friends used to attend the old *panigiri* festivities, but this made little difference to the exclusivity of those events. Advertised in Brasilia and announced to other Greek communities in Brazil mainly through social media and local journals, the 50th anniversary event was as an attempt at broadening participation and generating financial benefits for the community.

The event was successful and in the summer of 2016, the Community Board decided to organize the second edition of the *panigiri*, once again following a two-day celebration programme, on 26 and 27 August. Each of these *panigiri* festivals brought together about 2,000 participants from both the local Greek community and Brazilian society. Among the attendees were also many first-generation Greek immigrants who had kept their distance from the community's life in recent years. In addition there were younger members of the second and third generations without any patriotic or religious affiliation who joined the celebrations alongside their Brazilian relatives and friends. A first-generation immigrant shares this opinion about the new *panigiri* festivals, which now create the base for more collective activities among members of the Greek community and local Brazilians:

> The large-scaled *panigiri* festivals have now become an opportunity for the community to open its activities into the Brazilian society. The new generation of our members and the Brazilians as well need to have another idea of Greece, more in line with its contemporary vision and different from what they have learned from our conservative experiences. Besides, when one visits Greece today, one must have the same experiences with those which are provided in the community's life in Brasilia, otherwise upon arrival in Greece he will be confused discovering that customs and habits we still follow here do not exist there.

The new *panigiri* festivals also meant a new period for the community's actions and functioning. In the past, participation in the festival and its activities was limited to about 100 to 150 people, the majority of whom were first-generation immigrants. The new events, however, are seen as a great opportunity to gather almost all the families of the community alongside their Brazilians folks. Notwithstanding any kind of competitive differences among the families of the community, with regard mainly to their financial situation or their social outreach that kept them uninvolved in collective activities in the past, the participation in the *panigiri* appeared as an opportunity for recreating their relationships focusing on the common values of their Greekness and cultural heritage. A female second-generation immigrant whose life was always closely tied up with the community's activities because of her active parents describes this:

> At the last festivals, we saw more of the new generations of the community being involved and more Brazilians attending as well. Besides, most of the second-generation members are married to Brazilians. They returned to live a life reminiscent of the everyday life in Greece, as they originally had learned following the traditions of our parents, but finally discovered by themselves when they started visiting Greece.

Focusing on those cultural characteristics that unite the members of the community, rather than narrowly perpetuating conservatism and religiosity in order to preserve 'Greekness', the 'modernization' of the *panigiri* festival brought a new dimension into the community's functioning and promoted the participation of descendants. Indeed, the new generations took the initiative to emphasize the cultural aspects of their Greek identity, leaving aside the religious ones that used to create a disconnection for them and prevented them from being totally integrated into the host society. At the same time, that new dimension of the community's festivities eventually promotes Greece among the local population and potentially increases the number of Brazilians who attend the festival and may be inspired to travel to Greece. However, this shift towards a more open and secularly orientated festival was met with disapproval by many first-generation immigrants. One of them, who sees the community's development from multiple viewpoints as a first-generation immigrant, wife, mother and grandmother, explained:

> Today the community festivals are more like a cultural event. I guess that this is a consequence of what our children have experienced by themselves travelling to Greece and being close to the modern Greek life there. Since they came back they wanted to modernize our community too.

Greek culture revisited

Despite their parents' attempts to reinforce conservative traditions, the Brazilian way of life slowly influenced even the first generation of immigrants. Immigrants often have doubts about their precise identification, especially since the latter is inextricably linked to strong notions of the nation and nation-states, explain Sahoo and Sangha (2010: 87). As descendants came into contact with the local culture in Greece, they became aware of differences with the way of life of the immigrant community, which impacted on their sense of identity and lives among their Brazilian peers. Immigrants' children are naturally attached to the host country in which they are raised or even born, embracing automatically its norms and state institutions (Levitt, 2009: 1239). A second-generation immigrant explains:

> Greek culture was the first to learn until I went to school and I met with Brazilians. There I began to understand that I have two countries and two cultures. For the new generation, religion does not matter. Especially with mixed marriages, things have changed. Brazilian spouses, as they have a different religion, come closer to Greek culture through music, even the language, but certainly not because of the religion. Music keeps memories alive and through Greek music we remember our experiences from both the life in the community and our trips to Greece.

The ethnic identity aspect could be reinforced as a consequence of visiting the motherland, since during these visits immigrants have the opportunity to interact with their 'homeland culture' in its natural environment (Vathi & King, 2011: 505). As most of the second-generation immigrants began to visit Greece, they found that the model of 'Greekness' they had grown up with did not correspond exactly to the modern way of life in Greece. This has gradually led to confusion and rupture between old and new understandings of cultural identity and in particular regarding the emotions associated with community activities for younger members who have since developed their own understanding of Greek culture through travel. Eventually, through multiple interactions, people re-evaluate their national identities and reshape them as 'ethnic, transnational and diasporic ones', states Evergeti (2006: 361). This also means they will develop a new relationship towards their family's and community's social and cultural memory. By organizing the new *panigiri*, the second-generation immigrants reinterpreted that memory and appropriated it for their own needs of cultural belonging and identity. This occurred at a time when Greece as the homeland had long since begun – albeit slowly – to pursue a modernizing approach to tradition and religiosity. The new immigrant generation felt the need to keep pace with such developments and attempt to reformulate its perceptions of their national cultural heritage and their country of ancestral origin.

Conclusion

This chapter has explored the organization and celebration of the *panigiri* festival as identity practice by the Greek community of Brasilia. The *panigiri* has always been an integral aspect of the social and religious organization of life for Greeks; in the migration context, it moreover turns into a platform for celebrating cultural identity and a vehicle for collective remembrance. Associated with many embodied memories, this commemorative performance allows the community to act out, preserve and transfer memories of the home culture, while in the process constructing a unique social memory and migrant cultural identity.

For the first generation of Greek immigrants, this process was assisted by the characteristics of the community's specific location in Brasilia, a 'clean-slate' place that lacked a strong cultural identity posing threats of competition or interference. This situation changed for the second generation, who grew up in a developing capital city and many of whom married into Brazilian families. Their anchorage in Greek culture as defined by the pre-migration memories of their parents is expressed in their participation in the *panigiri* festival, but often becomes compromised, challenged or re-invented. The first immigrants regarded themselves as the sole bodies of an authentic cultural knowledge and memory which their children were expected to adopt and maintain. For those elderly people, the memory of Greece created a bridge between their past and present lives, while feeding the desire to return. For the second-generation immigrants, temporary visits rather than a permanent return to Greece became the basis for acquiring first-hand knowledge of Greek identity. It is through travelling back to Greece that they discover variances between the memories absorbed from their parents, the characteristics of the specific migrant culture their parents had formed and the evolving Greek culture in the motherland.

Travelling is often inspired by memories, which are inevitably re-evaluated at the destination; it also entails gaining new experiences that will in turn be remembered. The homeland trip allows descendants to gather their own experiences, and interrogate and perhaps confirm their special relationship with the motherland and the need to preserve their identity as Greeks. Most especially, the journey allows them to rediscover the significance of the *panigiri* festival and prompts them to relate to it in new ways. Connerton (1989) highlights commemorative performances and bodily practices as representations of social-habit memory and a group's collective memory. While discussing this in relation to different societal groups and categories, drawing on historical examples, he has not considered the specific context of migration, so topical today.

This chapter has illustrated how for each generation of immigrants, the festival – a pivotal point between migration and travel – represents a stage for the expression and negotiation of cultural identity, as well as the formation of social memory. Immigrants paradoxically try to protect themselves culturally in the social environment in which they are hosted, while simultaneously seeking to be integrated into the local population, albeit under their own rules. However, over time, efforts to maintain a national and cultural identity in the host environment become difficult because of the influence of local elements. This prompts the second generation to seek which aspects of their ancestors' identity should be kept in harmony with the cultural characteristics offered by their host-country context.

As scholars in the field of migration and diaspora studies, we should focus our attention on the creative initiatives of the younger generations of diasporic communities in devising innovative concepts and perceptions of their origin. These are essential strategies in order to negotiate and rediscover their position within a social environment that can be described as a hodgepodge of cultural elements and peculiarities from the country of origin and the host country. The staging of the new *panigiri* festival is an excellent example of this process. It illustrates the immense inventiveness of immigrants to preserve their cultural identity by enhancing common cultural characteristics, rather than narrowly preserving political and religious dogmatism, as their parents used to do.

Acknowledgements

I sincerely thank the teacher of the Greek School of Brasilia, Mrs Eleni Mangopoulou, for her help in conducting the interviews. My deepest gratitude, however, goes to the Greek immigrants of the community of Brasilia, who trusted me and opened their hearts in sharing memories and experiences.

References

Bitsani, E. (2016). Migration Memory, Cultural Heritage: A Vehicle of the Intercultural Identity of a City. The Case Study of the Eastern Greek Community and the Greek Museums of Trieste Italy. *Cogent Arts & Humanities*, 3(1182716), 1–15.

Bryant, E.P. (2016). *A Comparative Study of Language Attitudes, Use and Identity in Two Returnee Migrant Contexts: Greek-Brazilians and Greek-Germans in Greece*. Doctoral dissertation. University of Central Lancashire.

Connerton, P. (1989). *How Societies Remember*. Cambridge: Cambridge University Press.

Constantinidou, V.T. (2009). *Os Guardiões Das Lembranças: Memória E Histórias Dos Imigrantes Gregos No Brasil* (The Guardians of Memories: Memory and Stories of Greek Immigrants in Brazil). Sao Paulo.

Constantinidou, V.T. (2016). *Os Argonautas Do Cerrado: Memória e História Da Comunidade Grega De Brasília* (The Argonauts of The Land: Memory and History of the Greek Community of Brasilia). Sao Paulo.

Cudny, W. (2014). Festivals as a Subject for Reographical Research. *Geografisk Tidsskrift-Danish Journal of Geography*, 114(2), 132–142.

Evergeti, V. (2006). Living and Caring Between Two Cultures. *Community, Work & Family*, 9(3), 347–366.

Frost, N. (2015). Anthropology and Festivals: Festival Ecologies. *Ethnos Journal of Anthropology*, 81(4), 569–583.

Gailey, A. (1989). Migrant Culture. *Folk Life – Journal of Ethnological Studies*, 28(1), 5–18.

Garcia, A., Costa, L.Q.M. & de Oliveira, M.S.P. (2016). The Friendships of International Migrants in Latin America. In: A. Garcia, ed., *International Friendships: The Interpersonal Basis of a Worldwide Community*, 1st ed. Newcastle Upon Tyne: Cambridge Scholars Publishing, pp. 26–41.

Håland, E.J. (2014). The Legend and Popular Festival of Agios (Saint) Charalampos, and its Parallels in the Wider Greek Context, Ancient and Modern. *Folk Life – Journal of Ethnological Studies*, 52(1), 13–48.

Hirschman, C. (2004). The Role of Religion in the Origins and Adaptation of Immigrant Groups in the United States. *International Migration Review*, 38(3), 1206–1233.

Holston, J. (1989). *The Modernist City: An Anthropological Critique of Brasilia*. Chicago, IL: The University of Chicago Press.

Io, M.-U. (2014). Exploring the Impact of Past Memories on Tourist Experiences of Homeland Visit: The Case of the Chinese Immigrants in Macao. *Journal of Vacation Marketing*, 21(2), 191–204.

King, R., Christou, A. & Teerling, J. (2010). 'We Took a Bath With the Chickens': Memories of Childhood Visits to the Homeland by Second-Generation Greek and Greek Cypriot 'Returnees'. *Global Networks*, 11(1), 1–23.

Levitt, P. (2009). Roots and Routes: Understanding the Lives of the Second Generation Transnationally. *Journal of Ethnic and Migration Studies*, 35(7), 1225–1242.

Lewin, F.A. (2001). The Meaning of Home Among Elderly Immigrants: Directions for Future Research and Theoretical Development. *Housing Studies*, 16(3), 353–370.

Marcu, S. (2014). Geography of Belonging: Nostalgic Attachment, Transnational Home and Global Mobility among Romanian Immigrants in Spain. *Journal of Cultural Geography*, 31(3), 326–345.

Marschall, S. (2012). 'Personal memory tourism' and a wider exploration of the tourism–memory nexus. *Journal of Tourism and Cultural Change*, 10(4), 321–335.

McCabe, S. (1998). Contesting Home: Tourism, Memory, and Identity in Sackville, New Brunswick. *The Canadian Geographer / Le Geographe Canadien*, 42(3), 231–245.

Panopoulou, K. (2008). The Panegyri and Formation of Vlach Cultural Identity. *Dance Chronicle*, 31(3), 436–459.

Pearce, P.L. (2012). The Experience of Visiting Home and Familiar Places. *Annals of Tourism Research*, 39(2), 1024–1047.

Rosbrook, B. & Schweitzer, R.D. (2010). Meaning of Home for Karen and Chinese Refugees from Burma: An Interpretative Phenomenological Approach. *European Journal of Psychotherapy & Counseling*, 12(2), 159–172.

Rosenthal, D.A., Bell, R., Demetriou, A. & Efklides, A. (1989). From Collectivism to Individualism? The Acculturation of Greek Immigrants in Australia. *International Journal of Psychology*, 24(1–5), 57–71.

Sahoo, A.K. & Sangha, D. (2010). Diaspora and Cultural Heritage: The Case of Indians in Canada. *Asian Ethnicity*, 11(1), 81–94.

Silva, K. (2009). Oh, Give Me a Home: Diasporic Longings of Home and Belonging. *Social Identities*, 15(5), 693–706.

Skrbiš, Z. (2007). From Migrants to Pilgrim Tourists: Diasporic Imagining and Visits to Medjugorje. *Journal of Ethnic and Migration Studies*, 33(2), 313–329.

Smolicz, J.J. (2010). Greek-Australians: A Question of Survival in Multicultural Australia. *Journal of Multilingual and Multicultural Development*, 6(1), 17–29.

Vathi, Z. & King, R. (2011). Return Visits of the Young Albanian Second Generation in Europe: Contrasting Themes and Comparative Host-Country Perspectives. *Mobilities*, 6(4), 503–518.

Zorba, M. (2009). Conceptualizing Greek Cultural Policy: The Non-Democratization of Public Culture. *International Journal of Cultural Policy*, 15(3), 245–259.

5   Gallipoli revisited

Transnational and transgenerational
memory among Turkish and Sikh
communities in Australia

Burcu Cevik-Compiegne and Josef Ploner

Introduction

The word 'Anzac' may sound like an unintelligible collection of sounds to most people outside of Australia (or New Zealand). Yet, it is fair to state that all Australians, as well as citizens-to-be, are expected to know what 'Anzac' and 'Gallipoli' stand for as they constitute an intrinsic part of Australian national identity. 'ANZAC' was originally the acronym for Australian and New Zealand Army Corps. It was lexicalised as a word in its own right and is now interpreted as a national tradition, or more controversially, a 'national legend'. Predominantly associated with the First World War Gallipoli campaign (1915), the mythical birthplace of Anzac, Anzac Day (25 April) now officially commemorates all Australians who served and died in wars, conflicts and peacekeeping operations worldwide, as well as celebrating Australian national unity and identity. In recent years, this form of celebrating nationhood through military achievements (or indeed failure) has been repeatedly criticised not only for being militaristic and anachronistic, but also for its predominantly white, Anglo-Australian and masculine cultural connotations. At the same time, and somewhat paradoxically, certain minority and immigrant groups have started to view these commemorations as an opportunity to show that they are part of a more diverse Australian national community. Among those groups, we will focus on the Indian, Sikh and Turkish immigrants who take particular pride in being a part of the original Gallipoli myth and, consequently, Anzac Day.

In the last few decades, since the revival of Anzac Day, Turkish people secured themselves a place in the Australian national myth as the 'honourable' enemies in the campaign (Simpson, 2010). This status was supported by broad media coverage and the gradual rapprochement of the two countries through joint commemoration events on the Gallipoli peninsula in Turkey since the 1990s. To a large extent, this resulted in an increased awareness and sensibility among many Australians about the importance of the campaign for Turkish people. While bilateral forms of commemoration between Australia and Turkey have increased since the 1990s, the recognition and commemoration of other nationalities and minority groups among the Allied troops at Gallipoli remain scarce. This is particularly the case for Indian troops, and most notably the Sikhs among them, who fought alongside the Australians during the campaign and whose story has largely been forgotten. Anzac Day is the major event where the Sikhs endeavour to remember the history of their long-standing alliance with Australia while also displaying the military traditions embedded in their culture. They march separately from the Indian contingent, which consists of retired officers of the Indian armed forces. Sikhs are an eclectic group of ex-servicemen and descendants of servicemen who identify as Indian, Malaysian, Singaporean or Fijian Sikhs.

Our analysis is based on 19 semi-structured biographical interviews conducted in Sydney from 2014 to 2016 with active participants of the Anzac Day marches and other related commemorative events. (Participants' names have been changed to protect their privacy.) These interviews were conducted to generate original insights into the ways in which family histories intertwine, or potentially contrast with, 'official' commemorations of the Gallipoli campaign, and the Australian WWI experience more generally. Eleven participants were first-generation Indians or Sikhs, while all but one of the remaining male interviewees were first-generation Turkish migrants, most of whom are retired or semi-retired men. Only one Turkish and one Sikh woman participated in the research, both of whom were active in Anzac commemorative events and much younger than the average interviewees. Eleven participants knew of one or more relatives who participated in the First World War.

Since the participants in this research were chosen among those who march in the parade on Anzac Day, this research does not include the responses of the very many Turkish- and Sikh-Australians who do not wish to be associated with war commemoration or do not personally take part in the commemorative events. Focusing on both transnational and transgenerational practices of commemoration, this research affords a unique insight into how diasporic communities shape their narratives of self and memory in a way that bridges their past and present movements between two or more countries. While practices and experiences of travel and tourism only partially feature in this chapter (i.e. in the form of 'battlefield' or 'homecoming tourism'; see Marschall, 2017), it sheds new light on the complex ways in which memories 'travel' – not only between generations, but also between separate countries and places (Lacroix & Fiddian-Qasmiyeh, 2013). More than that, and focusing on the highly symbolic memorial site of Gallipoli, this study offers additional insights into Sheller and Urry's (2006: 214) assessment that places themselves can be seen as travelling 'slow or fast, greater or shorter distances, within networks of human and nonhuman agents'. As such, it adds depth and breadth to the overall content and scope of this edited volume.

All participants come from countries where the First World War has long been marginalised in commemorative calendars. Although some of the research participants have family ties to WWI soldiers, most of them discovered an interest in commemoration and the history of the war only after settling in Australia. Therefore, the rediscovery of their family histories is necessarily motivated by a need to make sense of their past through the lens of their current circumstances. Biographical interviews shed light on how they narrated their life stories before and after immigration and how the participation in the war created a sense of continuity within their family histories that encompasses a past predating their birth while giving meaning to their post-immigration lives.

Gallipoli in the context of transnational and intercultural memory

Although there is a wealth of literature exploring 'Gallipoli' and 'Anzac' as collective Australian *lieux de mémoire* (see Beaumont, 2015), the complex ways in which migrant and diasporic communities in the country relate to national WWI memory have received little attention in both academic and public debate (Bongiorno, 2014). In this context, the growing identification with Anzac Day among first- and second- generation Turkish- and Sikh-Australians raises new questions about how the formation of collective memory is played out in a culturally heterogeneous society and how it can be afforded by a particular, if largely contested, historical event.

A common theme within research on memory formation among migrant and diasporic communities is that, once settled in their 'host' countries, these communities develop highly selective forms of commemoration which tend to focus on nostalgic narratives of a shared past as well as ideas of a 'lost home' (Safran, 1991; Clifford, 1997). Drawing on Anderson's notion of 'imagined' communities (1991) and Ricoeur's work on memory, Lacroix and Fiddian-Qasmiyeh (2013) point out that such narratives tend to oscillate between 'remembering' and 'forgetting' and 'can be defined as identity narratives which merge "actual" and "mythical" past events with the aim of inscribing the group in a historical and spatial trajectory' (2013: 685). While forgetting is usually characterised by the exclusion of past events that could potentially jeopardise in-group cohesion and incorporation into the host society, practices of remembering are equally selective in that they privilege historical narratives that are accepted, if not shared by, both migrant community members and the wider 'host' society. In the latter case, memory can acquire both transnational and intercultural dimensions and serves as a vehicle to strengthen dialogue between groups that share a particular historical experience – however remote and mythical this may be. What adds complexity to the Australian case is that migration itself may become an important reference point for shared memory that forges (real or mythological) links between both recent and long-standing migrant groups.

Although contested (hi)stories of war, conflict and trauma (i.e. Gallipoli) are more likely to be eclipsed in the memory narratives of migrant communities, the emphasis on past alliances (Sikhs) or shared experiences (Turks) can become powerful means by which migrant histories are merged into greater narratives of national identity and belonging. According to Lacroix and Fiddian-Qasmiyeh (2013), the endorsement of a (transnational) collective memory can thus contribute to 'delimiting the boundary between "us" and "them"', but may still be exclusive in the sense that it 'distinguishes between those who can refer to this common past and those who cannot' (2013: 689).

The emergence of transnational and intercultural forms of memory in the field of memory studies is clearly underpinned by the influence of post-structuralist, post-colonial and post-feminist research paradigms, which have drawn attention to previously silenced or otherwise subaltern 'minority' voices (Hirsch & Miller, 2011;

Kennedy & Radstone, 2013; Waterton & Dittmer, 2016). According to Erll (2011), this development is paradigmatic for a renewed interest in 'cultural memory' which continues to move away from national and epistemologically flawed 'container-culture' concepts. Instead there is recognition of a plethora of transcultural mnemonic phenomena that 'do not come into our field of vision with the "default" combination of territorial, ethnic and national collectivity as the main framework of cultural memory' (Erll, 2011: 8). This assessment is particularly relevant in the context of 'official' Australian Anzac commemorations which, until recently, have been firmly associated with nationalistic sentiments and were criticised for primarily attracting 'chauvinistic, bellicose and intolerant' sections of the population (Bongiorno, 2014, cited in Waterton & Dittmer, 2016: 61).

The emergence of 'critical' cultural memory studies under the premise of post-colonial and post-feminist theory has also invoked a renewed interest in the contested narrative formation of intrinsically 'national' histories and invented traditions. To this end, it is clear that previously dominant and universalist narratives of 'nation' have become increasingly challenged by individual and familial (hi)stories that emphasise diversity, hybridity and cultural particularism. The continued interest in 'alternative' oral histories and biographical stories, such as those of migrant and/or minority groups, is but one characteristic feature of this ongoing trend and is equally reflected in the case studies presented in this chapter. However, as Bhabha (1990) argues, the increased emphasis on the particular and microscopic may in fact further substantiate the grand narratives of the nation state. It does so by adding familiarity and intimacy to previously hegemonic national discourses, and thus creatively 're-humanises' the abstract idea of the nation state. Typically, such micro-stories envisage personal historical milestone events (e.g. linked to war, migration, resettlement, etc.) but also tend to gravitate around particular localities and landscapes which hold the power to socially visualise communal expression of national belonging and affiliation. This 'spatialisation of historical time' (Bhabha, 1990) is certainly a central component in the contemporary commemoration of Gallipoli – not only as a physical landscape for transnational pilgrimage, but also as a site inscribed into numerous media reports, war memorials, museum exhibitions, school curricula and, not least, the annual Anzac Day parades across Australia.

Gallipoli and transgenerational memory

In line with the arguments outlined above, the autobiographical narratives presented in this research are constructed around personal milestone events but also mark turning points in life which convey a sense of continuity and (trans)national affiliation. Immigration is one of the important milestones that may transform the interpretation of past events and, in turn, transform the sense of self and community belonging. Of course, the focus of this study is not on the events that were directly experienced by the participants, but family histories that were narrated to them in different social contexts. The participants in this research have been reassessing the relevance of family histories that were transmitted to them, often in their childhood. While it may be reasonable to assume that second- (and third-) generation migrants gradually lose physical and emotional connections with their ancestral home and history, numerous studies have shown that these generations develop a keen interest in family histories – particularly when these relate to traumatic and disruptive events such as war, displacement or migration. Fischer (2015) has described this aptly as 'memory work', an active, if not therapeutic, strategy that enables individuals or groups to come to terms with past events that were often 'not spoken about' within private/family contexts. In a similar vein, and reflecting on the experiences of refugees, both Erll (2011) and Fiddian-Qasmiyeh (2013) have proposed the framework of 'travelling memory' to help trace the ways in which 'different scales of memory – ranging from the intimate and familial, to the collective and nationalist – "travel" both between the older and younger generations, and across space' (Fiddian-Qasmiyeh, 2013: 691).

In this reading, shared *lieux de mémoire*, whether 'real' or 'mythical', 'sacred' or 'profane', can become powerful sites that facilitate inter-generational ties and memory transmission. While young Australians who emanate from Sikh or Turkish backgrounds may indeed express an increased interest in their family's (Gallipoli) past, the way in which stories travel from one generation to another is obviously determined by complex processes of selection, filtering and forgetting which may alter not only the content of a particular story but also its meaning. At the same time, these stories are dependent on their relevance for a particular audience as well as the wider socio-political context in which they are placed (Kleist & Glynn, 2012). In view of the critically diagnosed 'memory orgy' that currently surrounds the Anzac 'legend' (Beaumont, 2015), it is perhaps not surprising that many Australians with Turkish or Indian/Sikh migration background seek to consolidate national history with private/family memory.

'The Anzacs' – a short history of selective and political commemoration

The Gallipoli landing started to be commemorated from its first anniversary in 1916, but the commemorations took different forms and contested meanings over the years and decades to come. This development can be traced in Australia through the war memorials that have dotted the landscape since the 1920s (Inglis, 2008). These memorials were not the exclusive sense makers of the war and historians have called upon other sources such as soldiers' accounts (Gammage, 1974) and historiography (Holbrook, 2014) to understand how the experience and remembrance of the war was shaped in Australia.

Various authors have diagnosed the curious upsurge of Anzac Day during the Whitlam government in the early 1970s (Simpson, 2010), after having been widely considered a fading tradition during the 1960s (Broadbent, 2009). The revival of Anzac Day as a central narrative in Australian national identity was accompanied by changing representations and perceptions of the war as a tragedy rather than a heroic feat. At the same time, previously overlooked Gallipoli contingents, among them nurses (Rees, 2008; Rae, 2004) and Aboriginal soldiers

(Watson, 2006), have since become the subject of many research projects, and their involvement is now officially recognised through a variety of commemorative practices and events. This growing demand for inclusiveness, which countered the prevailing myth of Anzac Day as being exclusively white, male and Anglo-Australian, enabled other voices to be heard and challenged previously dominant militaristic forms of commemoration. The recognition of alternative voices in the commemoration of Anzac is also reflected in Thomson's (1994) account of three radical left-wing Anzacs and their struggle to process their war and post-war experience against the backdrop of predominantly conservative and nationalistic Anzac traditions. Likewise, feminist activist groups such as 'Women Against Rape in War' used the increasing popularity of Anzac Day during the 1970s and 1980s to give voice to under-represented female protagonists and victims of war (Twomey, 2013).

In 1990, Bob Hawke became the first Prime Minister to capitalise on the upsurge of interest and participation in Anzac Day commemorations by organising an official trip to Gallipoli to commemorate the 75th anniversary of the landing. This first 'Gallipoli pilgrimage', as it is often called (McKenna & Ward, 2007), was attended by thousands of Australians and was broadcast live on national television. This new commemorative practice, a truly 'invented tradition', contributed significantly to the popularity of Anzac Day and, since then, has mobilised thousands of Australians to travel to Gallipoli every year. Ever since the politically driven reawakening of a collective Anzac myth under Bob Hawke, each Prime Minister has developed their own relationship to Anzac, thereby reshaping the politics of remembrance in the public Australian imagination. While this ongoing politics of remembrance has been challenged by a number of critical observers (McKenna, 2010; Lake, 2010) as being selective and ideology-driven, other authors have focused on the personal and collective experiences of the 'pilgrims' who travel to Gallipoli to attend the services (Basarin, 2011; Scates, 2006; West, 2005; Winter, 2009). However, literature focusing on the recognition of migrants and/or minorities in political Anzac narratives, as well as their participation in Gallipoli 'pilgrimages' and other commemorative events, remains scarce.

Turkish and Sikh migrant communities and 'Anzac Day'

Although national media regularly cover the participation of migrant and minority groups in Anzac Day, scholars have only recently started reflecting on the significance of Anzac Day for groups other than white Anglo-Australians (Broadbent, 2009; McKenna & Ward, 2015). There seems to exist an underlying assumption among both minority groups and critical observers that the place of Sikh and Turkish people in the Australian society is related to, if not largely dependent on, the historical significance that Gallipoli has for them. This is reflected, for instance, in a collection of conference papers focusing on Turkish-language texts about Gallipoli and addressing existing prejudice against Turkish immigrants in Australian society. Consider the opening paragraphs of the conference proceedings:

Many Turkish migrants in Australia have experienced prejudices and mis-conceptions about what it means to be Turkish. In view of this, it is hoped that this book will contribute towards the peaceful settlement of Turkish people in Australia.

(Akcelik, 1986: n.p.)

These conference papers, as well as other academic work emerging in the 1980s, aimed at communicating a more differentiated historical narrative relating to these groups and nationalities, assuming that it would help mainstream Australians understand who these people were. As Simpson (2010) observed, recent attempts to change attitudes towards Turkish-Australians may have also been under-pinned by changing representation of the 'Turks' in Australian popular culture, which saw them gradually transform from 'ruthless foe' (WWI), to 'noble enemy' (post-WWII), to 'national friend' (post-1980s). In line with these ongoing pro-cesses of re-contextualising established historical preconceptions, it is perhaps not surprising that people of Turkish background in Australia invested heavily in their Gallipoli heritage.

Sikhs are one of the oldest non-European groups in Australia, with a few thou-sand having settled in the country before the 'White Australia' policy encouraged European-only migration during the first half of the 20th century. However, most Sikhs who live in Australia today migrated during or after the 1960s, and contrary to the early immigrants came mostly from urban and professional backgrounds. As such, they have mostly been classified as 'skilled migrants' (de Lepervanche, 1984; Bilimoria, 1996). On the other hand, large-scale Turkish migration picked up after the 1967 agreement on *Residence and Employment of Turkish Citizens in Australia*, which mostly attracted unskilled workers (Senay, 2013). After the end of the agreed immigration period in 1974, Turkish migration to Australia slowed down substantially, and from the 1980s onwards was characterised by the influx of highly skilled and educated migrants. Most Sikh and Turkish migrants settled in Australia after the revival of Anzac Day and tended to perceive the event as an exclusive, highly regulated and predominantly white-Australian expression of national identity and self-sacrifice.

Despite a growing interest in participating in Anzac Day among Turkish- and Sikh-Australians, both communities were initially denied authorisation to march in the parade, which was, and still is, strictly regulated by the influential veterans' association Returned and Services League (RSL). During the 1980s, members of the oldest Australian-Sikh community in Woolgoolga were even refused access to the Dawn Service, the public and highly significant ceremony at dawn on Anzac Day, on the insubstantial grounds that their turbans were seen as inappropri-ate ceremonial attire. Sikhs were finally allowed to attend the services in 1993, and in 2005, a *Sydney Morning Herald* article quoted a Sikh participant saying: 'Growing up here as a Sikh, [Anzac Day] was always seen as not for anyone else but the white Australian people. We want our children to just feel a part of the community' (Lewis, 2005). This quote underscores the symbolic significance of

Anzac Day for Sikh-Australians and can be seen as paradigmatic for a gradually growing sense of belonging and national affiliation among this community. Gaining an active stake in Anzac Day commemoration thus denotes a particularly strong theme among immigrants who aim to build individual, familial and communal connections to Australian national symbols.

Anzac Day and the representation of migrant communities

Since, historically, Anzac Day has been predominantly identified as the domain of white Australians, the participation of migrant and/or minority groups in the commemoration is a powerful symbolic means to gain visibility and improve the standing of these communities within the wider 'host' society.

This underlying motive is certainly reflected in the narrative of Harnam Singh, who left India with his family in the early 1990s due to anti-Sikh violence, giving up a comfortable lifestyle for security. However, just as he managed to re-establish himself professionally in his new country, safety became the prime issue for his family once again with the rise of xenophobia after the 9/11 attacks in 2001. Harnam was even physically assaulted once because his turban 'looked like' Osama Bin Laden's and thus he was discriminated against as a terrorist. Many other participants either directly experienced or heard of similar incidents within the community. Becoming targets of violence in what they considered to be a safe haven, many Sikh community members actively started thinking about ways in which they could inform Australians about their distinct cultural heritage as well as their 'Australianness'. It was at this point that Harnam decided to attend Dawn Service, a part of the Anzac Day ritual, and lay a wreath at the local war memorial on his community's behalf every year. When Sikhs were finally granted permission to march in the parade in 2007, he was one of the first to join the group. All the participants believe that marching on Anzac Day gives their community visibility and therefore increases the Australian people's awareness of their culture.

As the previous example indicates, participation in Anzac Day is often seen as service to the community as well as to counter perceived racist and cultural discrimination. This also becomes explicit in the narrative of Kanwar Singh, who migrated to Australia in the mid-1970s. As a young man, Kanwar had served in the Indian army where he was involved in military operations against China and Pakistan, and it is worth mentioning that he had been a successful boxer who represented India in the 1972 Olympic Games in Munich. When he was visiting his relatives in Australia, he happened to get caught up in a recruitment rally for the Australian Army where the recruiting agents were very interested in his profile. They offered him Australian citizenship on condition that he served in the army. Agreeing to this arrangement, Kanwar found himself in Vietnam within a few months, only to return weeks later at the end of the war. Since then, Kanwar participated in Anzac Day marches with his Australian Army unit, but when the Sikhs were finally granted permission to march as a group, he did not hesitate joining them. Asked why he preferred to march with the Sikhs, he answered that he did so because he thought everyone should know that the fathers and grandfathers of Sikhs had fought side-by-side with Australians at Gallipoli. Indeed, Kanwar's great-uncle, who was like a grandfather to him, had fought at Gallipoli.

It becomes clear from Kanwar's narrative that marching with the Sikh Anzac Day contingent may be bound up with a strong wish to highlight the legacy and legitimacy of his community as a long-standing and loyal immigrant group in Australia. However, it is interesting to point out that Kanwar prioritised his forefathers' connection to Australian history rather than his own service in the Australian Army. Even if Kanwar's biography and migration history may not be representative of the wider Sikh community, his standpoint reveals that the symbolic significance of Gallipoli necessitates a demonstration and commemoration of the Sikh–Australian alliance. While this quasi-moral attitude may hark back to a mythical past, it equally constitutes a powerful expression of belonging and national affiliation among Sikh-Australians today.

Today, the National Sikh Council of Australia coordinates the Sikh participation in Anzac Day. In addition, they organised a photographic exhibition and an information leaflet, which was distributed during the march in 2015. All the material presented on both occasions emphasised Sikh troops' participation in the Gallipoli campaign and their status as an Australian ally. Turks, on the other hand, devote much effort to building a narrative that emphasises respect and friendly relationships between the Australian and Turkish soldiers who were opposed during the campaign. When large-scale Turkish immigration started with the Assisted Migration Scheme (1967), many of the newcomers were unaware that Australians had been among the Allied forces that landed in Gallipoli in 1915 (Fewster, Basarin & Basarin, 1985). During their first years in Australia, the former animosity between the two countries was a source of anxiety for many immigrants.

A well-known story goes that a Turkish person was once verbally harassed by an Australian co-worker who suggested that the Turkish person's grandfather may well have killed his. The Turkish person answered that, even if this was the case, his grandfather had no business invading the country in the first place. In the course of fieldwork for this study, many versions of this story emerged and each time it was attributed to a different person and setting. The story usually takes place either in a factory or schoolyard but the aggressor's anger and the Turkish person's self-righteous and confident response is always the same. The date is also invariably set sometime in the early 1970s. Regardless of whether this episode ever happened, the wide circulation and appropriation of the story may be indicative of the ways in which fear of hostility and perceived xenophobia were countered and negotiated among the Turkish community.

Since the 1970s, the narrative trope of the 'noble enemy' and 'national friend', born out of their assumed gentlemanly interactions during the Gallipoli campaign, has become an integral part of the Turkish-Australian Anzac legend. In addition to that, diplomatic rapprochement between the two countries around immigration and commemoration at Gallipoli, as well as the Turkish community's own grassroots efforts to contribute to commemorative events, has ensured them a privileged place in the Anzac legend. As indicated above, Turks reached the status of the honourable enemy who successfully defended their own country while also being chivalrous towards their enemies. Simpson (2010) pointed out that this myth partly harks back to the predominantly (if contested) neutral status of Turkey during the Second World War, as well as a growing disenchantment with outdated heroic war narratives among the post-WWII baby boomer generation. At the same time, the image of the 'noble Turk' has been complemented by popular media representations of the Australian soldiers at Gallipoli, who were often depicted as careless and naïve youngsters who gave their lives in a senseless and ill-fated campaign. Howsoever public imageries of Turkish and Australian soldiers may have changed in the public imagination, it is fair to state that within the commemoration of Anzac Day, the Turkish migrants in Australia have become the dominant stakeholders and beneficiaries of this symbiotic (and symbolic) relationship between the national myths of Australia and Turkey.

Retrieving and reinterpreting transgenerational memory fragments

The revival of Anzac Day from the 1970s onwards has been accompanied by the transformation of a nationalistic and generic 'Australian' grand narrative into a more approachable and intimate set of individual stories and experiences. In this context, the increased study of personal diaries and letters written by soldiers, as well as biographical interviews with Anzac veterans, became new and fruitful sources to understand the hitherto neglected human dimensions and consequences of the war. This renewed public interest also encouraged people to donate family memorabilia to heritage and educational institutions, which, in turn, called for donations to add to their gradually expanding collections. The nexus between military history and family histories was also promoted by the Department of Veterans' Affairs and the Australian War Memorial which have developed a range of research and educational resources to encourage national pride and interest in military history on the local level and among individual families (Damousi, 2010).

This gradual move from abstract and anonymous forms of national commemoration to more familiar and intimate forms has certainly influenced the ways in which Sikhs and Turks reapproached their Gallipoli memory. These communities, which had not benefited from the same resources as long-established Australian families, relied on first-hand accounts as prime sources for shaping their family histories. However, and together with the gradual loss of first- and second-hand informants, the stories about the war are few and far between. Since the interest in the individual experiences of Sikh or Turkish soldiers emerged only fairly recently, neither did the first-hand narrators deem them to be significant for the wider public, and the listeners did not think that these narratives were particularly relevant. Perhaps because both Sikhs and Turks had an extremely high recruitment rate during WWI, the recognition of family members as war veterans was hardly noteworthy among second- and third-generation migrants. With the increased interest in family and 'minority' war histories in recent years, the significance of these family experiences is assessed differently now. However, it remains diffi-cult to piece together different fragments so as to fully make sense of these stories.

The problem of fragmented war and family histories among migrant commu-nities is reflected in the narrative of Herman Singh, a Sikh man who arrived in Australia in 2005 after his retirement to join his children who had previously settled in Australia as skilled migrants. Asked about his family history and con-nection to the 'Great War', he recalls that his grandfather was in a cavalry unit deployed in the Middle East and he assumed that he might have been in Gallipoli. Herman never met his grandfather and his grandmother was the only source of information. However, his grandmother did not tell him much about his grand-father 'at that time', as Herman put it, regretting that it is too late now. The only thing he found out was that his grandfather would come home with his horse when he was on leave. Herman also mentioned the leather equipment of the horse, which was still in the house he grew up in. The mere randomness and episodic nature of this story makes it difficult to assess its significance, but as became clear in a follow-up conversation, that curious object turned out to be the only reason why Herman had heard about his grandfather's career in the cavalry and the fact that he had served overseas during the First World War. If there were other stories told about his grandfather, they were discarded from his memory, as they did not fit in any way with his or his family's position in society. In any case, Herman's attention focused on the leather equipment and the explanation was sufficient to satisfy his curiosity.

Three other participants of Turkish origin were vague about their fathers' war experiences even though they knew them very well. Saner came to Sydney with one of the first chartered flights that carried Turkish migrants in 1969. His father was a Gallipoli veteran who encouraged Saner to migrate to Australia rather than to Germany, since, in his view, the former enemy was still friendlier than the for-mer ally. He was influential in his son's decision. However, Saner did not feel that Australian Gallipoli veterans were particularly friendly to him when, sometime in the early 1970s, he introduced himself as the son of a Turkish soldier. By the time there was a keen interest in the Turkish stories about Gallipoli, his father had died. Saner holds detailed records and memories of his father's post-war activities but when it comes to the war, he is unsure about many details, emphasising that his father 'did not talk much about the war'. Saner's lack of knowledge about his father's experiences in WWI is partly due to the latter's illustrious post-war career as an influential public figure in Turkey. He met Kemal Atatürk during the War of Independence (1919–1922) and, through this connection, acquired land in Izmir. After serving as the mayor of Buca, he joined the President's Guard in Ankara where he worked more closely with Atatürk. He finished his career in the intel-ligence service. Saner has a comprehensive collection of memorabilia, including photos depicting his father with Atatürk, but there is little material evidence to shed light on his involvement in WWI and the Gallipoli campaign.

The complex interlinks between migratory histories and WWI family mem-ories are also implicit in the narrative of Elif, who only recently migrated to Australia from Turkey and who had a great-grandfather who fought at Gallipoli.

Although she never met him, she has gathered as much information as possible from her relatives. Despite the combined efforts of the family, the information about her great-grandfather's life during WWI remains limited. According to family accounts, he had been close to Mustafa Kemal in Gallipoli and was wounded in action, suffering the partial loss of sight. Elif's family likes to believe that he was wounded in an act of bravery that saved Mustafa Kemal's life, which might explain why he appears by the side of the Turkish supreme leader in a very well-known Gallipoli photograph. In 1984, Elif's uncle contacted journalists to tell the story of this unknown soldier in the picture and the story was published in *Milliyet*, one of the national daily newspapers. Beyond this newspaper article, nobody in the family seems to know much about him. Compared to Saner's father's story, Elif's great-grandfather's is much blurrier because of the widened generational gap. Only very few memories, if any, seem to have been passed on from the second to third generation in the family. However, the emphasis in both cases is on the close connection to Atatürk, which constitutes a significant element in merging private and seemingly insignificant family memories with the grand narratives of (inter-)national politics and historiography. Despite their fragmented and limited composition, both stories provide valuable insights into the ways in which different generations of Turks in Australia currently negotiate their identities by merging private family memories with more public and 'official' historical narratives.

Similar strategies of rediscovering and reinterpreting family histories related to Gallipoli are also prevalent among Australian-Sikh migrant communities. For example, Bikram Singh, who migrated to Australia in 1982, recalls his father to be very keen to talk about his war experiences. His father was a career soldier and continued serving several years after the First World War until his retirement. His experiences during the war overseas were something he was proud of and something he would frequently share with family and friends in India. Bikram grew up listening to a large collection of war-related stories, but only a few stood out in his memory. Some of these stories relate to Gallipoli, where his father had been deployed as a signaller and was given the challenging task of establishing contact between Australian troops and the British command. His mission appeared to be extremely dangerous, as many of his comrades had previously died on the job. He took the initiative and successfully delivered messages by choosing a different route but, on one fateful occasion, he was shot in the leg. According to the story, he waited an entire night for the rescue team, and just when he thought he was about to die, he was finally evacuated. He received the British War Victory Medal and Distinguished Service Medal for this particular action.

Although there are several evocative war stories that were left behind by his father, Bikram Singh considers Gallipoli the most relevant part of his father's experience today. Perhaps this is also the reason why he inadvertently attributes his father's injury to the Gallipoli campaign, even though military records indicate that his father was wounded in Mesopotamia much later in October 1918. As for family, relatives and friends in India, and perhaps for the storyteller himself, the remote locations where events took place seemed to be insignificant details in a much greater story of personal resilience and bravery. In this reading, Gallipoli was probably an abstract geographical idea for Bikram until the point he discovered that this was a major national memorial site for Australians. Ever since, Bikram is keen to emphasise the place of the story, while other elements are reinterpreted, modified or 'misremembered', such as the injury his father suffered in action.

Revisiting home country, rediscovering identity

None of the Sikh participants had any plans to visit Gallipoli, although some mentioned that they would like to. Kanwar Singh had heard that the Sikh cemeteries in Gallipoli were in utter neglect and asked if this was indeed the case. On a different occasion, he asked whether it was true that the Sikh cemeteries were at the hilltops, while the Australians were further down the slope and the British cemeteries lay near the beach. The response that there is no Sikh cemetery as such in Gallipoli and that Sikhs and other Indians are scattered across several well-maintained cemeteries was thus met with surprise. Reflecting on Kanwar's questions, it is easy to see that the way he imagines the Gallipoli peninsula is influenced by the popular yet erroneous representation of the place in the well-known film *Gallipoli* by Peter Weir (1981).

Depicting the disastrous 'sacrifice' of thousands of young Australians in a hopeless and futile offensive while the British failed to send reinforcements as they were having tea on the beach, the successful film has had a tremendous influence on the ways in which Gallipoli was formed in the public Australian national imagination. Following the coming-of-age of two Australian men, the film has also become a part of the Gallipoli pilgrimage ritual and has equally influenced anti-British sentiment that exonerates the Australians from any responsibility in the ill-fated campaign. While the film may have influenced Kanwar's personal imagery of Gallipoli, and nurtured his idea of a 'higher sacrificial order' of the Sikh soldiers in the campaign, it is also a striking example of what Landsberg (2004) has termed 'prosthetic memory'. This form of collective remembrance emerges from the absence of first-hand accounts about historical events and is increasingly afforded by popular culture and mass media. While prosthetic memory carries the risk of 'distorting' or 'romanticising' historical truths, it also has immense potential to challenge the ethnic or national essentialism of traditional identity politics.

For obvious reasons, it is more convenient for the Turkish participants to visit Gallipoli since it can be easily combined with family visits. However, many Turks who participate in Anzac Day are deeply committed to studying and understanding the war and its consequences, which involves repeated 'educational' visits to Gallipoli. One of these Anzac Day participants is Ahmet, who developed a profound interest in Gallipoli after being appointed to President of the Turkish Branch of the RSL in 2005. Because of his position, Ahmet has read extensively about the historical event as he felt obliged to answer any question about the war. He admits that his initial interest rapidly grew into an 'obsession', and he began to travel to Gallipoli regularly. Unlike other 'battlefield tourists', Ahmet does not travel to Gallipoli simply to discover the site or attend the ceremonies, but also to build local connections with Turkish community groups and commemorative organisations. During his last visit, he met several local officials as well as the academic staff at the university to talk about possible projects they can develop together in order to make the commemorations more meaningful for the Australian–Turkish friendship. This pragmatic approach yields returns to the community; however, the expectation of concrete or symbolic benefits introduces an emotional distance between the visitor and the place. In contrast, some other visitors experience a much more personal attachment to the place beyond their expectations.

Ahmet also said that his son, who grew up in Australia, went to Turkey recently and called him from Gallipoli in tears saying that, after all these years, he finally understood who he was. Asking the father about what might have triggered his son's emotional revelation, he thought that it might be a feeling of pride in his Turkish background and heritage. A similar moment of self-realisation occurred to Melih, who grew up in Australia and considered himself a 'real Aussie', until he went to Turkey for holidays with his family a few years ago. He chose Turkey as a holiday destination mainly for convenience and competitive prices. He had no interest in Gallipoli although his grandfather and great-grandfather had both fought there and only his grandfather had survived. The latter also served in the President's guard under Atatürk and much of his family history focuses on that part of his life. On his way back to Australia, Melih engaged in a conversation with an Australian man who was returning home after his visit to Gallipoli. He said that the conversation that took place during the eight-hour flight was a life-changing experience where he came to understand that he never could become a 'hundred-percent' Australian, because what he had to give up was too significant. Melih found this experience very hard to express in words but he described his flight from Istanbul to Singapore as a liminal space where he was feeling more Turkish the more he was moving away from Turkey.

The encounter and struggle with one's heritage and dual identity when travelling to the actual site of Gallipoli are also documented in a reflective auto-biographical account authored by second-generation Turkish-Australian history teacher Fevzi Cimen, who visited the site on Anzac Day in 2005 as part of a Gallipoli-themed scholarship award. Cimen's narrative generates fascinating insights into the ambivalent 'insider'/'outsider' positionality that characterises the journey which was much anticipated as an 'opportunity to merge my two worlds' (Cimen, 2005: 2). In his travel account, the narrator seems particularly surprised about how Turkish commemoration ceremonies differed from those attended by Turks in Australia, as well as the sincere (educational) interest that Turks of all generations showed towards learning about Australians' perspective on this fateful battle. In contrast, and observing the Australian national service at the iconic 'Lone Pine', Fevzi is irritated by the cheerful and casual behaviour of younger Australians, on which he comments: 'As an Australian, I was embarrassed. As a Turk, I was horrified' (Cimen, 2005: 4).

Drawing on Fevzi's travel account as well as direct conversations with several other research participants, there is a noticeable difference in attitude towards Gallipoli between the first- and second-generation immigrants. While the former appear to be rather preoccupied with the image of their community and culture as a means of integration in the 'host' society, the latter are rather focused on their ambiguous positionality as individuals in between the two cultures. The above examples also show that embracing their Turkish background seems to offer a feeling of peace and epiphany to these young persons, while it equally augments their sense of 'Australianness' and cultural belonging. The positive image associated with their family heritage in the context of the Anzac legend is indisputably a major factor in their experience. This is equally emphasised by a statement by Melih who believes that if he were from any other background, he would have never 'looked back'. In many ways, while the first-generation migrants endeavour to feel welcome in Australia as a community, the second generation is coming to terms with their dual identity.

While the place of Turkish-Australians is not easily negotiable in Gallipoli *in situ*, an Australian-Sikh may feel even more out-of-place. At least, this reflects the opinion of Manjeet Singh, who never travelled to Gallipoli and does not think that Australian-Sikhs should be attending Dawn Service there. He argues that it should be the Indian Government's responsibility to ensure Indian representation at Gallipoli, including Sikhs from India. On the other hand, Sikhs in Australia endeavour to obtain recognition 'not as a separate group, but as part of the group', meaning as part of the forces that fought in Gallipoli. De-territorialisation of the commemorations has a function in the Australian context: it removes the commemorations from an environment of protest (feminist and Aboriginal mainly), and from the imperial and colonialist overtones of the Anzac legend. It also gives an outlet to the Australians who would like to commemorate the war but are alienated by the militaristic and at times chauvinist parades of Anzac Day in Australia. However, the Sikhs' motivation to take part in the commemorations is tightly connected to their present and future in the Australian territory rather than to some obscure location in a foreign country where their forefathers fought in the past. Their struggle cannot be dislocated without losing its meaning.

Instead of taking part in battlefield tourism, some Sikhs and Indians travel to gather information about their families' experience of the war. One of the most common themes that emerged from the interviews was the feeling of regret about not having asked more questions about the war when relatives were still alive. As a consequence, many of the Sikh participants undertake private research to uncover the recorded details of their relative's experience. In their quest to shed light on their families' war history, unit histories and other history books, as well as archival documents, are frequently consulted. For example, Kanwar Singh has benefited from his contacts in the army who helped him locate documents about his uncle's unit.

Likewise, Herman Singh asked family members to undertake research on his behalf, through which he was able to find out that the Indian army regiment in which his grandfather served for 14 years had been deployed in Gallipoli.

Researching about their family in India is more difficult for those Sikhs who are not from India. Most attempts do not yield the expected or anticipated results. But visits to the home country are often combined with some inquiry into the oral and material family legacies of WWI. At this juncture, it is also interesting to point out that many participants of Sikh heritage felt disappointed about the lack of WWI-related commemorative events in India, compared to the national popularity and significance Anzac Day enjoys in Australia. While this judgement may fail to account for the complex socio-political development of Anzac Day from a small to a national event, it may lead to biased perceptions of one country being 'grateful' and the other being 'ungrateful' for the community's sacrifices and war efforts.

The above examples suggest that travel, either in the guise of 'battlefield tourism' or 'homecoming tourism', plays a significant role in the identity formation of many Australian-Sikhs and Australian-Turks. As Clifford (1997) indicates, such practices can be seen as constitutive of diasporic communities, whose cultural relations and allegiances are never purely 'nationalist', but always draw on transnational networks and imaginaries that are built from multiple attachments. While Clifford makes clear that diaspora is different from travel, diaspora discourses bend together both *roots* and *routes* to construct 'alternative public spheres, forms of community consciousness and solidarity that maintain identifications outside the national time/space in order to live inside, with a difference' (Clifford, 1997: 251).

Conclusion

Family histories about the First World War are narratives that enable many Sikhs and Turks to locate themselves in Australian history, thus reconciling their dual or multiple identities. It is the wider Australian commemorative context that has taken up momentum over the past three decades and has increasingly encouraged members from these communities to identify with their 'Gallipoli' heritage, and thus complement, if not challenge, the previously hegemonic white-Australian master narrative. Today, many persons with Sikh and Turkish background in Australia remain unaware of the fact that the Anzac legend is not a consensual narrative of Australian nationhood but continues to be challenged by a variety of under- or misrepresented groups. Historically, Sikh and Turkish cultural identity has been associated with a strong military heritage, and the predominantly militaristic nature of Anzac Day may thus be perceived as an appropriate (symbolic) entry point for those community groups. Drawing on interviews with Turkish- and Sikh-Australians, the shared history of Gallipoli with Australia seems to reassure first- and second-generation immigrants of their legitimate place within Australian society. Beyond being an event to celebrate both national and 'minority' community, Anzac Day commemorations provide a sense of continuity between their past and present, thereby consolidating Turkish and Sikh/Indian ties to Australia without compromising their cultural heritage and identity. As the participants understand the Australian commemorative tradition to be firmly anchored in the Australian national consciousness, they are often critical about the (lack of) public remembrance culture in their previous countries.

Although war memories may be considered contested or taboo within transgenerational contexts, many of the Sikh and Turkish Gallipoli veterans processed and transmitted their fading memories within a particular social framework to their descendants. These, in turn, often retrieved them after the process of immigration when these stories became more relevant to their increasingly hybrid identities. These new circumstances shaped and modified both the content and meaning of their memories, which were remodelled, reinterpreted and, at times, reinvented. With the impossibility of retrieving these stories or finding answers to questions never asked, there is also a feeling of guilt or inadequacy among second- and third-generation migrants to make up for lost memories.

The examples presented in this chapter thus highlight the limits of transgenerational memories as 'travelling' seamlessly from one generation to another (Lacroix & Fiddian-Qasmiyeh, 2013). At the same time, they shed new light on the workings of prosthetic memory (Landsberg, 2004) as a way of compensating for the lack of first-hand accounts with a new memory repertoire that merges familial memory fragments with mediated and popular imaginaries associated with a particular historical event. While the presented narratives provide valuable insights into 'bottom-up' attempts to negotiate identities between family memories and national affiliation, they equally challenge exclusive memory politics which continue to privilege some memories over others, and thus nurture processes of cultural othering and segregation. In the context of increasing xenophobia that permeates Australian society and institutions, Sikh and Turkish communities promote the proliferation of shared, transnational memories as a powerful tool to foster intercultural communication and understanding.

References

Akcelik, R. (1986). Foreword. *Before and After Gallipoli: A Collection of Australian and Turkish Writings*. Melbourne: Australian-Turkish Friendship Society Publications.

Anderson, B. (1991). *Imagined Communities: Reflections on the Origins and Spread of Nationalism*. London and New York: Verso.

Basarin, V. (2011). *Battlefield Tourism: Anzac Day Commemorations at Gallipoli: An Empirical Analysis*. PhD, Deakin University.

Beaumont, J. (2015). Commemoration in Australia: A memory orgy? *Australian Journal of Political Science*, 50(3), 536–544.

Bhabha, H. (1990). *Nation and Narration*. London: Routledge.

Bilimoria, P. (1996). *The Hindus and Sikhs in Australia*. Canberra: Australian Govt. Pub. Service.

Bongiorno, F. (2014). Anzac and the politics of inclusion. In: S. Sumartojo and B. Wellings, eds., *Nation, Memory and Great War Commemoration: Mobilizing the Past in Europe, Australia and New Zealand*. Oxford: Peter Lang, pp. 81–98.

Broadbent, H. (2009). *A Simple Epic: Gallipoli and the Australian Media – A Brief Survey*. Annual Lone Pine Lecture, Gallipoli Memorial Club, Sydney, 8 August.

Cimen, F. (2005). *Gallipoli: A Second Invasion* [doc]. NSW: Premier's Teacher Gallipoli Scholarship. Available at www.det.nsw.edu.au/media/downloads/detawscholar/.../ 2006/.../gallip_fer.doc [accessed 13 February 2017].

Clifford, J. (1997). *Routes. Travel and Translation in the Late Twentieth Century*. Cambridge, MA: Harvard University Press.

Damousi, J. (2010). Why do we get so emotional about Anzac? In: M. Lake and H. Reynolds, eds., *What's Wrong with Anzac: The Militarisation of Australian History*. Sydney: UNSW Press, pp. 94–109.

de Lepervanche, M. (1984). *Indians in a White Australia: An Account of Race, Class and Indian Immigration to Eastern Australia*. Sydney: Allen and Unwin.

Erll, A. (2011). Travelling memory. *Parallax*, 17(4), 4–18.

Fewster, K., Basarin, V. and Basarin, H. (1985). *A Turkish View of Gallipoli Çanakkale*. Crows Nest, NSW: Allen & Unwin.

Fiddian-Qasmiyeh, E. (2013). The inter-generational politics of 'travelling memories': Sahrawi refugee youth remembering home-land and home-camp. *Journal of Intercultural Studies*, 34(6), 631–649.

Fischer, N. (2015). *Memory Work: The Second Generation*. London: Palgrave Macmillan.

Gallipoli. (1981). [film]. Australia: Peter Weir.

Gammage, B. (1974). *The Broken Years: Australian Soldiers in the Great War*. Canberra: Australian National University Press.

Hirsch, M. and Miller, N.K., eds. (2011). *Rites of Return: Diaspora Poetics and the Politics of Memory*. New York: Columbia University Press.

Holbrook, C. (2014). *Anzac: The Unauthorised Biography*. Sydney: UNSW Press.

Inglis, K. (2008). *Sacred Places: War Memorials in the Australian Landscape*. Carlton, Vic.: Melbourne University Press.

Kennedy, R. and Radstone, S. (2013). Memory up close: Memory studies in Australia. *Memory Studies*, 6(3), 237–244.

Kleist, J.O. and Glynn, I. eds. (2012). *History, Memory and Migration: Perceptions of the Past and the Politics of Incorporation*. Basingstoke: Palgrave Macmillan.

Lacroix, T. and Fiddian-Qasmiyeh, E. (2013). Refugee and diaspora memories: The politics of remembering and forgetting. *Journal of Intercultural Studies*, 34(6), 684–696.

Lake, M. (2010). How do school children learn about the spirit of Anzac? In: M. Lake and H. Reynolds, eds., *What's Wrong with Anzac: The Militarisation of Australian History*. Sydney: UNSW Press, pp. 135–156.

Landsberg, A. (2004). *Prosthetic Memory: The Transformation of American Remembrance in the Age of Mass Culture*. New York: Columbia University Press.

Lewis, D. (2005). Bad blood set aside as Sikhs join parade. *Sydney Morning Herald* [online]. Available at: www.smh.com.au/news/National/Bad-blood-set-aside-as-Sikhs-join-parade/2005/04/25/1114281508433.html [accessed 21 February 2017].

Marschall, S., ed. (2017). *Tourism and Memories of Home: Migrants, Displaced People, Exiles and Diasporic Communities*. Bristol: Channel View.

McKenna, M. (2010). Anzac Day: How did it become Australia's national day? In: M. Lake and H. Reynolds, eds., *What's Wrong with Anzac: The Militarisation of Australian History*. Sydney: UNSW Press, pp. 110–134.

McKenna, M. and Ward, S. (2007). 'It was really moving, mate': The Gallipoli pilgrimage and sentimental nationalism in Australia. *Australian Historical Studies*, 38(129), 141–151.

McKenna, M. and Ward, S. (2015). An Anzac myth: The creative memorialisation of Gallipoli. *The Monthly* [online]. December 2015 to January 2016. Available at: www.themonthly.com.au/issue/2015/december/1448888400/mark-mckenna-and-stuart-ward/anzac-myth [accessed 21 February 2017].

Rae, R. (2004). *Scarlet Poppies: The Army Experience of Australian Nurses during World War One*. Burwood, NSW: College of Nursing.

Rees, P. (2008). *The Other Anzacs: Nurses at War, 1914–18*. Crows Nest, NSW: Allen & Unwin.

Safran, W. (1991). Diasporas in modern societies: Myths of homeland and return. *Diaspora*, 1(1), 83–99.

Scates, B. (2006). *Return to Gallipoli: Walking the Battlefields of the Great War*. Cambridge: Cambridge University Press.

Senay, B. (2013). *Beyond Turkey's Borders: Long-Distance Kemalism, State Politics and the Turkish Diaspora*. London: I. B. Tauris.

Sheller, M. and Urry, J. (2006). The new mobilities paradigm. *Environment and Planning*, 38, 207–226.

Simpson, C. (2010). From ruthless foe to national friend: Turkey, Gallipoli and Australian nationalism. *Media International Australia*, 137, 58–66.

Thomson, A. (1994). *Anzac Memories Living with the Legend*. Melbourne: Oxford University Press.

Twomey, C. (2013). Trauma and the reinvigoration of Anzac: An argument. *History Australia*, 10(3), 85–108.

Waterton, E. and Dittmer, J. (2016). Transnational war memories in Australia's heritage field. *Media International Australia*, 158(1), 58–68.

Watson, L. (2006). *Aboriginal and Torres Strait Islander Soldiers of the First World War*. Zillmere, QLD: Kurbingui Youth Development Association.

West, B., ed. (2005). *Down the Road: Exploring Backpacker and Independent Travel*. Perth: API Network, Curtin University of Technology.

Winter, C. (2009). Tourism, social memory and the Great War. *Annals of Tourism Research*, 36(4), 607–626.

6   'To live in France'

The confluence of tourism, memory, migration and war

Bertram M. Gordon

Introduction

'To live in France', wrote Richard Cobb, an Englishman who served in France during the Second World War and settled there afterward, 'was a source of joy' (Cobb, 1969: 18). Although he later returned to England, Cobb devoted the remainder of his professional life to the study of French history. His expression encapsulates the sentiments and memories of those who arrived in France as foreign soldiers from abroad and either stayed on or later returned there to live, in the words of the German essayist Friedrich Sieburg (1929), 'as God in France' (unless otherwise noted, all translations are my own). Decisions by Second World War veterans were made for many reasons but often involved the interactions of tourism imaginaries engendered by a land that had become a tourism icon before the war, together with the memory of their war-time experiences there, often linked to romantic attachments.

This chapter explores the connections linking tourism, migration and memory by focusing on foreign veterans of the Second World War in France, both German and Allied. While stationed there, these servicemen managed to do some sightseeing during off-hours that arguably contributed to their later return as migrants or as tourists, revisiting places where they once served but also memorable sites encountered during their war-time touristic explorations. The current chapter may be viewed as a contribution to the niche area of 'vet tourism' (Nishino, 2017), but it goes beyond this by including former soldiers who returned to France to settle there. The reasons for such migration to places of former military service are manifold and may not be articulated in sources readily available to the historian. They include economic opportunity and romantic liaisons, with the two sometimes intermixed. Hopefully, this chapter will encourage future research, especially into the often hidden private diaries and letters that will help provide fuller answers to some of the questions raised here.

Memory and the Second World War

Johann Michel and others have noted that memorial and memory studies have received significant attention during recent decades (Michel, 2010: 2). A possible factor might be an aging population in the industrialized Western world drawing attention to issues of memory and its many expressions. The impact of Sigmund Freud and Freudian studies has also played a role in the development of memory studies, much of which has focused on trauma and its subsequent effects on what Roger Kennedy called 'unconscious memory' (Kennedy, 2010: 179; see also Eley, 2011: 558 and 570). This work has been enriched by the work of Marianne Hirsch and many others examining the forms of memory of the Holocaust among survivors and subsequent generations of those impacted directly.

In addition to the focus on trauma, much of this attention, as Alon Confino pointed out some twenty years ago, centres on what might be called 'top down', or the construction of memory by political, heritage and academic communities, paralleling the paradigm in the field of social history in the 1960s and 1970s. Calling for more attention to the study of private memories – including about tourism experiences – Confino wrote:

> We miss a whole world of human activities that cannot be immediately recognized (and categorized) as political, although they are decisive to the way people construct and contest images of the past. We can think of the family, voluntary association, and workplace but should also include practices such as tourism and consumerism.
>
> (Confino, 1997: 1395)

There is, of course, a wide range of memories from the traumatic to the sublime. As Erika Apfelbaum (2010: 88) writes, many memories are happy as well as traumatic and private as well as public, though they may become public when written about and published as, for example, Marcel Proust's memories of the *madeleine*. Gastronomical recollections also played a role in the memories of ex-servicemen and women returning to France, as will be seen later in this chapter, highlighting the role of private memory in history.

Relationships between war and tourism and their impact on the memories of participants are an area that has been little studied until recently. The connections among happy memory, tourism, objects and war first came together for me during an interview I had in Paris with Jacques Schweizer, who had led the pro-German war-time *Groupe Collaboration*'s youth affiliate, the *Jeunesse de l'Europe Nouvelle* during the German occupation in France. When, after a two-hour interview in his law office in Paris on 28 June 1974, I thanked him for his generosity, he led me to a cabinet, showed me some ceramic souvenirs of his visit to a Nuremberg Nazi Party rally, and said, 'No, it is I who thank you, for allowing me to relive some of the happiest moments from my youth' (Gordon, 1980: 236). In an essay on communicating memory, Birgit Braasch (2008: 5) suggests the importance of including material objects as well as photographs taken by tourists in the study of memory. Indeed, the memories of both German and Allied soldiers who served in France during the Second World War and recalled these days as times of pleasure are at variance with the many examples of nostalgic memory of place and loss so frequently addressed elsewhere.

Memory is itself a complex phenomenon based on the physiology of the brain and the attendant role of the hippocampus that has only recently begun to be understood (Carey, 2016). Steven Rose divides memory into procedural and declarative, the former referring to recalling how to do something, such as riding a two-wheeled object, the latter referencing something from the past, namely its being called a bicycle. He further subdivides declarative memories into semantic, meaning a storehouse for information, and episodic or autobiographical, relating to 'episodes in one's own life' (Rose, 2010: 200). War-time memories of travel and tourism fit most clearly into the autobiographical subcategory. Arguing that memories are not merely stored in the brain as information might be in a computer, Rose (2010: 207) writes: 'Each act of recall is itself a new experience. Reactivated memories are subtly changed each time we recall them'.

Episodic memory has also been described, by Endel Tulving, as 'mental time travel' (Sutton, Harris & Barnier, 2010: 211 and 489), or 'Chronesthesia', to use the more technical term, another hint in the direction of linking memory to travel and, by extension, tourism. Episodic memory has now been redefined by some to mean future-oriented mental time travel or 'pre-experiences' of future events; in other words, the view that remembering the past and imagining the future are connected in a single process (Perrin & Michaelian, 2017: 228–229). Either way, a tourism of the mind may be likened to the tourism imaginary described by Rachid Amirou as the 'totality of images and evocations tied to tourism' (Amirou, 2012 [1995]: 25–26). We are arguably touring the past in our memories or the future in our 'pre-experiences'. Often 'memory' is construed as that of an event, or episode, to use Rose's term, or a homesickness type of nostalgic or diasporic longing (Boym, 2001: 251). In episodic memory, however, we may also be touring an alternative present or future, a form of spatial touring. As my examples will show, former soldiers in France may look back to some of their happier experiences in that country, including romance, as well as to a future of settling there.

In this chapter, I suggest that memory, however defined, may look back as well as forward to a happy time. An individual experience of France is blended into a cultural memory formed over time by the development of France as a tourism icon sufficiently strong as to induce a return visit or even permanent move to France. Where such memory is formed around a romantic relationship, it may be asked whether this would have occurred had not touristic images, contributing to the subsequent development of memory, induced the soldiers to wander around in their spare time, providing the opportunity to meet the persons with whom they created relationships. Recent work by Karen Shanton and Alvin Goldman (2010) depicts remembering as a process of imagining past events, a process in which a causal connection to the remembered event is at best incidental. In other words, the distinction between autobiographic or episodic memory and the tourist imaginary is blurred at best.

Memory and tourism

The development of memory studies as a field has been paralleled by that of tourism studies (Gordon, 2015: 135–156). There is clearly a connection between tourism imaginaries and experiences and memory, although it has not often been studied. Addressing collective forms of memory, such as 'social memory' (Sutton *et al.*, 2010: 221–222), Vida Bajc asked:

> What kinds of cultural and social dynamics underlie the processes through which certain types of actors come to play a role in how collective memory is presented through tourism? What are the various capacities with which these actors operate? . . . How does tourism enable their roles to endure or change through time?
>
> (Bajc, 2006: 7)

His questions highlight the role of tourism in the creation of memory both for individuals and within groups, and suggest the development of such touristic memories that ultimately helped colour the perceptions of soldiers serving in France during the Second World War. Braasch references the possibility of a social or collective memory among war veterans, arguing:

> On a group level, war veterans' meetings can be taken as an example. In these meetings, where veterans are in the same group in which they made their war experiences, much more is remembered than, for example, in interviews.
>
> (Braasch, 2008: 13)

As Stéphanie Nkoghe (2008: 55) points out, tourists receive a wide variety of stimuli and in effect will 'see, hear, touch, taste', thereby creating an experience stored in their memories. A tourist's memory includes information from before, during and after travel. It is this collection of memories of a France already present in the tourism imaginary of many that led some to return to live there after the war.

As with memory studies, tourism has received growing academic attention and it, too, has been the subject of a variety of definitions. Tourism, however, or more specifically, the tourist gaze, to use John Urry's term, is in its essence the act of seeing, of looking with curiosity at the world (Urry, 1990: 1–2). Studying the admittedly fragmentary source material from the war veterans will not only narrate some fascinating personal stories of sentiment and relocation but also help insert the phenomenon of tourism imaginaries as they inform tourism circuits into the even larger phenomenon of memory as a whole.

Those who fight in wars bring their own cultural perspectives with them, including tourism gazes and images, even if these words are not always used and these perspectives are incorporated into their memories. The iconic tourism images associated with France and especially Paris by the time of the Second World War affected the behaviour of the foreign troops stationed there, both German from 1940 through 1944 and Allied after the Liberation of 1944 (Gordon, 1996: 287–298; 1998: 616–638). Lost in the carnage and destruction of war, however, are the ways in which the experiences of travelling and, by implication, touring in foreign and often occupied lands may have impacted the lives of the soldiers who experienced these areas, and inspired them to return either to view again the sites they saw during their military service or, in some cases, to settle there.

The tourism iconicity of France

The attraction of France in general and Paris in particular as international tourism destinations was well established by the time of the Second World War. Paris especially had acquired tourism iconicity with the rebuilding of the city during the 1860s by Baron Georges-Eugène Haussmann and the coming of the railway during the second half of the nineteenth century. Cinema also focused on and magnified the appeal and attractions of Paris. Harald Welzer emphasized the impact of films on soldiers, noting that interviews of German veterans of the Second World War indicated that their memories of service were frequently traceable to well-known films and that 'scenes from these films provided images and a language to put the war experiences into stories' (Welzer, 2005: 37, cited in Braasch, 2008: 14).

Sutton *et al.* (2010: 215) remind us that 'self-identity goals influence which events from our lives are recalled and the way in which these events are recalled'. Tourism and travel as matters of status are well known and the iconic status of France as a tourist destination by the time of the Second World War most certainly enhanced its image in the minds of foreign soldiers serving there. The links between tourism and war can be difficult to trace retrospectively because touring is so often seen as an ordinary or 'normal' activity, requiring no special commentary especially when occurring in the context of war or migration when seemingly larger issues of life and death may be at stake. The tourist imaginary of France as the land of living well, however, continued through the Second World War when both Germans and Allies designated it as a rest and recreation area. Although Hitler made clear his wish that occupied France not become an *Etappenstadt* [city of malingerers] (Torrie, 2011: 316; von Kageneck, 2011: 71), the reality was quite different as thousands of Germans toured Paris and, in effect, vacationed in occupied France (Müller (Leutnant), 1940; Gordon, 1998: 622–623). They had created sets of memory that were shared in the manner indicated in Maurice Halbwachs' concept of 'collective memory', while at the same time retaining their individual memories of their war-time experiences.

Post-war Germans touring formerly occupied territories were frequently able to make connections with places they had seen as soldiers during the war, recalling memories of youth, adventure and domination (Confino, 2000: 109). The earlier mentioned example of Jacques Schweizer reliving some of the happiest moments from his youth in recalling his activities before and during the war comes to mind. Again, the memories of the former soldiers must be considered in the larger context of the frequently middle-aged men remembering nostalgically the exploits and glories of their youth.

Among the elements of memory sometimes overlooked in the emphasis on the political has been the memory of a sense of place or what Nancy Wood (1999: 3) called a 'symbolic topography'. Halbwachs had also considered memory in terms of landscapes and objects, linking 'history and geography' (Apfelbaum, 2010: 91). German and later Allied soldiers' memories of Paris, together with the prewar tourism imaginaries they carried into the war, led some of them to return to visit or live in Paris. Often such memories are not written or if they are, they are likely to be in private letters, diaries and sources rarely available to the historian. They may be transmitted in later years, perhaps in altered form as the years pass or through the stories of children and grandchildren. None of this makes them any less real or significant as factors to be considered in reconstructing, or attempting to reconstruct, the historical past. The stories available attest to the powerful role of memory in creating small communities of expatriate veterans living in France with yet an additional layer of memory – their own recollections of the homes they left – itself an area for further research and all highlighting the tensions and complementarities of group and individual memory.

Remembering interwar France

In an anonymously written article in 1927, an unnamed former American soldier from the First World War then living in Paris had immigrated there, in his own words, seeking 'the Blue Bird of Happiness': the allure of France but specifically of Juliet, a woman he had met while serving there. He had left Saint-Nazaire in July 1919, he wrote, expecting that if he ever returned to France it would be 'as a tourist or an A.E.F.' [American Expeditionary Forces] pilgrim but, in fact, it was love for Juliet that had brought him back to France (Former American Soldier, 1927: 20). Describing the differences between France and the United States, he wrote:

> The Frenchman takes time to live; he is not overly ambitious; he is not constantly in a hurry; and he extracts from the routine events in life – the evening aperitif, the beefsteak smothered in onions, the friendly intercourse of the family counsel – every bit of enjoyment that they can possibly bestow. We American exiles are fortunate in receiving instructions from these specialists in the science of living.
>
> (Former American Soldier, 1927: 86)

English-speaking soldiers who served during the war in France and returned subsequently include Richard Cobb, mentioned at the outset of this chapter, who had studied in France between 1935 and 1939 and later became one of England's most highly respected historians of France. He described himself as a '*boulevardier*', someone who spent his time strolling and presumably touring the grand boulevards of the Right Bank in Paris (Cobb, 1969: 48). Cobb had acquired a deep love not only for Paris but also for many of the small towns where he learned French and studied French history (Cobb, 1969: 5). Later, he described his weekends in Lyon:

enhanced by a trip up the Saône, by the Blue Train to L'Ile Barbe, or by the *ficelle* [funicular] to Saint-Just, thence to Vaugneray, in the Monts du Lyonnais, in a Wild West sort of train: both places to which the Lyonnais would flock in great numbers *en famille*, in couples, or as solitary fishermen.

(Cobb, 1969: 9)

Returning to Britain in 1939, Cobb served subsequently in the army and following the Liberation was stationed in Normandy, although he did not see action there. While in Normandy, he edited a newspaper for the local French and visited war cemeteries there. After spending time in Belgium, he was based in Roubaix, where he stayed with families and for a time considered settling (Cobb, 1969: 24–25 and 32). Following demobilization, Cobb remained in Paris, where he supported himself by teaching English in a variety of public and private schools. In 1952, he married Françoise Richard, a French woman by whom he had a son. In Paris, Cobb met the budding historian Albert Soboul. Both were students of Georges Lefebvre, a well-known specialist in the history of the French Revolution. A Communist, Soboul arranged for local sympathetic families to feed Cobb and may have encouraged him to become a Communist supporter. Cobb attended a memorial service for Stalin in 1953 and reportedly wept at the occasion (Cobb, 1969: 37–39). He left France, and his second wife and child, in 1955 to take an academic position in Wales (Thomas, 1996). Later, Cobb, who by now had become a well-known historian of France, married an English woman, renounced any association with Communism and broke with Soboul (Friguglietti, 2016). He appears to have been unsuccessful in attempts to gain French citizenship (Mansel & Colton, 1996), indirectly thereby raising another area for exploration, namely the reactions of the local people to the returning veterans. Looking back nostalgically on his years in France, Cobb later wrote:

To live in France is to live double, every minute counts, the light of the sky of the Île-de-France is unique and a source of joy, there is joy too in a small rectangle of sunshine at the top of a tall greying, leprous building, the colour of Utrillo, and in the smell of chestnuts that brings the promise of autumn, la Rentrée, and the beloved repetition of the Paris year.

(Cobb, 1969: 18)

Migration: quantitative and qualitative

Studying the former military personnel who on the basis of their memories of France later took up residence there is a qualitative narrative; although the French government maintains statistics on immigration, they do not include the immigrants' motivations, which in any case will have been complex, varying by individual. France's INSEE [*Institut national de la statistique et des études économiques*], its statistical agency, defines as immigrants persons living in France who are born to non-French citizens outside the country, whether or not they have acquired French citizenship ('Qu'est-ce qu'un immigré?', 2004: 3).

Passports, while in one form or another dating back to antiquity, became generalized in France and the rest of Europe only during the First World War, becoming standard during the interwar years. In 1921 there were some 300,000 immigrants in Paris (Martineau, 2011). From the interwar years onward, it is likely that at any given time several hundred thousand foreigners were living in France. Americans were estimated at more than 100,000 permanent residents in France in 2016 (Americans in France, n.d.). Although the documentation provides estimates of the numbers of immigrants, it offers little information on the individuals and their reasons for entering the country.

There is, however, a qualitative argument to be made on the basis of individual stories and biographical memory often in the case of exceptional individuals. An example is the story of a stash of handwritten letters exchanged between a certain Johann, a German soldier stationed in Paris, and Lisette, a French secretary there during the Occupation. The letters were discovered in a Paris flea market in 2007 and were described six years later in the *Economist 1843* magazine. Research on the couple indicated that they had met at the Paris World Exposition in 1937. Johann, the soldier, was already married. They apparently met again by chance in a Paris café during the summer of 1940 and subsequently became lovers in a France that, the article noted, had lost some two million men to German prisoner of war camps. Tourism in Paris contributed to the romance between the couple then in their twenties:

> Whenever he could get away from his duties, Johann visited her. On fine days, they did the sights together with all the other Germans who had arrived in Paris, and who had grown up to think of France as beautiful and culturally impressive, but at the same time insufficiently martial and somewhat decadent. *Gott in Frankreich?* (1929), Friedrich Sieburg's bestselling book, warned France to adopt German ways in terms that would be familiar to Frenchmen today, lest it fail to find a place in the new European order.
>
> (Moorehead, 2013)

In her history of women's lives in occupied Paris, Anne Sebba described Lisette and Johann as 'strolling around the sights of Paris together, walking up the Eiffel Tower (the Resistance had put the lift out of action) and eating in romantic restaurants à deux' (Sebba, 2016: 57). In April 1941, Johann was sent to German-occupied Poland to help prepare for the coming invasion of Soviet Russia. Becoming ill in Russia, he was sent back to Germany and, in the spring of 1942, returned to Paris. The letters tell harrowing stories of Johann's becoming a prisoner of war following the liberation of France in late 1944 and Lisette accused of what became known as 'horizontal collaboration', or having had an affair with a German soldier. She was apparently spared punishment, however, because of evidence showing she had aided the Resistance. Johann divorced his German wife and he and Lisette were ultimately married in 1949. They became managers of a hotel and restaurant on Lake Constance in Germany. 'From time to time', the story continues, 'Lisette returned to Paris, to window-shop for the elegant clothes she so loved', but they refused to return permanently to France, reversing the model of the former soldiers moving to the sites they had toured. They remained together until Johann's death in 1986. Lisette died fourteen years later (Moorehead, 2013; Sebba, 2016: 358–359).

At least a few German soldiers stationed in the occupied Channel Islands, some on leave and/or convalescence, returned there after the war to marry local women they had met. One such former German soldier married an Islander woman and ended up running a guesthouse in Saint Helier on the island of Jersey (O'Sullivan, 2016). In his study of the German prisoners of war in post-war France, Fabien Théofilakis observed an improvement in relations between the prisoners, especially those who eventually found work in the private sector there, and the local French as memories shifted with the passage of time after the war. One such prisoner, who had lost his original home town, Danzig, now in Poland, and who was fluent in French, was employed in a Lyon tannery, where he eventually fell in love with the boss's secretary and was warmly invited into her family (Théofilakis, 2014: 364–365).

From enemies to brothers: two combatants return to Normandy

Another outstanding and very different case in point is the story of Johannes Börner, a German soldier who became a resident and citizen of France as a result of his meeting and marrying a French woman. Born in 1925 in Leipzig, Börner served as a private in the 3rd Paratrooper Division of the German army and in July 1944 was sent to Normandy to help fight the Allied invasion (Börner, n.d.). Captured and then kept in prisoner of war camps in Normandy, Börner seized an opportunity to work on a local farm in April 1946 (Stasi, 2014: 139–140). Given the choice of remaining in France in 1947 or returning to his native Leipzig, now in the Soviet occupation zone of Germany, Börner chose to stay in France, where he worked for a time in Paris, paralleling the decision of the former German soldier who settled in France rather than return to his native Leipzig. Describing Börner's personal trajectory, Jean-Charles Stasi writes that the former parachutist had come to appreciate the 'imagination' and 'flexibility' of the French in contrast to German 'discipline'. In 1954, Börner met a local woman in Normandy whom he married (Stasi, 2014: 147–148). His story is especially striking because his military career paralleled that of Léon Gauthier, also from Normandy, who had joined the Resistance early in the war and had served in it in London during the Occupation, where he enlisted in the Kieffer unit of the Resistance, a commando brigade of 177 men who participated in the Normandy landings (Stasi, 2014: 66–67).

The stories of Gauthier and Börner, who fought on opposite sides in the summer of 1944 and years later became friends, participating jointly in D-Day landing commemorations in Normandy, exemplify the ways in which private memory may transition into public history over time when they were published in 2014 in Stasi's book, *Ennemies et Frères du Jour J à aujurd'hui, au-delà de la guerre* [*Enemies and Brothers from D-Day to the Present, Beyond the War*]. The two former soldiers celebrated Christmas together in 2012 and in 2014 participated in ceremonies marking the seventieth anniversary of D-Day, in this case becoming part of the official memory celebrations discussed by Michel and Confino (Gayle & Reuters, 2014). In a recent book on the memories of the Vichy past in France today, Richard J. Golsan (2017: xiii) suggests: 'For anyone familiar with the ferocity of the fighting' in Normandy, the meeting in 2014 of the two former soldiers 'seemed strained and artificial'. Their story, however, highlights the role of individual memories and their potential over time to alter dominant narratives (Apfelbaum, 2010: 89).

It is highly likely that Börner's progressive embrace of France, even before meeting his wife, was related to tourist experiences in Paris and Normandy. In total, nearly one million German soldiers remained as prisoners of war in France between 1944 and 1948 (Launet, 2012). Börner appears to have been very much the exception among German prisoners of war as most were repatriated by the late 1940s.

Sex, romance, tourism and migration back to France

Very different from Börner's story was the behaviour of German soldiers who used occupied France as a venue for sex tourism, leaving some 200,000 babies born to local women in France (Picard, 2009). Focused on sexual activity reflecting imbalances of power or 'militourism', a term used more recently in reference to this phenomenon in Polynesia (Teaiwa, 2016: 850–851), much of the tourism of German soldiers and their Allied successors (Roberts, 2013) in war-time France focused on sex and romance. August von Kageneck, a German soldier aged eighteen, who arrived in France shortly after the June 1940 invasion and visited several sites in the country, remembered soldiers who had climbed the Eiffel Tower and had carved the names of their wives into its beams. He recalled especially the odyssey of a soldier from Hamburg who wrote 'we were shown a series of things that we knew only in our wildest imaginations'. This soldier had also found his way to a brothel and noted 'Ah, soldiers. They always find a brothel more readily than a church' (von Kageneck, 2011: 70–71).

In a commemoration marking the sixty-fifth anniversary of the end of the war in Europe in 2009, and similar to Confino's 'top-down' construction of memory events (Confino, 1997: 1394, n. 22), a group of those born to German fathers and French mothers gathered at the Mémorial de Caen in Normandy for a study day on 'war childhoods, broken childhoods'. Those assembled had often endured childhood taunting as 'bastards' or '*têtes de boches*' [literally 'heads of Germans' in a highly disparaging sense]. Participants in the Caen study day also included children of French soldiers stationed in Austria and Germany after the war, all of whom were in search of 'the other half', in the words of Gerlinda Swillen, a professor at the Free University of Brussels who had recently learned of the death of her German father half a century earlier. In the words of Jean-Jacques Delorme, the founder of the Franco-German organization *Cœurs sans frontières* [Hearts without Borders] and who himself had located his other family in Mainz, 'we wish to be able to say: I am Franco-German with a French passport in one pocket and a German in the other' (Picard, 2009). Swillen eventually found out that upon learning that a child was on the way, her father, a *Wehrmacht* soldier, had offered to marry her mother but had been refused. He was later stationed in France, where he married a local woman. He had returned to Germany after the war.

Memories of 'dying to be sent to Paris'

One of the more well-known stories of Americans serving in the military who ended up living in France is that of the singer Josephine Baker, who spent much of the interwar period in Paris, then served as a spy for the Free French during the war, and afterward settled at the Château des Milandes, a Renaissance castle over-looking the Dordogne River in the Périgord region, where she raised a family of twelve children adopted from different countries. Baker, who ultimately became an iconic figure in African American history as well as among the American expatriate community living in France, had become a well-known singer and dancer, starring in 'Shuffle Along', an early all-black musical, in the United States before leaving for Paris, looking for a world without racial segregation in 1925, where she performed in *La Revue Nègre* (Crosley, 2016).

Another American settling in France was Harold Kaplan, who had studied French literature at the University of Chicago and then worked for the Voice of America [*La voix de l'Amérique*] radio in 1942. Sent to Algiers and then to metropolitan France, Kaplan stayed in France after the Liberation (Kaplan, L., 2013; Kaplan, A., 2016). In a 1990 interview, he recalled 'dying to be sent to Paris' and complained that he had been made to stay too long in North Africa (Kaplan, H., 1990: 9). Americans who participated in the 1944 landings and stayed on or returned to live in France were also included among the some 8,000 living and working in Châteauroux, the largest American military base in Europe until General de Gaulle withdrew France from NATO in 1966. A *New York Times* article of 2009 recalled that:

> For many here in Châteauroux of the older generation, the years at the NATO base were the good old days, with well-paying jobs plentiful at the base and splotches of colour – as off-duty Americans sported Hawaiian shirts and tooled around in their brightly collared Chevrolets and Oldsmobiles – in the dreary greyness of post-war France. About 450 weddings were celebrated between American servicemen and Frenchwomen in City Hall.
>
> (Tagliabue, 2009)

Even in 2009, however, some of the Americans remained. They included Joseph Gagne, a native of Augusta, Maine, who had participated in the Normandy landings. In January 1952 Gagne had learned of the plans to build a base in Châteauroux. Together with his French wife, Jeanine, he had opened a hamburger restaurant there, called 'Joe from Maine'. Gagne died at the age of eighty-six in 2009, but, as the newspaper reported, his daughter Annette continued to serve hamburgers, hot dogs and Tex-Mex dishes at the restaurant (Tagliabue, 2009). The gastronomic memories of the United States served by a second-generation daughter born and raised in France added yet another layer to the history of migration and memory in France. They also imply another area for further study, namely the degree of assimilation of the immigrant war veterans and their descendants; in other words, to what extent did they become French in contrast to clustering in more identifiable expatriate communities?

Veterans remember

Following the Liberation in 1944, a 'French Welcome Committee' office in Paris offered visiting Allied military personnel information about the city as well as guided tours (Leveque, 1945: 3–4), and the city of Metz was used for rest and rehabilitation as American forces moved towards Germany (Haahr, n.d.). Quasi-military personnel during the war had included the 'grey mice', the German military women's auxiliaries, followed by their successors among the Allied personnel both referenced in *For You*, a post-Liberation French publication aimed at promoting local tourism by Allied personnel (Paris ***** 1945: 6–7).

In a book, *Veterans Recall*, Hilary Kaiser, an American by birth, living in France and the daughter of an American soldier who had fought in Asia during the Second World War, collected several examples of autobiographical or episodic memory stories of Allied participants in the war, including some Americans who later immigrated into France. Ridgway B. Knight, born and raised in France, subsequently acquired a Master's in Business Administration from Harvard University in 1931 and thereafter settled into a business career in the United States. He then served with the American forces in North Africa and France, beginning in 1943 (Kaiser, 1994: 17). Knight, who later had a career working with the American State Department, eventually retired to France, where in comments again attesting to the power of gastronomic memory, he recalled arriving in Paris in early September 1944, shortly after its liberation:

> I had two marvellous days in Paris, and I'll always remember them. The monuments, the clouds, the beautiful girls and women in flowered skirts riding bicycles. It made an absolutely heavenly sight. I also remember one of my meals there. It was at Prunier's. The Normandy coast had been liberated, so there were oysters, but there were no lemons available in Paris and we were given vinegar to put on them.
>
> (Kaiser, 1994: 28)

William Jay Smith, born in Louisiana, had studied French in France prior to the war. Sent to Casablanca, he was subsequently assigned as liaison officer to the French ship *La Grandière* and sailed with it to the South Pacific. As of the publication of Kaiser's book in 1994, Smith and his French wife split their time between New York and Paris. Another American, included in Kaiser's book, is Roger Lantagne who landed as a parachutist on D-Day in Normandy and retired to France in 1973. Lantagne later remembered applying with some friends for two-day passes to see Paris after the war had ended but while he was still there. They ended by staying six days in Paris and during this tour Lantagne met his future wife (Kaiser, 1994: 49–50 and 45).

Kaiser also tells the story of another American soldier who was sent to England and France, and who recalled driving on days off to tour Fontainebleau, Versailles and Rouen, none of which had suffered significant damage from the war (Kaiser, 1994: 64). Yet another visited newly liberated Saint-Lô, which had been 95% destroyed by the bombings on 5 and 6 June and the subsequent fighting in July 1944 (Lemay, 2014: 168). The Cathedral had been destroyed and few civilians were left in the town. 'We drove through St. Lô in the morning with the sun shining and then again at night with the moonlight on it. It was really a horrifying sight' (Kaiser, 1994: 83). He also visited the Chartres Cathedral, whose stained-glass windows had been removed for their protection. 'It was extraordinary to see the Cathedral with transparent glass. You could see all the statues inside' (Kaiser, 1994: 83–84).

In an example of reverse migration, Charles Lemeland, who as a boy experienced the liberation of his hometown of La Haye du Puits in Normandy, and became fascinated with the Americans, eventually emigrated to the United States in 1954 where he made a career in teaching (Kaiser, 1994: 87 and 95). Phyllis Mitchell, an American woman who served in the United States Women's Army Corps and was sent first to Britain, then in November 1944 to liberated Paris, ended by marrying a Frenchman and living there. The role of romance in memory extends beyond the scope of this chapter but the two are clearly linked and, in this instance, blended into tourism imaginaries as well. Mitchell remembered taking off from her office work in a building on the Champs-Élysées on occasional afternoons to shop for perfume requested by friends and relatives back in the United States. The little available was generally labelled 'artificial'. She and her friends enjoyed shopping in the little stores along the Rue du Bac and then strolling along the Seine nearby (Kaiser 1994: 149 and 152).

What is noteworthy about the stories collected by Kaiser is the extent to which the American veterans' decisions to immigrate into France were based on marital relations and how little they said about their having seen French sites as tourists either prior to the war or during their engagement there. Romantic attachments could well have developed from a tourist gaze formed while strolling, dining or shopping in Paris. Led to sites that enhanced their affection for Paris and France, the soldiers also increased the likelihood of creating romantic liaisons. These many recollections of sites, romances and youthful exuberance, combined with those of war, trauma and death, are all interlayered in the soldiers' memories. When one considers the pleasures of tourism and romance mixed with the horror of carnage and destruction that marked the war, one might ask if the various kinds of memory expand and develop one another or, instead, whether one kind of memory may conceal another. One is reminded of the ubiquitous warning signs posted at railway crossings in France: '*un train peut en cacher un autre*' (one train may hide another).

Memory in succeeding generations

In interviews and contacts I have come across many migrants from Central Europe, Germany, North America and elsewhere who have held some form of residence permit in France associated with the Second World War. Sometimes the interview is by second generation, or 'post-memory', to use Marianne Hirsch's term referring to 'the generation after', meaning that information comes from the sons or daughters of the immigrant involved (Hirsch, 1997: 22). Although Hirsch used the term 'post-memory' in reference largely to the generations that followed Holocaust survivors, Elizabeth Syrkin suggests that it might also be used to describe the formation of communities among those born of parents who had survived other traumatic events (Syrkin, 2017). Recent research has, indeed, moved in the direction of confirming the possibility of post-memory with changes in DNA in what is clinically better known as transgenerational epigenetic memory (Lim & Brunet, n.d.; American Friends of Tel Aviv University, 2016). These developments in both cultural and physiological studies open the door to the possibility that transgenerational epigenetic memory or post-memory might also include happier recollections, passed down in altered and fragmentary forms to second and third generations from former soldiers who had served in France and had found the experience pleasurable enough to later migrate there.

Many of the military personnel did not survive the war or live long after, so their children and now grandchildren have become the only sources for their stories, with gaps and uncertainties in their own memories, a phenomenon growing as the years go by and the war generation passes away. Increasingly, this means that the memories, perhaps on occasion nostalgic, of their service time in France that drew them to return to live there will be filtered through the lenses of their children and grandchildren with potential gaps and reinterpretations, again illustrating the shifts in memory that occur in succeeding generations.

Dr Marion Pluskota of the Institute for History at Leiden University, for example, noted that her grandfather Adam Pluskota, born in 1907 in Klonowa, now in Poland, was a soldier in the French army during the early days of the Second World War. Taken prisoner with the defeat of France in 1940, he was interned in Switzerland where he met her grandmother. Dr Pluskota believes that he later settled near Mulhouse in Alsace where factory jobs were relatively plentiful after the war. The Red Cross had told her that he was repatriated to France on 6 November 1945. The relatively large community of Polish immigrants from the interwar years in France may have been a motivating factor in her grandparents' decision to relocate there afterward (Pluskota, 2016). Shifting over time and space, the evolving memories of the Polish immigrants and their succeeding generations are additional striking reminders of the heterogeneity of those who settled in France and their constructed memories after the Second World War.

A story recalled in a telephone conversation in 2016 by Ian C. Dengler represents the memory passed on to a second generation of American expatriates, in his case one involved in the 1968 French student revolt. His father had worked in the tourism trade in France and elsewhere in Europe during the interwar years, resuming residence shortly after the war to renew his business there. Dengler told the story of a German military family who had served in France and had subsequently moved back 'near Paris'. He recalled seeing silverware stamped with the swastika, perhaps from the German embassy of the occupation years, in their home in France in the mid-1960s (Dengler, 2016). The memory of swastika-marked silverware in the home of the German family living in France, paralleling Jacques Schweizer's Nuremberg rally mementos, highlights the role also played by war tourism objects in the creation and transmission of memory (Apfelbaum, 2010: 91–92). As Mark D. van Ells writes in his essay about the souvenirs collected by American service personnel during the Second World War,

> In essence, military service – like travel – is an extraordinary experience distinct from 'home' life, and also conferred a kind of special status apart from the rest of society – and thus also worthy of memorialization through souvenirs.
>
> (Van Ells, forthcoming)[1]

Material objects spoke to the soldiers' status as historical actors during a dramatic time in history while at the same time grounding their memories in materiality as if they needed somehow to prove to themselves that their memories were real (Van Ells, forthcoming). Autobiographical memory is, after all, selective and linked to the present and to issues of perceived status.

Who were the migrants back to France?

There was also a working-class relocation to France, for example of Polish workers, including perhaps Dr Pluskota's grandfather, during the interwar years, but it is more difficult to document possible tourism images among them. Most memory does not pass into written history that can be readily traced. Soldiers from the working classes were arguably least likely to relocate as they were often unfamiliar with France and less likely to know the language. In contrast to the relatively less affluent and less well-educated workers who needed to earn money and find a job, many of the veterans who returned to France were more affluent and did so in retirement and from interests in the arts and the culture generally, as in the case of the Smith couple splitting their time between New York and Paris, mentioned by Kaiser. Migrants into France also include those with second homes there, a phenomenon called 'lifestyle migration' characterized by those who, in Nelson Graburn's (2017: 275) words, 'decide to go and live in those desirable places they had previously encountered as tourists or mobile workers, after retirement or even before as a second home'.

Those most likely to marry local women and remain in France would have been officers who had the privilege of spare time to fraternize with the local population. Officers billeted with the upper and middle classes and with more leisure time would have more likely attracted fraternization by the locals than conscripts assigned to the Atlantic Wall, evidenced also in post-war American as well as German war movies. In occupied Paris, officers might dine at Maxim's whereas conscripts would have had to settle for canteens. Gerhard Heller, for example, assigned as Lieutenant in charge of literature for the German *Propagandastaffel* [Propaganda Staff] in occupied Paris, was acquainted with the most prominent literary circles in Paris. In his post-war memoir, he recalled having been invited to remain in Paris in the spring of 1944 by a French acquaintance there. Tempted though he was, Heller decided to return to Germany to be with his family and share with them the coming 'abyss' (Heller, 1981: 201–202; Ory, 2011: 105). Ernst Jünger, whose 1920 memoir *In Stahlgewittern* [*Storm of Steel*] had focused on his experience of trench warfare during the First World War, was also posted as an officer in Paris during the German occupation. Jünger's gastronomic memory was written into history when he wrote of dining on the famous duck at the Tour d'Argent restaurant in 1942, and how he reflected on the sense of power he felt in contrast to the hungry Parisians in the buildings across the street (Jünger, 1965: 147). Strolling with a female friend from l'Étoile along the Rue du Faubourg Saint-Honoré and ending at Place du Tertre and Sacré-Cœur, he added in words echoing Sieburg's that Paris had become for him 'a second spiritual fatherland, the ever deeper image enveloping all that is dear and precious to me in the old civilization' (Jünger, 1965: 161). Having also visited Paris during the interwar years, Jünger, like Heller, was tempted to stay on but ultimately returned to Germany (Jünger, 1965: 111).

There is a gender issue for consideration as well. To be stationed in France, a German, or later Allied, woman needed to be a secretary or translator to be assigned to come to France in the first place, as in the case of Phyllis Mitchell, in the United States Women's Army Corps doing office work on the Champs-Élysées in Paris. Instead, local Frenchwomen might end up working as translators first for the Germans, and then the Allies, in France, contributing to the many marital liaisons in the romantic tourism that brought the soldiers back to France. The issues of cultural, social, generational and gender differences all highlight the challenges remaining to be explored in attempting to uncover the stories of soldiers who as by-products of their service time spent in France during the Second World War, internalized and remembered their experiences of touristic icons such as the streets, restaurants and cafés of Paris or the old churches and oysters of Normandy. Memories of sites, sounds and smells all merged together as the tourist gaze blended into the personal memories of the veterans who returned.

Each veteran had his or her distinct memory of service in France, altered undoubtedly as the years went on and yet again in the memories passed down to children and grandchildren as personal memory became generational memory. One might consider as a collective memory the recollections shared by the Americans who served in the war, and then returned to live and work in Châteauroux. The migrants chose France voluntarily as it represented a new and more fulfilling lifestyle, most likely with a marriage partner as well. Trauma was not the only type of memory that lingered in the minds of the Second World War veterans. The recollections that these veterans carried with them were what Astrid Erll (2011: 11–12) called 'travelling memory', ranging 'from everyday interaction among different social groups to transnational media reception and from trade, migration and diaspora to war and colonialism'. In this context Erll discussed travel and migration, which also opens the door to the less well-studied phenomenon of the migrations of war veterans returning to France (Erll, 2011: 11–12). As with others, Erll addressed this issue largely in terms of trauma such as the Holocaust but the same process may be seen at work in very different sensibilities among the war veterans returning to France.

Conclusion: looking ahead

Looking ahead, it may be anticipated that an increased availability of letters and diaries, together with a heightened interest in tourism history and memory studies among researchers, will enhance our knowledge of the relationships between tourist perspectives regarding France and the desire to relocate permanently there. Remaining open to question are the forms in which the many subjective personal memory accounts of individuals of the kind Confino proposed to study will be transformed into a body of written history that can be passed on to future generations or instead will be lost in favour of the public memory of commemorations so much more readily accessible to researchers. This chapter should be seen as suggesting a direction of research in cultural history that will ultimately produce more evidence than is currently available. It should also be seen as a step towards the integration of the study of the tourist imaginary with that of migration and cultural memory, both personal and collective.

Note

1 My thanks to Mark D. Van Ells for sharing an advance copy of his text with me.

References

American Friends of Tel Aviv University (2016). Biological Mechanism Passes on Long-Term Epigenetic 'Memories': Researchers Discover the on/Off Button for Inheriting Responses to Environmental Changes, *ScienceDaily*, 28 March, viewed 13 August 2017 from www.sciencedaily.com/releases/2016/03/160328133534.htm.

'Americans in France' (n.d.). Embassy of the United States, Paris, viewed 15 February 2017 from https://web.archive.org/web/20150418070413/http://france.usembassy.gov:80/us-france-americans.html.

Amirou, R. (2012) [1995]. *L'imaginaire touristique*. Paris: CNRS Éditions.

Apfelbaum, E. (2010). Halbwachs and the Social Properties of Memory. In: S. Radstone and B. Schwarz, eds., *Memory: Histories, Theories, Debates*. New York: Fordham University Press, pp. 77–108.

Bajc, V. (2006). Introduction to Collective Memory and Tourism: Globalizing Transmission through Localized Experience. *Journeys: The International Journal of Travel and Travel Writing*, 7(2), 1–14.

Börner J. (n.d.). Johannes Börner, 2nd Paratrooper Corps, 3rd Paratrooper Division, 15th Infantry Company, 5th Paratrooper Regiment. *Ceremony in Marigny – Normandy – France [online]*. Available at: www.normandytothebulge.be/JohannesBorner.html [accessed 15 February 2017].

Boym, S. (2001). *The Future of Nostalgia*. New York: Basic Books.

Braasch, B. (2008). Communicating Memory: The Creation and Retrieval of Memory. In B. Braasch, ed., *Major Concepts in Tourism Research: Memory, CTCC Research Papers, Current Research in Critical Tourism Studies* [online]. Available at: www.york.ac.uk/media/sociology/MEMORY%20PAPER.pdf [Accessed 15 August 2017].

Carey, B. (2016). Suzanne Corkin, Who Helped Pinpoint Nature of Memory, Dies at 79. *New York Times* [online], 27 May. Available at: www.nytimes.com/2016/05/28/science/suzanne-corkin-who-helped-pinpoint-nature-of-memory-dies-at-79.html?emc=edit_th_20160528&nl=todaysheadlines&nlid=65406266&_r=0 [accessed 28 May 2016].

Cobb, R. (1969). Experiences of an Anglo-French Historian. In: R. Cobb, *A Second Identity: Essays on France and French History*. London: Oxford University Press, pp. 1–50.

Confino, A. (1997). Collective Memory and Cultural History: Problems of Method. *American Historical Review*, 102(5), 1386–1403.

Confino, A. (2000). Traveling as a Culture of Remembrance: Traces of National Socialism in West Germany, 1945–1960. *History & Memory*, 12(2), 92–121.

Crosley, S. (2016). Exploring the France that Josephine Baker Loved, the American Entertainer had a Rich Relationship with her Adopted Country – and It with Her. *New York Times Travel* [online], 12 July. Available at: www.nytimes.com/2016/07/17/travel/josephine-baker-paris-france.html [accessed 17 July 2016].

Dengler, I. C. (2016). Telephone conversation, 16 December.

Eley, G. (2011). The Past under Erasure? History, Memory, and the Contemporary Author(s). *Journal of Contemporary History*, 46(3), 555–573.

Erll, A. (2011). Travelling Memory. *Parallax*, 17(4), 4–18.

Former American Soldier. (1927). Why I Live in Paris, by a Former American Soldier. *The American Legion Monthly*, 2(5), 20–21 and 85–86.

Friguglietti, J. (2016). Email to the author, 16 July.

Gayle, D. and Reuters. (2014). We Fought Each Other on D-Day in the Town Where We Both Now Live: WWII French and German Soldiers are Best Friends 70 Years after Normandy Landings. *Daily Mail* [online], 12 May. Available at: www.dailymail.co.uk/news/article-2626309/We-fought-D-Day-town-live-WWII-French-German-soldiers-best-friends-70-years-Normandy-landings.html [accessed 25 July 2016].

Golsan, R. J. (2017). *The Vichy Past in France Today: Corruptions of Memory*. Lanham, MD: Lexington Books.

Gordon, B. M. (1980). *Collaborationism in France during the Second World War*. Ithaca, NY: Cornell University Press.

Gordon, B. M. (1996). Ist Gott Französisch? Germans, Tourism, and Occupied France, 1940–1944. *Modern and Contemporary France*, NS4(3), 287–298.

Gordon, B. M. (1998). Warfare and Tourism: Paris in World War II. *Annals of Tourism Research*, 25(3), 616–638.

Gordon, B. M. (2015). Touring the Field: The Infrastructure of Tourism History Scholarship. *Journal of Tourism History*, 7(1–2), 135–156.

Graburn, N. (2017). Epilogue: Home, Travel, Memory and Anthropology. In: S. Marschall, ed., *Tourism and Memories of Home: Migrants, Displaced People, Exiles and Diasporic Communities*. Bristol, UK: Channel View Publications, pp. 269–282.

Haahr, J. (n.d.). The 'Yankee' Division in World War II, the 26th Infantry Division History – W.W.II. [online]. Available at http://yd-info.net/page2/index.html [accessed 15 February 2017].

Heller, G. (1981). *Un Allemand à Paris 1940–1944*. Paris: Seuil.

Hirsch, M. (1997). *Family Frames: Photographs, Narrative and Postmemory*. Cambridge, MA and London: Harvard University Press.

Jünger, E. (1965). *Journal de Guerre et d'Occupation 1939–1948*, translated from the German by Henri Plard. Paris: René Julliard.

Kaiser, H. (1994). *Veterans Recall: Americans in France Remember the War*. Paris: Graphics Group.

Kaplan, A. (2016). Email to the author, 12 July.

Kaplan, H. (1990). Interviewed by Schmidt, G. L., 10 October 1990, © 1998, *ADST, The Association for Diplomatic Studies and Training Foreign Affairs Oral History Project Information Series* [online]. Available at: http://adst.org/OH%20TOCs/Kaplan,%20 Harold.toc.pdf [accessed 4 September 2017].

Kaplan, L. (2013). Writing Moves the Sky. *Public Seminar, New School for Social Research*, 22 November [online]. Available at: www.publicseminar.org/2013/11/ writing-moves-the-sky/#.WKTuZhRh28q [accessed 17 July 2016].

Kennedy, R. (2010). Memory and the Unconscious. In: S. Radstone and B. Schwarz, eds., *Memory: Histories, Theories, Debates*. New York: Fordham University Press, pp. 179–197.

Launet, E. (2012). Grand Angle, 1944–1948, l'autre cohabitation Franco-Allemande [Wide Angle Lens, 1944–1948, the Other Franco-German Cohabitation]. *Libération* [online], 17 May. Available at: http://next.liberation.fr/culture/2012/05/17/1944-1948-l-autre-cohabitation-franco-allemande_819477 [accessed 11 July 2016].

Lemay, K. C. (2014). Gratitude, Trauma, and Repression: D-Day in French Memory. In: M. R. Dolski, S. Edwards and J. Buckley, eds., *D-Day in History and Memory: The Normandy Landings in International Remembrance and Commemorations*. Denton, TX: University of North Texas Press, pp. 159–188.

Leveque, J. (1945). The French Welcome Committee. *For You*, 1, 3–4.

Lim, J. P. and Brunet, A. (n.d.). Bridging the Transgenerational Gap with Epigenetic Memory, *Semantic Scholar* [online]. Available at: https://pdfs.semanticscholar.org/ 1d4b/1b19cffccf2ac427659faa04728b984bcb35.pdf [accessed 13 August 2017]. Subsequently published in *Trends in Genetics* (2013) 29(3), 176–186.

Mansel, P. and Colton, T. (1996). Obituary: Richard Cobb. *The Independent*, 16 January [online]. www.independent.co.uk/news/people/obituary-richard-cobb-1324236.html [accessed 3 March 2017].

Marschall, S. (2017). Introduction. In: S. Marschall, ed., *Tourism and Memories of Home: Migrants, Displaced People, Exiles and Diasporic Communities*. Bristol, UK: Channel View Publications, 1–31.

Martineau, M. ed. (2011). Cours 1ère Histoire: Mutations des sociétés depuis 1850 (3) [First Year History Course: Social Changes since 1850]. *Museclio* [online], 31 August. Available at: http://museclio.over-blog.com/article-cours-1ere-histoire-mutations-des-societes-depuis-1850-3-82965500.html [accessed 16 February 2017].

Michel, J. (2010). *Gouverner les mémoires, Les politiques mémorielles en France*. Paris: Presses Universitaires de France.

Moorehead, C. (2013). Sleeping with the Enemy. *The Economist 1843* [online], September–October. Available at: www.1843magazine.com/content/features/anonymous/sleeping-enemy [accessed 11 July 2016].

Müller (Leutnant). (1940). *F. d. R. d. A., Kommandur 30. Division. Kommandant der Stadt Paris, 16 July*. Archives nationales, Paris, AJ/40/451 [Folder 5, #8], M. B. F. C. 59 L. Vii AG. 102, 1 Juli 1940–30 Juni 1941.

Nishino, R. (2017). 'Vet Tourism': Memories and War-Related Travel. *Call for Papers, H-Travel* [online], 28 April. Available at: https://networks.h-net.org/node/15531/ discussions/177594/cfp-'vet-tourism'-memories-and-war-related-travel [accessed 2 September 2017].

Nkoghe, S. (2008). *La Psychologie du Tourisme.* Paris: L'Harmattan.

Ory, P. (2011). Sept haut lieux parisiens de la Collaboration. In: *Les Collabos / Pluriel Histoire,* no editor indicated. Paris: Athème Fayard/Sophia Publications, pp. 101–107.

O'Sullivan, A. (2016). Email to the author, 14 July.

Paris ***** (1945). Paris ***** this fortnight. *For You,* 3, 6–7.

Perrin, D. and Michaelian, K. (2017). Memory as Mental Time Travel. In: S. Bernecker and K. Michaelian, eds., *Routledge Handbook of Philosophy of Memory.* London and New York: Routledge, pp. 228–240.

Picard, M. (2009). 200 000 enfants de soldats allemands seraient nés en France [200,000 Children of German Soldiers were born in France], *Le Figaro* [online], 30 November. Available at: http://www.lefigaro.fr/actualite-france/2009/11/30/01016-20091130ART-FIG00413-200000-enfants-de-soldats-allemands-seraient-nes-en-france-.php [accessed 20 February 2017].

Pluskota, M. (2016) Emails to the author, 18 and 21 July.

Qu'est-ce qu'un immigré? (2004). *Histoire de l'Immigration en France.* Grenoble: Collectif des luttins. Available at: www.preavis.org/formation-mr/Luttins/brochure_immigration_1-0.a5.pdf [accessed 21 November 2017].

Roberts, M. (2013). *What Soldiers Do: Sex and the American GI in World War II France.* Chicago, IL: University of Chicago Press.

Rose, S. (2010). Memories Are Made of This. In: S. Radstone and B. Schwarz, eds., *Memory: Histories, Theories, Debates.* New York: Fordham University Press, pp. 198–208.

Sebba, A. (2016). *Les Parisiennes: How the French Women of Paris Lived, Loved, and Died under Nazi Occupation.* New York: St. Martin's Press.

Shanton, K. and Goldman, A. (2010). Simulation Theory. *WIRE's Cognitive Science* [online], advanced review. Available at: http://fas-philosophy.rutgers.edu/goldman/ Simulation%20Theory.pdf [accessed 10 August 2017].

Sieburg, F. (1929). *Gott in Frankreich? ein Versuch.* Frankfurt am Main: Frankfurter Societäts-Druckerei.

Stasi, J-C. (2014). *Ennemies et Frères du Jour J à aujurd'hui, au-delà de la guerre.* Bayeux, France: Heimdal.

Sutton, J., Harris, C. B. and Barnier, A. (2010). Memory and Cognition. In: S. Radstone and B. Schwarz, eds., *Memory: Histories, Theories, Debates.* New York: Fordham University Press, pp. 209–226.

Swillen, G. (2016). *De Wieg van WO II: Oorlogskinderen op de as Brussel-Berlijn.* Brussels: ASP, Academic and Scientific Publishers.

Syrkin, E. (2017). Postmemory. *CoHab Diasporic Constructions of Home and Belonging* [online], 28 November. Available at: www.itn-cohab.eu/wiki/postmemory [accessed 1 August 2017].

Tagliabue, J. (2009). After 43 Years, a French Town's Nostalgia for Harry and Joe Lingers. *New York Times* [online], 26 April. Available at: www.nytimes.com/2009/04/27/world/ europe/27france.html [accessed 11 December 2016].

Teaiwa, T. (2016). Reflections on Militourism, US Imperialism, and American Studies. *American Quarterly,* 68(3), 847–853.

Théofilakis, F. (2014). *Les Prisonniers de guerre allemands: France, 1944–1949.* Paris: Fayard.

Thomas, R. M. Jr. (1996). Richard Cobb, 78, an Authority on the French Revolution, Dies. *New York Times* [online], 23 January. Available at: www.nytimes.com/1996/01/23/arts/richard-cobb-78-an-authority-on-the-french-revolution-dies.html [accessed 3 March 2017].

Torrie, J. S. (2011). 'Our Rear Area Probably Lived Too Well': Tourism and the German Occupation of France, 1940–1944. *Journal of Tourism History*, 3(3), 309–330.

Urry, J. (1990). *The Tourist Gaze: Leisure and Travel in Contemporary Societies*. London: Sage.

Van Ells, M. D. (forthcoming). An Amazing Collection: American GIs and Their Souvenirs of World War II. In F. Jacob and K. Pearl, eds., *War and Memorials. The Second World War and Beyond*. Ferdinand Schöningh.

Von Kageneck, A. (2011). *La France Occupée*. Paris: Perrin.

Welzer, H. (2005). *Das kommunikativ Gedächtnis: Eine Theorie der Erinnerung*. Munich: C. H. Beck.

Wood, N. (1999). *Vectors of Memory: Legacies of Trauma in Postwar Europe*. Oxford: Berg.

7 Pajouste Forest, 23 August 1941

Memory, migration and massacre

Aron Mazel

Introduction

On Saturday 23 August 1941, the German Nazis and their Lithuanian collaborators massacred my paternal grandparents, Mashe and Mordechai Mazel, and
significant numbers of my other maternal and paternal relatives. That day witnessed the killing of 7,523 Jews in Pajouste Forest about eight kilometres east of
the city of Panevėžys, in the northern part of Lithuania (Neumärker, 2005: 145;
Figure 7.1). Combined, there were six recorded episodes of killing between 21
July and 23 August 1941 in the vicinity of Panevėžys, which included the Nazis
and Lithuanians killing 8,837 people, 99% of whom were Jews (Levinson, 2006a:
146–148). My father's family came from Panevėžys, while my maternal relatives
were from Ramygala, a small town about 30 kilometres south of Panevėžys. The
Ramygala Jews had been relocated to the Panevėžys ghetto in mid-July 1941 as
the Jews from adjacent 'towns – Raguva, Ramygala, Krekenava etc. were also
forced into the [Panevėžys] ghetto. They were brought here by truck to be exterminated' (Yahadut Lita, 1984, cited in Levinson, 2006b: 107). The Ramygala
Jews were, therefore, also murdered in Pajouste Forest on 23 August 1941. It is
likely, however, that my maternal great-grandmother, Sarah Nochemovitz, died
in Ramygala because the aged and unwell were left in a Beit Midrash (Jewish
study hall), which was set alight and they were burned to death (Rosin, 1996).

Setting out from the United Kingdom, where I live today, I visited Lithuania
with my daughter Nicola in August 2011 to honour the memory of my family
members and particularly my paternal grandparents and to recite kaddish (the
Jewish prayer for the dead) for them on the 70th anniversary of their killing in
Pajouste Forest. Ironically, as we entered the clearing in the Pajouste Forest where
the massacre had occurred, we heard a series of gunshots. The sounds were rico-
cheting off the trees, which prevented us from knowing which direction they were
coming from and how far away the shooting was taking place. We learned that
the shots were being fired by troops of the Lithuanian Armed Forces, who were
unlikely to have been aware of the significance of the day. Nonetheless, it was a
poignant reminder of what Pajouste Forest might have sounded like on that fateful
Saturday 23 August 1941 when over 7,500 Jews were shot and their bodies shoved
into pits. It exacerbated the already heightened emotions we were experiencing

when visiting this place which had witnessed such horrific slaughter, and which – seven decades later – continues to have a significant impact on my family.

Being in the Pajouste Forest, Panevėžys and Ramygala has roused in me a set of emotional responses about the Holocaust and made me reflect on the ongoing impact it has had on my family. The experience must be seen in relation to the insights that were captured in two interviews undertaken with my parents by my oldest brother Monty Mazel in Israel in May 1989 and by myself in South Africa in July 1997. These were not formal investigations with a questionnaire schedule of any kind. Instead, they took the form of informal dialogues between my parents and two of their children desiring to learn more about their past, with a strong emphasis on their lives in Lithuania and, in my father's case, the time he spent out of Lithuania, between 1915 and 1922. Both conversations occurred in a single sitting, around a mealtime, with other members of the family present, i.e. children moving in and out of the room, and food being served and eaten. The 1989 conversation, which lasted 54.21 minutes, occurred in Monty's home on Moshav Sde Ilan in northern Israel. The event was captured with a video camera and the footage has subsequently been digitized and transferred to a DVD. The 1997 interview with my parents took place in their flat in Vredehoek in Cape Town and included Ann Macdonald, my partner of 40 years, and myself. The interview was recorded on two sides of a 60-minute cassette tape, which has also been digitized.

Although both parents took part in the conversation, it would be fair to comment that in both instances the focus was largely on my father's past. This is perhaps due to his more intense and dramatic history, which included, for example, a personal memory of the First World War (WWI) and the Russian Revolution, as well as the above-mentioned murder of his parents. No photographs or other objects were used as prompts in the interviews and, as will be evident later, our parents were not encouraged to reveal or discuss material that they appeared to feel uncomfortable about.

This chapter addresses various facets of Nicola's and my trip to Lithuania in relation to public and private issues of memory and experience. This trip, the 1989 and 1997 interviews and, in fact, the writing of this chapter were not part of a formal research project guided by pre-defined objectives. Rather, the narrative below emerged and evolved as an attempt to embed autobiographical memory and personal experience into a larger context and analyse it in relation to the academic literature on communicative and cultural memory. Similar to Marschall's (2015: 332) personal search for family history, this chapter is in large part based on 'autobiographical reflexivity and auto-ethnography'.

The chapter brings together various strands of knowledge and insights generated through this family journey. They have been framed around three themes: (i) memory and silence when dealing with traumatic events; (ii) the feeling of 'homecoming' that I experienced in Lithuania and especially Panevėžys, although it was my first visit; and (iii) the emotions and thoughts that emerged during Nicola's and my walk down M Valančiaus Gatve, the street where my father, Morris Mazel, was raised for much of his early life. The text below follows its own internal flow, structured along these three themes, without necessarily attempting to comply with the conventions of academic writing in the social sciences.

Memories of movement and migration but silence about death

> The work of postmemory defines the familial inheritance and transmission of cultural trauma.
>
> (Hirsch, 2001: 9)

Using this definition provided by Hirsch (2001), it is evident that I belong to the Holocaust 'postmemory' generation. For her, this

> characterizes the experience of those who . . . have grown up dominated by narratives that preceded their birth, whose own belated stories are displaced by the powerful stories of the previous generation, shaped by monumental traumatic events that resist understanding and integration.
>
> (Hirsch, 2001: 12)

Hirsch (ibid.) believes that postmemory portrays the connection of the new generation to the happenings of the previous generation. In particular, it reflects their inquisitiveness and wish to 'own' the knowledge and memories that their parents hold along with the 'ambivalences' that accompany this.

At a personal level, this has meant absorbing the hurt and trauma that my parents suffered from the death of close family members during the Holocaust. My parents were not – strictly speaking – Holocaust survivors in that they were not in Lithuania at the time, but in South Africa. They were, however, both born in Lithuania and, as will be shown below, had either lived in or visited Lithuania and Eastern Europe within five years of the outbreak of the Second World War (WWII). Consequently, they had deep emotional connections to Lithuania and to their family who remained and were murdered there in 1941. Growing up, I knew that my grandparents had been killed in the Holocaust and that it was on either 23 or 24 August 1941. I did not know until 2006, when I came across the Einsatzgruppen report of the killings in Panevėžys and surrounding areas, that the massacre had taken place on the 23rd (Neumärker, 2005; Figure 7.1). My emotional connection to the Holocaust, which was initially established through my home environment, was intensified by my attendance at Herzlia primary and high schools, Jewish day schools in Cape Town. The shadow of the Holocaust was ever present there through, for example, commemoration days and ceremonies, educational initiatives and visits by survivors of Auschwitz with numbers branded on their forearms.

It should be noted, however, that while the Holocaust was a powerful backdrop to my life from as early as I can remember, the injustices of apartheid and the struggle against it provided a parallel and equally potent narrative in my life. Not only was my father's grocery shop in District 6, on the outskirts of Cape Town's central business district, torn down in 1974 as part of the implementation of the Group Areas Act, but I also participated in the struggle against apartheid in Pietermaritzburg in the 1980s and early 1990s. At the time I worked as an archaeologist at what was then called the Natal Museum. Therefore, Hirsch's definition of the 'postmemory' generation does not completely resonate with

                                                                    11'2

Blatt 3.

                    -Übertrag: 16 152

22.8.41 Aglona   Geisteskranke: 269 Männer,
                                   227 Frauen,
                                    48 Kinder   544

23.8.41 Panevezys   1312 Juden, 4602 Jüdinnen,
                    1609 Judenkinder   7 523

18.bis
22.8.41 Kr.Rasainiai 466 Juden, 440 Jüdinnen,
                    1020 Judenkinder   1 926

25.8.41 Obeliai   112 Juden, 627 Jüdinnen,
                    421 Judenkinder   1 160

25.und
26.8.41 Seduva   230 Juden, 275 Jüdinnen,
                    159 Judenkinder   664

26.8.41 Zarasai   767 Juden, 1113 Jüdinnen, 1 lit.Kom.
                    687 Judenkinder, 1 russ.Kommunistin   2 569

26.8.41 Pasvalys   402 Juden, 738 Jüdinnen,
                    209 Judenkinder   1 349

26.8.41 Kaisiadorys alle Juden,Jüdinnen u.J.-Kinder   1 911

27.8.41 Prienai   "   "   "   "   "   1 078

27.8.41 Dagda und
        Kraslawa   212 Juden, 4 russ.Kr.-Gefangene   216

27.8.41 Joniskis   47 Juden, 165 Jüdinnen,
                    143 Judenkinder   355

28.8.41 Wilkia   76 Juden, 192 Jüdinnen,
                    134 Judenkinder   402

28.8.41 Kedainiai   710 Juden, 767 Jüdinnen,
                    599 Judenkinder   2 076

29.8.41 Rumsiskis u.
        Ziesmariai 20 Juden, 567 Jüdinnen,
                    197 Judenkinder   784

29.8.41 Utena und
        Moletai   582 Juden, 1731 Jüdinnen,
                    1469 Judenkinder   3 782

13.bis
31.8.41 Alytus und
        Umgebung   233 Juden   233

Monat September:

1.9.41 Marismpole   1763 Juden, 1812 Jüdinnen,
                    1404 Judenkinder, 109 Geistes-
                    kranke, 1 deutsche Staatsangehörige,
                    die mit einem Juden verheiratet war,
                    1 Russin   5 090

                                                     _____

                    -Übertrag: 47 814

Figure 7.1 A single page from the 'Report on mass murder of 1 December 1941 by the
            Commander-in-Chief of the SS Security Police and the Security Service in
            Kovno, SS-Standartenführer (SS-Colonel) Dr. Karl Jäger'

Available at: http://biblioteka.teatrnn.pl/dlibra/dlibra/doccontent?id=19733 [accessed 16 November 2017] my experiences as, for me, the 'traumatic events' of both the Holocaust and the unfolding of apartheid were interwoven in my mental landscape. This was reflected in a newspaper piece I had written, shortly before Nicola and I visited Lithuania. It described my role as a witness in the fight against apartheid, using photography, and created a link between the two phenomena:

> Just as my father's pain at losing his parents and community, murdered by Nazis and their collaborators during WW2, had pervaded my life, the parents, family and friends who came to mourn in the Edendale Valley [outside Pietermaritzburg] reached right into my being.
>
> (Mazel, 2010: 10)

Both 'monumental traumatic events' of the past and 'powerful stories' of the present were hence entwined in my lived, communicative memory and postmemory. The trip to Lithuania did, however, compel me to re-think the context in which my postmemory of the Holocaust was framed. This involved reflecting on the pain and trauma my parents suffered from the murder of close family members and their communities. In addition, in the case of my father, it included the upheavals he experienced previously when growing up in Lithuania and Eastern Europe during WWI and in the prelude to and aftermath of the Russian Revolution, during which his education was totally disrupted.

My father did not instinctively talk about growing up in Panevėžys. He could, however, be encouraged to share remembered stories and anecdotes, especially when looking at old photographs of Zionist youth and football teams in his hometown. Furthermore, he was happy to talk in detail, where he could remember, about his formative years, particularly the time between 1915 and 1922, between the ages of seven and 14. This was the time when his family was forced to leave Panevėžys during WWI as the retreating Russians believed that the Jewish occupants of the town were spying on them for the advancing Germans. The Jews were given 24 hours to leave, which many did, including my father's family, i.e. his parents and his brother, who was two years older than him. The absence from Panevėžys involved a few years with his paternal family in Minsk (1915–1917) and then time in the Crimea (1917–1922), after which he returned to Panevėžys at the age of 14.

Then, in 1929, at the age of 21, my father left Panevėžys and migrated to South Africa where he lived for the rest of his life. He moved away because of the lack of work opportunities in Lithuania; as he noted, in 1997, 'I can't walk about here [i.e. Panevėžys] doing nothing so I went to South Africa'. Reflecting on the migration process, he explained, in 1989,

> I went to a chap what used to get you papers to go to South Africa . . . mostly the chaps used to go to South Africa . . . easier to go in . . . we paid £5, English pounds . . . he wrote out a letter that somebody asked me to come, he needs me [which was a fabrication] . . . We showed it in the English Consulate in Kovno [Kaunas]. Then they gave me a visa for that.

He had considered going to Palestine but indicated that the British would not let Jews into Palestine, although after many attempts his brother managed to migrate there in 1935. My mother Lily Mazel (née Wainer) had a different migration story. Her father had migrated alone to South Africa from Ramygala in 1929, when my mother was seven years old. He worked to raise money and only in 1935 was he able to bring my mother, her mother and her three younger brothers to join him. By then she was 13.

In 1937, after an absence of eight years, my father travelled back to Eastern Europe to see his parents, without realizing this would be the very last time (Figure 7.2). He decided against entering Lithuania because, as he explained in 1997, when he was in London, en route to Lithuania, he 'went to the Lithuanian consul there . . . They had a book . . . they say they want me there . . . to go to the army in Lithuania; they were looking for me to go in the army'. Instead, he travelled to Latvia and called his parents to join him. He covered the costs of his parents' travel and accommodation and they spent a fortnight together in Dvinsk, close to the border of Lithuania.

In order to get to Latvia and then back to London, my father travelled through Germany by train. In 1989, when asked, 'what was the feeling going through

Figure 7.2 The author's father and grandparents in Dvinsk, in 1937. From left: Mashe Mazel, Morris Mazel and Mordechai Mazel

Photographer unknown

Germany?', he responded, 'I was sitting in third class . . . and the Germans were sitting and I was watching them and . . . they were talking German and they say what a wonderful man Hitler is . . . what a big man'. In 1997, he was asked whether he had any sense of what was coming in Europe during his trips through Germany. He commented that as a 'foreigner on the trains you didn't feel it yet . . . and then they started their nonsense'. My father's relationship to the event of 23 August 1941 was extremely distressing, and as children, we just knew not to go there. Significantly, in both interviews, we changed the subject after asking what it was like while travelling through Germany in 1937. Despite knowing what had happened to my father's parents, we could not ask questions about this in the independently conducted interviews of 1989 by my brother, and in 1997 by myself.

The silence about the family killed in the Holocaust was not absolute, however, as I can recall him and my mother mentioning that some of the Lithuanian youth that he had played soccer against in Panevėžys had participated in the harassment and killing of Jews. Moreover, I recall my mother speaking emotionally, and justifiably so, about the death of her Uncle Gerson. He had been a tailor and was shot by the Germans in Lithuania in 1941 (I do not know the specific place), and left to die out on the street. No one could tend to him and try to save his life for fear of being shot themselves. Regretfully, I never asked my mother how she knew these details and neither were they raised in the interviews of 1989 and 1997. Even though my parents had shared these particular memories, the overwhelming experience regarding the Holocaust was that of silence and avoidance.

The silence described above is by no means unusual. Robins (2016), whose father migrated from Germany to South Africa in 1936, described a similar pattern. In 1989, Robins (2016: 2) interviewed his father about his family history and reflected that

the interview, while enlightening, had one gaping hole. While I asked my father questions about almost every aspect of his life in Poland and Germany, none of my questions addressed what happened to Edith and the rest of his family . . . But there seemed to be an agreement that the rest of his family were not to be spoken about.

This 'black hole of silence' has been addressed by many authors (for example, Hass, 1990, 1996), but a particularly poignant representation of it was expressed by Fresco (1984: 421), who noted that the 'silence formed like a heavy pall that weighed down on everyone. Parents explained nothing, children asked nothing'. This phenomenon was certainly evident in the two interviews conducted with my parents.

The story does not, however, end with the 'black hole of silence'. There was a twist. In 2005, a cousin, my mother's younger brother's daughter, told me a puzzling story. She and her husband had stayed with my parents in Cape Town, in the early 1990s, and my father confided in the husband a story he said he had never told his children. He said he was there, in the Pajouste Forest, and watched the massacre from behind the trees when his parents were killed and could do nothing about it. Not knowing my father's life story, they believed it to be true. It was not true. In 1941, my father was in Cape Town running his small grocery shop in District 6, which as mentioned earlier he did until it was razed to the ground in 1974. My father's 'false memory' is not an uncommon phenomenon. Bublitz and Dresler (2015: 1284) described how the 'process of selective consolidation of a fraction of our experience and the repeated reconsolidation of these memory traces suggest that our memories may be less veridical than we expect'. This interesting perspective is supported by many years of false memory research in which the substance of memories could be changed or fresh memories embedded through several and rather simple ways, such as narrating untrue stories about the past. Unsurprisingly, Brainerd, Stein, Silveira, Rohenkohl and Reyna (2008: 919) noted that '[r]emembering negative events can stimulate high levels of false memory, relative to remembering neutral events', which would have been the case when I believe my father's sense of guilt combined with his thoughts, later in his life, about the Holocaust and the murder of his parents.

My parents never went back to Lithuania and never expressed a desire to do so. In fact, I recall them indicating, in no uncertain terms, that this is something they would not want to do. Moreover, I do not believe that my father properly mourned the loss of his parents despite the fact that he could be a very emotional person in relation to family matters. I suggest that the reasons for this were, in part, reflected in the comments that Hass made in a radio interview with Fredinburg (1997/2015) about the experience of Holocaust survivors in the United States of America. He commented:

After they migrated . . . they were so focused on making it . . . so focused on developing a new family – raising a new family of their own, giving some rebirth to the Jewish people, that they didn't allow themselves the luxury of mourning.

This strongly resonates with a view expressed by my mother when I questioned her, in 2005, about why she and my father had seven children when their sole income derived from a small grocery shop in District 6. Her unequivocal response was that my father had a strong drive to repopulate the Jewish people following the Holocaust. Moreover, in terms of the lack of mourning, Hass (in Fredinburg, 1997/2015: n.d.) noted that there is 'one other more subtle reason' for this:

One very interesting aspect about holocaust survivors that differentiates them from other trauma victims; most trauma victims need to resolve the trauma, need to forget about it and move on. But, holocaust survivors, because they are so committed to remembering the holocaust, can never fully grieve, can never fully mourn, can never fully resolve that trauma.

I do not believe that my father resolved the trauma of the murder of his parents. He took this to the grave along with feelings of guilt that he survived and they did not, and along with the false memory he created of watching them being murdered and feeling utterly helpless. It is not known what transpired between him and his parents when they met for the last time, in Dvinsk in 1937. Did he ask them to return with him to South Africa or was this matter not discussed at all? Either way, I believe the fact that they did not join him in South Africa and that he did not prevent their deaths probably contributed to him leading the rest of his life with feelings of guilt. Hass (1996: 24) has commented that in many ways the guilt experienced by Holocaust survivors represents the 'embodiment of anger directed toward the self'. I suggest that this applied to my father.

The uneasy feeling of being at 'home'

> Did I dare say it? In some ways I felt very much at home in this land of bears and forebears.
>
> (Cassedy, 2012: 70–71)

As I had foreseen, visiting Lithuania was accompanied by substantial pain and anger, given the devastation the Holocaust had wrought on both my maternal and paternal families and the long-lasting emotional suffering it has caused my family. However, the visit also unexpectedly generated a sense of homecoming inside me, especially in Panevėžys. Despite being cognizant of the academic literature describing this sensation, I did not foresee that it would affect me and I was unprepared for this response. As I have stated previously (Mazel, 2014: 152):

> this unexpected emotion crystallised in Panevėžys when Gennady Kaufman, Chairman of the Jewish community, asked me to give a brief presentation, on my experience of visiting the town and the Pajouste Forest and on my experience in the anti-apartheid struggle in South Africa, at a workshop on tolerance on 24 August 2011 (i.e. the day after we had visited Pajouste Forest).

This spur-of-the-moment invitation encouraged me to consider my relationship with Lithuania and especially Panevėžys. It became clear that I had a strong sense of 'return' to this 'foreign' town, which is about 10,000 kilometres from Cape Town in South Africa, where I was raised.

I told the gathering in Panevėžys that even though I grew up in Cape Town and have resided in the United Kingdom since 2002, Panevėžys has been ever present in my life. Most of my father's friends, who we saw mostly at family occasions such as batmitzvahs and barmitzvahs, were from Panevėžys. They were known as 'landslites', the Yiddish word for someone who is from the same place. Furthermore, as noted earlier, my father could be encouraged with photos to recall memories of his youth and his experiences of WWI and the Russian Revolution. Later in his life, he attended the Ponevez, one of the Yiddish spellings of Panevėžys, synagogue in Cape Town, where I understand he was the last living connection to the town. It has been remarked by Ann Macdonald, my partner, that I was 'marinated' in a Jewish Panevėžys reality and that it 'is central to my identity and how I belong and function in the world' (Mazel, 2014: 153).

This is not something my daughter Nicola feels to the same degree and is reflected in our different responses to being in Lithuania. Significantly, Nicola did not share the feeling of homecoming, despite being acutely aware of our family's connections to these places. In a recent conversation with her, she explained to me:

> The Lithuania I saw wasn't the one I imagined that my grandparents had grown up in. My strong impression of it was its emptiness and that it was flatter than I expected it to be. My reaction to the landscape was very much conditioned by my grandparents because within the emptiness of the landscape there was 'missingness'. Like, I was aware of the disappearance of my great-grandparents and their whole communities, it was culturally empty. So, for example, where I would have expected content there was a lot of blandness. In Panevėžys, I spent time sketching old synagogues that were now offices and a pub. While doing this, two girls, possibly 12 or 13 years of age, asked me what I was doing and I told them I was there because 70 years ago, there had been a massacre in the town and I'd come to mark the occasion. They were utterly unaware that such a thing had happened and did not appear to engage with this, or ask any further questions. Another example of the 'missingness' is that at the National Museum of Lithuania there was no reference to Jewish history – it was like they had been cut out. I could see the holes and feel the emptiness, but other people who did not even know to look would never have known that they had been there in the first instance. I felt the same emptiness walking down my grandfather's street and visiting my grandmother's village.

Nicola's and my experience of visiting Lithuania both reflected pain and hurt and the damaging impact it had on our family (Figure 7.3). For me, it was the feeling of 'homecoming' in which I 'populated' the places we visited, particularly Panevėžys and Ramygala, with the people that my parents had spoken about and who I had seen in old photographs from the 1920s and 1930s. Nicola, meanwhile, who was present during the interview with my parents in 1997 but was only 13 at the time, had a memory of my father's and his family's journey through the Ukraine to the Crimea, and could recall seeing old family photographs, but significantly not those taken in Lithuania in the 1920s and 1930s. She did not, therefore, have the same visual cues as I had with which to frame her response to our visit to Lithuania.

Tolia-Kelly (2004: 314) has defined the concept of re-memory as 'an alternative social narrative to memory as it is a form of memory that is not an individual linear, biographical narrative'. Rather, it is a 'conceptualization of encounters with memories', inspired through everyday smells, noises, textures and material objects. Furthermore, Tolia-Kelly (2004: 322), referring to Morrison (1990), notes that the significance of re-memory is as 'an embodied narration' of what has gone before. With this in mind, it is evident that the powerful and evocative

Figure 7.3 The author and his daughter, Nicola, at the Pajouste Forest murder site on
        23 August 2011

Photographer: Larry Mehl

're-memories' I absorbed through the stories told by my parents and occasionally
their 'landslites' about their lives in Panevėžys and Ramygala; family photographs (of which there were only a few); the odd piece of material culture; and
the day-to-day living, in what my partner has defined as a 'Jewish Panevėžys
reality', formed part of the 'emotional luggage' I had carried with me to Lithuania,
especially Panevėžys and the Pajouste Forest. My father's stories of his travels
through Germany in 1937 also impacted powerfully on me, as did those dealing
with his family fleeing Panevėžys in 1915, during WWI, and returning in 1922.
Although I was conscious of the impact of these stories on my identity when I
embarked on the journey to Lithuania, I did not anticipate how strongly it would
define my response to the sense of 'homecoming' I experienced.

According to Čiubrinskas (2006, cited in Dargufiytë, 2010: 49–50), increasing numbers of Jews, probably like myself, have been travelling to Eastern Europe 'to honour their ancestors, out of nostalgic reasons or even to be of use to one's own country'. This has not happened in isolation. Sandri (2013) notes that Jewish heritage and culture has become progressively 'popular' around Europe. According to Sandri (2013), '[n]ew Jewish museums, exhibitions, festivals, workshops of all types, conference and academic study programs now abound'. Following Gruber (2002), the author adds a caveat, saying, 'what passes for Jewish culture, or what is perceived or defined as Jewish culture', suggesting that there has been a certain amount of creativity or embellishment in the framing of what constitutes past Jewish culture in Europe. The key point, however, is that there are numerous and growing opportunities to participate in tours to visit Jewish heritage sites in Europe. This is in part reflected in Gruber's response to the question from Hoare (2017) about what she would recommend to the 'eager traveller' about the 'best of Jewish heritage in Europe'. To this she replied: 'There is so much to see, that that's a difficult question!' and then recommended visiting restored synagogues and associated Jewish buildings in the Czech Republic among a number of other suggestions.

These visits are, however, not without complications, as Dargufiytë (2010: 50) explained: 'Inevitably, these East European "homelands" are loaded with traumatic memory for the majority of the Diaspora people, and this is always the case for the descendants of East European Jews'. In an associated comment, Aviv and Shneer (2005: 8) noted that:

> In a post-Holocaust world, many American Jews [I believe this applies more broadly] came to see Eastern Europe no longer as the real place from which to draw roots but one that they want to bear witness to. It is a land of Jewish ghosts and lost cultures.

Drawing on these views, Dargufiytë (2010: 52) maintains that 'precisely this "nostalgic sacredness" is becoming the main motive which draws Jewish roots tourists to their cultural and familial lands'.

Concerning other situations, commentators provide various reasons as to why people travel to the land of their birth or that of their ancestors. Basu (2004) proposed three primary reasons for Scotland: homecoming, pilgrimage and the quest for, for example, ancestral homes and gravestones. Bohlin (2011: 290) commented that especially in cases of 'ancestral' or 'roots' return to a physical place where their ancestors once lived, the experience of a 'shared past lies at the heart of accounts of homecoming, whether personal narratives, public discourses or state policy'.

According to Timothy and Teye (2004), African-American trips to West Africa are a form of appreciation of the cultural and family legacy of one's community, while Austin (1999) noted that Africans in the diaspora on trips to Africa view themselves as 'coming home'. The feeling of 'homecoming' and the reconnection with the land of their forefathers represent the spirit of their trip. The analogy is sometimes drawn between these trips to Africa and those undertaken by Jews to Eastern Europe. According to Dargufiytė (2010), the Holocaust has left its imprint on the 'very tropes' of Jewish heritage and identity in the same way as Ebron (1999) claimed that such phenomena have impacted on Africans who were removed from their continent as slaves to many other parts of the globe. These understandings are strongly linked to the concept of place identity: 'The construction of identity for or by people(s) through reference to place and/or the construction of identity for places through reference to their morphology, histories, cultures and inhabitants' (Whitehead, Eckersley & Mason, 2012: 14).

When I embarked on my journey to Lithuania in 2011, I was unaware of the growth in the Jewish heritage and roots tourism referred to above. I did not see my trip as a touristic venture. I did not aim to look for my roots or explore my heritage. I had no positive feelings or sense of longing towards Lithuania. I did not go there to visit cemeteries or death sites in general (i.e. thanatourism). Instead, I sought to commemorate the 70th anniversary of a traumatic event in my family, which has left a legacy that remains a burden for my family. Once there, however, I desired to be in the spaces where my father and mother had lived and grown up and where my grandparents had perished and to take in their meaning in a way that utterly surprised me, something that I could call 'homecoming'. I regarded myself as more akin to Marschall's (2015) travellers who may not consider themselves as 'tourists', or be defined in this way by tourism authorities: 'The destinations of their journeys may not be declared heritage sites or dark tourism attractions, but rather they are idiosyncratic places of subjective meaning, associated with memories of trauma' (Marschall, 2015: 332).

There are signs to the Pajouste Forest massacre site (Figure 7.4) and the site is demarcated by short concrete uprights and wooden poles; within the massacre site the areas of the pits where the bodies of the victims lie buried are demarcated with ground-level concrete blocks, and there are also memorial stones (Figures 7.3 and 7.5). Nevertheless, I do not believe that it is 'recognized, branded and marketed by tourism authorities' and it lacks 'all the hallmarks of "heritagization", restoration and touristic commodification' (Marschall, 2015: 336). There is an abundance of such sites scattered all over Lithuania and its adjoining countries, and it is unlikely that people visit them on a regular basis. At least, that was the impression I obtained during our visit, especially as Nicola and I appeared to be the only people who had travelled to Panevėžys and the Pajouste Forest to commemorate the 70th anniversary of the massacre. Gennady Kaufman, who took us to the site, did not mention any other visitors to the Panevėžys Jewish community for that purpose and there were no other people at the massacre spot during our visit.

Lastly, in the framework of Jewish visits to Eastern Europe, Dargufiytė (2010: 52) has alluded to the concept of 'nostalgic sacredness'; this only partly resonates with my feelings: 'sacredness', yes, but not 'nostalgic'. There was nothing 'nostalgic' about a trip that was imbued with sadness and pain, along with the unanticipated emotion of 'homecoming' and a sense of belonging. All these emotions were intense in the walk we did down the street my father grew up on, to which we turn next.

Figure 7.4 Road sign to the Pajouste Forest massacre site

Photographer: Aron Mazel

Walking M Valančiaus Gatve: troubling and unknown memories

> At subsequent stages of ghettoization, deportations, and eventually extermi-
> nation, Jewish victims were gradually deprived of everything.
>
> (Stola, 2007: 241)

In 1997, one of my brothers, Herzel Mazel, travelled to Panevėžys with his son;
the first Mazels to return to the town since August 1941. Before the trip, my father
in Cape Town conveyed to him, via a fax sent by our brother, Abraham Mazel,
that his

> grandfather [i.e. Abram Abelski] owned a few houses on Vishkopevelensis
> Gatwe where he [i.e. my father] lived with his family until he left for SA.
> The grandfather had his own shul [i.e. synagogue] on that street – apparently

a second-hand car dealership on that spot now. If there is a 16th of February Street (Main Road of Ponevez then). Your grandmother had her grocery shop there.

Moreover, in my 1997 interview of my parents, my father commented: 'Yes, there were a lot of houses. My grandfather had a whole suite of houses'. With this knowledge in mind and given my family's strong connection to M Valančiaus Gatve, Nicola and I walked the length of the street, some 360 metres between Respublikos Gatve and Naujamiesčio Gatve, on the morning of the 70th anniversary of the massacre.

It seemed to us that many of the homes pre-dated 1941, while the above-mentioned synagogue was still standing. Concerning the ownership of the houses, an interesting insight has been provided by Yoffee (1998), who referred to it as 'Ruta's Rule' after his guide from Vilnius University. Jewish houses usually had street-facing main entrances, normally with the same number of windows on either side in order to enable the public to visit the shop usually situated within the house. In contrast, Christian houses usually had side entrances to enable entry to vegetable gardens and/or animal pens and barns. If accurate, this 'rule' implies that there are houses currently on M Valančiaus Gatve that retain the architectural characteristics of their Jewish holders. As we made our way down the street, we considered whether Abram Abelski, my great-grandfather, had owned one or more of the houses we were passing. We even wondered about whether

Figure 7.5 Pajouste Forest massacre site

Photographer: Aron Mazel

my father grew up in one of the dwellings and whether there might even still be my family's objects in one or more of them. These were disconcerting thoughts.

As we proceeded down the street, people appeared from some of the houses and observed us. I believe they were aware that we were not there as conventional visitors to this part of town. This is not a tourist area and we were walking slowly and stopping from time to time, pointing at places and photographing them, and clearly conversing about the houses. Furthermore, it is conceivable that they would have recognized us as being of Jewish origin. We discussed what was occurring and made a deliberate decision not to avert our eyes, but looked back. Consequently, this resulted in an unanticipated passive-aggressive 'standoff' with some of the residents of M Valančiaus Gatve.

I believe that this experience was underpinned by the question of memory. Nicola's and my memories revolved around the questions of ownership, theft and restitution informed in part by my father's fax. These issues were uppermost in our thoughts during this walk. Contextualizing the theft of Jewish properties, Dean (2007: 28) observed that there could be no uncertainty about the fact that the seizure of Jewish property was 'primarily a state-directed process linked closely to the development of the Holocaust'. Furthermore, he proposed that the widespread 'participation' of the local population as beneficiaries of this theft 'served to spread the complicity' with and 'acceptance' of German Nazi actions against the Jewish population beyond a small circle of offenders. 'In this way the Nazis and their collaborators were able to mobilize society in support of Nazi racial policies to a greater extent than the spread of racial antisemitism alone would have permitted' (Dean, 2007: 28). In Panevėžys, the appropriation of Jewish properties and belongings was likely to have taken place between early July 1941, when the Jews were instructed to relocate to the ghetto, and 23 August 1941, when the Jewish population was finally exterminated.

It is possible that some, many or perhaps even all of the people we encountered on M Valančiaus Gatve are descendants of beneficiaries of stolen Jewish property. What of their memories, especially when considering that restitution appears to be a problematic issue for Lithuania? Especially because, as Block (2009: 73), notes, 'officials are never eager to return property to Jewish claimants, often due to concerns about negative reactions from local residents'. According to Jansen (2011: 88), after the ethnic cleansing in post-war Croatian villages, the ways of dealing with what had occurred 'relied on strategies of vagueness and selective amnesia'. Could it be that these sentiments also characterize the Lithuanian occupants of previously Jewish houses on M Valančiaus Gatve and elsewhere in Panevėžys and Lithuania? Support for this possibility derives from observations made in a recent book by Lithuanian author Ruta Vanagaite (2016). In her book entitled *MUSISKIAI: knyga, sukretusi Lietuva! (Our People: Journey with an Enemy!)*, Vanagaite notes that although there have been increasing attempts to confront the memory of the Holocaust past in Lithuania during the last decade (Vitureau, 2013), it remains inadequate to date. Vanagaite's book is only available in Lithuanian at this point. In an interview with Gerstenfeld (2016), however, she explained how her interest in the history of the Holocaust in Lithuania derived from her participation in the 'Being a Jew' educational project for young Lithuanians who were unaware of the killings, in much the same way that the young girls who Nicola engaged with in Panevėžys, in 2011, appeared to be unaware of the massacre that had taken place in their town 70 years previously.

Vanagaite noted that many of these young Lithuanians encountered anti-Semitic attacks from 'friends or relatives after they shared their experiences from the project' (Gerstenfeld, 2016). The project led her to appreciate the current depth of anti-Semitism in Lithuania even though there are very few Jews left in the country. Through her research into the Lithuanian Holocaust, together with Efraim Zuroff of the Simon Wiesenthal Center, she discovered that even 'some' of her own relatives had 'played a role' in the Holocaust. She asserts that it is probable that her family was not 'actively involved' in 'violence' but that they supported the Nazis in identifying Jews and possibly even 'isolating' them prior to their murder. Moreover, she believes that the 'official' Lithuanian view is that gangs of 'monsters' killed the Jews. Linked to this, she has discovered that the graves of the victims are often neglected and memories of them have largely been removed from 'public sight'. Lastly, she has noted that older people appear to have found her publication 'quite offensive' as by implication it denies them and their parents from being acknowledged as the 'victims of the war'.

Vanagaite's insights regarding older people resonate with a conversation I had with a Lithuanian educator, whose name I failed to record, following the work-shop on tolerance on 24 August 2011. He told me that he had tried to enlist older members of the Panevėžys community to interact with his students about WWII and the Holocaust and noted that they 'are not able to talk about what happened'. Similarly, Vanagaite commented to Gerstenfeld (2016) that it is 'incredibly pain-ful for Lithuanians to face their country's past'. I would suggest that this also applies to the residents of M Valančiaus Gatve, my father's street, who observed Nicola and myself making our way slowly along the road on 23 August 2011.

Conclusion

This chapter is an analysis of a trip I made to Lithuania in August 2011 with my daughter Nicola to commemorate the memory of relatives who were murdered by the Nazis and their Lithuanian collaborators on 23 August 1941. It explores our combined experience of the visit as a platform for examining the historical and family context regarding the migration of my parents from Lithuania to South Africa. Moreover, it looks at issues of memory and the feelings associated with second- (myself) and third-generation (Nicola) descendants visiting the land of our parents and grandparents together with the memories of my parents, and primarily my father, through the interviews conducted in 1989 and 1997. Unsurprisingly, what emerges when comparing the perspectives are intergenerational differences regarding our relationships to Lithuania.

As mentioned earlier, my parents never returned to Lithuania and, in fact, showed no desire to re-visit the land of their birth. Reflecting on this, I suspect that it would have been unbearable for them given the emotions it would have unleashed, particularly considering that the people they had known as children and, in my father's situation, as a young adult had been totally obliterated in the most horrific way. In contrast, I had a desire to visit Lithuania to commemorate the death of my grandparents. During the trip, I filled the landscape, particularly in Panevėžys and Ramygala, with my relatives and Jewish people in general. These were people associated with the memories that were absorbed in the home primarily through storytelling, anecdotal memories and photographic references, part of what Tolia-Kelly (2004) has referred to as 're-memory'. In contrast, for Nicola there was emptiness to the landscape where people were missing.

These disparate intergenerational views require us to consider whether the children and grandchildren of migrants necessarily have a 'collective memory' of their homeland, especially when that memory involves a series of traumatic events. There may be some sense of collectivity to the memories within families but it is likely that there will also be intergenerational differences as revealed by Nicola and myself. It is also possible, however, that the memories associated within the same generation may vary according to the position of the children in the family. For example, it is possible that first-born children have a different perspective as they may have absorbed the most intense feelings of grief and devastation so soon after the event, before family life consumed parental energy, and have different responsibilities and sets of obligations within the family. This issue has not been explored here but would certainly be worth investigating to develop a more nuanced understanding of the impact on family memories with regard to migration, trauma and memory itself.

The massacres of Jews in Lithuania, of which the Pajouste Forest event formed part, completely decimated the country's Jewish community. Unsurprisingly, the memory of these events still bears heavily on Lithuanian society, particularly since its independence from Soviet rule in 1992 (Sužiedėlis, 2001). As Vanagaite has noted, although there have been increasing efforts in Lithuania to address the memory of the Holocaust past during the last decade (Vitureau, 2013), these remain inadequate. I believe this insufficient response was reflected in the 'interaction' that Nicola and I had during our walk down M Valančiaus Gatve. While this was a highly localized experience, it has broader consequences as reflected by Sužiedėlis (2001: n.p.), who commented that the

> only way for Lithuanians to lighten the load of the difficult history of 1941 is to embrace it . . . [However] artfully presented, the strategies of denial and evasion, the finger-pointing and righteous indignation directed at the Other, serve only to further weigh society down.

It might not be possible for older Lithuanians to come to terms with what happened, but succeeding generations of Lithuanians would do well to heed Sužiedėlis's (2001: n.p.) comment that as 'a general proposition, attempts to evade, deny, minimize or misrepresent historical offenses are unsuccessful in the long run'.

Acknowledgement

I thank Ann Macdonald for commenting on this chapter and her editorial assistance.

References

Austin, N. K. (1999). Tourism and the Transatlantic Slave Trade: Some Issues and Reflections. In: P. U. C. Dieke, ed., *The Political Economy of Tourism Development in Africa*. New York: Cognizant, pp. 208–216.

Aviv, C. & Shneer, D. (2005). *New Jews: The End of the Jewish Diaspora*. New York: New York University Press.

Basu, P. (2004). Route Metaphors of 'Roots-Tourism' in the Scottish Highland Diaspora. In: S. Coleman & J. Eade, eds., *Reframing Pilgrimage: Cultures in Motion*. London: Routledge, pp. 150–174.

Block, H. (2009). The Restitution of Holocaust-Era Jewish Communal Property: An Unfinished Item on the Jewish Diplomatic Agenda. *Israel Journal of Foreign Affairs*, 3(1), 71–79.

Bohlin, A. (2011). Idioms of Return: Homecoming and Heritage in the Rebuilding of Protea Village, Cape Town. *African Studies*, 70(2), 284–301.

Brainerd, C. J., Stein, L. M., Silveira, R. A., Rohenkohl, G. & Reyna, V. F. (2008). How Does Negative Emotion Cause False Memories? *Psychological Science*, 19(9), 919–925.

Bublitz, C. & Dresler, M. (2015). A Duty to Remember, a Right to Forget? Memory Manipulations and the Law. In: J. Clausen & N. Levy, eds., *Handbook of Neuroethics*. Dordrecht: Springer, pp. 1279–1307.

Cassedy, E. (2012). *We Are Here: Memories of the Lithuanian Holocaust*. Lincoln, NE: University of Nebraska Press.

Čiubrinskas, V. (2006). 'To Be of Use for Your Own Country': Missionary Identity of the Lithuanian Transmigrants. *Social Sciences*, 53(3), 25–32.

Dargufiytė, Z. (2010). Jewish Roots Tourism and the (Re)Creation of Litvak Identity. *LCC Liberal Arts Studies, Volume III: Responses to Cultural Homogeny: Engagement, Resistance, or Passivity*, 47–53.

Dean, M. (2007). The Seizure of Jewish Property in Europe: Comparative Aspects of Nazi Methods and Local Responses. In: M. Dean, C. Goschler & P. Ther, eds., *Robbery and Restitution: The Conflict over Jewish Property in Europe*. New York: Berghahn Books, pp. 21–32.

Ebron, P. A. (1999). Tourists as Pilgrims: Commercial Fashioning of Transatlantic Politics. *American Ethnologist*, 26, 910–932.

Fredinburg, R. (1997/2015). Interviews Dr. Aaron Hass about His Books: *The Aftermath of Living with the Holocaust* and *In the Shadow of the Holocaust*. Posted online on 20 April 2015 by Christian Zionist. Available at: https://exposingmodernmugwumps.com/2015/04/20/the-holocaust-we-must-remember-dr-aaron-hass-the-aftermath-of-living-with-the-holocaust-and-in-the-shadow-of-the-holocaust [accessed 18 May 2017].

Fresco, N. (1984). Remembering the Unknown. *International Review of Psycho-Analysis*, 11(4), 417–427.

Gerstenfeld, M. (2016). Exclusive Interview: 'Journey with an Enemy' on the Lithuanian Shoah. *Israel National News*. Available at: www.israelnationalnews.com/Articles/Article.aspx/18437 [accessed 20 May 2016].

Gruber, R. E. (2002). *Virtually Jewish: Reinventing Jewish Culture in Europe.* Berkeley, CA: University of California Press.

Hass, A. (1990). *In the Shadow of the Holocaust: The Second Generation.* Cambridge: Cambridge University Press.

Hass, A. (1996). *The Aftermath: Living with the Holocaust.* Cambridge: Cambridge University Press.

Hirsch, M. (2001). Surviving Images: Holocaust Photographs and the Work of Post-memory. *The Yale Journal of Criticism*, 14(1), 5–37.

Hoare, L. (2017). *Ruth Ellen Gruber Reflects on Five Years of Jewish Heritage Europe.* Available at: http://ejewishphilanthropy.com/ruth-ellen-gruber-celebrates-five-years-of-jewish-heritage-europe [accessed 18 May 2017].

Jansen, S. (2011). The Violence of Memories: Local Narratives of the Past after Ethnic Cleansing in Croatia. *Rethinking History*, 6(1), 77–93.

Levinson, J. (2006a). The Shoah and the Theory of the Two Genocides. In: J. Levinson, ed., *The Shoah (Holocaust) in Lithuania.* Vilnius: The Vilna Gaon Jewish State Museum, pp. 322–353.

Levinson, J. (ed.). (2006b). *The Shoah (Holocaust) in Lithuania.* Vilnius: The Vilna Gaon Jewish State Museum.

Marschall, S. (2015). Touring Memories of the Erased City: Memory, Tourism and Notions of 'Home'. *Tourism Geographies*, 17(3), 332–349.

Mazel, A. D. (2010). Capturing Conflict on Film. *Natal Witness*, 20 March, p. 10.

Mazel, A. D. (2014). Troubled 'Homecoming': Journey to a Foreign yet Familiar Land. In: I. Convery, G. Corsane & P. Davis, eds., *Displaced Heritage: Dealing with Disaster and Suffering.* Woodbridge: The Boydell Press, pp. 151–161.

Mazel, M. (1989). Personal Communication (Interview between Monty Mazel and his Parents, Morris and Lily Mazel), Sde Ilan (Israel).

Mazel, M. (1997). Personal Communication (Interview between Aron Mazel and his parents, Morris and Lily Mazel), Cape Town (South Africa).

Morrison, T. (1990). The Site of Memory. In: R. Ferguson, M. Gever, T. Minh-ha & C. West, eds., *Out There: Marginalisation and Contemporary Cultures.* New York: The New Museum of Contemporary Art and MIT Press, pp. 299–324.

Neumärker, U. (2005). Strategies of Terror. In: Anon., ed., *Materials on the Memorial to the Murdered Jews of Europe.* Berlin: Nicolaishe Verlagbuchhandlung GmbH, pp. 138–155.

Robins, S. (2016). *Letter of Stone: From Nazi Germany to South Africa.* Cape Town: Penguin Books.

Rosin, J. (1996). Ramygala. In: D. Levin, ed., *Encyclopedia of Jewish Communities in Lithuania.* Yad Vashem, Jerusalem. Available at: www.jewishgen.org/yizkor/pinkas_lita/lit_00640.html [accessed 16 November 2013].

Sandri, O. (2013). City Heritage Tourism without Heirs: A Comparative Study of Jewish-Themed Tourism in Krakow and Vilnius. *European Journal of Geography* [online]. Available at: https://cybergeo.revues.org/25934 [accessed 16 May 2017].

Stola, D. (2007). The Polish Debate on the Holocaust and the Restitution of Property. In: M. Dean, C. Goschler & P. Ther, eds., *Robbery and Restitution: The Conflict over Jewish Property in Europe.* New York: Berghahn Books, pp. 240–258.

Sužiedėlis, S. (2001). The Burden of 1941. *Lituanus: Lithuanian Quarterly Journal of Arts and Sciences*, 47(4) [online]. Available at: www.lituanus.org/2001/01_4_04.htm [accessed 27 October 2013].

Timothy, D. J. & Teye, V. B. (2004). American Children of the African Diaspora: Journeys to the Motherland. In: T. Coles & T. Dallen, eds., *Tourism, Diasporas and Space*. London: Routledge, pp. 111–123.

Tolia-Kelly, D. (2004). Locating Processes of Identification: Studying the Precipitates of Re-Memory through Artefacts in the British Asian Home. *Transactions of the Institute of British Geographers, New Series*, 29(3), 314–329.

Vanagaite, R. (2016). *MUSISKIAI: knyga, sukretusi Lietuva!* Vilnius: Alma Littera.

Vitureau, M. (2013). *Restoring the Nazi-Decimated Heritage of Lithuanian Jews*. Available at: http://artdaily.com/news/65188/Restoring-the-Nazi-decimated-heritage-of-Lithuanian-Jews#.UojWdY3GI7C [accessed 6 November 2013].

Whitehead, C., Eckersley, S. & Mason, R. (2012). *Placing Migration in European Museums: Theoretical, Contextual and Methodological Foundations*. Milan: MeLA Books.

Yahadut Lita (1984). Vol. 4. Tel Aviv: Association of Lithuanian Jews in Israel.

Yoffee, B. (1998). *My Recent Jewish Heritage Roots Tour to Lithuania and Belarus: Moving and Inspiring*. Available at: www.litvaksig.org/index.php/litvaksig-online-journal/my-recent-jewish-heritage-roots-tour-to-lithuania-and-belarus-?task=article [accessed 19 May 2013].

8 Old homes made new

American Jews travelling to Eastern Europe from 1920 to the present

Oskar Czendze and Jason Francisco

Introduction

The contested relations between homeland and diaspora are traditionally mediated by states of memorial longing and varieties of exile consciousness. Hebrew names these as *galut* and Yiddish as *golus*, a condition of removedness, alienatedness, loss, spiritual emptiness. In traditional Jewish religion, *golus* is basically a permanent Jewish situation, indeed a human situation, to be ended only with the arrival of the Messiah and the return to the biblical Zion (Zemel, 2015: 7). However, this is not to say that living in diaspora disables the normal processes of human attachment, dissolving everyday life into a dream of an (imagined) homecoming to the (imagined) homeland. It is not that diasporic places resist becoming home. On the contrary, as Caryn Aviv and David Shneer (2005: 7) argue, to live in diaspora is to charge the lost and the dispersed with the urgency and the expectation of return; in effect to create multiple centres in concatenated relations. As a result, one place substitutes for another in a self-extending and transmutable experience of home. In a phenomenon that Jonathan and Daniel Boyarin (2002: 11) term "rediasporization", Rio de Janeiro might serve as a proxy for the remembered Cairo, as Cairo the remembered Córdoba, just as Los Angeles might serve as a proxy for the remembered Johannesburg, which served the remembered Kaunas, all of these lineages eventually underpinned by the (mythic) remembered Jerusalem. In some contrast to the traditional view, diaspora, in this way of understanding, is understood as a positive power of inspiration and dynamic cultural transformation across time and space. The complications of decentralized and recentralized, imagined and real homelands are enough to prompt Aviv and Shneer (2005: 22–3) to call to dissolve the antagonism of centre and diaspora. Instead, they are speaking of global Jews, who are making a home in a global, not diasporic, world.

This essay examines the memorial or memory practices of American Jews from Eastern European towns over the last century, from the 1920s to the present, specifically the forms of their remembering what should properly be called diasporic homelands in what is today Poland and Ukraine. In this chapter, we argue that Jewish memorial practices operate in four distinct modalities: nostalgia, trauma, amnesia and invention. We examine these forms by bringing them into conversation with the historical issue of migration and the representation of Eastern Europe as homeland in the diaspora. Underpinning our reading is the concept of collective memory, which sociologist Maurice Halbwachs (1992: 25) defines as the process by which individual memory is given shape by present social interaction, shared experiences and the continuous discourse about the past. In this sense, the past is never an exact historical reconstruction, but can only be seen through the lens of memory.

Specifically, we look at the historical and current development of *landsmanshaftn* (Jewish hometown associations) which were established by Jewish immigrants from various Eastern European towns or cities at the height of the mass migration to the US in the late 19th and early 20th century. *Landsmanshaftn* kept ties to, and memories of, the old home, while helping immigrants to meet their substantial needs in the New World. In the early 1900s and late 1930s, there were thousands of such societies in the New York City area alone, perhaps 20,000 in the rising industrial centres of the Northeastern and upper Midwestern United States (Soyer, 1997: 201). Each *landsmanshaft* was a dynamic and organic entity: some formed religious congregations; others promoted their members' radical politics or fostered the Americanization process. In general, they offered Jewish immigrants a sense of cultural and emotional stability, belonging and community. Moreover, as memorial groups, they manifested multiple dimensions of memory and diaspora across time and space. Therefore, they offer a special window into the dynamic phenomenon of migration, specifically the dialectic between loss and reinvention of Jewish collective memory and identity.

Nostalgia and the myth of the *shtetl*

> When someone leaves his native city, he leaves behind so many joys of youth, so many sweet and heartfelt memories, that he brings his memories along with him so that he can recall them joyfully. But what kinds of youthful memories did I bring with me? Kalush gave me nothing. No education. No one bothered with a poor orphan. Many Jewish orphans wandered in the streets in tatters, half naked, and the respectable Jews did not even want to take notice. They were immersed in themselves. And yet, I felt a longing upon leaving my native town.
>
> (Reisman, 2006: 65)

Ben Reisman emigrated from the Galician town of Kalush to New York in 1896. In his autobiographical essay from 1942, he recounts the emotions that accompanied the departure. Although the poverty, misery and indifference of his native social environment marked the individual memory of the East European hometown, he maintained feelings of rootedness and attachment to the place of his birth. In the United States, many Jewish immigrants like Reisman shared these emotions which stood in a dynamic tension with the desire for rapid economic and social mobility in the new society. However, as we will see, the mental distance to the old home increased, especially in the interwar period. Therefore, often nostal-gic pictures of Eastern Europe replaced the growing distance to the real homeland in the collective memory.

Distance from home does not necessarily produce longing for home; rather, it does so under certain conditions. The 1920s and 1930s represented a turning point in the lives of many Jewish immigrants from Eastern Europe, especially for members of *landsmanshaftn*. The First World War caused huge destruction in their hometowns; famines and the pogroms during the Ukrainian Civil War shattered communal organization and the possibility for immediate help in the Jewish communities. These blows effectively sealed the demise of the tradi-tional *shtetl*, which had begun a steep decline in social and economic viability by the 1860s, as Yohanan Petrovsky-Shtern (2014), Eva Hoffman (2007) and Yehudah Bauer (2013) have shown. In contrast, Jews in the American diaspora were spared by these events, and a key part of American Jewish nostalgia after the First World War can be understood as a reactive approach to one's own good fortune. Being in a comparatively comfortable situation while friends and rela-tives suffered immensely across the ocean motivated *landsmanshaftn* to intensify their contacts and launch an effort to rebuild the Jewish communities in their old home (Polland & Soyer, 2012: 165–6).

The Rymanower Young Men's Benevolent Association (1937), for example, commented that a spirit of 'patriotism and self-sacrifice' dominated the American Jewish community after the war. Likewise, the obvious differences between *land-slayt* in America and Eastern Europe were erased by creating a unity which the United Brisker Relief expressed in a call to its members 1917: 'We, the fortunate Briskers, who are here in this free country . . . must take an interest in our Briskers and our brothers and sisters suffering from the war' (cited in Soyer, 2007: 55). *Landsmanshaftn* mobilized an impressive amount of material help together with other Jewish organizations like the American Joint Distribution Committee. The archives of the AJDC Landsmanshaftn Department (n.d.) show the dimensions of the effort: between 1920 and 1938, for example, the Felsztyner Relief Committee issued a countless number of invoices amounting to between 50 and 200 dollars with the reference line 'economic aid'. The National Origins Act in 1924, which led to a migration ban of Jews from Eastern Europe, functioned as an additional catalyst for initiating the actual help for friends and relatives in the old home (Diner, 2004: 78; Soyer, 1986: 6).

On the one hand, American Jews did realize how far away they actually were from the events and thus from their families in Eastern Europe; on the other, this very distance reinforced feelings of attachment to their native place and put the old home into a central position in their new lives in the United States. If some important part of nostalgia is due to a sense of danger – the prospect of current events loosening ties and generating a psychological gap between life in America and the old home, a gap wider and potentially more difficult to bridge than the (considerable) physical distance – in response to that danger, many American Jews intensified not only their material aid, but also their commemorative work. Indeed, memorial efforts in time became the binding element of *landslayt* in the United

States from the 1920s on, in keeping with Halbwachs' observation (1992: 25) that a group maintains unity by thinking of the old home and its layout.

Svetlana Boym (2001: 19) defines nostalgia as 'longing for a home that no longer exists or has never existed, a sentiment of loss and displacement, but also a romance with one's own fantasy'. The longing of the members created positive pictures of their town, images full of charm, pictures that reflected their own desires. A myth of the *shtetl* arose as a lost idyll of a simple and harmonious Jewish community destroyed by the modern world (Roskies, 1999: 43–4). In some measure, such an image arose independently of the mass migration from Eastern Europe that began in the late 19th century, and the devastation of the First World War, but was already a key feature of the renascence of high literature in Yiddish, especially in the works of Sholem Aleichem, and later of Peretz Markish, Fishl Bimko, Shmuel Halkin and Itsik Fefer, among others (even as many other Yiddish writers did not romanticize the *shtetl*). By the 1920s, the trend of mythicizing the *shtetl* had taken root among memoirists. Saul Miler, a member of the First Dobromiler Young Men's Sick and Benevolent Association, portrays his native town in his memoirs as follows:

> The little Jewish shtetl Dobromil was a little shtetl like all the other little shtetls of Galitisia, but yet it lay in a setting of scenic natural beauty. It nestled there in a valley, this shtetl, ringed around with lofty green hills, with bountiful orchards, with flower gardens, an atmosphere fragrant with bracing fresh air.
>
> (Miler, 1980: 3)

Although in the Galician town of Dobromil Poles, Ukrainians and Germans made up half the population before the First World War, Miler draws a picture of a genuine Jewish village with beautiful and idyllic natural surroundings. This 'restorative nostalgia' emphasized a transhistorical and universal reconstruction of home (Boym, 2001: 31). However, some *landslayt* reflected on the aspect of longing and the contradictions it produced. As a Brisker *landsman*, Paul Novick, formulated: 'Just what is Brisk? The truth is that Brisk is what we want it to be' (cited in Soyer, 1997: 196). It is a reconstruction of a past that had never altogether existed, only in the way memory saw it. However, since the radical changes that took place in the interwar period, the myth of the *shtetl* as a common place of origin functioned as a new cornerstone of a specific American Jewish identity.

Tourism in the interwar period

Beyond memorializing and connecting with the past on an abstract level, travelling to Eastern Europe strengthened the emotional ties with the old home in the 1920s and 1930s. Tourism was a growing phenomenon at a time when the old country became more and more central not only within the immigrant societies, but also in American Jewish society at large (Shandler, 2013: 31). For some

American Jews, as a result of the October Revolution 1917, the new Soviet Union represented a dynamic and in many aspects more innovative alternative to the monotonous life in the US (Soyer, 2000: 125). In this respect, an anonymous Jewish immigrant, who participated in the revolutionary years at the beginning of the century in Russia, wrote to the editor of the column *Bintel Brief* in the Yiddish newspaper *Forward* in 1917:

> From time to time, however, I had the desire to visit Russia . . . But in America one is always busy . . . so I never went. But now everything is changed . . . The ideal for which I fought has become a reality, and my heart draws me there more than ever now . . . and I'm ready to go home now.
>
> (Metzker, 1990: 132)

Going back to Eastern Europe, however, did not always mean travelling to a new future; often it was a very personal journey into the past. In 1932, Rose Schoenfeld visited her native town of Drohobycz in interwar Poland to see her mother, whom she had not said goodbye to before leaving for the new country. She recounts this visit as follows:

> I did not enjoy the trip at all, because I found great poverty and desolation there . . . Each person cried, pleaded for help, and begged me to look up their friends and their landslayt in America so they could help them . . . My brother did not even have a tablecloth to lay on the table for the Sabbath. From all his wealth, only a mountain of ash remained, because the Russians had burned his houses.
>
> (Schoenfeld, 2006: 186)

Although Schoenfeld had always remembered her hometown as the place of a happy childhood and family, she was now shocked by the poverty and misery in Drohobycz. Similarly, the Yiddish humourist Chune Gottesfeld (1937) wrote about the muddy streets and backward way of life he witnessed during his visit to Skala, Poland. He further portrayed his old friend Zalmen as 'a man with a large, wild beard (the kind of beard you see in America only in the movies, on a wild man wrestling with lions in Africa). He . . . looked ancient, a real old geezer' (cited in Kugelmass & Shandler, 1989: 16). Both realized that, while on the one hand their emotional ties to the old home never completely vanished, on the other, the visits had revealed how foreign the East European society and its environment, which they shared in their memories, had become.

Tourism offered *landslayt* the possibility to confront their fascination for Eastern Europe and their nostalgic images of the *shtetl* with the real place. These dynamic cultural interactions connected the two antagonisms of new and old home, past and present (Shandler, 2014: 39–41). The private visits therefore symbolized, in most cases, a journey back in time to an imagined past. American Jews captured these moments not only in diaries and travel reports, but also in

Figure 8.1 Julius Blackman (second row from top, fourth from left) during his visit to Petroverovka (Zhovten) in the Soviet Union, 1932

From the Archives of the YIVO Institute for Jewish Research, New York

photographs which were often shared with family or friends. In these pictures, American Jews posed, for example, in front of a farm, surrounded by a pictur-esque landscape or together with old friends and relatives (see Newman, 1993).

Group pictures with people from the native town illustrated clearly the grow-ing cultural distance between American Jews and their families and friends in the old home. For example, Julius Blackman, a Jewish immigrant and businessman from the US, posed with a group of men during a visit to his Russian hometown Zhovten in 1932 (Figure 8.1). In this photograph, he features in very fine dress with a smile in the middle of a group of men whose miserable circumstances are almost literally written on their faces. During these trips, Jewish immigrants realized their personal transformation in American society, their cultural distance to the old home, and this confirmed their experience of migration. At the same time, the feeling of foreignness in the own former homeland was often mutual. In their elegant clothes and with their modern cameras, many American Jews were regarded as 'the other' by the townspeople (Newman, 1993: 225).

Members of Jewish hometown associations also went back to Eastern Europe to document the situation of their former neighbours and families in Eastern Europe. In the 1920s and 1930s many *landsmanshaftn* raised funds to send delegates with money and personal letters to their hometowns (Soyer, 1997: 175–80). During their mission, these members also documented their experience of the old home in film. For example, Pesach Zuckerman (*A Pictorial Review of Kolbishev*, 1929) from the Kolbushover Relief Committee and Aleksandr Harkavy (*Novogrudok*, 1931) from the Nowogrodek Relief Committee made movies of their respective hometowns, Kolbuszowa and Nowogródek in Poland. They filmed the daily life and appearance of people, familiar places and architecture and captured greetings from people passing by. These moving images were unique not only as they functioned as a personal and intimate glimpse into the East European Jewish culture for the *landslayt* and the broader public across the ocean, but also as they seemed to immortalize the hometowns.

Moreover, these short movies reflected a specific intention by the filmmaker. In the introduction to *A Pictorial Review of Kolbishev* (1929) the narrator addressed the audience in the United States as follows:

> Although we have made this glorious country as our second home, living under far better conditions and enjoying more freedom under the American flag, we still feel and consider in the depths of our hearts our native towns with all its shadows and faults as the sunny spot of the first happy years. Looking upon the schools, synagogues and all the other unique features prevalent in our idyllic towns, we feel as a shock of pride would touch us and many a tear relieves our very sensitive hearts while looking at these pictures and recalling the first episodes of our early lives.

In his movie, Pesach Zuckerman reproduced a sentimental image of an East European *shtetl* as a shared space of Jewish origin based on the emotional memory of a happy childhood. Thus, scenes of traditional Jewish everyday life appear throughout the video: Jews buying and selling at the marketplace, children going to the traditional school, the *heder*, or Jews going to the synagogue. The filmmaker's personal appearance in front of the camera – for example, praying at the gravestones of family members – further emphasizes the emotional tribute to the old home. As a result, the movie increased both the nostalgic memory and the myth of the *shtetl* as a place of a more authentic Jewish life which were shared by the audience in the United States.

Aleksandr Harkavy described this nostalgic attachment to the old home in a letter after his first visit to Nowogródek in 1921:

> After 3 hours I finally arrived in my beloved and wonderful town. Looking at Nowogrodek made me cry . . . It's almost 43 years ago when I left this place where my cradle stood, where I dreamed my youth, and where I left my mother's grave.
>
> (cited in Sztyma, 2013: 17)

His short movie *Novogrudok* (1931) ten years later, however, conveys a more nuanced picture. Although he also portrays a simple and harmonious traditional

Jewish life, Harkavy shows modern Jewish infrastructure such as Makabi sport clubs or political parties. Moreover, he presents himself in front of the camera as delegate of his *landsmanshaft*, distributing money to the townspeople. By using common nostalgic images of East European Jewish life, and showing modern Jewish institutions together with American relief packages, Harkavy's video seems to be aimed at encouraging American Jews to foster their actual help for the old home.

Visual and written travel reports confronted *landslayt* in the United States with their nostalgic longing for an imagined home, the *shtetl*. Like the travellers, the American audience shared the dynamic emotions between attachment to the former home and its people and obvious feelings of foreignness upon arrival. On the one hand, facing the simple life in these pictures contributed to a stronger nostalgic view of the *shtetl* as the place of common origin and a more authentic Jewish way of life. On the other hand, seeing and reading the reports of delegates about how they became 'the other' made Jewish immigrants more confident and secure that they, in fact, had become Americans in the new country. However, at the same time, this process of Americanization had the paradoxical effect of making the *landslayt* turn more determinedly towards their former homes in Eastern Europe, intensifying the material help and relief work (Soyer, 1993: 362). Together, the nostalgic memory, the transatlantic tourism and the practical relief work placed Eastern Europe in a central position in shaping the *landslayt* Jewish identities constructed in the dialectic between their new and old homes.

Trauma: commemorating war, destruction and loss

Sombre and traumatic forms of memory could also define the American Jewish immigrant community in the interwar period. Acts of commemoration became central in this case, and revealed the deep emotional connections the members retained to their places of origin. For example, the *landsmanshaftn* published *yizker bikher* (memorial books) which memorialized the destruction of their hometowns after the First World War and, in particular, the pogroms during the Ukrainian Civil War (see Fischer, 2008; Magocsi, 2007: 203–9). The Felshtiner *yizkor bukh*, for example, published by First Felshtiner Progressive Benevolent Association (1937), gives a detailed account of the landscape of *shtetl*-life in Felshtin and the pogrom of 1919. Together with the Proskurov *yizkor bukh* from 1924, this document, with its archetypical pattern tracing the community's experiences from the mythologized and flowering *shtetl* to suffering and mass martyrdom and closing with the rebirth in the Promised Land, served as model for post-Holocaust *yizker bikher* (Roskies, 1999: 57–61). Furthermore, those books often had a sacred character in the community. They served as substitute gravestones by including lists of names of the dead along with illustrations of tombstones and funeral iconography (Baker, Boyarin & Kugelmass, 1998: 25–7).

After the Holocaust and the complete destruction of Jewish communities in Europe, the transformation of Jewish hometown associations into societies of memorialization and documentation was furthered, based on loss. In her analysis of the case of Białystok, Rebecca Kobrin (2010) demonstrated how the *landslayt* struggled with their identity as Białystoker when Jewish Białystok no longer existed. American *landslayt* could no longer travel to visit the old home as they had in the interwar period, because this home no longer existed as a real space. The mission then became to create a physical and mental space to bear witness to their home's legacy.

This effort incorporated many different aspects. Most *landsmanshaftn* continued to write *yizker bikher* and these became the biggest projects of memorialization and documentation of vanished life until the early 1960s (Diner, 2009: 48–50). The effort was international and even attracted new members into the societies. The books appeared in the United States, Canada, Israel, Latin America, South Africa and Europe, and in different languages, in Yiddish, English or Hebrew. Up to the present day, they mainly serve as portable memorials to commemorate the vanished places and its people by reconstructing East European Jewry on paper and collectively giving testimony to the events during the Holocaust. Furthermore, American *landslayt* held annual commemorations (*haskore*) on the anniversaries of the hometown's destruction or on specific dates to mark events like pogroms and massacres. Such calendar events not only recalled the past in the present and held the community together, but also strengthened a specific version of collective memory, in this case a traumatic one, across time and space. Up to the present day, the Fraternal Order of Bendin-Sosnowicer, for example, hold such calendar events with the slogan 'Remember and Never Forget!' (Fraternal Order of Bendin-Sosnowicer, 2008), including services and lectures. Jewish hometown associations further erected monuments commemorating the victims of the Holocaust in their own cemeteries in America or Israel. These monuments played a major role in constructing memory (Young, 1993: 6–7). By visiting the cemeteries, members of the societies were always confronted with the central monument and its inscription, and thus the destruction of the hometown's community across the ocean. Together with the *yizkher bikher* and annual commemorations, traumatic forms of memory were emphasized and this resulted in a specific type of memory, based on the notion of loss and absence.

In the postwar period, Jewish commemorative impulses were forced to contend with broader trends that psychically distanced and indeed 'othered' Eastern Europe according to Cold War ideology. The concomitant rise of Zionism as a dominant aspect of American Jewish consciousness made it easy for American Jews from the 1950s to come to view the Ashkenazic homeland as a kind of anti-homeland except within the provinces of a specific type of bereft memory, an expression of attachment to Eastern Europe built largely from anger and rejection. As an example of a new type of *landsmanshaft* that arose after the Second World War, the New Cracow Friendship Society, established in 1965 in New York and still active today, stands for a postwar type of Jewish communal solidarity in response to the experiences of the Holocaust. The organization describes itself as a Holocaust survivor group for Jewish Polish survivors from the Kraków district including members of the second and third generations. The founders' vision was to speak out about the Holocaust in American society, and never forget what had happened to the European Jewry. They also aimed to provide a comfortable and secure place for their members, and to support those survivors in need, both in an emotional and material sense (The New Cracow Friendship Society, 2015: iv). Like other *landsmanshaftn*, they held annual memorial services and erected monuments at cemeteries in the US and Israel in memory of the Jewish community in Kraków and all of those who perished in the Holocaust. For example, in 1970 they erected a monument at Beth Moses Cemetery in Pinelawn, NY, which contains soil from the concentration camps in Auschwitz and Płaszów in the foundations (The New Cracow Friendship Society, 2015: 20–1).

Importantly, the New Cracow Friendship Society understands the injunction never to forget the Holocaust concomitantly as an injunction to emphasize the estrangement of Jews from their non-Jewish neighbours during the catastrophe, such that the traumatic aspect of memory is linked to a bellicose attitude, and often a tendency towards collective blame of non-Jews in an ancestral Jewish place. Asked about the connection to their original hometown, one of the founders of the New Cracow Friendship Society, Steven Morrow, replied in an interview for the 50th Anniversary Journal in 2015: 'We are from Krakow but the Poles treated us horribly. So we don't want to use their spelling. We'll use a 'C' as a protest, and our people will know what that means' (The New Cracow Friendship Society, 2015: xiii). In this respect, today's city of Kraków has an ambivalent role as a carrier of heritage for following generations. The real space functions as an abstract reference point for a common place of origin. At the same time, the society dissociates themselves from the Polish past as a heritage which is worth sharing with future generations.

Steven Morrow's response reflects a common attitude among many American Jews towards East European countries in the decades after the Second World War. In the 1950s, American Jewish newspapers published articles which accused specifically Poles, Hungarians, Lithuanians, Ukrainians and other East European people of the murder of the Jewish people during the German occupation and collaboration with the Nazi regime (Diner, 2009: 253–6). These public statements were not meant to diminish the German atrocities, but to show how people of other nations took part in the annihilation of the European Jews and supported or benefited from the Nazi regime. Many testimonies reveal that survivors and their descendants in America developed a stronger dislike against people from East European countries than against Germans. The sociologist Barbara Engelking (2001: 36–7) argues in her study on Polish-Jewish survivor testimonies that in many cases, antisemitic violence by Poles left a deeper wound than the German terror. According to her, the reason is that during the occupation, the relationship of Jews in Poland to the Nazis was clear – it was one between two enemies. In this relationship, they could only expect violence and oppression. Poles, in contrast, lived for centuries as neighbours with the Jews and shared the same enemy. Jews expected solidarity or, at least, empathy in the fight against the Nazis. In addition, anti-Jewish violence after 1944 and the 'anti-Zionist' communist campaign in 1968 further deepened the negative attitudes against Poles in general (Polonsky, 2015: 26–8).

In this case, American Jews travelled back to Eastern Europe to see the sites of Jewish martyrdom. With the wave of liberalization in Central and Eastern Europe, in April 1989 the New Cracow Friendship Society (2015: 58–60) organized a trip to the holy sites of martyrdom in Poland, a 'homeland that never was', further deepening sombre and traumatic forms of memory. Up to the present day, the Kieltzer Sick and Benevolent Society of New York holds annual trips to the Polish town of Kielce where on 4 July 1946 a group of Polish soldiers, policemen and civilians murdered the town's Jews (Gross, 2008: 134–6). In August 1987, the *landsmanshaft* went to Kielce to hold a service on the site of the massacre. Rabbi David Blumenfeld (1987), a member and former president of the society, noted an incident during his visit:

> This slogan was shouted at Cantor Cooperman (Toronto) and me on the street when we went to re-visit his home in Kielce. 'Nasze kamienice – wasze ulice' / 'We (Poles) are in the houses – you (Jews) are in the streets'. This slogan was a reversal in language from what was said by them before the Holocaust, namely: . . . 'You (Jews) are in the houses – we (Poles) are in the streets'.

Blumenfeld gives here the impression of a historical continuity of Polish antisemitism and thus of traumatic experiences for Jews in Poland then and now.

Traumatic forms of memory which are based on the notion of loss and absence dominated the *landsmanshaftn* and American Jewish society in general after the Holocaust. American Jews constructed a specific image and memory of Eastern Europe which William Mandel (1985: 18–19), member of the Kieltzer Society, impressively describes during his trip across several East European countries in 1985:

> If a Jew who comes from that area and now lives somewhere else in the world, were to pass by those towns now, it would seem to him that he was in a deep trance. Often it seems as if the doors and windows of those houses will open and the faces of Jewish men, women and children would be looking out again . . . But, soon though, one comes out of the trance and sees immediately the tragic and bloody truth . . . there is not even one Jewish person.

Eastern Europe is perceived as a space of suffering and destruction, a Jewish cemetery, which only hosts the ghosts of the past. Travelling to these places and entering this space can be a traumatic experience which conflates and confronts memories of the past with the reality. Therefore, Eastern Europe is no longer an imagined homeland of the future, as in the interwar period, but a lost home of the past.

Amnesia: the influence of assimilation and Zionism

Throughout the decades of the postwar period, however, we can also identify a radical opposite phenomenon within American Jewish society, the forgetting of

Eastern Europe as a Jewish homeland. Two major forces pushed this process as the old home increasingly became a hazy homeland: on the one hand, the growing assimilation of Jewish immigrants into American society and, on the other, Zionism and the strong focus on Israel as the actual home for all Jews around the world.

In the late 19th and early 20th century, political Zionism with its roots in the discourses of acculturation and antisemitism in modern Europe got little attention from American Jews, except for a few intellectual circles which promoted a spirit of pioneering in the land of Israel (Katz, 2015: 19–20). After David Ben-Gurion announced the creation of the State of Israel in 1948, however, American Jews showed growing emotional ties with the new state in the Middle East. They started to travel to the biblical country and to report their experiences. A *landsman* from the Rohatyner Young Men's Society, for example, described Israel during a meeting as an 'incredible flourishing . . . pulsating land, fuel of green fields, citrus forests' (Rohatyner Young Men's Society Inc., 1966). This sentimental view of Israel characterized American Zionism in contrast to the traditional political Zionism which put the Jewish state at the centre of all political, economic, cultural and social life. On the one hand, it seems that the early American Zionists shifted the nostalgia from the old home to *eretz yisroel*. On the other, they were also less ideological than their European forefathers because they saw Israel as a mirror image of America with shared values of freedom and democracy (Katz, 2015: 4–9).

This type of romantic Zionism dramatically changed after the Six-Day War in 1967 (Brenner, 2016: 162–6). American Jews feared that the military clash between Israel and its Arabic neighbours would result in a second Holocaust and that traumatic memories and experiences of the past would be repeated (Katz, 2015: 7). Facing these emotions of fear and powerlessness in the face of a renewed threat against the Jewish people, American Jews started a material and financial aid campaign for Israel. The New Cracow Friendship Society (2015: 13), for example, sent ambulances, promoted Israeli state bonds and offered stipends for Israeli students and financial packages for Israeli war veterans. This material help resulted in strong political support for Israel which the president of the Fraternal Order of Bendin-Sosnowicer, Morris Drexler (1984: 4), formulated as follows: 'Israel's struggles are our own struggles as well. As Jews and as survivors of the Nazi brutality, we are obligated to aid Israel in whatever ways we can'. This absolute solidarity with the State of Israel turned into a 'religion of American Jews' (Brenner, 2016: 164), which is strongly connected with the traumatic memory of the Holocaust.

In the postwar decades, the processes of suburbanization and assimilation further supported this transformation of the collective identity and memory of American Jews. Professionalization and high social mobility made economic success possible for Jewish immigrants, and opened up many opportunities in this era which soon became known as the golden age (Diner, 2004: 283–8). Most American Jews left behind their ethnic subcultures in the big cities, their migration experience and their old ties with the Eastern European Jewish tradition and culture. In the suburbs, in contrast, questions of Jewish identity, cultural practice or social networks now became a matter of choice. As a result, new collective identities emerged out of intermarriage with non-Jews, belonging in non-Jewish social networks and other processes of assimilation (Moore, 1981: 233–6).

These post-urban settings of an American Jewish society which left their roots behind opened a space within the construction of Jewish self-awareness. The State of Israel, especially after 1967, filled this gap by creating a modern secular American Jewish identity with Israel as a type of civil religion (Aviv & Shneer, 2005: 12). *Landsmanshaftn*, for example, celebrated annual events related to the State of Israel like the Independence Day, *Yom ha'Atzmaut*. In contrast to the interwar period, *landslayt* replaced Eastern Europe with Israel in providing the content and expression of their Jewish identities. Lorraine Kaufman, a *landsfroy* of the Fraternal Order of Bendin-Sosnowicer, stated during a meeting in 1984: 'For two thousand years Jews have waited and prayed for a homeland. Imagine how often our grandparents in Bendin and Sosnowice prayed "Next Year in Jerusalem". And for all of us we can say, "Tomorrow in Jerusalem!!!"' (Drexler, 1984: 6). In this respect, the memory of the biblical Israel, the mythic homeland, was transformed into a physical and actual home for all Jews worldwide, anticipating the arrival of the Messiah and thus fundamentally questioning the traditional definition and meaning of diaspora. In contrast, Eastern Europe, the physical and ancestral homeland, lost its role as a source of inspiration in the collective memory of Jewish immigrants and became a faded memory.

Some of the *landsmanshaftn* that are still active reflect this amnesia. Once central to the immigrant life of Eastern European Jews in the US, the processes of assimilation, post-urbanization and Zionism caused the decline of Jewish hometown associations by over 90 per cent. The few remaining members of the Rohatyner Young Men's Society, for example, do not meet outside of their biannual dinners. In fact, they function only as a burial society today. In 2008, 24 out of 32 households voted in favour of disbanding the group (Brostoff, 2008). However, some members strongly opposed the vote, mainly because of their cemetery plots. Ruth Brown, for example, who never attends any of the meetings and lives in Florida, said: 'I just want to know I'm going to have a place to rest. My grandparents are there, my parents are there, my husband is there' (ibid: 4). According to the president, Bernard Hulkower, 'there's a general feeling that we're not going anywhere' (ibid: 4). The *landsmanshaft* today seems to be only a forum for discussions about the two cemeteries in Queens. The Eastern European hometown does not play a role anymore.

However, members of the *landsmanshaftn* sometimes travelled back to Eastern Europe, for example to find out where their hometown was located. The Rymalower Young Men's Benevolent Association, for example, established by young immigrants from the small Galician town Grzymałów in 1913 in New York, follows classical patterns of a *landsmanshaft*: a mutual aid society for young men providing benefits, such as burial service and friendships. The memory of their hometown Hrymayliv in today's Ukraine (pol. Grzymałów, yidd. Rimalov), however, is lost. In 1965, member Morris Weissbrot went on a trip to Ukraine to locate the town (Drucker). He found an elderly couple in the Husiatyn region who remembered a town called Grzymałów without any further specific data. The reason was that Grzymałów served as a municipal settlement during the Soviet Period. After the fall of the Iron Curtain in 1989, the town appeared once again on the map as Hrymayliv in today's Ukraine. Ironically, the association does not stay in contact with their hometown and does not provide support, for example, for the rundown 18th-century synagogue (Virtual Sztetl, 2016). It seems that the society is more concerned with documenting their own history as an American organization than maintaining any physical or imaginative ties with its hometown.

However, assimilation and Zionism were by no means automatic social processes and could also lead to a feeling of disorientation among descendants of Jewish immigrants, as an anonymous letter to *Forward* in 1967 shows:

> Dear Editor . . . I am a young man twenty years of age. My grandparents brought a precious heritage of Yiddishkeit from Eastern Europe . . . I still remember how they used to sing Jewish songs, speak Yiddish, and prepare delicious kosher meals . . . My parents and I now reside in the suburbs in an area which lacks the Jewish traditions and customs that I knew as a child. Very few except the older Jewish people speak Yiddish . . . Most of the young ladies I meet are not the type of Jewish girl I would like. I feel like a stranger among the Jewish girls who are interested only in rock'n'roll and wear mini skirts . . . I want to know how my family and I can perpetuate our traditions.
> (Metzker, 1990: 211–12)

The young author seems to be lost in the new American Jewish world of the suburbs and tries to find a more authentic Jewishness by reviving a nostalgic longing for his grandparent's East European *yiddishkayt*. Similarly, although in a different context, since the 1990s, descendants of Jewish immigrants are searching for their own ethnic identity by looking to their ancestral homeland, Eastern Europe. They adapt their growing interest in family history and increasing fascination for the old home to the dynamics of a modern society, in the real as well as virtual world, and thus are changing forms of American Jewish collective memory and identity.

Invention: the search for roots in the real and virtual world

> The children haven't got the same need as our parents had . . . But I think there'll always be a need for knowing where you came from.
> (cited in Kliger, 1986: 35)

In 1986, a *landsman* from the Antopoler Young Men's Benevolent Association knew, deliberately or not, that social processes of assimilation and Zionism would not diminish the general interest in questions of family history. Since the 1990s, in addition, globalization and flexibility have increased American Jews' awareness of the diversity of Jewish culture worldwide and diasporic identities (Aviv & Shneer, 2005: 16). Moreover, a growing political and cultural distance from Israel has increased the desire and search for an alternative American Jewish vision which goes beyond the dominant secular identity with Israel as civil religion (Gitelman, 2016: 4).

At the same time, however, this notion of diversity made descendants of Jewish immigrants more aware of issues relating to their own ethnic identity, a general phenomenon of the American society (see Conzen *et al.*, 1992). To solve this problem, American Jews started to search for their roots in archives, and to talk with family members or peers in the digital world of the internet. As with many other diasporic communities, they also took part in the phenomenon of 'roots-tourism' (see Coles & Timothy, 2004; Marschall, 2015) by travelling to their ancestors' homeland in Eastern Europe which, since the fall of the Iron Curtain in 1989, was much easier to visit.

As a result of this growing interest in questions of ethnic identity and family history, *landsmanshaftn*, which already 'were viewed as relics of the Old World' (Weisser, 1985: 5), have been recently re-established after many years of inactivity. The Felshtin Society, for example, emerged from the First Felshteener Benevolent Association dating from 1905. After nearly 20 years of inactivity, descendants of Felshtiner Jews refounded the society in 1998. At the official reunion celebrations in 1999 and 2009, over one hundred people with roots in the East European town gathered. Currently, there are around 240 members. As the president, Alan Bernstein, recalled during an interview on 17 May 2016, their main purpose was to translate and publish an English version of their *yizkor bukh*, and to provide a space for social and educational interaction among members and the broader public. With the help of younger descendants, a website offers further resources for genealogical research such as photographs and written documents. In 2015, the *landslayt* launched their digital Oral History Project which collects testimonies of first-generation American Felshtin Jews to study the acculturation process of Jewish immigrants and to relate the 'experience of our ancestors to current global issues regarding immigration and refugees from distressed places' (Fischkin, 2016: 3).

With their original purpose, the Felshtin Society shows, on the one hand, a degree of continuity with the work of their forefathers. They are translating the *yizkor bukh* for people who are not able to read Yiddish and perform common acts of commemoration. In April 2019, for example, the Centennial Event at the Museum of Jewish Heritage will commemorate the Felshtin pogrom of 1919. On the other hand, they have shifted the focus of their work towards their East European hometown, today's Hvardiyske in Ukraine. In contrast to the activities of their forefathers, which erected a Holocaust-monument in Dimona, Israel, the reunited *landsmanshaft* dedicated a memorial to the victims of the pogrom at the place of the old Jewish cemetery in former Felshtin in May 2010. Prior to this event, they organized a trip for the *landslayt* to their old home, including meetings with current Jewish leaders and the local population (Bernstein, 2010). Even for the Centennial Event the priority is given to dedicate a 'significant part of the day . . . to Felshtin and for Felshtiners' (Bernstein, 2016b: 2) and to celebrate its cuisine and music. Those activities show that the Felshtin Society have reoriented their activities towards the commemoration of their past, partially in the US, but mainly in their ancestors' hometown in contemporary Eastern Europe.

The World Society of Częstochowa Jews and their Descendants is another example of the 'renaissance' of *landsmanshaftn*. Established in New York in 2004, the society explicitly tries to be global by having an international advisory board with hundreds of members who can trace their roots to Częstochowa in Poland and its surroundings. The *landslayt* foster research on the history of Częstochowa Jews, organize conferences and social activities, and run several projects including the restoration of the Jewish cemetery in their Polish hometown (Rajcher). In addition, reunions held every three or four years in Częstochowa demonstrate that the global society's work is strongly linked with contemporary Poland and their hometown.

In contrast to the Felshtin Society, however, the World Society did not emerge or take inspiration from previous Czenstochover *landsmanshaftn*. The organization grew out of a trip to Poland in 2002 which Alan Silberstein and his cousin Sigmund Rolat, the president, took to see the traces of their family history. In particular, the meeting with Jerzy Migalski in Częstochowa played a decisive role, as Silberstein explained when interviewed on 19 May 2016. During his research in the 1990s, the Polish scholar had found out that prewar Częstochowa, contrary to the Polish historical narrative, was home to a well-established Jewish community with schools, hospitals, companies and political parties. Silberstein and Rolat decided to support Migalski's project of an exhibition on Jewish life in Częstochowa from the 1700s to current times. Together with the help of Częstochowa survivors around the world, the cousins found documents and photographs from various archives for the project. With the support of local authorities, the formal opening of the exhibition *The Jews of Częstochowa: Coexistence, Holocaust, Memory* was attended by *landslayt* from around the world. It was then decided to form the World Society and to use the internet to keep people connected. The exhibition subsequently travelled throughout North America, further attracting membership to the World Society. During the fifth reunion in September 2016, the exhibition's materials were incorporated into a permanent exhibit in an annex to the Municipal Museum in the Polish city (Steinhagen, 2016).

When interviewed, Alan Silberstein stated his motivation as follows:

> To me it was never about genealogy or my family, it was preserving the role of Jews in the development of this important city, and cultivating the interest of the Polish citizens in learning about their Jewish neighbours and roots.

The society's work goes beyond preserving the memory for its own sake or satisfying the members' interest in identity, genealogy and understanding their parents' stories. Today's *landslayt* construct a memory which is grounded in the interaction of Jews and Gentiles in Eastern Europe and based on invention. As Silberstein further explains:

I am interested in Poles understanding that what they take for granted as their culture, as their city, as their industry was one in which Jews played a significant role. Jews have much heritage in Poland, as much as in Israel.

The case of the World Society shows a new dimension of *landsmanshaftn* with the active support of knowledge about the Jewish heritage in Eastern Europe and the building of mutual understanding across the ocean. They are constructing a new collective American Jewish identity with the specific notion of Poland as Jewish homeland, against the common view of Eastern Europe as a Jewish cemetery.

The rediscovery of Eastern Europe as homeland in the collective memory is therefore strongly connected with the dimensions of travel. During an interview on 25 May 2016, Mark W. Kiel, born and raised in the US as the son of a Jewish family from Częstochowa, identified himself strongly as a Czenstochover Jew. As a member of the World Society, he recalled in his speech at the official reunion in 2004 the cultural shock of seeing the Jewish non-presence and degenerated memory in the old home:

> I never come as a tourist to Poland but as pilgrim visiting the sanctified sites of memory and martyrdom . . . I urge the children to come to Poland to see the empty streets and feel the presence of the ghosts.
>
> (Kiel, 2004)

Travelling back symbolized a pilgrimage based on the traumatic memory of the past. However, twelve years later in the interview, Kiel remembers that although he first came to Poland full of hate, he was amazed by the efforts of Poles to commemorate the Jewish heritage. Further interactions with the local non-Jewish population strengthened this impression. Moreover, Kiel states that he regrets the loss of Polish heritage and language. His mother, in contrast, maintained a connection to her past in the United States through the Polish language. Kiel modified his conception of Poland based on personal experiences by going there. Felshtiner Jews report on their trip to Ukraine in a similar manner. They were overwhelmed by the friendliness of Ukrainian students, who welcomed them to the town with music. Bernstein remembers: 'It took us completely by surprise and its heartfelt warmth spoke to our hearts in a way that our different languages were irrelevant' (Bernstein, 2010). In both cases, as in the example of the World Society, the interaction with non-Jewish people gave a stimulus which made Eastern Europe central, no longer in a traumatic sense, to constructs of Jewish identity and memory.

Similarly to what happened in the interwar period, today's *landslayt* are travelling back and forth between the old and new country. On their trips, they interact with local people in their ancestral homeland which confronts them with different collective memories. This dynamic process challenges their understanding of themselves and makes American Jews conscious of their own identity and the meaning of home in the diaspora. In the interwar period, these cultural confrontations resulted in fostering both the Americanization process and, at the same time, the ties with Eastern Europe, increasingly considered as the lost home. After the Holocaust, going back symbolized a traumatic return to the places of destruction, loss and death. Cultural interaction with the local population was not part of these trips. Political change in the early 1990s, however, reduced the mental distance to the old home. This allowed for a closer interaction with locals which put Eastern Europe in a more central position to concepts of Jewish memory and identity. These examples across time and space show how perceptions and memories of home, based on different experiences in the Jewish diaspora, can change, and ethnicity can thereby be rethought. It conforms to the idea that ethnic identity is socially constructed, grounded in the diasporic experience (Conzen *et al.*, 1992: 4–5).

The virtual diaspora in the global world of the internet is a very recent example for the social construction of Jewish collective memory and identity. Digital media immensely improved the range and quality of social communication. An individual interest in genealogy could therefore result in a collective experience in a social network. Since the 2000s, Jews worldwide have created dozens of public or private groups, for example on the social platform Facebook, which connect people with the same roots in a specific Eastern European hometown or people with a general interest in the history and culture of the local Jewish population. Some of these 'virtual *landsmanshaftn*' are explicitly devoted to genealogy and the family history of towns, while others preserve and discover the local Jewish heritage.

In contrast to most of the genealogical groups, heritage groups often travel to Eastern Europe to discover and preserve the Jewish heritage of a specific town in the real world. In 2008, for example, descendants of Jewish immigrants from Rohatyn in today's Ukraine founded the virtual group Rohatyn Jewish Heritage (originally called Rohatyn Shtetl Research Group), since 2017 a registered NGO (Osborn, 2017). With the help of social media, Marla Raucher Osborn, one of the main figures in the organization, connects Jewish and non-Jewish people worldwide for the group's activities in Rohatyn. In particular, this project has involved an exceptionally active collaboration with a local activist historian in Rohatyn, Mikhailo Vorobets. A child witness to the massacres of Rohatyn's Jews, and to his parents' (unsuccessful) efforts to save his family's Jewish neighbours, Vorobets has spent decades painstakingly learning the precise locations of Rohatyn's buried Jewish headstones. His research forms part of a larger project to write a detailed integrated history of Rohatyn's Jewish, Polish, Ukrainian and Austrian populations from the mid-19th century through the Second World War. Beginning in 2008, Vorobets partnered with Rohatyn Jewish Heritage to put his research into action. With funds provided by Osborn's group, Vorobets has to date recovered well over two hundred *matsevot*. As of this writing, recovery work continues, and Rohatyn Jewish Heritage plans eventually to build a memorial with the reclaimed headstones. Additionally, Rohatyn Jewish Heritage organizes occasional programs in Rohatyn schools. Thus, in contrast to genealogical groups which are dedicated to the individual interest in family history, the Rohatyn organization is overtly connected with the local Ukrainian population. By acting explicitly and simultaneously in the real and virtual world, they create a community of Jews and non-Jews in their ancestral home in today's Ukraine.

Conclusion

In the wake of the Second World War, as the new State of Israel rapidly became not just a place of asylum for Jews worldwide but a Jewish homeland – and compensatorily so, as if to redeem the losses of the Holocaust, in the standard Zionist narrative – the effect was that Israel superceded Eastern Europe and replaced it as an ethnic homeland in the American Jewish imagination, if not altogether so in Jewish memory. However, in recent years, another shift has become apparent, as we have traced here. Once again, Eastern Europe has emerged as central to American Jewish conceptions of a Jewish homeland.

While examples of old-fashioned *landsmanshaftn* have survived the decades, the renewal of American Jewish interest in Eastern Europe owes significantly to the age of digital media, and new opportunities for travel after the fall of the Iron Curtain in 1989. Digital media has opened new possibilities for connecting *landslayt* worldwide by making genealogical research and actual trips to Poland or Ukraine easier and feasible. In the digital age, the century-old words of the editors of the *Jewish Daily Forward* echo with new relevance: 'We have to be Americans. We will be', they wrote in 1916, 'but you will not be able to erase the old home from our heart', (cited in Roskolenko, 1971: 127).

Exactly why this renewal is occurring for American Jews remains elusive. Inasmuch as we are still in the middle of it, perhaps it is not yet for us to understand. To ask directly: how to characterize the emotional dimension of the renewal of Jewish interest in Eastern Europe? Is it a matter of more or less simple curiosity, much like the interest of Americans of many ethnic and national backgrounds in their ancestries? Or does it show that Jews in America have remained somehow incompletely assimilated even as they have become fully acculturated? Have American Jews retained an internal place for a 'truer' or deeper identity connected to the homes of their ancestors (Chase & Shaw, 1989: 3)? And behind these questions lurks an even murkier question: how to distinguish between curiosity and emotional need in the first place, between degrees of assimilation, and between true and truer identity?

In this chapter, we have shown that Jewish memorial practices in historical perspective operate in distinct modalities, namely nostalgia, trauma, amnesia and invention. We have roughly periodized these modalities, presenting them as emerging successively in time, such that nostalgia best characterizes the pre-Holocaust period, followed by trauma in the decades after the genocide, followed by amnesia and then invention in recent years. We hope it is also clear, however, that these modalities are interpenetrative. Each contains aspects of the others. The nostalgia of the early 20th century and the interwar period involved significant powers of invention, for example, reflecting a need to remember the old homes not just as they were, but as Jews wanted them to have been. Likewise, trauma overtly involves amnesia, both in the sense that traumatic events are by definition incompletely recalled and perhaps unrecallable, and in the sense that the Holocaust in memory functions to obscure the prewar past, especially the positive aspects of relations between Jews and non-Jews. Amnesia, in turn, is not a simple condition of blankness. Rather, it is a combination of passive distance and active disavowal, and thus is shot through with chains of substitution, representation and misrepresentation, invention and misinvention.

The dialectic between loss and invention that has significantly shaped the collective memory of Eastern Europe in the American Jewish diaspora from the 1920s to the present day could also be called a dialectic of Jewish death and Jewish life. In our view, what distinguishes the current moment is the particular balance between them: it seems to us that the re-emergence of Eastern Europe in American Jewish consciousness in the digital age admits consciousness of Jewish death and Jewish life in equal parts, in contrast to earlier eras that more strongly favoured one side or the other. Eastern Europe is, today, at once a Jewish ruin and a place of Jewish return. It is a place of unpurged Jewish pain and a place where Jews enrich their lives with deeper and more tangible forms of memory, in the form of new contacts between Jews of shared ancestry, and in some cases the creation of relations between Jews and non-Jewish Poles and Ukrainians who also live with – contend with – Jewish absence.

Altogether, the Eastern Europe that is now emerging in American Jewish consciousness seems to us to contain three distinguishing characteristics. First, it is a place capacious enough to contain a full spectrum of Jewish responses to the past century of Jewish history – Jewish fortitude, self-help and success, as well as the trials of migration, assimilation and persecution, not to mention genocide – without the geopolitical pressures and implications that attach to debates around contemporary Israel. Second, Eastern Europe as a homeland is comparatively free from the redemptive discourse so deeply a part of the Zionist narrative, which is to say that the homeland stakes are comparatively lower. Third, and following from the previous point, Eastern Europe turns out to be a uniquely productive place, perhaps the best place, to confront the unhealed wounds of the Holocaust, which persist in unexpected ways across generations.

In tracking the various forms of American Jewish memory of Eastern Europe over many decades, we note, finally, a certain hard-to-name aspect of Jewish diasporic consciousness more broadly, a dimension of *golus* consciousness that might be called a generative lack, or the persistence of loss that gives as much as it takes away. In different forms for different generations, we see rupture that shelters revival within itself, and revival that does not explain away rupture. We see renewal that is both intracommunally Jewish, and intercommunally Jewish and non-Jewish. We see a spirit of reckoning that is constantly dissatisfied and productively non-conclusive, allowing both closure and re-opening. Foregone forms of American Jewish imagination of Eastern Europe contained all these things, and the emerging forms of American Jewish imagination of Eastern European homelands contain them still.

Acknowledgements

Thanks to the Tam Institute for Jewish Studies at Emory University for supporting the research on which this chapter is based. Also, thanks to Alan Bernstein, Gaëlle Fisher, Eric Goldstein, Leo Greenbaum, Mark Kiel, Deborah Lipstadt, Sam Norich, Elissa Sampson, Rivka Schiller, Alan Silberstein and Daniel Soyer for sharing their expertise and providing insightful comments.

References

AJDC Landsmanshaftn Department (n.d.). *Communication with the Felsztyner Relief Committee* [letters and invoices]. YIVO Institute for Jewish Research, RG335.7, Box 3, Folder 99. New York.

Aviv, C. and Shneer, D. (2005). *New Jews: The end of the Jewish diaspora.* New York: New York University Press.

Baker, Z.M., Boyarin, J. and Kugelmass, J. (1998). *From a ruined garden: The memorial books of Polish Jewry.* Bloomington, IN: Indiana University Press.

Bauer, Y. (2013). *Der Tod des Schtetls.* Berlin: Suhrkamp-Verlag.

Bernstein, A. (2010). The Felshtin trip. *The Felshtin Society* [online]. Available at: http://felshtin.org/the-felshtin-trip-may-20-2010 [accessed 27 April 2017].

Bernstein, A. (2016a). *Interview with O. Czendze on 17 May.* New York.

Bernstein, A. (2016b). President's message. *The Felshtin Society Newsletter*, 1(5), 2.

Blumenfeld, D. (1987). *My visit to Kielce, Poland in 1987* [report]. YIVO Institute for Jewish Research, RG1056, Box 1. New York.

Boyarin, D. and Boyarin, J. (2002). *Powers of diaspora: Two essays on the relevance of Jewish culture.* Minneapolis, MN: University of Minnesota Press.

Boym, S. (2001). *The future of nostalgia.* New York: Basic Books.

Brenner, M. (2016). *Israel: Traum und Wirklichkeit des jüdischen Staates. Von Theodor Herzl bis heute.* München: Verlag C.H. Beck.

Brostoff, M. (2008). Last call for landsmanshaften? Aid societies fold as old country ties fade, *The Forward* [online]. Available at: http://forward.com/news/14060/last-call-for-landsmanschaften-aid-societies-fold-02414 [accessed on 22 April 2017].

Chase, M. and Shaw, C. (1989). *The imagined past: History and nostalgia.* New York: Manchester University Press.

Coles, T. and Timothy, D.J., eds. (2004). *Tourism, diasporas, and space.* London: Routledge.

Conzen, K.N., Gerber, D.A., Morawska, E. *et al.* (1992). The invention of ethnicity: A perspective from the USA. *Journal of American Ethnic History*, 12(1), 3–41.

Diner, H.R. (2004). *The Jews of the United States, 1654 to 2000.* Berkeley, CA: University of California Press.

Diner, H.R. (2009). *We remember with reverence and love: American Jews and the myth of silence after the Holocaust, 1945–1962.* New York: New York University Press.

Drexler, M. (1984). *Meeting for this month* [journal]. YIVO Institute for Jewish Research, RG1198. New York.

Drucker, R. (n.d.). The first 90 years! *First Rymalower Young Men's B.A. Inc.* [online]. Available at: www.rymalower.com/id14.html [accessed on 23 April 2017].

Engelking, B. (2001). *Holocaust and memory: The experience of the Holocaust and its consequences. An investigation based on personal narratives.* London: Leicester University Press.

First Felshtiner Progressive Benevolent Association (1937). *Felshtin: Zamulbukh, lekoved tsum ondenk fun di Felshtiner kedoyshim*. New York: Posy-Shoulson Press.

Fischer, L. (2008). Whither *pogromshchina*: Historiographical synthesis or deconstruction?. *East European Jewish Affairs*, 38(3), 303–320.

Fischkin, B. (2016). Summary of informal meeting of Felshtin Society. *The Felshtin Society Newsletter*, 1(5), 3.

Fraternal Order of Bendin-Sosnowicer (2008). *The 65th annual Yizkor commemoration, 5 October* [letter]. YIVO Institute for Jewish Research, RG1198. New York.

Gitelman, Z. (2016). Introduction: Homelands, diasporas, and the islands in between. In: Z. Gitelman, ed., *The new Jewish diaspora. Russian-speaking immigrants in the United States, Israel, and Germany*. New Brunswick, NJ: Rutgers University Press, pp. 3–19.

Gottesfeld, C. (1937). *Mayn rayze iber Galitsye*. New York: Signal Press.

Gross, J.T. (2008). *Strach: Antysemityzm w Polsce tuż po wojnie. Historia moralnej zapaści*. Kraków: Wydawnictwo Znak.

Halbwachs, M. (1992). *On collective memory*. Chicago, IL: University of Chicago Press.

Hoffman, E. (2007). *Shtetl: The life and death of a small town and the world of Polish Jews*. New York: Public Affairs.

Katz, E.A. (2015). *Bringing Zion home: Israel in American Jewish culture, 1948–1967*. Albany, NY: State University of New York Press.

Kiel, M.W. (2004). Ambivalence and hope: Some reflections of a son of Czenstochover Jews. *The World Society of Częstochowa Jews and their Descendants* [online]. Available at: www.czestochowajews.org/papers/2004/kiel_eng.pdf [accessed on 23 April 2017].

Kiel, M.W. (2016). *Interview with O. Czendze on 25 May*. New York.

Kliger, H. (1986). Traditions of grass-roots organization and leadership: The continuity of landsmanshaftn in New York. *American Jewish History*, 76, 25–39.

Kobrin, R. (2010). *Jewish Bialystok and its diaspora*. Bloomington, IN: Indiana University Press.

Kugelmass, J. and Shandler, J. (1989). *Going home: How American Jews invent the old world*. Exhibition catalogue. New York: YIVO Institute for Jewish Research.

Magocsi, P.R. (2007). *Ukraine: An illustrated history*. Toronto: University of Toronto Press.

Mandel, W. (1985). *A visit to my hometown* [journal]. YIVO Institute for Jewish Research, RG1056, Box 1. New York.

Marschall, S. (2015). "Homesick tourism": Memory, identity and (be)longing. *Current Issues in Tourism*, 18(9), 876–892.

Metzker, I., ed. (1990). *A Bintel brief: Sixty years of letters from the Lower East Side to the Jewish Daily Forward*. New York: Schocken Books.

Miler, S. (1980). *Dobromil: Life in a Galician shtetl, 1890–1907*. New York: Loewenthal Press.

Moore, D.D. (1981). *At home in America: Second generation New York Jews*. New York: Columbia University Press.

The New Cracow Friendship Society (2015). *50 years of achievement*. New York: The New Cracow Friendship Society.

Newman, R. (1993). Pictures of a trip to the old country. *YIVO Annual*, 21, 223–239.

Novogrudok. (1931). [video recording]. New York: Aleksandr Harkavy.

Osborn, M.R. (2017). About the Rohatyn Jewish Heritage Program. *Rohatyn Jewish Heritage* [online]. Available at: http://rohatynjewishheritage.org/en/info/about [accessed on 23 April 2017].

Petrovsky-Shtern, Y. (2014). *The golden age shtetl: A new history of Jewish life in East Europe*. Princeton, NJ: Princeton University Press.

A Pictorial Review of Kolbishev. (1929). [video recording]. New York: Pesach Zuckerman.

Polland, A. and Soyer, D. (2012). *Emerging metropolis: New York Jews in the age of immigration, 1840–1920*. New York: New York University Press.

Polonsky, A. (2015). From Johannesburg to Warsaw: An ideological journey. In: C.R. Browning, S. Heschel and M.R. Marrus, eds., *Holocaust scholarship: Personal trajectories and professional interpretations*. London: Palgrave Macmillan, pp. 20–47.

Rajcher, A. (n.d.). The World Society. *The World Society of Częstochowa Jews and their Descendants* [online]. Available at: www.czestochowajews.org/eng_world_society.htm [accessed on 23 April 2017].

Reisman, B. (2006). Why I came to America. In: J. Cohen and D. Soyer, eds., *My future is in America: Autobiographies of Eastern European Jewish immigrants*. New York: New York University Press, pp. 35–105.

Rohatyner Young Men's Society Inc. (1966). *Minutes, 1 March* [minutes]. YIVO Institute for Jewish Research, RG1016. New York.

Roskies, D.G. (1999). *The Jewish search for a usable past*. Bloomington, IN: Indiana University Press.

Roskolenko, H. (1971). *The time that was then: The Lower East Side 1900–1914. An intimate chronicle*. New York: Dial Press.

Rymanower Young Men's Benevolent Association (1937). *35th Anniversary Banquet in Brooklyn, 24 October* [letter]. YIVO Institute for Jewish Research, RG123, Box 12, Folder 272. New York.

Schoenfeld, R. (2006). What drove me to America and my experiences in Europe and America. In: J. Cohen and D. Soyer, eds., *My future is in America: Autobiographies of Eastern European Jewish immigrants*. New York: New York University Press, pp. 160–188.

Shandler, J. (2013). Ponownie spojrzenie przybysza. In: Muzeum Historii Żydów Polskich, ed., *Listy do tych, co daleko*. Warszawa: Muzeum Historii Żydów Polskich, pp. 30–39.

Shandler, J. (2014). *Shtetl: A vernacular intellectual history*. New Brunswick, NJ: Rutgers University Press.

Silberstein, A. (2016). *Interview with O. Czendze on 19 May*. New York.

Soyer, D. (1986). Between two worlds: The Jewish landsmanshaftn and questions of immigrant identity. *American Jewish History*, 76(1), 5–24.

Soyer, D. (1993). The travel agent as broker between old world and new: The case of Gustave Eisner. *YIVO Annual*, 21, 345–368.

Soyer, D. (1997). *Jewish immigrant associations and American identity in New York, 1880–1939*. Cambridge, MA: Harvard University Press.

Soyer, D. (2000). Back to the future: American Jews visit the Soviet Union in the 1920s and 1930s. *Jewish Social Studies*, 6(3), 124–159.

Soyer, D. (2007). Transnationalism and Americanization in East European Jewish immigrant public life. In: J. Wertheimer, ed., *Imagining the American Jewish community*. Waltham, MA: Brandeis University Press, pp. 47–66.

Steinhagen, D. (2016). Wystawa "Żydzi Częstochowianie": Oni tworzyli historię tego miasta. *Gazeta Wyborcza Częstochowa* [online]. Available at: http://czestochowa.wyborcza.pl/czestochowa/1,48725,20721650,wystawa-zydzi-czestochowianie-oni-tworzyli-historie-tego.html [accessed on 22 April 2017].

Sztyma, T. (2013). "Tam" i "Teraz": Filmowe plenery z przeszłości. In: Muzeum Historii Żydów Polskich, ed., *Listy do tych, co daleko*. Warszawa: Muzeum Historii Żydów Polskich, pp. 16–27.

Virtual Sztetl (2016). Synagoga w Grzymałowie. *Virtual Sztetl* [online]. Available at: www. sztetl.org.pl/en/article/grzymalow/11,synagogues-prayer-houses-and-others/42296, synagoga-w-grzymalowie [accessed on 23 April 2017].

Weisser, M.R. (1985). *A brotherhood of memory: Jewish landsmanshaftn in the new world*. New York: Basic Books.

Young, J.E. (1993). *The texture of memory: Holocaust memorials and meaning*. New Haven, CT: Yale University Press.

Zemel, C.M. (2015). *Looking Jewish: Visual culture and modern diaspora*. Bloomington, IN: Indiana University Press.

9   The Macanese *Encontros*

Remembrance in diaspora 'homecomings'

Mariana Pinto Leitão Pereira

Introduction

This chapter highlights the interplay between memory, 'homecomings' and migrant associations in the context of a diaspora with affiliation to more than one 'place of origin'. It focuses on the Macanese diaspora gatherings, known as *Encontro(s)* and Youth *Encontro(s)*, which have taken place in Macau every three years since 1993 and since 2009 respectively; and the involvement of migrant associations, mostly known as *Casas de Macau* (CM) – translated as home(s) or house(s) – in organizing these gatherings and perpetuating remembrances of and connections to 'home'. Currently, thirteen *Casas*, located in diasporic places of settlement all over the world, are recognized by the Macanese Communities Council (CCM) as being officially involved in preparing the 'homecomings'. This chapter shows how Macanese personal and shared identity perceptions before, within and after the *Encontros* are influenced by the *Casas*' role of shaping the understanding and remembrance of one's roots.

In the first section, a summary of the Macanese migration is presented, followed by a brief discussion of the term 'homecoming' as a conceptual framework underlying the case study. The findings derive from archival research and analysis of 393 newsletters published online by the *Casas*, specifically of references related to the gatherings (see Arnone, 2017, for a similar methodology). Supplementing the study of the *Casas*' newsletters are data gathered from a two-hour semi-structured interview with the current President of the CCM, Mr J. Sales Marques; from a review of local newspapers in Macau; from informal conversations with three conveniently sampled participants of the 2016 *Encontro*; and consideration of an email contribution by a participant in the latest International Youth *Encontro* (referred to as Participant A). The three young adults (whose names are also withheld to protect their anonymity) were all born in the diaspora and shared their opinions, feelings and insights about the homecomings and their journey to Macau.

It is important to acknowledge that this research is also the result of self-reflective engagement and observation. I identify myself as a member of the Macanese diaspora, having been born and raised in Macau. As a teenager, shortly after the Handover, I emigrated to Portugal with my parents, where I joined the *Casa* in Lisbon. I moved back to Macau in 2014 and attended my first *Encontro* there in 2016, yet my only interaction with participants was during the opening dinner, for which I purchased a ticket. I was unable to join the rest of the events, as they were organized during working hours. In fact, the *Encontros* do not really cater much for locally resident Macanese, who are largely excluded from the events, unless they have contacts or volunteer in its organization. Despite much talk about (re)connecting with the local place and its social world, the *Encontros* are, in essence, about the journeying and gathering of the diaspora in Macau, a place constructed as 'home', and – as will be shown below – the assertion of Macanese identity.

The Macanese diaspora

Macau, a city located on the Southeast coast of China, was officially declared a Portuguese colony in 1887, although the Portuguese presence dated back to the mid-sixteenth century. In 1999, a new phase in Macau's history was marked by 'the Handover', as the city became a Special Autonomous Region of China. While the Portuguese presence shaped Macau in many ways, the Portuguese population never constituted the majority of the city's residents. Current data from the Statistics and Census Service (SCS) of Macau and from the Portuguese Migration Observatory (PMO) (SCS, 2016; PMO, 2017) show that 1.4% of the total population holds Portuguese nationality. Identifying the Macanese, however, poses several challenges.

Known as *filhos da terra* (sons of the land), the Macanese, a heterogeneous Eurasian ethnic minority, are traditionally defined as those born in or with ancestors from Macau; being descendants of intermarriages between Portuguese and Asians, they are of very diverse physical appearance and characterized by hybrid cultural traits embedded in their behaviour and lifestyle (Gaspar, 2015). Because Macau is not a nation-state, the Macanese have various nationalities besides Portuguese, making it almost impossible to identify and quantify the community, both those resident in Macau and those in the diaspora. In 2016, according to the SCS (2016: tables 35 and 36), around 8,500 people in Macau were local-born Portuguese, and around 10,698 people claimed to have Portuguese ancestors. This does not mean they identify themselves, or are seen, as Macanese. In fact, and with more than half of Macau's population being of recent migrant origin, the largest communities from mainland China, the Philippines and Vietnam, the Macanese minority is often mistaken as immigrant, given their physical appearance. Nevertheless, the Government of Macau is not only very much aware of the Macanese, but has provided support in many aspects, including for the *Encontros*, and has recognized its diasporic community.

Macanese emigration was driven during the second half of the nineteenth century by political, economic and social transformations in Asia. The spatial dispersion of the Macanese migrant population, many of Portuguese nationality, entailed moving almost exclusively to Hong Kong, Shanghai and other Chinese Treaty Ports, where local-born Macanese descendants began forming their own communities. During the Second World War, Macau became a neutral Portuguese haven, but also a host territory, with Shanghai and Hong Kong refugees seeing the land of their ancestors for the first time. After the War, Macau again experienced major migration outflows, including refugees who were Macanese descendants, in search of jobs, education and better livelihoods, this time beyond the borders of China (Dias, 2016: 21, 22). Based on this, Dias describes the Macanese migration as a diaspora, for entailing: a geographical scattering of long duration, linked by social networks and connections; awareness of the various dispersed communities; intergenerational transmission of common cultural traits; and integration processes, with the family playing a relevant role as source, maintainer and consolidator of the migratory fluxes and networks.

The 'multiple origins' of the Macanese diaspora have to be emphasized, and Macau has been, at different periods, both the origin of and host for its diaspora. In a previous study on the Macanese community following the Handover, Koo (2004: 33) questioned whether the diaspora's 'home' could be identified, not only given the change that Macau underwent after 1999, but also because of the imbricated temporal and spatial relations of the Macanese movements.

Although only partially comparable, Iorio and Corsale's (2013, 2017) research on the Transylvanian Saxons' homecomings is noteworthy here. Originating from Germany, this community settled in Transylvania (modern-day Romania) during the Middle Ages, but their descendants moved 'back' to Germany after the collapse of the Soviet Union. These Transylvanian Saxons living in Germany, and their descendants, then (re)visit Romania as their homeland. Iorio and Corsale (2013, 2017) speak of a 'double diaspora' to express this complex movement between two different 'places of origin' and the affiliations established both with Germany and Transylvania. The authors distinguish the first-generation migrants as 'homesick travellers' and the generations born in Germany as 'roots tourists'.

Part of the Macanese migration could be analysed as a 'double diaspora', but it becomes complex to understand how different migrant generations negotiate memories of Macau when this distinction depends on choosing which place is 'the origin'. Participants in the *Encontro* include Macanese born and raised in Macau; others who emigrated very young and established 'roots' elsewhere; some who were born outside Macau, yet, as returning refugees, temporarily called it 'home'; and others descending from the various waves of Macanese emigration dating back to the nineteenth century, many of whom have never even been to Macau.

Another specificity of the Macanese *Encontros* is the key position of the migrant associations within the diaspora. This parallels the involvement of clan associations in the homecomings of the Scottish diaspora (Basu, 2004), which have also benefited from official support from the government (Sim & Leith, 2013). Likewise, the Eritrean migrant associations and the Eritrean government function as active promoters of the connection to 'home' and between the diaspora (Arnone, 2017). However, these case studies do not involve more than one 'place of origin', and the role of the associations does not appear as central as in the Macanese *Encontros*. In short, the current research focuses on some singularities and unique permutations that contribute to nuancing the framework of 'homecomings', notably through the notion of multiple roots.

'Homecomings': a conceptual framework

'Homecomings' have been conceptually approached in different ways and by a variety of scholars. Traditionally, members of diaspora were defined in relation to a specific territory of origin or 'home', and their desire to return has been coined as 'homecoming', but the diaspora concept has shifted, along with the definition of a single unchanged 'home' (see e.g. Axel, 2004; Brah, 2005; Brubaker, 2005). 'Home' is no longer thought of as a static element, and the meaning and relevance of 'homeland' is constantly negotiated (Weingrod & Levy, 2006; Jansen & Löfving, 2007). The concept of 'home' is an inconsistent, contingent or fluid notion that can refer to multiple places, movements and conceptions at the same time; it is momentary and 'atemporal', embedded and constructed through feelings, memories and experiences; but it is also a concept that can portray a stable physical space which roots and frames (Basu, 2004; Bhandari, 2017; Golob, 2013; Marschall, 2017). The purpose here is not to define 'home', but to acknowledge that while it is changeable by its various temporalities, network of actors and spatialities, 'home' is still individually and collectively negotiated and constructed in the context of each diasporic reality and its attachment to 'roots'. Importantly, a shifting notion of 'home' affects the way members of diaspora relate to their attachments and ultimately define themselves.

Axel (2004: 27) perceives diaspora as a 'mobile category' of identification, encompassing different temporalities and characterized by networks connecting various micro-territories. In the 'diasporic condition' (Ang, 2011), identity is both in one's roots and the routes journeyed between places. Personal and shared remembrances become a key component in travel, especially in journeys undertaken to what is identified as a formal/ancestral 'home', as in the *Encontros*, where diasporic identities are negotiated and group consciousness and social networks (re)created.

While identities are felt and reworked in the present, diasporas tend to have a nostalgic relationship with 'homeland' (Sim & Leith, 2013: 260). In fact, the interplay between mobility, nostalgia and belonging is often understood as an underlying characteristic of the homecoming phenomenon, in parallel to the entwining of temporal dimensions of movement with geographical concepts of 'here and there' (Golob, 2013: 157). Nostalgia, however, does not always entail return (Jansen & Löfving, 2007: 9), and having a 'homing desire' differs from wishing to visit, or even have, a 'homeland' (Brah, 2005: 177), a significant insight in the current understanding of diaspora. Nevertheless, nostalgia can become a vehicle through which people without personal recollections of the 'ancestral home' establish a connection to places they have never seen. Those who return to this 'home' with personal memories might have to deal with the altered state of the remembered environment, the changes in its inhabitants (in comparison to how one remembered them) and the changes of the self. In what Marschall (2017: 8) terms 'the memory gaze', they scrutinize the former home, finding both contrasts with and affirmations of their remembrances.

Diaspora 'homecomings', then, express a process of journeying and encountering, entailing the negotiation of relations to certain shared places; the (re)collecting, (re)making and (re)evaluating of memories and narratives; and the unfolding and shaping of social networks that bind the dispersed communities (Marschall, 2017). But as Jansen and Löfving (2007) concluded, it is not whether people are able to go where 'home' is, but whether there is, in the present, a connection and willingness to have a 'homeland orientation'. This is vital for approaching the Macanese diaspora, characterized by having multi-layered identity affiliations, as a dual-roots relationship is held both with Macau and Portugal, considered to be ancestral homes, while Hong Kong or Shanghai are described as 'home' for some; moreover, a third-level affiliation exists for these people's descendants born in countries like Australia. The point is not 'which is home for whom', or 'who was born where', but to take as a baseline how Macau was chosen for the *Encontros*, as a mediating space for the multiple attachments that bring the dispersed communities together. From these attachments, it might be possible to reflect on what kind of relationship the migrants then establish with the mediating place.

Considering such understanding of 'homecomings', the following section will present an analysis of the *Casas'* newsletters, as they unfold the intricacies of the *Encontros* and the trips undertaken by hundreds of Macanese from different generations and, let us say, origins. The research shows *Casas* as major actors in organizing and defining the character of the homecomings, and mediating the processes of identity and remembrance formation within what initially appear to be pilgrimages of nostalgia, but are in fact much more.

The *Casas de Macau*

Before 1999, the *Casas* were established with support from the Portuguese Government to strengthen the Macanese diasporic network outside of Macau. After the Handover, the associations were acknowledged by, and have received support from, the Chinese Government of Macau. The following list of associations, their establishment date and locations, reflects the dispersion of the Macanese communities: Hong Kong (Club Lusitano, 1866); the United States of America (*União Macaense Americana*, 1959 – UMA; *Casa de Macau* Inc, 1995; Lusitano Club of California, 1984 – LC); Portugal, 1966 (CMPT); Canada (in Toronto, 1993 – CMT; the Macao Club, 1993; the Macau Cultural Association of Western Canada, 1989; in Vancouver, 1995 – CMV); Brazil (in Rio de Janeiro, 1991 – CMRJ; in São Paulo, 1989 – CMSP); Australia, 1990 (CMA); and the United Kingdom, 2015 (Almeida, 2013). (References to the *Casas'* newsletters below are identified by the acronyms provided here.)

Notwithstanding the Macanese elusive character and its multi-local origins, the overall guiding principles of membership acceptance to the *Casas* are the requirements of either having been born in Macau or being of Macanese ancestry.

Since their inception, the associations have celebrated Macau as the diaspora's roots; they strive to safeguard, promote and foster interest in and awareness of Macanese culture, heritage and history. All *Casas'* mission statements, values and activities reflect not just how they mediate the fluidities of belonging and being, but also their contribution and effort to form and sustain group consciousness, while negotiating and fostering shared Macanese cultural references and memories (Augusto, 2016; CMA, October 2013; CMA, 2017a, 2017b; CMPT, website, 2017; CMV, 2017a, 2017b; UMA, Spring 2008). The *Casas* implicitly define 'Macaneseness', a term previously employed by Koo (2004), as selected cultural aspects are re-enacted and constructed in the association's context, both physically and in the members' memories.

Despite a somewhat specific structure, each association includes elected members of different generations, who volunteer to join the executive board or organizational team and are responsible for specific aspects such as the cultural section or the newsletters (Augusto, 2016; LC, Winter 2013). Membership fees are due in all *Casas*, apart from the recently created one in the UK, and the collected funds are used for running the association and organizing activities. In some cases, foundations were established (e.g. in Portugal) to assure that donations and financial subsidies provided by private and public entities after the Handover would be well managed and spent in supporting the association and its members (e.g. in the form of bursaries) (CCM, *Estatutos*, 2017a, 2017b; Fundação CM, website).

One of these entities is the Macanese Communities Council (CCM), who is responsible, among other things, for raising sponsorship for the *Encontros*, the most desirable and costly of organized activities taking place in Macau. The partial funding, distributed to those attending the homecomings, derives not from membership fees but an array of international and Macau-based sponsors (CMT, December 2003; CCM, *Estatutos*; Marques, 2017). The CCM was created in 2004 as an umbrella private institution that represents, in Macau, the interests of all Macanese communities, and serves as a supporting platform when dealing with the local Government of Macau or other associations. With its coordination and supervision, preparations for each gathering are made concurrently by the associations it encompasses: in 2017, CCM included thirteen *Casas* and eight Macau-based entities, none of which was considered a 'migrant' association, but instead targeted the overall Macanese (CCM, Governing Bodies).

Most significantly, being a member of a *Casa* recognized by the CCM became the baseline for eligibility to receive the specially allocated subsidies for the *Encontro*. The newsletters show that some participants joined the associations primarily to get the financial support for the homecoming, which prompted *Casas* to announce that subsidies would only be given to members paying subscription fees for the past two consecutive years (CMA, April 2013; CMT, March 2007; UMA, July–September 2015). Since subsidies can increase depending on the events' attendance levels, these became a reflection of the success of the *Encontros* themselves (Barbosa, 2 December 2010). The associations gained a pivotal and somewhat governing role in organizing the *Encontros* (CMV, July 2004). The homecomings, then, create the opportunity for the *Casa* leaders to personally meet with other CCM members, to make joint decisions and prepare for the next years of activities (CMA, April 2014; Marques, 2017).

In parallel to the CCM, other collaborators, such as Macau's Tourism Office (MGTO), provide support at organizational and infrastructural levels, the *Encontros* being a way to promote Macau as a destination. The Institute of Tourism Studies has been involved in organizing many events, mainly related to Macanese culture and gastronomy (CMA, Winter 2008; CCM, 2016; UMA, Winter 2010). The *Casas* themselves are expected to promote Macau at touristic, economic and entrepreneurial levels in the countries where they are established, justifying part of the financial support provided by the government (Pereira, 2007: 21). The event is certainly significant for the local tourism industry, as hundreds of people must be accommodated, even some of those with family in Macau, preferring to stay in hotels for various reasons (Anonymous B, 2016). Apart from the accommodation providers, revenue is moreover generated through catering services and transport companies, but the comprehensive impact the *Encontros* and Youth *Encontros* have on an already highly touristic city is still to be determined.

The *Encontros* of the Macanese communities

The first *Encontro*, whose mentor was the Macanese Lourenço da Conceição, himself a migrant (Pereira, 2010a), happened on 1 November 1993, with official support from the Portuguese Government. Subsequent gatherings occurred in 1996, 1999, 2001 and then every three years thereafter, the next one being planned for 2019. Since 2009, Youth *Encontros* have taken place triennially under more specific conditions than the general *Encontros*, to target the *Casas'* young members. Overall, all *Encontros* last almost one week and are an intense combination of sponsored organized activities, such as debates on identity, history, genealogy and language; book launches; guided tours; Catholic masses; cultural performances; and, most of all, opportunities to socialize and refresh memories. At the centre lies Macau, a physical space, for many associated with personal memories; or an imagined and symbolic one, created through descriptions and shared narratives of belonging and being, as with so many other host-country-born members of diasporas (e.g. Tie, Holden & Park, 2015), and – importantly – narratives perpetuated through the activities of the associations.

Staging the *Encontros* along similar configurations, while also offering some novelties, was the result of several decisions that structured the homecomings; for example, to always take place towards the end of the year; lasting no more than eight days; with all meals, and some shows, being provided free of charge (CMV, December 2000; CMV, July 2001). Typically, participants with identifying badges are taken around to presentations and performances prepared jointly by the associations in Macau and the *Casas*; guided tours to historical places are on offer, as well as book launches or homages to relevant figures in the community. During the *Encontros*, multilingual groups of people with diverse physical features can be seen excitedly strolling in the streets, recalling lost places and finding known faces (LC, Winter 2013).

The largest participating groups usually come from the USA, Canada and Australia, in comparison to Brazil, Portugal or Hong Kong. Between 1993 and 1996, the number of participants doubled (circa 600 and 1,200 respectively), and from then onwards the number fluctuated around 1,500 (UMA, Winter 2007). However, not all members of the *Casas* join the homecoming. For instance, in April 2017, the Casa in Toronto registered 213 membership renewals, but only sixty travelled to Macau for the 2016 *Encontro* (CMT, June 2017). Although there is not necessarily a direct correlation between identity and the frequency of 'homecoming' trips (Sim & Leith, 2013), the attendance rate of participants from Hong Kong (e.g. forty-four in 2010; Pereira, 2010b), a city not even one hour away by boat, raises the question of how one's distance from 'home' influences people's identity, decision about joining migrant associations and homecoming events. The contextual experiences created in the *Encontro*, the social bonding, sense of belonging, nostalgia and shared stories (Almeida, 2013: 17; LC, Summer 2012), might become relevant enough to justify the presence of those living close.

In fact, whereas the homecomings were devised to target the diaspora, there appears to be rising participation by 'locals', those residing in Macau. For instance, 894 diaspora-based participants versus 646 locals were recorded in 2016 (Almeida, 2016), although the figure only reflects residency, not whether these 'locals' consider themselves Macanese. It also does not distinguish people who continued to be part of a migrant association even after having 'moved back' to Macau, and who join the *Encontros* through their diasporic *Casa*, not least perhaps to access the associated financial advantages. As mentioned earlier, most Macau-based Macanese, on the contrary, appear to have little contact with the homecomings, unless they are involved in organizing or attending specific activities. Similarly to Sim and Leith's (2013) research on Scottish homecomings, Macanese homecomings appear to be more about connecting the diaspora with Macau than connecting with local Macanese. For those in the diaspora who cannot attend, most of what is debated during the conferences and events remains largely unknown, except for basic newspaper coverage or sporadic comments through the newsletters. The impact the gatherings have on the local population or the wider diaspora community is largely undocumented. The same applies to the extent of contact between diaspora participants and locals, including the frequency of meetings and activities with family or friends outside the events.

Most participants join the *Encontros* in the context of the *Casas*, rarely on their own initiative. Some Macanese travel to Macau outside the *Encontros*, as for them the associations and concept of diasporic community are not primary motivators. Little information is available about these travellers, mostly because of the difficulty in identifying them based on their nationality or immigration status. The structure of the triennial events, though, offers many advantages in terms of transportation, accommodation, participation in subsidized activities and possibilities of meeting others from the community. Participants also have high expectations regarding the individual events and the overall success of the gathering, since their aim is usually to enjoy Macau and be with fellows (CMT, December 2004).

Concerns surrounding the definition of Macanese identity, and the relations between the various diasporic communities and between the diaspora and Macau-based Macanese, are some of the aspects debated during these *Encontros*. The endangered language Patuá, music, religion and gastronomy form focal points for workshops and various events, all of which contribute to constructing these cultural expressions as common traits that unite the Macanese dispersed in diaspora. Moreover, the gatherings are opportunities for the *Casas* to showcase their involvement and vitality in safeguarding their concept of Macanese culture, while local organizations and institutions take the opportunity to solidify relations with the diaspora associations, establishing agreements of cooperation, exchange and joint projects (CMT, February 2007; Rangel, 2006: 26). Participants represent themselves and the *Casa* they belong to, which essentially means that the *Casas* expect these members to join all the *Encontro*'s events. Nevertheless, some 'home-comers' wander in search of their own places of memory and childhood, ending up skipping the scheduled programme (Anonymous C, 2016; CMA, March 2007).

Narratives of the *Encontros*

Written testimonies share the general view that the *Encontros* are 'a kind of pilgrimage . . . a chance to reaffirm . . . identity as Macanese and re-establish links' (UMA, Winter 2010), especially through encounters with friends and relatives. Symbolically charged events and ritualistic actions – e.g. the traditional group photo on the iconic Ruins of St. Paul's stairway or placing flowers on the Monument to the Macanese Diaspora in Macau – show how the gatherings (re)confirm the connection between the diaspora and Macau and become a platform for defining and affirming 'Macaneseness'. Inaugurated in 2004, the monument moreover represents an official acceptance of the Macanese community and its diaspora on behalf of the Chinese Government of Macau (LC, Fall 2013; Pereira, 2007: 21).

Debates and decision-making about matters concerning the Macanese communities and the diaspora are purposefully planned to coincide with the gatherings. For instance, in the 1996 *Encontro*, representatives in a deliberation on identity made the significant decision to accept those born outside of Macau as being Macanese. In July 2000, following the Handover, the presidents of the recognized *Casas* at the time met in Portugal, confirming their close ties with that country and the uncertainties of where the diasporic community could root itself. Among the topics for discussion was the definition or affirmation of who could be considered Macanese, now understood as either someone born in Macau or in the diaspora, but also anyone desiring or aspiring to be Macanese (CMV, July 2000). By clarifying this position anew, the message was that Macau's new political status would not mean the end of the Macanese communities. Place-bound identities were thus re-shaped and reaffirmed as part of a multi-local diaspora, even though the significance of Macau for those born elsewhere can be ambivalent.

An expression of this multi-locality are the optional pre- or post-*Encontro* trips that some *Casas* began organizing to Hong Kong, Shanghai or other Asian places with ties to the Macanese diaspora (UMA, Summer 2010). Referred to as 'pre- or post-reunion tours' by the *Casa* in Australia (CMA, March 2007), the newsletters provide little explanation about the choice of these destinations. Hong Kong and Shanghai are the birthplace of many Macanese in diaspora, but these tours do not appear to entail such emotionally charged activities as revisiting places related to one's past. An exception is perhaps the socializing events at the Club Recreio, a Portuguese association in Hong Kong, which was frequented by many Macanese around the period of the Second World War (UMA, Winter 2013).

Attachments are differently experienced during the *Encontros*, depending on the participants' own situation: as mentioned earlier, some visit Macau for the first time; others return after long absences; others routinely come to Macau but organize their trips to coincide with the triennial gatherings (Anonymous A, 2016). Participants describe missing Macau when living far away, but when in Macau, their country of residence becomes a place of belonging, based on comparisons induced by the visit (Anonymous A, 2016). Recent urban developments in Macau render familiarity even more challenging. A fondly remembered or imagined Macau clashes with its current physical appearance witnessed during the *Encontro*, with the disappearance of 'places and buildings of my memory' in the name of development (CMA, July 2011). In the context of the 2007 *Encontro*, some participants described the experience not as revisiting Macau, but as getting to know the new Macau, albeit with the past remaining present through legacy and heritage (Pereira, 2007: 21).

Changed geographies are commonly addressed in the newsletters, accompanied by feelings of sadness, grief and astonishment, and for some, the memories of a past Macau create greater 'homesickness'. As a coping mechanism, past geosocial references, such as the place where someone's old house was, are used for orientation in arranging meetings and understanding where venues are during the *Encontros*. Macau also becomes synonymous with its people, implying that Macau can be wherever Macanese people are. Encountering familiar faces in Macau, even mere acquaintances, is described as one of the most significant moments of all *Encontros*, creating a diasporic intimacy. As Boym (2001: 245) observed, such encounters lead participants to recognize and (re)connect with one another, something which in other contexts or under different circumstances would likely have a far less meaningful impact.

Participants who failed to have such experiences expressed sentiments of disappointment and loneliness; a lack of purpose in visiting Macau. Moreover, the physical changes in the place of origin may be perceived as so profound and the rupture felt so deeply that some can only make connection with selected cultural elements, such as the local food. Some participants confessed not wanting to return, because Macau had nothing to do with them anymore (Almeida, 2013: 4; Diniz, 6 December 2013b; Doré, Almeida & Moura, 2001: 267, 278–280, 284; Gaspar, 2015: 222). Such sentiments – migrants travelling to their 'home' and finding that it has changed too dramatically to still be 'theirs' – are of course far from unique to the Macanese community (Graburn, 2017: 270).

The Youth *Encontros*

The relationship to Macau is felt very differently between those who were born or had lived there, and the descendant generations, who are visiting the city for the first time. Some insights on the perceptions of the latter are provided from the recently created Youth *Encontros*, organized by the CCM and the Macau-based Macanese Youth Association. While structurally resembling the main *Encontros*, the Youth gatherings are focused on presenting to the younger members of the associations what are considered core traits of Macanese identity. Carefully chosen events, speeches and workshops provide the best of Macau's cultural heritage, while also featuring modern developments and future projects. They are organized to show how traditions can be carried out and ties to Macanese culture can be strengthened in the diaspora through the diasporic associations (UMA, Summer 2012).

In this context, the *Casas* are indispensable. In the pre-Youth *Encontro* stage, young participants who would like to join must send an application letter to their *Casa*, guarantee their participation in all activities organized while in Macau and submit a report upon return from the gathering. This process, which does not apply to the normal *Encontros*, is justified because accommodation and airfares are totally covered for three young representatives from each *Casa*. It is meant to be an incentive for the younger generations to get involved with the migrant associations and deepen their sense of 'Macaneseness' (CMA, December 2009; CMT, September 2007). Of course, anyone paying for their own trip and fitting the category of 'young' is most welcome to join. In 2015, the criteria to apply for funding were age (between eighteen and thirty-five), being of Macanese descent or being a voting member for a period determined by each *Casa* (CMA, April 2015). The *Casa* in Portugal announced that the selected youths would also have to reside permanently in Portugal and have Portuguese nationality (CMPT, February 2009).

Members who apply, however, are not necessarily limited to second, third or fourth migrant-descendant generations living in diaspora. Young Macanese who were born in Macau, but left in their teens, can become part of a *Casa* while living or studying abroad, and potentially receive funding from there to join the Youth *Encontros* (Anonymous C, 2016). Still, for the majority, the experience of the Youth gatherings is quite different from that of the general *Encontros*, as the focus is really on those who have no attachments or social networks in Macau. While Youth *Encontros* are a way to meet other young people from the Macanese diaspora, all events are carefully designed to provide experiences and contacts that pave the way to take an interest in the future of the associations and of the dispersed communities themselves (CMT, January 2014). The *Casas*, older members of the community and even previous participants of the *Encontros* play a role in disseminating certain narratives and images of Macau, exposing the youth to what Macau 'really is' and hence creating expectations of the place before the young members embark on their trips. As one youth participant summed up: 'Not having ever participated in an *Encontro*, I was very curious to learn what all the talk was about . . . why the word '*Encontro*' seemed all mystical' (CMT, December 2015; CMV, May 2013).

A constructed notion of Macau is hence created in the context of the associations; Macau is presented as the root of one's identity, the place where one can experience 'what [it] is like to truly be Macanese' (LC, Winter–Spring 2008). Genealogy is a significant element here; it confirms the ancestry of those attending and is enhanced through acknowledgement by other participants, most especially when meeting previously unknown relatives (CMV, May 2013; UMA, Winter 2007). For many of the youth participants, the place of their ancestors' roots is an unknown, new and yet somewhat familiar destination. They hold an idealized image based on photos and the older generation's personal memories, but they can experience a sense of discomfort when their visit reveals divergence from how they have pictured the place (Doré *et al.*, 2001: 286).

In the Youth *Encontros*, much attention is thus paid to actively crafting the participants' experiences, as opposed to the normal *Encontros*, which rely on providing contexts where members create their own experiences and remembrances. What participants encounter is important to all these diasporic gatherings, but the goal of the Youth *Encontros* is more specifically to encourage the formation and refreshing of memories based on personal experiences; for family stories to be reaffirmed and attachments created to places previously only known through mediated sources. Most significant is for youngsters to confirm their Macanese identity, reassure them about their fitting in with a dispersed (imagined) community, and realize their own role in the migrant association they represent (CMT, July 2012; see also Huang, Norman & Ramshaw, 2016; LC, Fall 2009).

In 2009, during the youth plenary session, participants gathered to discuss issues faced by young Macanese in the diaspora. Some of the addressed key points focused on improving the *Casas*' activities, communication and the direct relationship between the associations' youths with Macau (Silva, Ribeiro, Reid & Narciso, 2009: 6). *Casas* and the CCM expect youth representatives to help define, in their own way, the mission and values of the *Casas*, and devise governance models in which youths can have a voice. The experiences of the *Encontro* are used to improve the functioning of each association and contribute to its aims, justifying the very membership of the youths (CMT, June 2009 and September 2011).

The local government in Macau has shown enthusiasm for the *Encontros* in general and has especially involved itself in the Youth *Encontros*. Both for Macau and for China, these young members might develop a professional interest in the region, representing a future potential for enhancing the role of Macau, and contribute to China's development, both nationally and internationally. The fact that the youths represent sources of expertise, with the capacity to connect to the local Macanese, and are in theory able to adapt more easily to the society in Macau, has also been acknowledged by the diaspora itself. It is not only the link to their ancestor's place of origin but also the branding of Macau as a land of business opportunities that is strategically mobilized to draw these youths' attention in carefully structured plenary sessions and roundtables within the Youth *Encontros* (Almeida, 2012; CMA, December 2009; CMT, July 2012; UMA, July–September 2015).

Upon returning to their country of birth or residence, youth representatives are greeted with much hope and perceived as ambassadors for the diaspora's opportunities in the future. The gatherings are catalysts in this process and an invaluable personal experience benefiting both the participants and the *Casas* (CMV, May 2010). Individual accounts of what happens after the *Encontro* have not been collected for this research, but one of the testimonies in the association newsletters described how a youth representative from UMA decided to return to Macau for a whole year to conduct research and learn Portuguese (UMA, Fall 2009). This is very exceptional, as few participants of both types of *Encontros* consider moving to Macau, having established a family abroad and adapted to their new livelihoods (Diniz, 4 December 2013a).

Trends for the future

Whereas the *Encontro* is an appealing event, associated with sponsored travel, excitement, encounters and entertainment, joining the associations and participating in their regular activities is a very different matter. The difficulty in attracting members, especially youths, and motivating them to become active is a constant topic of concern for most *Casas* (CMT, December 2003). The *Encontros* are also only attended by a portion of the general membership, on account of time constraints or financial difficulties. For instance, about one third of the members of the Lusitano Club went to the 2016 *Encontro* (LC, 2017a, 2017b; LC, Winter 2016). This Club is known for having some of the highest participation levels. Its focus lies on events specially targeting youngsters and organizing family-based functions, i.e. creating contexts in which Macanese heritage and cultural characteristics (e.g. food or language) form an integral part of the activities (LC, Winter 2013). Conversely, in the *União Macaense Americana*, it appears that membership among the younger members is not really sought for its social networking character, but for deepening knowledge of one's ancestry, stories and Macanese identity and culture (UMA, Fall 2007). Joining the *Encontros* could be the consequence of an existing curiosity instilled by the family and the *Casas*, and potentially the beginning of a deeper interest in the associations, given the sense of belonging that the gatherings engender (CMT, September 2011; UMA, July–September 2015).

If the older generations are the carriers of knowledge and memories of the past, and the younger members represent the future, it is understandable why in 2012 the three *Casas* in the USA proposed that both types of *Encontros* should be organized in parallel, hence creating opportunities for the stories told in the diaspora to be contextualized. So far, this step has not yet been taken. The presidents of the *Casas* noted that many youths have in fact shown an interest in joining the Youth *Encontros*, but had to be excluded due to limited subsidies (UMA, Winter 2012). Perhaps bringing these younger members into the general

Encontros would ease the fatalistic references to the disappearance of the community, and loss of its culture, given the reduced involvement of the younger generation. The notion that the Macanese are in extinction has been voiced elsewhere (e.g. Carvalho, 2015), yet some rather see this as an identity adaptation to current times and changed circumstances.

Curiously, in the newsletters, a complex intergenerational dialogue surfaces. While the older generation generally perceives that the future of Macau and Macanese identity is dim, members of the younger generation exhibit a range of divergent responses. Some are completely disinterested; others are aware of their responsibility to be actively involved (with their family's support) and may even complain about not being able to do more (Augusto, 2016: 77; LC, Fall 2009; LC, Winter 2013). However, what transpires widely across the community is the sense of losing the collective cultural identity. This can be observed both in Macau, where this identity is undergoing a metamorphosis due to the changed socio-political situation, and in the diaspora, where descendants want to blend in cultural aspects of their own country of birth. Clearly the issue is primarily one of mentality and not lack of support, as we have seen that funding is provided by various sources, including the Chinese Government (see Unknown, 2010; UMA, April–June 2016).

Meanwhile, a most recent event may show a change in the way the *Casas* further negotiate the notion of diaspora. The first International Youth *Encontro*, which took place from 13–20 August 2017 in San Francisco (USA), was solely organized and partially funded by the Lusitano Club of California, targeting young Macanese adults over twenty-one (LC, Fall 2017). According to one of the participants (Participant A, email correspondence), any young Macanese, not necessarily related to an association, could have joined. This, in itself, was quite a significant decision, possibly opening the path for Macanese non-affiliated with associations to be integrated in some of the events. An important emphasis was given in the newsletter when describing the purpose of this gathering: 'to learn more about our unique Portuguese Macanese heritage' (LC, Fall 2017: 2). Identifying this heritage within the context of a gathering that was not organized in any of the spaces considered to be an 'ancestral home' or 'place of origin' is quite significant for a diaspora that is characterized as having multi-local roots.

Participants included representatives from the three *Casas* in the USA, as well as some young adults from Macau and Portugal. The aim of what the organizers call a 'mini *Encontro*' (LC, Fall 2017: 12) was to create a precedence and encourage other *Casas* to organize similar events for the young Macanese outside of Macau to meet, a strategy in which the associations can assume a more central role in supporting and strengthening the diasporic network and identity, as well as interconnecting various pockets of the diasporic community. Beyond the logistical reasons prompting the decentralization, one may interpret this decision (especially if sustained in the future) as a significant symbolic gesture that tells us much about perceptions of roots, home and the future of Macanese identity in the diaspora.

Discussion and final remarks

Compared to individually arranged types of diasporic 'return' travel, typically centred on visiting significant sites and social relations, the *Encontros* of the Macanese diaspora resemble in many ways the organized homecoming tours of other diasporas discussed in the scholarly literature. For instance, they are based on a sense of nostalgia and a quest for identity and belonging; they are focused on visceral, emotional experiences of home/land; and they include highly symbolic and ritualistic performances. However, this chapter has also illustrated how the Macanese *Encontros* are different from other case studies.

Perhaps the most unique characteristic is that they bring together participants with triple or more identity affiliations. Unlike other homecomings that involve dispersed members of diaspora identifying partly with their country of residence and partly with one specific place of origin, the Macanese ultimately descend from two ancestral 'places of origin' (Portugal and Macau), and possess more complex and multiple identity affiliations.

Other distinguishing features are the fundamental change of the socio-political landscape in Macau and the fact that the *Encontros* have received continuous governmental support from two different states: the Portuguese, before 1999, and the Chinese Government, following the Handover. The change of political status caused notions of belonging to tremble, but this was surpassed by reassurances of new possibilities and governmental support, which so far have indeed continued. The diaspora's acceptance and adaptation to Macau's new position may be reciprocal to this support and to the new Government's acknowledgement of the community's importance and connection to Macau.

The chapter has moreover highlighted the exceptionally powerful role played by the *Casas*, whose activities construct contexts for sharing and (re)working memories of Macau, as well as placing certain fluid cultural traits, notably language and gastronomy, as bonding elements at the core of 'Macaneseness'. Most important among these activities are the *Encontros* and understandings of 'roots', irrespective of whether Macau is one's place of origin, which are gained through personal and recounted homecoming experiences. These are partly staged by the organizers, who seize the opportunity to showcase how they safeguard Macanese traditions and cultural identity. The newsletters contain a variety of accounts that express multifarious experiences at the homecoming events. They emphasize the central role of memory and its sharing and revival as the condition for the community's continuity; genealogies and family stories; feelings of connection, identity reaffirmations and cultural (re)encounters; and the challenges in finding one's place within the community, the migrant associations and sometimes one's sense of belonging. These narratives ripple back to the *Casas* when members return from the gathering and are then included in strategies for perpetuating and affirming the community's cultural and social features, which in turn influence the organization of the next *Encontro*.

Despite the difficulty in separating different generations of *Encontro* participants (based on the methodology of the current research), some relevant distinctions were noted. For first-generation emigrés, or those who lived in Macau and created their own first-hand narratives, the multifaceted, well-structured and carefully planned one-week gatherings provide opportunities for re-encountering what was once familiar, and recapture, confirm or challenge one's memories of Macau and perceptions of themselves and others as Macanese. These are the foundations for revisiting and for greater emotional attachments or disappointments to be felt. The gathering embodies the epitome of a nostalgic return, of an event to be remembered, but also sometimes of an experience not to be repeated, due to expectations not being met. While the *Encontros* have become a social obligation for some, others do not feel the need to go back. Besides the Handover, the decreasing chance of meeting familiar people, the disappearance of commonly known places and changes in the urban landscape distinguish the Macau of the present with personal memories of the past.

Those who have never lived in Macau take homecomings as an opportunity to build their personal relationship; to create experiences to be remembered; and to confirm or rework their images of 'Macau as roots', derived from the stories of parents and activities of the *Casas*. This is especially seen in the Youth *Encontros*: whereas the general *Encontros* provide a context for the participants' memories and 'Macaneseness' to be reasserted, 're-lived' and even updated, the Youth *Encontros* are focused on identifying and presenting core traits and narratives of being Macanese to those with little or no personal memories of Macau. While the general *Encontros* focus on Macau as 'roots in the present' and on connecting participants with past experiences and memories, in the Youth *Encontros*, the past and its heritage are presented as incentives for the future and Macau is branded a place of opportunities.

Among youth participants are feelings and a sense of belonging shaped before the trip, partly by the *Casas*, which are then affirmed during the homecomings – not least perhaps because there is a certain expectation to feel them. What is remembered of the Youth *Encontro*'s experience is then re-enacted in the associations when participants return, a kind of reassurance of the belonging, which is expressed in the reports submitted as a pre-condition for the fully paid event trip – again diverging from general *Encontros*, where participants do not have to share their experiences with the *Casas*.

Despite drawbacks and challenges, the Macanese homecoming events are still regarded as important. However, the first International Youth *Encontro* organized in San Francisco also indicates the potential for different future directions. It will be interesting to see how future events will shape the 'longing' and nostalgic discourses centred on Macau and how this will influence the diaspora's perceptions of its own multi-rootedness. Lastly, this chapter has also highlighted a number of unanswered questions and shown that the *Encontros* and their local and diasporic impacts are yet to be fully understood. Empirical research based on interviews or other qualitative methods would need to be conducted to explore in depth how the *Encontros* influence participants' relationship with Macau, their sense of diasporic belonging and various other dimensions of the homecomings that could not be assessed through the methodology of this research.

To the Macau of today, of yesterday, of forever.

(Almeida, 2013: 3)

Acknowledgement

I would like to acknowledge the comments made by António R. J. Monteiro.

References

Almeida, F. (2012). Jovens macaenses descobrem terra de oportunidades. *Jornal Tribuna de Macau* [online], 11 April. Available at: http://arquivo.jtm.com.mo/view.asp?dT=400303010 [accessed 18 June 2017].

Almeida, H. (2013). Cuza ta fazer!?! Encontro 2013 reúne Macaenses de todo o mundo. *Jornal Tribuna de Macau* [online], 12 December. Available at: http://jtm.com.mo/record/2013/12Dec/Revista%20Encontro%20Macaenses%202013.pdf [accessed 18 June 2017].

Almeida, I. (2016). Um encontro 'vivido por cada um à sua maneira'. *Jornal Tribuna de Macau* [online], 25 November. Available at: http://jtm.com.mo/local/um-encontro-vivido-por-cada-um-a-sua-maneira [accessed 17 June 2017].

Ang, I. (2011). Unsettling the national: Heritage and diaspora. In: H. Anheier & Y. R. Isar, eds., *Heritage, Memory and Identity*, 1st ed. London: Sage, pp. 82–94.

Anonymous A, Anonymous B & Anonymous C (2016). Oral testimonies, 30 November. Encontro 2016, Macau.

Arnone, A. (2017). Returning, imagining and recreating home from the diaspora: Tourism narratives of the Eritrean diaspora in Italy. In: S. Marschall, ed., *Tourism and Memories of Home: Migrants, Displaced People, Exiles and Diasporic Communities*. Bristol: Channel View Publications, pp. 156–177.

Augusto, P. (2016). *As Festas da Casa de Macau do Rio de Janeiro*. Macau: Instituto Internacional de Macau, Real Gabinete Português de Leitura.

Axel, B. K. (2004). The context of diaspora. *American Anthropological Association*, 19(1), 26–60.

Barbosa, P. (2010). Pela renovação. *Jornal Tribuna de Macau* [online], 2 December. Available at: http://arquivo.jtm.com.mo/news/20101206/news_images/00_06_12_2010.pdf [accessed 16 June 2017].

Basu, P. (2004). My own island home: The Orkney homecoming. *Journal of Material Culture*, 9(1), 27–42.

Bhandari, K. (2017). Travelling at special times: The Nepali diaspora's yearning for belongingness. In: S. Marschall, ed., *Tourism and Memories of Home: Migrants, Displaced People, Exiles and Diasporic Communities*. Bristol: Channel View Publications, pp. 112–130.

Boym, S. (2001). *The Future of Nostalgia*. New York: Basic Books.

Brah, A. (2005). *Cartographies of Diaspora: Contesting Identities*. London: Routledge.

Brubaker, R. (2005). The 'diaspora' diaspora. *Ethnic and Racial Studies*, 28(1), 1–19.

Carvalho, R. (2015). Macau: The rise and fall of an empire? *South China Morning Post* [online], 12 November. Available at: http://multimedia.scmp.com/macau [accessed 17 June 2017].

Casa de Macau Inc. Australia (CMA) (2017a). *Casa Down Under Newsletter* [online]. Newsletters available at: www.casademacau.org.au/newsletter/newsletter.htm [accessed 10 June 2017].

Casa de Macau Inc. Australia (2017b). *Welcome to Casa Downunder: Official website for Casa de Macau Australia* [online]. Available at: www.casademacau.org.au/default.htm [accessed 16 June 2017].

Casa de Macau Portugal (CMPT) (2017). *Qui Nova* [online]. Newsletters available at: www.casademacau.pt/comunidade/publicacoes-cm/qui-nova [accessed 11 June 2017].

Casa de Macau Toronto (CMT) (2017). *Casa de Macau Toronto* [online]. Newsletters available at: www.casademacau.ca/news.php [accessed 12 June 2017].

Casa de Macau Vancouver (CMV) (2017a). *Casa de Macau Club (Vancouver) Home* [online]. Available at: www.casademacau.org [accessed 12 June 2017].

Casa de Macau Vancouver (2017b). *Voz dos Macaenses de Vancouver* [online]. Newsletters available at: www.casademacau.org/newsletter.php [accessed 13 June 2017].

Conselho das Comunidades Macaenses (CCM). (2016). *Encontro das Comunidades Macaenses 2016*. Macau: Conselho das Comunidades Macaenses.

Conselho das Comunidades Macaenses (2017a). *Estatutos*. Chapter I, Article 3; Chapter III, Article 20 [online]. Available at: www.conselhomacaense.com/estatuto-do-conselho-das-comunidades-macaenses [accessed 14 June 2017].

Conselho das Comunidades Macaenses (2017b). *Governing Bodies* [online]. Available at: www.conselhomacaense.com/orgaos-sociais [accessed 14 June 2017].

Dias, A. (2016). *Diáspora Macaense: Territórios, Itinerários e Processos de Integração (1936–1995)*. Macau: Instituto Cultural.

Diniz, S. (2013a). A fé inabalável na comunidade macaense. *Jornal Tribuna de Macau* [online], 6 December. Available at: http://jtm.com.mo/especiais-jtm-column/encontros-macaenses-2013/a-fe-e-inabalavel-na-comunidade-macaense [accessed 13 June 2017].

Diniz, S. (2013b). Passeio pelo património reavivou memórias e orgulho. *Jornal Tribuna de Macau* [online], 4 December. Available at: http://jtm.com.mo/local/passeio-pelo-patrimonio-reavivou-memorias-orgulho [accessed 13 June 2017].

Doré, A., Almeida, A. & Moura, C. (2001). *Macau somos nós: Um mosaico da memória dos Macaenses no Rio de Janeiro*. Macau: Instituto Internacional de Macau.

Fundação Casa de Macau (CM) (2017). *Apresentação* [online]. Available at: www.fundacaocasamacau.org/historia_dois.html# [accessed 12 June 2017].

Gaspar, M. (2015). *No tempo to Bambu: Identidade e Ambivalência entre Macaenses*. Lisboa: Instituto do Oriente.

Golob, T. (2013). Imagining a home in a world of flux: Challenging individualisation and transnational belongings. *Polish Sociological Review*, 182, 153–163.

Graburn, N. (2017) Epilogue: Home, travel, memory and anthropology. In: S. Marschall, ed., *Tourism and Memories of Home: Migrants, Displaced People, Exiles and Diasporic Communities*. Bristol: Channel View Publications, pp. 268–281.

Huang, W., Norman, W. & Ramshaw, G. (2016). Homecoming or tourism? Diaspora tourism experience of second-generation immigrants. *Tourism Geographies*, 18(1), 59–79.

Iorio, M. & Corsale, A. (2013). Diaspora and tourism: Transylvanian Saxons visiting the homeland. *Tourism Geographies*, 15(2), 198–232.

Iorio, M. & Corsale, A. (2017). Travelling to the homeland over a double diaspora: Memory, landscape and sense of belonging: Insights from Transylvanian Saxons. In: S. Marschall, ed., *Tourism and Memories of Home: Migrants, Displaced People, Exiles and Diasporic Communities*. Bristol: Channel View Publications, pp. 178–198.

Jansen, S. & Löfving, S. (2007) Introduction: Movement, violence, and the making of home. *European Journal of Anthropology*, 49, 3–14.

Koo, B. (2004). *The survival of an endangered species: The Macanese in contemporary Macau*. Sydney: University of Western Sydney.

Lusitano Club of California (LC) (2017a). *Lusitano Club of California: A Casa de Macau* [online]. Available at: www.lusitanousa.org [accessed 12 June 2017].

Lusitano Club of California (2017b). *Bulletins* [online]. Newsletters available at: www. lusitanousa.org/bulletins [accessed 11 June 2017].

Marques, J. (2017). Interview, 29 February. Macau.

Marschall, S. (2017). Introduction: Tourism and memories of home. In: S. Marschall, ed., *Tourism and Memories of Home: Migrants, Displaced People, Exiles and Diasporic Communities*. Bristol: Channel View Publications, pp. 1–31.

Participant A. (2017). Email correspondence, 28 October.

Pereira, L. (2007). A grande festa. *Revista Macau* [online], 9, 16–24. Available at: https:// issuu.com/revista-macau/docs/rm_issue_09/6?ff=true [accessed 12 June 2017].

Pereira, O. (2010a). A génese das reuniões da 'família' macaense. *Jornal Tribuna de Macau* [online], 27 November. Available at: http://arquivo.jtm.com.mo/view.asp?dT=367103012 [accessed 13 June 2017].

Pereira, O. (2010b). Casas dos EUA com presença em peso. *Jornal Tribuna de Macau* [online], 27 November. Available at: http://arquivo.jtm.com.mo/view.asp?dT=362103000 [accessed 14 June 2017].

Portuguese Migration Observatory (PMO) (2017). *China-Macau* [online]. Available at: http://observatorioemigracao.pt/np4/paises.html?id=147 [accessed 13 November 2017].

Rangel, J. (2006). *Falar de nós – II. Macau e a comunidade Macaense – acontecimentos, personalidades, instituições, diáspora, legado e futuro*. Macau: International Institute of Macau.

Silva, K., Ribeiro, C., Reid, T. & Narciso, S. (2009). Report: Encontro da Comunidade Juvenil Macaense. *Casa de Macau* Australia [online]. Available at: www.casademacau. org.au/news/newsdocs/YouthEncontroJul09%20Report.pdf [accessed 13 June 2017].

Sim, D. & Leith, M. (2013). Diaspora tourists and the Scottish Homecoming 2009. *Journal of Heritage Tourism*, 8(4), 259–274.

Statistics and Census Service (SCS) (2016). *By-Census* [online]. Available at: www.dsec. gov.mo/Statistic.aspx?NodeGuid=ee77eb29-fd1b-4f13-8a2d-3181e93adb05 [accessed 31 October 2017].

Tie, C., Holden, A. & Park, H. (2015). A 'reality of return': The case of the Sarawakian-Chinese visiting China. *Tourism Management*, 47, 206–212.

União Macaense Americana (UMA) (2017). *Bulletins* [online]. Newsletters available at: www.uma-casademacau.com/index.php/bulletins [accessed 11 June 2017].

Unknown (2010). Nova geração deve ter 'mais arrojo'. *Jornal Tribuna de Macau / Lusa*. 29 November. Available at: http://arquivo.jtm.com.mo/view.asp?dT=362203004 [accessed 18 June 2017].

Weingrod, A. & Levy, A. (2006). Social thought and commentary: Paradoxes of home-coming: The Jews and their diasporas. *Anthropological Quarterly*, 79(4), 691–716.

10 Dinner in the homeland

Memory, food and the Armenian diaspora

Carel Bertram

Introduction

In 2012, Stephan travelled to Anatolia to look for his mother's lost house in the Ottoman Armenian village of Goteh. In the genocide of 1915, his mother, Satenig, had been Goteh's sole survivor. Her husband had been taken away with the men and shot; one of her children was bayonetted in front of her, the other died on the death marches that were the fate of the rest of the village. Saved by missionaries, in 1919 an Armenian man brought her to Massachusetts as a wife for his brother, who had come to the United States (U.S.) as a sojourner and whose own wife and three children had been massacred. This brother would become Stephan's father. Stephan travelled on his 'pilgrimage' to Goteh with his wife Angele and three of his four children, whom his father had asked him to name after the children he had lost. However, Stephan had named his oldest daughter for his mother, that sole survivor of Goteh. On their pilgrimage to her village, the young Satenig, her sister, Sona, and her brother, Stephan stopped at the entrance to the village, where they were welcomed by women baking bread. With a rush of warmth, they accepted, and ate, the bread of the village of their grandmother (Figure 10.1). It tasted 'Armenian', and somehow familiar.

This chapter explores the experiences of U.S.-based Armenians who travel as self-described pilgrims to their ancestral homeland in Turkish Anatolia in search of their family's lost houses, and what they ate when they were there. It uses examples from an extensive archive that I have constructed, comprising over 400 travellers' accounts including videos, photographs, maps and memoirs that span a period of well over 40 years. Since the early 1990s, most of these visitors to Anatolia have travelled in small groups led by Armen Aroyan from Glendale, California. After a pioneering journey to his family's village in the late 1980s, Aroyan began to answer the pleas of fellow Armenians who longed to see their own family's village, but had not even dreamt it possible. By 2016, when Eastern Turkey was again becoming inhospitable, several thousand pilgrims had found him by word of mouth, to be shepherded in small, village-focused groups. One such group included Stephan and his family.

I was also on that trip. In fact, I travelled on 12 Aroyan-led group pilgrimages in addition to accompanying several individual travellers to their home villages

Figure 10.1 Sona eats 'hatz', the bread of her grandmother's village

Photograph by Satenig Ghazarian, May 2012

between 2007 and 2015. I began with no experience as an ethnographer, only with an interest in how, for the Turkish population of the early 20th century, memory was deeply connected to place. This was a population with roots in the same time and place as the Armenian groups, but with very different memories. My intention was originally discursive and focused on the reading of written reports or creative responses (poems, plays, documentaries) to these trips. I soon realized that I could actually go on a pilgrimage myself to see how it operated. On my first excursions, I sat quietly on the bus, unsure of what I was seeing or where it would lead. I took notes on the back of envelopes. On later trips, I carried a notebook, also writing furiously and listening carefully, transcribing in the evenings. I took very few photographs, hoping to concentrate on what others were photographing, and many later shared their annotated photographic journals with me. I often assisted Aroyan, carrying luggage, relaying daily itineraries or taking individuals on side trips. I felt very much a part of the later trips, and many of the pilgrims have become dear friends.

These trips allowed me to observe the emotional tenor and the variety of moods elicited by the physical experience of the diasporic homeland. I was introduced as an academic with the hope of publishing a scholarly interpretation of these 'returns'. Sharing my own story, especially my academic background as a scholar in Turkish studies, sometimes made the building of trust precarious. Aroyan's support here was crucial.[1] On the other hand, the ability to relate my own grand-parents' history of Russian pogroms and exile created a sense of commonality. Almost everyone I spoke with soon seemed eager to have me tell their story as they felt it needed to be told and were comforted that a non-Armenian would take this on.

Given the way in which my research was conducted and evolved over the years, some of the conversations cited in this chapter had to be re-created from memory and notes, but all of these have been personally verified by the respec-tive speakers and their use for this publication approved. Apart from personal observations and conversations, I draw extensively on what are essentially archi-val sources, namely the reflections composed by travellers themselves over the years. Hundreds of these have been collected by Armen Aroyan and will soon be published in a book (Aroyan forthcoming). I also draw on the many first-hand travel accounts published in articles, books or web travelogues. I have, more-over, viewed many of Aroyan's tour videos as well as the home videos taken by pilgrims and sent to me later, along with letters about their thoughts. It is in this larger context that I interpret what I saw and heard, beginning with the example of Stephan and his family's vignette. I argue that the stories of the past, including food-related associations, are part of a memory chain that ties exilic peoples and their subsequent generations to their lost home in a lost homeland (Bertram, 2015; Gieryn, 2000; Tuan, 1990, 2014).

Certainly in the Armenian diaspora, homeland-food and 'food-ways' (food stories, preparation, tastes, recipes, and the social customs of eating and serving) associated with their Anatolian parents or grandparents stand as 'memory' in the inner circle of what are considered true markers of identity. During the travel to their Anatolian homeland, the descendants of Ottoman Armenians are continually confronted by familiar foods that they knew from their parents (or grandparents) in the United States or other lands of diaspora, and considered their own. This is hardly surprising, especially if their mother or grandmother was born in an Anatolian village, and their father or grandfather in an Anatolian town. However, although the food they find on their homeland trip is decidedly both familiar and delicious, the circumstances and location make their experience fraught. Since their ancestors, whose lost homes they seek, left this place because of the fears and instability caused by 19th or early 20th-century massacres, or as survivors of the genocide of 1915, they are now eating familiar foods in a land enveloped by a memory chain of pain, a land often thought of as that of the enemy. It is certainly difficult to conceive of a shared heritage in a country where the long history of the Armenian presence has been rewritten in official sources such as school cur-ricula; where village churches have been turned to mosques, or more frequently, to stables; where the Armenian names of home villages have been Turkified; and where their monasteries and schools have been destroyed. This chapter examines this dilemma, and one approach to its resolution.

Memory

Scholarship on memory burgeoned in the 1980s, making memory a 'metahistorical category' (Klein, 2000: 138) that has subsumed the analyses of many formerly separate genres such as autobiographies, culinary memoirs, nostalgia cookbooks (Bardenstein, 2002; Salmaner, 2014: 1, 2006; Sutton, 2006), ethnographies and oral histories, lost village/city memory books (Davis, 2011), personal and communal rituals and commemorations (Nora, 1989) and, especially, memoires of return (Hirsch & Miller, 2011). Particularly productive for the study of diasporic memory is a focus (as is this chapter) on personal images of family food practices and food-related stories that create and support home and homeland as an affective, emotional – rather than political or national – place. This approach yields both a humanizing and nuanced understanding of what it means to 'be', say, part of a Jewish (Bahloul, 1992), Palestinian (Abu-Lughod, 1991, 2007) or Armenian (Bakalian, 2011; Pattie, 1999) diaspora. This is especially true when memory is investigated as the impetus for travels of 'return' and analysed when memory actually meets the object of its desire. For the impulse of heritage or legacy travel flows from these place-related 'memories', becoming spatial extensions of identity, both for displaced natives and for their descendants (Coles & Timothy, 2004; Palmer, 2005; Stephenson, 2002). Some heritage tourists hope to find a material reality as a supportive scenography for their inherited stories of 'the old country' (Pattie, 1999). Travellers who are refugees, exiles and displaced peoples may also wish to fulfil a vow to parents; others travel with an urgency to commune with family spirits; or to pray for their souls in the places where these spirits and souls are believed to reside (Bertram, forthcoming). Although there can be no closure to genocide, some travel for a type of closure to an inherited melancholia (Eng & Kazanjian, 2003). Because of these intensely personal yet spiritual quests, most of the travellers in my study – along with many others who travel to sites of loss – refer to themselves as pilgrims, prompting me to use the term here. Scholars of tourism and pilgrimage agree that the distinctions between heritage tourism and pilgrimage may be difficult to describe, but pilgrimage always includes travel to places that have the possibility of offering specific spiritual rewards. For the pilgrim, the reward may simply be felt as a psychological or somatic experience of 'traces of some absent or ineffable quality of being' (Morinis, 1981: 284) at the heart of their Armenian identity.

In this chapter, I address the psychological and somatic reactions to encountering foods or food-ways that embody this ineffable 'quality of being' in a vulnerable setting; for here, the foods of their homeland, in their homeland, are being prepared and claimed by people whom the pilgrims see as descendants of the perpetrators who exiled them. In fact, all of Turkey is seen as a landscape of denial, one in which the Turkish government has worked to erase the genocide from national memory (Çandar, 2017). Drawing on Bachelard's (1964) seminal *The Poetics of Space* and especially his insight that the poetic essence of one's childhood house is captured in adult daydreams, or *reverie*, I discuss how the encounter with familiar foods in this sensitive setting induces a home-centred reverie that serves to 'protect' against a variety of memories and emotions. It hence protects the pilgrim from being overwhelmed by negative emotions.

Following Hage (2010), I identify the affective meaning of home that these reveries strategically and poetically access. In Part One, I use Yervant as an exemplar of how encounters with familiar foods expose the affective components of the lost home for pilgrims who were born in Anatolia; that is, the native-born who autobiographically remember eating these foods in this place of their origin. I argue that their memories and experiences are distilled through reverie to provide a screen of security and wholeness in the face of loss. However, for the pilgrim-generations that did not personally experience either the life of 'the old country' or the brutality of its loss, and yet who feel this 'memory' as their own – that is, the 'postmemory' generation (Hirsch, 2012) – reveries cannot call forth the ancestral village as they were never there. However, in response to their remembered stories of the village and why it is no longer theirs, the food encounters of the descendant generation engender protective images from their home in the host land, the autobiographical source of their sense of wholeness. To illustrate this, in Part Two, I discuss the experience of a 1.5-generation traveller, Alberta, and her cousin, Aurora, a descendant; and in Part Three, I return to the family from Goteh, adding other examples of descendant pilgrims to give a fuller account of the distinctive, protective effect of reverie when it evokes a home in the host land.

Part one: Yervant, the native-born pilgrim

In 1951, Yervant Küçükyan, under cover of his business credentials as a tobacco merchant, travelled the 300 miles from Beirut on Lebanon's Mediterranean coast to Antep (Armenian Aintab; today: Gaziantep) in south central Turkey in order to be close, once again, to his childhood home. He had left in 1916, at the age of 13, among the last of the Armenian deportees. Into the 1950s, post-genocide return was made next to impossible by Turkish laws, which also stood behind the Ottoman appropriation of Armenian properties (Akçam & Kurt, 2015). The few who did return rarely wrote about it, making Yervant's published memoir extremely precious.[2] Writing in Armenian, in Beirut, he was no doubt certain that the history of the genocide, and its details in Antep, were fresh in the minds of his Armenian readers, so he went into no detail. Yet the genocide frames every moment of his trip, as he begins his article by writing how its events were engraved on his brain. Speaking to his readers as fellow exiles, he notes how they would understand how 'a deep longing for my homeland' pulled him 'toward Antep with an inexplicable force' (Küçükyan, 1952: n.p.). On arrival, he sought and found all the houses of his past, some of which he visited several times: the house where he had been born in the Armenian neighbourhood of Kayacığa; his mother's family house (the Noraduryan house) and his uncle's house on Reyhan Street. But on first reaching Antep, he had headed first for his grandfather's home (the Gözüküçükyan house) in the Armenian neighbourhood of Kastel Başı (Figure 10.2). He and his family had lived there after returning to Antep in 1913, having first fled in 1910 from

Figure 10.2 The Gözüküçükyan House, Antep

Photograph by Murad Uçaner, June 2017

possible repercussions of the Adana massacres of 1909. He found this imposing house easily, still resonating with his family's presence.

> with excitement and devotion, we stopped in front of [my] father's house. I raised my eyes, and in my view, through the four windows, my grandfather, Hagop Gözüküçükyan, and his two much beloved sons, Arenag and Nezar, still lived . . . just like in all my dreams.
>
> (Küçükyan, 1952: n.p.)

This dreamlike state was revived at lunch at the home of the son of one of his father's former business partners. Unlike his other encounters, which were full of conversations and impressions, it seems that all he remembered of this lunch was the food, which he itemized: köfte (meatballs), dolma (stuffed vegetables) and two specifically Antep specialties, the Güllü family's baklava and pistachio soup. Everything else seemed to come and go from his consciousness, where, seated 'around that magnificent table, I am in a dream'. In fact, instead of engaging with his Turkish host, or describing the foods made by this Turkish family, this meal elicited a reverie that transported him to another meal, one in the paternal family home of his Armenian childhood, which was at the centre of all his Antep thoughts.

> It seems that I am at our old Armenian house. It's snowing outside. We are sitting on a rug (savan) around the coal-brazier (tandir). In that warm room my grandmother and my grandfather, with their heads uncovered, are eating together with their children, all spooning soup from a giant pot, eating as a whole family in that house that was inherited from generation to generation.
>
> (Küçükyan, 1952: n.p.)

Reverie

Yervant's memoir introduces and explores the 'dream state' that Bachelard (1964) calls a reverie, and which, unlike nocturnal dreams, involves the conscious mind. In *The Poetics of Space*, Bachelard shows how, when directed towards the house of childhood – which I expand here to include the family home in general – the substance of reverie is the archetypical 'felicity' of home. In other words, although the substance of reverie is spatial, it is not architectural but affective, and although it seems to take place in a nostalgic past, it is not specific to a time; rather, it is timeless. Thus, the archetypical quality of this 'reveried' or day-dreamed house (Bachelard's *oneiric* house) comes not from the specific stories or memories or even the emotions that the dreamer superimposes on a place, but, instead, from the deepest qualities of that space, which are the actions and activities that perform home, and thus bring the space of house to life. When reverie calls forth practices and embodied relations with home, the dreamer 'inhabits' the house's archetypical qualities, summarized by Game and Metcalfe (2011: 44) as well-being, felicity, tranquility and love. By tying together the 'immemorial and recollected', reverie allows for a spiritual return to 'the fullness of the house's being' (Bachelard, 1964: 8).

Tellingly, however – as Yervant found when the new owners of his grand-father's house invited him in – reverie's spiritual return cannot function among intruders; and the house, once a 'structure of feeling' (Bertram, 2008: 184), reverted to its architecture.

> With searching eyes I examined the modest, dusty building of my father's house, and its garden; these strangers in our old house are not my family, and the house under its roof is not our home, but just an ordinary stone building . . . what I wanted from that house was to go inside and to sit in the corner where I had done my lessons, where my dear mother had prepared bread by the stove, where I had savored homemade cheese, raisins and figs.
> (Küçükyan, 1952: n.p.)

Foods were central to reliving his past in reverie. But it was not the taste of the food that Yervant was after; the homemade bread and cheese and the raisins and figs were available in Antep, and probably in Aleppo at that time, and perhaps even Beirut, too. The longing was to relive the *experiencing* of these foods in the family setting, to re-experience the act of their preparation, which gave meaning to the act of savouring. He knew – or hoped – that by 're-experiencing' these actions in the old house, 'traces', at least, 'of some absent or ineffable quality of [his own] being' (Morinis, 1981: 284) would be restored. His impulse, then, was for a desire for wholeness as protection against a feeling of existential discon-tinuity and loss. If this happened, his reverie might become satisfying. Yervant planned to (and did) return to his house several times to 're-experience' it alone.

> I will lean against my father's house and stroke the walls, I will knock with the door's iron doorknocker; and the faces of my mother and my sisters will come alive in the eyes of my soul; and I'll meet with them again and, saying welcome to those names I cannot forget, I will visit once again the stories that my father always told us, about his father's and his grandfather's life, and about the markets, the schools, the places where my ancestors led their ordinary lives.
> (Küçükyan, 1952: n.p.)

Here we see how reverie is active dreaming and how participation in it makes it performative: the activities of reverie restore the house to life – at its essence. We might then say that in the selected traces that make up reverie, one inhabits the deep structure of the house as 'an allusive and fragmentary story whose gaps mesh with the social practices it symbolizes' (de Certeau, 1984: 102).

The protective power of reverie

Even as fragments and traces, such as Yervant's mother's baking of the bread that he will soon eat, or perhaps because of these fragments' ability to evoke one's own place in the archetypical, the house that is brought to life elicits security and protection. Experienced as a timeless cocoon, the house as it appears in reverie might be the only refuge that allows the pilgrim-dreamer to be safe from the entirely real anguish and anger of a place that might otherwise only be experienced as loss. Certainly, the impulse for protection is clear; yet, although Yervant's reverie seems not to be clouded by memories of eviction, when the family was forced to sell everything on the street before leaving, the success (of this performative reverie) is not clear at all. As Hage would suggest, when an exile's memories of the homeland are triggered by what is emotionally missing and emotionally *irreplaceable* – that is, beyond the existential irreplaceability of lost childhood or losses due to time – nostalgic memory is essentially depressive (Hage, 2010: 42).

Although Hage (2010) only addresses experiences in exile rather than, as here, on journeys of return, he relates the preparation or eating of foods from the homeland to an attempt to re-create the sense of security associated with 'back home'. For Hage, creating security (through nostalgic food preparation, for example) is an affective building block of the diasporic home, which, when successful, can be considered an aspect of *positive* nostalgia. Along with security, additional 'affective building blocks' are, according to Hage, a sense of familiarity and a sense of community. Nostalgic activities that do not contribute to security, familiarity and/or community leave the exile feeling lost and disconnected, or, as Bachelard (1964: 7) would say, a 'dispersed being'. This defines what Hage (2010) calls a '*negative* nostalgia'; in fact, what the pilgrim's reverie guards against.

Thus, Hage's affective building blocks are useful to us in defining the positive aspects of home activated by the pilgrim for protection, as well as in identifying what causes a sinking feeling of loss. They also help us understand how descendant pilgrims who are able to situate their reveries in the host land, unlike the native-born, also gain from reverie's protective power, but by conflating a living host land's warmth with the lost village home.

Part two: descendants of survivors

In 2007, Alberta,[3] shepherded by Armen Aroyan, made a pilgrimage to Bitias, one of the six villages of Musa Dagh ('Mt. Moses'), the mountain of villages made famous by Franz Werfel's 1933 historic novel, *The Forty Days of Musa Dagh*. That story chronicles how two thirds of its villagers resisted the 1915 Ottoman deportation orders by hiding on the mountain, finally to be rescued by the French Marines. Alberta's mother and her family, however, were part of the other third, those who were sent on an enforced march to Syria, the survivors ending up in Hama. In 1920, Alberta's grandmother, her mother and her mother's sister, the only three to survive of a family of 10, returned to live in Bitias, which, as part of the former Ottoman Syrian province of Iskenderun/Alexandretta, had come under the protection of France. Thus, after the genocide, the Armenian villages of Musa Dagh, now outside of Turkish control, began to revive. The man who would become Alberta's father returned to Bitias in 1924. He and his brother had been sent as sojourners to America in 1910 by their father, who feared that the all-too-close Adana pogroms of 1909 would be repeated. On his return, he found that only two of his seven immediate family members had survived. Alberta's parents met in Bitias and married that year, and Alberta was born a year later, in 1926; a second daughter arrived in 1929. But in 1939, with the loss of safety due to the immanent transfer of the area from a French protectorate to the new Republic of Turkey, all the Armenians of five of the villages of Musa Dagh left as refugees, most to resettle in Lebanon. The villagers of the sixth village, Vakef, chose to stay, and Vakef is now the only Christian village left in Turkey (Magzanian, 2008; Shemmassian, n.d.).

In 1939, Alberta was 13, the same age that Yervant had been when he left Antep in 1916. In 1951, when Yervant was making his 'pilgrimage' at age 48, having been away for 38 years, Alberta, at age 26, was moving with her family from Lebanon to New Jersey. She did not return to Bitias until she was 82, not having seen it for 68 years. Although both Alberta and Yervant longed to see the houses of their youth, another reason for Alberta's trip was that she was in the process of writing a Musa Dagh cookbook, together with her two younger sisters: Anna, who had also been born in Bitias, and Louisa, who had been born three years after the exile. Anna did not accompany Alberta on this pilgrimage, but Louisa and her husband Richard and their son Alex came, along with another relative, Aurora, whose grandparents were from Bitias, but whose parents were from the Musa Dagh village of Kheder Bey, and who had been, herself, born in America. This group, whose story is chronicled in the Magzanian (2008) cookbook or captured on video, acts as a cross-over between the experiences of native-born pilgrims who return to their birthplaces and the experiences of pilgrim descendants. Like Yervant, Alberta may be considered a part of what has been termed the 1.5 generation, those who immigrate as children or adolescents, and thus have autobiographical memories of the homeland, yet whose young adulthood and maturity is part of the diaspora (Rumbaut, 2012).

The affective components of home

A sense of familiarity and community were a component of what had made Yervant's neighbourhood 'home' in Antep, made clear as he walked through the town identifying Armenian churches and schools as well as each house by its Armenian owner. But, noting that these places were all emptied of Armenians, he lamented, 'We were still foreigners in the place where we were born' (Küçükyan, 1952: n.p.). Alberta remembered the cohesive social life of her entirely Armenian village, which resembled Yervant's neighbourhood when it was thriving. On village paths, Alberta, too, had identified houses by their former Armenian occupants. Furthermore, for her, an entire section was made up of her own relatives, such that she could even identify the house of her 'dad's aunt's granddaughter's cousin's son' (Aroyan [video], 2007). This awareness gave a homey sense of security as well. As Alberta remembered it, the 'homeyness' of this cohesive life was epitomized by the food-ways that connected its houses to each other and to Chaghlaghan, the orchard that supplied it with food. Her mother's morning chores were interrupted by daily visitors, many of whom were relatives who visited frequently, even daily, often for a cup of 'Kahfo', the word used for thick, sweet coffee in the Musa Dagh dialect of Kristinik. Alberta attributed many of these comings and goings among households to her family's relative wealth, although they also reflect the way in which food-ways, as a performance, solidify ties, and, as 'a lived space that is "embracing and embraced"' (Game, 2011: 43, paraphrasing Bachelard, 1964: 8), performs home.

> Because we were one of the families whose larder was always full, we helped those less fortunate when they came to our door. Some visitors asked for a favor or for much-needed items that we readily fulfilled; 'Auntie,' (every married woman in Bitias was everyone's auntie) 'could we borrow a cup of sugar?'; 'a loaf of bread?'; 'how about a bowl of pickles?'; 'do you have any leftover fruit from Chaghlaghan?'
>
> (Magzanian, 2008: 155)

The sense of Bitias as a community was punctuated by a sense of separateness from town-folk (in this case, also Armenians) who came by the thousands from Aleppo to spend the summer holidays in the cool mountain air, but who looked down on village ways, including, or perhaps especially, its food. On her pilgrimage, while standing near her own Bitias house, Alberta related the story of how two such visitors had been received as unexpected guests by their Bitias classmate. The young host cautiously asked his Aunt, 'what have you made for dinner?'

> And she said, 'Turkhanoom Shoorbo.' Well, they're city folks, they are not going to eat what is called Turkhanoom Shoorbo. She said, 'don't worry, I will serve it to them and they will gobble it up.' So she brought a big bowl of the Shoorbo and said, this is called *Soup de Paris*! And they gobbled it up, sure enough!
>
> (Aroyan [video], 2007 and see Magzanian, 2008: 48)

Apart from speaking of the quality and taste of a 'homey' cabbage soup, recalling this oft-told local story in the place where it happened communicates a sense of pride in local cleverness, even the educated-ness of the verbal ploy (this aunt worked as a cook at the French Consulate in Aleppo during the winter). It also identifies this place as one of loss. It was the loss of a parochial childhood in houses safely separated from a larger world, where in winter Alberta's mother took part in a monthly book club, and her daughters would sit in the corner and listen to Victor Hugo's *Les Miserables* (Magzanian, 2008: 155). But now, standing in Bitias, the story was like the useless house-deeds that other pilgrims carried. Thus, I suggest that for Alberta, any protection afforded by this reverie – of how Turkhanoom Shoorba performed home – was in its connection to the diaspora, where it had become a part of diaspora life, an active building block of positivity.

There, Louisa, the descendant, had demanded that not only the recipe of a food she loved, but its story become a part of the cookbook to ensure that 'home' would be kept alive.[4]

The diasporic home

In fact, to some extent, the Magzanian home in New Jersey attempted to replicate Bitias: the food items their mother prepared were the ones she had made in Bitias; their father had terraced and planted their garden to allow him to still 'feel' the beauty, tastes and homeyness of their Bitias orchard, Chaghlaghan. As another resident put it, 'Living in Paterson, NJ during the 1940s was like living in Musa Dagh, and not in the US' (Shemmassian, n.d.: 211). When Alberta and her parents moved again, from New Jersey to Maryland to be near Louisa, their mother, at age 75, continued to cook her ancestral foods, and her father, at age 93, designed a new, terraced Chaghlaghan. Louisa called the old village skills (and chores) that were part of her Paterson, NJ life, such as making yogurt, 'maintenance' (Magzanian, 2008: 152). 'Each meal we prepare dates back to Bitias and the region of clustered villages on Musa Dagh' (ibid.: 164). Here, Turkhanoom Shoorba, and the elements of Bitias life that it represented, were now associated with its cooking and retelling in America, where their sister Anna learned it from their mother, teaching it to her sisters who would make it a part of their cookbook. Their immediate hope was that the book would preserve the food and life of Bitias for Louisa's son, Alex, who, at age 26, travelled to Bitias as a third-generation pilgrim; in fact, in the book, Alberta reports proudly that he could make the flaky, coiled bread called baghash (ibid.: 164). But a second goal was to preserve these food-ways for other descendants of Musa Dagh. It would be safe to say that every Musa Dagh villager had relatives in other Musa Dagh villages, where all spoke the same dialect of Armenian and even ate, as the three sisters would say, in the same 'dialect' of food. Their cookbook's subtitle was *An Armenian Cookbook in a Dialect of its Own*. Their life in their home in the diaspora now represented hope for the future, and all three sisters' agency in it. In fact, Hage (2010) suggests that when the needs of security, familiarity and community are met by exilic home-builders, a fourth building block of home becomes possible, and that is a sense of hope, or positive expectations for the future.

Positive and negative reveries

I suggest that the protection afforded to pilgrims who inhabit reveries grounded in their diasporic host land home is more successful than that grounded in the homeland because it includes this positive aspect of future. Reveries that call forth the violently and forever lost home are like negative nostalgia; they cannot have this sense of hope unless they are expanded to include the diasporic home. Thus, for first and certainly 1.5-generation pilgrims from the diaspora, local foods and food memories have the potential of inducing reveries rooted in overlapping places. Turkhanoom Soup identifies Bitias, but its preparation continued in the Magzanian home kitchens in Syria, Lebanon, New Jersey and Maryland. Returning to Bitias to tell this story cements this link. The expanded space is a corrective that may even protect against what might be called a negative reverie. Instead of associating foods only with homes that had been wrenched away, food reveries now include those homes built by exiles to promote a sense of an affective Bitias that was ongoing in the future, with a continuing protection, agency and happiness.

A counter-example is Alberta's associations with the water of Bitias, which evoked a negative reverie related to an inherited memory, passed on by her mother. The waters of Bitias and Chahglayan were part of the familiarity that made Bitias 'home'. As a village child, Alberta had learned the sources of the four major springs, and how blue faucets indicated 'mother water', or water that came straight from the springs, without accumulating. Standing by one of these springs, Alberta said, 'I just drank some of it, I'm going to drink some more' (Aroyan [video], 2007). Then she told this inherited story:

> My sister [Anna] told me that I should have two drinks of water here. One for me, and one for my grandfather who died in Hama [according to our mother], soon, within a few months after they got there. And his observation was, 'I would be OK if someone could bring me a glass of cold water from my favourite orchard,' which was Chaghlaghan.
>
> (Aroyan [video], 2007)

Although her reverie, induced by drinking the beloved, life-giving water of Bitias, could be considered an attempted spiritual healing of her grandfather's anguish, and even of her family's inherited memory of his anguish, it could provide no emotional protection from the loss that had caused it, as the water she was drinking was undeniably still not hers. Even if her reverie of the spring waters of her childhood included an immemorial happiness, the taste of this water had lost its 'felicity', as her grandfather had died when its loss began.

Pilgrimage itself is a way to connect the next generation to the homeland, which Alberta understood when her familiarity with the landscape opened a reverie for her cousin, Aurora. Alberta had, in fact, been hunting for a wild pistachio bush, with crunchy shells that enclosed a spicy berry called 'peevig' [terebinth; menengiç in Turkish]. For Alberta, it called forth memories of eating these as a child, especially when roasted as a treat for guests . . . and children. But *Aurora*'s memories of peevig were from the United States, when her Bitias grandmother's sister would send this 'taste of home' from Lebanon. Unlike exilic or survivors' food memories, a descendant's 'memory' of the ancestral home is always inherited, and can only be known from stories and mediated sources. For Aurora, then, as with other inherited stories, finding and eating this berry would induce a reverie of a home in the diaspora, where her grandmother's nostalgic stories of eating peevig in Bitias seemed to emerge with their scent from a box that was opened in New Jersey.

In both cases, food-induced reveries may be analogous to Proust's, whose taste of a madeleine in Paris sent him into a surprising reverie about eating madeleines in his childhood. Unlike Proust, who then forgot about the madeleine he was actually eating in the present, the pilgrim's food-invoked reverie is neither unconscious nor unexpected. In fact, it is searched for in order that the pilgrim may consciously participate in the authenticity of their ancestral place. The searched-for authenticity that grounds the pilgrim in this place is arguably best served by the senses, which go deeper than collected narratives, as the sensual experience of food, or even sensual memories of food, may bequeath a 'culinary citizenship' (Mannur, 2007: 13) that allows the pilgrim the possibility of imagining themselves living or inhabiting fragments of their ancestral stories. Furthermore, unexpected and probably unnoticed, but absolutely inherent, are the new connections to the diaspora made by these authenticating senses: *Soup de Paris*, once served by its simpler name in Bitias, is imagined on a table in New Jersey, where the cookbook writer calls on it to perform the work of legacy. This process of tying visceral reactions in the homeland to a home in the host land creates a new, enlarged imaginative space. Preparing Bitias foods in New Jersey is an act that performs the lost Bitias house, but the eating of Bitias foods in Bitias also performs a New Jersey home. Although this arguably gives the two homes a new, common memory, for the second and third generations it also, as we will see below, irrefutably displaces memory to a protective space in the diaspora.

It is true that Yervant's reveries, which returned him to what Bachelard calls the 'fixations of happiness' of childhood, offered some protection from a world that had erased that life so brutally. As Bachelard (1964: 6) reminds us, when we enter reveries of our childhood house, 'we travel to the land of Motionless Childhood, motionless the way all Immemorial things are. We live fixations, fixations of happiness. *We comfort ourselves by reliving memories of protection*' (my emphasis). But the dead-end quality of that protection seems obvious when compared to reveries that call forth the protection of an ongoing chain of memory that keeps one's values alive. As the pilgrim, Carolann wrote on finding family foods in her ancestral Kharpert (Harput/Elazığ), food that she knew from Massachussetts:

> [These foods] validated the values [that the survivors] brought from the yerkir [homeland]: of hard work, honesty, hospitality, and devotion to community, family, church, and nation. They carried these values with them as they journeyed on foot over mountain ranges, through valleys and across rivers – and passed them on to their new families. They suffered but they managed to survive. Their food connected them to the yerkir and all the yerkir meant to them.
>
> (Najarian, 2005: n.p.)

Clearly, what the pilgrim understood was that the survival in the host land of the food of the homeland was more than a symbol of an ideal past; it was a symbol of a strong future.

Part three: descendants – 'inherited memory' in a hostile environment

The second and third-generation descendants of survivors inherited deep connections to their family villages through a heritage preservation culture and,
especially, from beloved family members who had endured exile. This is the
'postmemory' generation who, as the poet pilgrim Alidz expressed it,

– grew up

With the idea that we should go back to this land.

The vision of the land, the homeland

was, from my childhood, inscribed on my soul

(Agbabian, 2018: n.p.)

Yet the sense of homecoming that food engenders in the pilgrims is shared with an
unending bombardment of other emotions generated not just by family genocide
stories, but by either a tenuous welcome or a continuing hostility to their presence.

Figure 10.3 Pilgrims eating 'Armenian food' at a Turkish restaurant

Photograph by Sona Gevorkian, May 2012

We see this, for example, with Stephan and his family in Goteh. As the family searched for traces of their ancestral house, Stephan carrying a hand-drawn map and his two daughters their 'hatz', the bread of their grandmother's village, they were followed by locals. These villagers were not unfriendly, yet they were certain that Stephan's map would lead to the gold that most Turkish citizens have been trained to believe was stashed by 'the wealthy Armenians' as they were sent to death; and they kindly offered to help for a percentage of the find. At a restaurant in Kharpert, as another group of pilgrims ate a meal made of the Kharpert specialties that they knew from home, I watched as a friendly local family at an adjacent table asked who they were and where they were from (Figure 10.3). When they heard the answer, 'We are Armenians, we are from Kharpert', they offered a confusing welcome: 'We are glad to see you here! But . . . why did you leave?' This common response cut more deeply than the almost farcical certainty that the Armenians had returned for their gold; and the pilgrims could only answer with dismay: 'we were deported'. What made up the pilgrims' deepest reality was often unknown in their own homeland, or more frequently denied. But for the pilgrim at dinner, the events were fresh: before dinner in this same restaurant, Carolann wrote that she had stood looking up at the hillside where the famous Euphrates College once stood, and where, she was certain, several women in her family had been educated.

> We held a photo of what was once Euphrates College taken from the point where we now stood and with the empty hillside behind us . . . In my mind's eye I saw yet another photo, one I had seen in books about Kharpert and in various exhibitions, of Armenian men being marched out of the town, most likely along the street where we were standing. It was here where we would be eating dinner tonight, in a small restaurant overlooking Mezireh [Elazig].
>
> (Najarian, 2005: n.p.)

Hirsch's work (2012) suggests that this postmemory generation feels the anguish of genocide as if they had experienced it themselves; that is, *as if it were the pilgrims' personal history*. This may or may not be true. However, I suggest that the actual, autobiographical pain of hearing the genocidal stories from one's own parents or grandparents is pain enough. Added to this is the anguish the pilgrim feels on their journey when they visit other pilgrims' villages and hear their stories, or see collective sites of Armenian culture, with a ravaged history still raw almost 100 years later. In 2004, Isabelle, whose father was from Jerman (Yedisu), a village of Keghi (Erzerum), wrote:

> Along our way, we visited many villages. We were hospitably received by the Kurds, who now dominate the region. They offered us tan [a cold, diluted yogurt drink; Turkish 'ayran'] and madzoon [yogurt], tea, bread, and even Keghetsi beorag [local Keghi pastry]. In village after village, we saw ruined churches and monasteries. Some had been converted to mosques;

others, partially standing, served as stables or garbage dumps. Still others were totally laid waste, their stones littered about as if being reclaimed by the mountains.

(Kaprielian-Churchill, 2006: n.p.)

It is a credit to their ancestors' memory that, in a landscape of denial and erasure, the food they ate did not stick in their throats. Perhaps in part this was because of those Turkish citizens who welcomed them; those who remembered or knew the truth; those who said, 'I am not the government'; or those who lamented, as had the woman in the Musa Dagh village of Yoghunluk, encountered by the poet pilgrim Alidz:

Aghhh, she says

When the Armenians left this area

They took its Bereket [blessedness] with them.

(Agbabian, 2018: n.p.)

In fact, when meeting sympathetic Turks or Kurds, pilgrims often felt a puzzling sense of brotherhood, especially with those who expressed a kinship because their own grandmothers had been Armenian – daughters left behind for protection, or grabbed as booty from the death marches of the genocide.

Enlarging the imaginative space of home

Whether or not there were signs of denial or erasure, or possibilities of brotherhood, a sense of rootedness was frequently established by identifying as 'Armenian' the many Turkish foods that were recognized from homes in the Armenian diaspora. In 2012, Barlow walked into a cheese market in his ancestral town of Van and said, 'it's full of Armenian cheese!', at which point stories of his own family became linked to it:

My grandmother used to make this cheese, which is a cheese made with vegetables, panchareghen, which is greens, basically. And it's called jajig in Armenian, and it's a cheese that she made that I remembered, and they're still eating it and they are known for it in Van today.

(Personal communication with author, December 2012)

For second and third-generation pilgrims, this 'Armenian food' elicits a wellspring of memories and associations that flow not from the ancestral village itself, but from their homes in the *diaspora*. Typically, this generates friendly arguments among pilgrims about whose recipe is truly authentic; yet the warmth of the memories from their diaspora source comes less from ingredients and flavours than from their performative power to evoke home and family, i.e. they centre on the activities of making or enjoying the food.

When Carolann and her aunt (her mother's sister) Hasmieg entered the restaurant in Kharpert, they were anticipating a treat that Armen Aroyan had ordered for them:

> Armen had already told us two local specialties would be served: Kharpert kufteh [stuffed meat balls] and surum [a dish of flatbread baked with butter and garlic-flavoured yogurt]! Surum! My aunt Hasmieg and I couldn't wait! For years we have enjoyed surum (or serim) in our family [in the U.S.], but today, few people are familiar with this dish – it is not in any recipe book or on any menu. It is a forgotten food! Hasmieg and I simply could not believe that surum was here, in this desolate town. During the summer, on the days our grandmother baked the flat round bread on the sheet of zinc – the sahje – over the outdoor fire, she would make surum for lunch. Some of the flat rounds of bread would be cooked until thoroughly dried and hard, making it possible to store the breads for weeks while others were taken off the sahje while still soft. These she rolled and placed in a large baking pan layered with garlic, butter, and with her own madzoon [yogurt], and then baked. This is surum!
>
> (Najarian, 2005: n.p.)

It was these *processes* of the old country that were handed to the new, which would become the performance of what family meant. That is, as a reified positive nostalgia, or 'maintenance', as Louisa had called it, these food performances would become the affective building blocks of home in the host land. Carolann understood well that this performance was a part of a chain of memory that linked each generation to the other.

> Maybe my grandmother had those thoughts about her own mother, her village, her other life, each time she rolled out the dough for 'hatz' [bread]. I can see her bent over the floured board, rolling the thin dowel back and forth over the dough, shaping to the right thickness and size, then flipping it over the dowel and taking it to my grandfather, who would take the dowel from her and slide the round of dough onto the sahje over the hot wood fire. It was our family's ritual; my grandmother and grandfather performed it, then my mother and father, and now my nephew and niece.
>
> (Najarian, 2005: n.p.)

Carolann's narrating or conceptualizing this performance brought her diaspora family to life on her visit in the homeland, expanding the imaginative space of home to include both places. In fact, her images and narrative operate in a way similar to cookbook writing in which the 'narratives are highly performative as the author would attempt to create a scene in which the reader actively, yet imaginatively, re-creates the dish in question' (Salmaner, 2014: 38), but also allowing Kharpert and Massachussets to merge into one affective place.

Anto was also transported by the taste of surum to the process of making it: On the bus, he told me, 'I make it the way that I learned it from my mother from Sepastia, [Sivas]. My mother used to make the bread early in the morning [in Providence, RI] and dip it in the coffee. What was left at night was used for the surum'. He then relived the experience, describing how he would replicate his mother's actions.

> You roll the lavash [Armenian flat bread] into a long coil and cut into one inch small coils [pinwheels]. Put them in a pan and put it in the oven for a couple of minutes. Then you heat madzoon [yogurt], a big container, or more, on low. Add some water to the madzoon and keep stirring. Then you get the butter and melt it separately. If you like garlic, chop it in. I put garlic on the side. Pull the bread out of the oven and ladle the whole madzoon over it. Fill the cracks! Add the butter and garlic and put it back in 2–3 minutes; if it's too hot it boils and curdles.

Watching his mother in Providence brought Sivas to life. Eating surum in Kharpert brought Providence to life in Anatolia. It was surprising to have a non-local (Anto was not 'from' Kharpert, he was 'from' Sivas) claim a Kharpert dish; for pilgrims' memories and attachments to foods are village and town specific, and linked to strongly held local identities that are linked, in turn, to the reason they came. Perhaps Sivastzies claim surum, too.

In Kharpert, Carolann ate 'Kharpert kufteh that were close seconds to my Mom's' (Najarian, 2005: n.p.). Kharpert Kufteh/kuftah, lamb and bulgar meat balls that are hollowed out so that the walls are evenly thin and strong, then stuffed with a meat, onion, and pine-nut mixture and boiled in broth, are a prized dish that takes skill to make. Another pilgrim pronounced her dinner in Kharpert as 'authentic', 'with Kharpert kufteh and the works' (personal correspondence with author, January 2012). It was authentic because the food was prepared just as her grandmother had prepared it, and eating it, she felt the presence of her grandmother and grandfather whom she had known in the United States. In fact, many meatball flags of identity were raised. In Lidge, in the province of Diyarbakir, Zaven's thoughts about kuftah were different. As he explained to me in Lidge, first of all, they had a flat bottom.

> They'd start with a ball like this, and then they'd put a hole in it, and they'd take the insides and they'd stick it in this way, so the bottom was flat and [gesturing to his mother's cultural prowess, or her 'maintenance'], if you weighed them, they were all *exactly* the same.

Zaven had come several times to the Diyarbakir village of Lidge, eventually finding the spot where the family house had stood. Standing there, Zaven mused on his family, the survivors of the Lidge family house, and their American children, who had gathered on weekends either in New York or in Rhode Island.

They were all first cousins, and they were all from this same house [in Lidge]. It was like that every week. Every Sunday, for years it was like that, together. They rotated houses. But every Sunday it was all the same people. All the women would cook; the men would eat first.

Thus, as we have seen, associating food in Turkey as 'Armenian', and connecting it to the places and people in the diaspora who keep or kept it alive, works in two directions: first, while eating or making ancestral foods in the diaspora, an exile or descendant imaginatively 'inhabits' the lost home as a method of building a successful new home. There, foods from the homeland act as 'imagined metonymies' in that these 'tastes and actions are fragments or traces of an equally imagined homely whole, the imagined past "home" of another time and another space' (Hage, 2010: 422).

Protective reveries in a space of hope

Second, however, while eating or relating to Armenian/Turkish food, especially in proximity to one's ancestral house, descendant pilgrims open a realm of reverie that takes them back to their home in the diaspora. This is a protective reverie because it completely removes the dreamer from a place that is the source of pain to a place that is a source of pride. Whereas Yervant's protective cocoon, sitting, as it were, on the edge of eviction, could never provide full security, those that take place in the diaspora can offer a productive sense of wholeness. As Hage suggests for exiles, a positive nostalgia is possible when new homes are made up of the affective building blocks that make one 'feel at home where they actually are' (2010: 419). In the case of the pilgrim, a reverie of the host land that takes place in the homeland is not just autobiographical and real, it recalls the building blocks of the Armenian home that serve the possibilities of an Armenian future.

Thus, Zaven's Lidge-conjured family in Providence contains his mother and aunts in the kitchen making Lidge-perfect kuftah, Sunday after Sunday; his father and uncle singing Lidge-learned Armenian and Kurdish songs that Zaven loved but could not always understand; the raki [a clear, anise-flavoured liquor] being passed in the living room; the children under foot who will absorb and continue their culture, albeit in their own ways. All hover in his reverie as he stands with his cousin, or one of his daughters, at the top of the hill, where nothing remains except the view that his father remembered seeing from his grandfather's house.

Conclusion

To paraphrase Ruth Klüger (2012), a recipe for Kharpert Kuftah is not a recipe for dealing with the genocide;[5] and the stories, recipes and food-ways that come to life during dinner in the homeland are not an avenue or a strategy to bring the genocide's political or ethical repercussions to the table. But they *are* relevant to the discussion of its continuing pain. Clearly, exilic communities have used the preservation and presentation of 'old country' foods as affective building blocks in the successful construction of a secure sense of home in their host lands. I have explored here how this productively affectionate relationship between home, food and food-ways can re-surface as solace and protection when exiles are exposed to the sources of that painful fracture as they travel to the home that was lost. This is because food-related stories are almost always ones of wholeness; they speak to the sympathetic and emotion-laden values of the life that was lost rather than to the loss itself. Finding the foods and food-ways of their families in this ancestral setting could have several additional outcomes. Because this is their homeland, the foods that are encountered might be considered a wellspring for authenticating or rejuvenating their repertoires when they return. This does not happen, however, because what might seem an encounter feels like a confrontation with a perpetrator culture. I know of no pilgrim who collected Turkish cookbooks. When Priscilla compared the foods that she found in the Republic of Armenia to the foods that she found in Turkey, she said,

> here, in Turkey, we are going back to our childhoods, and that makes me feel happy. It's true, we don't eat the same food as in Armenia. *This* is our food, and *this* is our culture. But what they did to us changed everything. Our culture turned on us.
>
> (Personal correspondence with author, March 2014)

Hers was a sober assessment that did not attempt to erase affinities that could not be celebrated. Thinking that 'we are the same because we eat the same' does not happen (Mannur, 2007: 27). Instead, these foods generate a protective urge: if only in reverie, the pain of loss becomes a way to restore the wholeness of this place in the wholeness of one's real or imagined past. Dehistoricized in the timelessness of reverie, the foods become solely Armenian, prepared in a time of rootedness. With this established, the foods reclaim the land as the wellspring of homey values at the heart of self and culture. At the heart of this reclamation is reverie, the creative daydreaming that takes the dreamer to their own remembered home, the place that allowed them to dream in the first place, consolidating experiences into an archetypical image of home as security, felicity and wholeness. Without this reverie,

> man would be a dispersed being. It maintains him through the storms of the heavens and through those of life. It is body and soul . . . Therefore, the places in which we have experienced daydreaming reconstitute themselves in a new daydream, and it is because our memories of former dwelling-places are relived as daydreams that these dwelling-places of the past remain in us for all time.
>
> (Bachelard, 1964: 6)

For the native-born pilgrims, reverie is a return to the original house, becoming a protective cocoon that shields them momentarily from the realities of the present.

In a still hostile environment associated with an era of near ethno-cultural annihilation, pilgrims from the next generation are also in need of protection. But never having lived in Turkey, familiar foods generate reverie-images of a home in the diaspora where these foods were essential components of their deepest 'sense of being', as well as of their identity (Bakalian, 2011; Hirsch, 2012; Pattie, 1999). Because the diasporic home of this second group (along with that of the 1.5 generation) is one that was not cut off, but is still alive, its distillation in reverie supports the pilgrims' agency in valorizing and nurturing their fundamental values, providing an unequivocally protective, spiritual strength. Called into play through the essential tie between food and the deepest meanings of home, the performative nature of this reverie brings this spiritual essence to life. A reverie, then, is not a withdrawal into memories of the past as a refuge (Game, 2011). Rather, as an ongoing creation of an intimate yet idealized place of the past that nurtures their deepest sense of being, it is able to provide the pilgrims with a persistent and protective spiritual strength. This is the larger spiritual reward that the pilgrims can take home, allowing them, perhaps, to experience dinner in the homeland as an integration of the values of a lost past with gratitude for the present and confidence in the future.

Notes

1 I am ever grateful to Armen Aroyan for his kindness and generosity in welcoming me on these trips and for supporting my work, including sharing historical and personal source material.
2 I am deeply grateful to the Antep architect Murad Uçaner for sharing his translation of Yervant's article from Armenian into Turkish and for information about Yervant's neighborhoods and houses.
3 All names associated with published sources are as they appear in the publications. For others, when permission was granted, those with whom I have corresponded, personally interviewed, observed on trips or watched in videos are identified only by their real first name. Those whom I was unable to reach for permission are anonymously referred to as 'one pilgrim'.
4 See Salmaner (2014: 18) for 'how food's performative nature is analogous to the performative nature of identity and how such performativity is manifested in a cookbook genre'. See Hass (2011) for thoughts on how, for the native-born at least, the diaspora complicates the meaning of the real home.
5 'Recipes for gefilte fish are no recipe for coping with the Holocaust' (Klüger, 2012: 30).

References

Abu-Lughod, L. (1991). Writing against culture. In: E. Lewin, ed., *Feminist anthropology: A reader*. Hoboken, NJ: Wiley Blackwell.

Abu-Lughod, L. (2007). Return to half-ruins: Memory, postmemory, and living history in Palestine. In: A. Ahmed and L. Abu-Lughod, eds., *Nakba: Palestine, 1948, and the claims of memory*. New York: Columbia University Press, pp. 77–104.

Agbabian, A. (2018). My hand on stone [in Armenian]. In: A. Aroyan, *The pilgrim speaks*. Glendale, AZ: A. Aroyan. Forthcoming, trans. Gulesserian, L.

Akçam, T. & Kurt, Ü. (2015). *The spirit of the laws: The plunder of wealth in the Armenian genocide*. Trans. Aram Arkun. New York: Berghahn.

A pilgrimage to historic Armenia and Cilicia: June 2007 (2007). [VHS/film]. Glendale, AZ: Armen Aroyan.

Aroyan, Armen. (forthcoming). *The pilgrim speaks.*

Bachelard, G. (1964). *The poetics of space*. Boston, MA: Beacon Press, Trans. Jolas, M.

Bahloul, J. (1992). *The architecture of memory: A Jewish-Muslim household in colonial Algeria, 1937–1962*. New York: Cambridge University Press.

Bakalian, A. P. (2011). *Armenian-Americans: From being to feeling Armenian*. New Brunswick, NJ: Routledge.

Bardenstein, C. (2002). Transmissions interrupted: Reconfiguring food, memory, and gender in the cookbook-memoirs of Middle Eastern exiles. *Signs: Journal of Women in Culture and Society, 28*(1), 353–387.

Bertram, C. (2008). *Imagining the Turkish house: Collective visions of home*. Austin, TX: University of Texas Press.

Bertram, C. (2015). Armenian Americans and Anatolian identity: The encounter with home. In *Critical approaches to Armenian identity in the 21st century: Vulnerability, resilience, and transformation*. Hrant Dink Vakfı, October 2015. Available at: hrantdink. org/en/activities/projects/history-program/329-21-yuzyilda-ermeni-kimligine-elestirel-yaklasimlar-konferansi-2017.

Bertram, C. (forthcoming). Coming to terms with home and homeland. *Journal of the Society for Armenian Studies.*

Çandar, C. (2017). How Turkey went back to square one 10 years after murder of Armenian intellectual. *Al-Monitor*, January 19. Available at: www.al-monitor.com/pulse/originals/2017/01/turkey-hrant-dink-assassination-anniversaire.html [accessed March 23, 2017].

Coles, T. & Timothy, D. J. (2004). *Tourism, diasporas and space*. London and New York: Routledge.

Davis, R. (2011). *Palestinian village histories: Geographies of the displaced*. Stanford, CA: Stanford University Press.

de Certeau, M. (1984). *The practice of everyday life*. Berkeley, CA: University of California Press.

Eng, D. L. & Kazanjian, D. (2003). Introduction: Mourning remains. In: D. L. Eng & D. Kazanjian, eds., *Loss: The politics of mourning*. Berkeley, CA: University of California Press, pp. 1–28.

Game, A. & Metcalfe, A. (2011). 'My corner of the world': Bachelard and Bondi Beach. *Emotion, Space and Society*. Available at: www.sciencedirect.com/science/article/pii/S1755458610000502 [accessed September 20, 2015].

Gieryn, T. F. (2000). A space for place in sociology. *Annual Review of Sociology, 26*, 463–496.

Hage, G. (2010). Migration, food, memory, and home-building. In S. Radstone & W. Schwartz, eds., *Memory: Histories, theories, debates*. New York: Fordham University Press, pp. 416–427.

Hass, A. (2011). Between two worlds. In: M. Hirsch & N. Miller, eds., *Rites of return: Diaspora poetics and the politics of memory*. Cambridge: Cambridge University Press, pp. 173–184.

Hirsch, M. (2012). *The generation of postmemory: Writing and visual culture after the Holocaust*. New York: Columbia University Press.

Hirsch, M. & Miller, N. (eds.) (2011). *Rites of return: Diaspora poetics and the politics of memory*. Cambridge: Cambridge University Press.

Kaprielian-Churchill, I. (2006). Keghi: Yesterday, today and tomorrow. *Western Armenia Forum*. September 30. Available at: http://armenie-occidentale.forumactif.fr/t450-keghi-geghi [accessed June 1, 2017].

Klein, K. L. (2000). On the emergence of memory in historical discourse. *Representations, Special Issue: Grounds for Remembering, 69* (Winter), 127–150.

Klüger, Ruth. (2012). *Still alive: A Holocaust girlhood remembered*. New York: Feminist Press at the City University of New York.

Küçükyan, Yervant. (1952). *100 Jam Aintabi: Huşer Yev Dıbarivorutner*. Beirut. Zanaser. Trans. into Turkish by Murad Uçaner. Gaziantep: Uçaner archive, 2014.

Kugelmass, J. & Shandler, J. (1989). *Going home: How American Jews invent the old world*. New York: Yivo Institute for Jewish Research.

Magzanian, Alberta, Magzanian, Anna & Magzanian, L. (2008). *The recipes of Musa Dagh: An Armenian cookbook in a dialect of its own: The recipes of Victoria Chaparian Magzanian*. Lulu.com, n.p.

Mannur, A. (2007). Culinary nostalgia: Authenticity, nationalism, and diaspora. *MELUS: Multi-Ethnic Literature of the United States, 32*(4), 11–31.

Morinis, E. (1981). Pilgrimage: The human quest. *Numen, 28*(2), 281–285.

Najarian, C. (2005) Our trip to historic Armenia. Available at: www.bvahan.com/armenianpilgrimages/najarian1.htm [accessed May 28, 2014].

Nora, P. (1989). Between memory and history: Les Lieux de Memoire. *Representations, 26*(1), 7–24.

Palmer, C. (2005). An ethnography of Englishness: Experiencing identity through tourism. *Annals of Tourism Research, 32*(1), 7–27.

Pattie, S. (1999). Longing and belonging: Issues of homeland in Armenian diaspora. *Political and Legal Anthropology Review, 22*(2), 80–92.

Rumbaut, R. G. (2012). Generation 1.5, educational experiences of. In: J. Banks, ed., *Encyclopedia of diversity in education*. Available at: http://ssrn.com/abstract=2182167 [accessed June 2, 2017].

Salmaner, M. (2014). *The bittersweet taste of the past: Reading food in Armenian literature in Turkish*. University of Washington, Seattle, Ph.D. dissertation.

Shemmassian, V. L. (n.d.). The experience of the Musa Dagh Armenian immigrants in the United States during the 1910s–1940s. *Haigazian Armenological Review*, 195–227. Available at: www.haigazian.edu.lb/Publications/Documents/HARVol31fullcontent/195–226 [accessed April 10, 2016].

Stephenson, M. L. (2002). Travelling to the ancestral homelands: The aspirations and experiences of a UK Caribbean community. *Current Issues in Tourism, 5*(5): 378–425.

Sutton, D. E. (2001). *Remembrance of repasts: An anthropology of food and memory*. London: Bloomsbury Academic.

Tuan, Y. (1990). *Topophilia: A study of environmental perception, attitudes, and values*. New York: Columbia University Press.

Tuan, Y. (2014). *Space and place: The perspective of experience*. Minneapolis, MN: University of Minnesota Press.

Werfel, F. (2012 [1933]). *The forty days of Musa Dagh* (G. Dunlop & J. Reidel, trans.). Boston, MA: David R. Godine.

11 Memoryscapes of the homeland by two generations of British Bangladeshis

Md Farid Miah and Russell King

Introduction

In this chapter, we interpret and compare memories of life, landscape and kinship-based socialities in Bangladesh on the part of two generations of British Bangladeshis, namely first-generation immigrants born in Bangladesh but now living in London, and their British-born children. The research material was collected via in-depth interviews with members of the Bangladeshi immigrant community in East London, the major concentration of Bangladeshis in the UK, and in Sylhet, the peripheral, north-eastern region of Bangladesh, from where most of these immigrants originate.

According to Gardner and Mand (2012: 971), the British Bangladeshi community is a 'transnational community *par excellence*', notable for the vibrancy of the links which are maintained with Bangladesh, despite the long distance. Such links include continuous exchanges of goods, gifts, ideas and, above all, visits. We interpret these visits and other connections to the Bangladeshi homeland through the lens of memory. We propose the notion of 'memoryscapes' (cf. Phillips & Reyes, 2011) to connote the real and tangible, but often nostalgic and idealised, recollections of places, landscapes and people remembered from the distant past of childhood, or from more recent experiences of visits. Beyond the addition of memoryscape to Appadurai's (1990, 1996) exploration of the various 'scapes' which represent contemporary global cultural exchange, other innovative features of this chapter are its cross-generational and gendered comparisons, and its multi-sited fieldwork in London and Bangladesh.

We therefore analyse two 'memoryscapes' associated with this long-distance migration and the visits back and forth. The first, for the first generation only, is about memories of their early lives in Bangladesh. For most, this entails nostalgic recollections of childhood in rural Sylhet, but also, for some, more harrowing memories of political struggle and economic hardship which led to the decision to leave. The second memoryscape refers to visits 'home', both of the first and the second generation. These visits take place at fairly regular intervals, depending on the family's financial circumstances, the strength of their transnational ties and the geographical distribution of kin. Annual visits are typical, but they can also take place more, or less, frequently. They fall into a category of mobility known as 'visiting friends and relatives' (VFR) but, beyond this kinship and social network function, they can also have a touristic expression, since the journeys are seen as holidays and may involve visiting other parts of Bangladesh in addition to the place of origin. Moreover, some of these trips have an economic dimension, as opportunities are taken to check on investments in land and housing, and to resolve matters of inheritance.

In synthesis, we argue that the experiences and practices of VFR mobilities demonstrate that the transnational social field linking London and Bangladesh is highly interactive and performative. Memories are on balance positive, fuelled by nostalgia, the reinforcement of kinship and family solidarity, and a strong sense of connection to the 'homeland'. However, our findings also suggest that the transnational bond between Bangladesh and its London diaspora is at a critical juncture. In particular, disputes around land and properties are threatening the continuation of the British Bangladeshi transnational way of life, and the depth of the relationship between host and home country is in danger of being diluted.

The chapter is structured as follows. In the next section we introduce the reader to the British Bangladeshi community in East London. This is followed by a brief section on the methods used to collect research data. We then review the literature on the intersections between memory, diaspora and visits to the homeland, including justification for our use of the notion of memoryscape. The empirical findings are presented in two parts. The first concentrates on memoryscapes of the first generation, looking back to their pre-migration lives in the homeland. The second part is about visits 'home' and their powerful significance for transnational identities and kinship networks, with comparisons drawn between the generations and between men and women participants. In the conclusion we stress the key findings and their originality, and speculate briefly on the future of British Bangladeshis' relationship with the homeland.

British Bangladeshis

Although there is a less extensive literature on Bangladeshi migration to Britain than there is on the Indians and Pakistanis, the historical presence of Bengalis, in London especially, is long-established. Already by the 19th and early 20th centuries Bengali seamen, called *lascars*, recruited to work as cooks and deckhands by the East India Company, had jumped ship and set down the roots of their community in degraded housing close to the London docklands. The vast majority of the *lascars* came from Sylhet, the north-eastern region of Bangladesh (then still part of British India), and subsequent chain migration has preserved the link with this region of origin (Adams, 1987; Gardner, 1995).

The Bangladeshi community of East London received a significant numerical boost in the decades immediately after the Second World War, when Britain recruited workers from Commonwealth countries – who were at that time British passport holders – to rebuild infrastructure and work in various industries and services in the fast-growing postwar economy. These early postwar migrant workers were mostly men. However, the Commonwealth Immigration Act of 1962, designed to control immigration, in many ways had the opposite effect, as it encouraged Bangladeshi men to stay put and to bring over their wives and families. Investments were made in houses and businesses, the second generation was born, and the 'myth of return' (cf. Anwar, 1979) became the complex reality of the community's attitudes and behaviours. In other words, the notion of return was continually held as an ideology, at the same time as the Bangladeshi families moved towards settling down in Britain, knowing that, in reality, they would probably not return. The contradiction is partly resolved by a generally intense transnational identity and contacts, including regular visits 'home'. Meantime, the Bangladeshi war of independence (1971) had also contributed to the further inflow of migrants who were escaping the chaos and atrocities of the conflict.

The Bangladeshi migrant-heritage population in the UK is now well established, with a multi-generational structure. Identified as a separate ethnic category for the first time in the 1981 census, the population has continued to grow rapidly, reaching more than 450,000 in 2011, 222,000 of whom are in London, mainly concentrated in East London where the original focus in Tower Hamlets, near the old dockland area, still exists, alongside an eastward suburban drift towards Ilford and Barking. In the 2011 census, both UK-born and non-UK-born populations of Bangladeshi origin were categorised as 'Asian British-Bangladeshi'; as a result, contemporary researchers, including ourselves, use the term 'British Bangladeshi' in a wider sense regardless of birthplace, citizenship or immigration status.

Despite the fact that Gardner (1995, 2002; also Gardner & Mand, 2012) observed that Bangladeshi migrants in London maintain strong transnational ties with their homeland, there has been little systematic exploration of the memories of the places left behind. Zeitlyn's recent research (2012, 2015) on Bangladeshi transnational childhoods does include participation in the children's visits with their families to see their extended kin and places of origin in Bangladesh, and we will summarise this research later in the chapter. We include our own material on children's homeland visits, in the form of memories of such visits held by adult-age second-generation British Bangladeshis; but we also analyse a fuller spectrum of the VFR phenomenon, comparing the experiences of first- and second-generation visitors to the homeland.

Note on methods

Fieldwork, carried out both in London and Sylhet, consisted mainly of semi-structured interviews but also more informal participation within the community, including on family visits in Bangladesh. The interviews were the responsibility of the first-named author. The second author contributed by shaping the research design and theoretical frameworks, based on previous research on visits to the migrant homeland in other geographic contexts (Christou & King, 2014; King & Lulle, 2015; King *et al.*, 2013). Both authors participated equally in the analysis and interpretation of the interview scripts.

Prior to conducting the formal interviews, contact was made with potential interviewees via the first author's personal networks within the Bangladeshi community living in East London and at various social, cultural and community events. These initial contacts and preparatory meetings were necessary to gain trust, and set the boundaries and expectations for participating in the research, including following standard ethical procedures of informed consent. Over a six-month period in 2016–17, 30 interviews with first- and second-generation Bangladeshis were carried out in London, followed by another 30 interviews with visiting migrants and their non-migrant relatives in Sylhet during a three-month field trip in 2017. Interviews were more or less evenly distributed across generations and by gender. The first-generation migrants were interviewed in Bangla, the second-generation participants in English. All interviews were subsequently transcribed and those in Bangla translated into English. We use pseudonyms to respect participants' confidentiality.

Memoryscapes, diasporic space and visits to the homeland

In their text *Global Memoryscapes*, Phillips and Reyes (2011: 2) explore the practices of memory as they relate to globalisation – the movement of people, ideas, technologies and discourses across national boundaries and the consequent emergence of new transnational social structures that are not bound by national borders or identities. These authors envision memoryscape as 'a complex landscape upon which memories and memory practices move, come into contact with, and are contested by, other forms of remembrance' (2011: 13). Whilst Phillips and Reyes' book is mainly about public memory, the memories of our participants are personal, private (albeit often shared) and spatially localised.

Our notion of memoryscapes introduces a material, spatio-temporal and aesthetic dimension in which experiences of earlier life-stages or recent visits sited in the diasporic homeland are narrated, often with warm nostalgia, but sometimes laced with tension or disappointment (cf. Christou & King, 2010: 645). In this way, we add memory to the litany of 'scapes' – ethnoscapes, ideoscapes, technoscapes, financescapes and mediascapes – specified by Appadurai (1990, 1996) as demonstrative of how media, ideas and travel (to which we add memory) fuel individual and collective imagination in the practice of everyday lives. Representing multiple realities, Appadurai's scapes are fluid and constantly shifting, and completely intertwined with each other, especially when connected to important global processes like international migration. Here the key 'scape' is ethnoscape, which is the result (also in the imagination) of the movement of people across borders and cultures, reshaping those cultures along the way. Appadurai claims that his scapes

> are not objectively given relations which look the same from every angle of vision, but rather . . . they are deeply perspectival constructs, inflected very much by the historical, linguistic and political situatedness of different sorts of actors . . . [including] intimate face-to-face groups, such as villages, neighbourhoods and families.
>
> (1990: 296)

Migration – especially in the minds of migrants – leaves behind a trail of memories of times and places in the past. Often these memoryscapes are idealised, but for the migrants themselves they are also real and tangible, and refer to the minutiae of places and landscapes, and to the social contexts and relations that inhabit these landscapes of memory. These principles are nicely brought out by Butalia's (2011) chapter in *Global Memoryscapes*, which chronicles an emotional journey undertaken by an elderly Indian Sikh back to his pre-partition village in Pakistan.

Memory, meanwhile, can be regarded as an act of remembering which creates new understandings of both the past and the present (Agnew, 2005: 8). In this chapter we construct Bangladesh as a geographic and psychic space of 'home', or perhaps better, 'homeland', in which that diasporic hearth, especially its landscape and people, is remembered or imagined by many diasporans as a space of familiarity and safety, but by others as a locus of unfamiliarity and disillusionment.

In her classic text *Cartographies of Diaspora*, Avtah Brah writes that the concept of 'diaspora space' represents 'the intersectionality of diaspora, border and dis/location', as well as 'a point of confluence of economic, political, cultural and psychic processes' (1996: 181). Brah's argument is that diaspora space as a conceptual category is inhabited not only by those who have migrated and their descendants, but equally by those who are represented as indigenous, as sedentary non-migrants. Brah concludes (1996: 181, her emphasis), 'the concept of *diaspora space* (as opposed to that of diaspora) includes the entanglement of genealogies of dispersion with those of "staying put"'.

The interwoven notions of diaspora, home and homeland are intricately connected with, and contingent upon, 'memory work'. The diasporic landscape of the homeland and the people 'left behind' hold a particular attraction to migrants and their descendants, and this is what goads them to make repeated return visits, which in turn reshape those memories. As Marschall points out (2017: 6):

> The revisit can be a vehicle for the systematic pursuit of memories; an extension of the process of remembering itself; an opportunity for reconstructing one's own past and affirming or reshaping one's identity. As the traveller encounters the old home, memories are recaptured, refreshed and verified; distorted memories are exposed and adjusted; embodied memories are relived through bodily experiences; long-forgotten memories can suddenly resurface and cause deeply emotional reactions; memories may be spontaneously shared with companions. After the journey, memories are re-evaluated, consolidated, synthesized and narrated; in the process, they may be compared and partly merged with other people's memories and perhaps one's own memories from previous journeys.

According to Brah (1996: 182), 'the image of a journey' is 'at the heart of the notion of diaspora'. But then she goes on to more narrowly specify that 'diasporic journeys are essentially about settling down, about putting roots "elsewhere"'. Two important critiques of this statement can be made. The first is the implication that the diasporic journey is inevitably a journey of migration, of settlement and (reflecting the origin of the term 'diaspora') of scattering. We question this assumption on two counts: one, that the journey is only one-way; and two, that the journey ineluctably leads to permanent settlement. There is now a substantial body of recent research which documents the fluidity of diaspora as a social and geographic formation, with evidence of onward migration or 'rediasporisation', and 'counter-diaspora' or return to the diasporic homeland (see, *inter alia*, Christou & King, 2014; King & Olsson, 2014; Tsuda, 2009; Wessendorf, 2013).

The second critique of Brah's formulation is to point out that 'diasporic journeys' can be both multi-directional and multi-temporal, including short-term visits. Indeed, visits 'home' are considered a fundamental constitutive element of the Bangladeshi diasporic experience – of being a migrant, or a migrant descendant, long-term settled in a foreign land. In terms of the temporal rhythms of movement, visits to see relatives and friends in the homeland are enfolded within the longer rhythms of lifetime migration and diaspora formation (cf. Williams *et al.*, 2011). Indeed the practice of making regular homeland visits may facilitate the continuance of long-term settlement abroad and abrogate the necessity to confront both the existential dilemma of the migrant ('where do I belong?') and the binary decision of whether to return-migrate.

Ignored in the migration and diaspora literature until relatively recently, visits made by migrants to their countries and communities of origin have now become the focus of a substantial body of empirical research: see Baldassar (2001) for a pioneering ethnographic study of Italo-Australians and Janta *et al.* (2015) for a literature review. As pointed out in our introduction, travel within the diasporic space created by the history and geography of Bangladeshi migration can be classified as part of VFR mobilities. Theoretically, these diaspora-defined visits can be of three types: migrants and their descendants visiting the homeland – the '*desh*'; non-migrants from the homeland visiting their relatives abroad in the diaspora; and diasporans visiting relatives and friends in other diasporic locations outside the homeland. Our analysis in this chapter is limited to homeland visits.

Baldassar (2001: 3) characterises the visit home as a 'secular pilgrimage' of enormous importance to migrants, not only for the first generation, for whom the return travel is to their place or district of birth, but also for the second generation, for whom the journey has a different resonance – a connection to their family's geographical and cultural origins. For the first generation, visits are mainly about reinforcing their Bangladeshi, or more precisely Sylheti, identity, keeping in touch with kin and community, demonstrating their success abroad, checking up on land and property, and perhaps investing in new acquisitions. For the second generation, the homeland visit can be (but is not always) a 'transformatory rite of passage' (Baldassar, 2001: 323) which unveils the ethnoscape of their ancestral past, but also poses soul-searching questions about the exact nature of their hybrid British Bangladeshi identity.

Memoryscapes of childhood

The most evocative remembrances of the physical and social landscape of the home country were narrated by older first-generation Bangladeshis thinking back to their childhood and early-adult lives in Sylhet. The memories were undoubtedly sharpened by the contrast between what they recalled, often vividly, of their youthful rural milieu, and their subsequent working lives on British merchant ships or later in industries and low-status service jobs in England. These memoryscapes covered several interlinked themes: the love and care they received from their family and kin; the air and its smells; the fresh food and fruits they savoured; the friends they played with in and out of school; the teachers they were taught by; the paddy fields, gardens and open yards around their modest houses; the ponds they bathed and swam in; playing in the rain and mud; and many other things. Each of these themes and topics was contained in several nostalgic narrative accounts. Below are a few typical examples.

We start with Alim who, like most first-generation older migrants, had been living in England for many decades. In the following extract from his interview, he first gives a good description of the homestead that he remembers, and then moves on to highlight some more specific memories of his Sylheti childhood.

> There used to be ponds, both in front and behind most of the houses in our village, but many have disappeared now. We use to bathe in those ponds, and sometimes we would start with one pond and then move to swim in another until we finished swimming in all the ponds. And when the ponds were running out of water in the dry season, we'd run to catch the fishes there . . . some of them we put in water tanks at home and fed them too . . . I had a cycle, an Indian one, and my cousin had one too, a British-made one, so we used to do cycle racing with each other on our way to school. After school, we played in the late afternoon, chasing one another, playing hide and seek.

For Siddik, below, the physical landscape of the village and its rural economy is palpable, as is his memory of the warmth and humour of the older villagers.

> I remember hosting people at home, helping the labourers during the harvest in the Bengali new year, processing the paddies in our yard . . . watching people travel to and from the market. Touring the entire village is unforgettable, entering from one end and then walking past one house after another. People were more caring then, old people were very funny – there was this old grandmother, she used to joke with us all the time. We had mangos, berries and many other fruits, whatever was in season, from different households, and so many other things we did, and came back home before sunset.

According to Renu, a first-generation British Bangladeshi woman, the memories of the homeland, including specific micro-details of the local landscape, are felt if anything more strongly as time passes; and she spoke of these memories not so much in a tone of nostalgic regret, but almost as an expression of rejoicing:

I hear from other people that one's country is one's motherland, but I feel this in real terms . . . I miss my country and my mother . . . The air, the water, and even the trees are still dear to me . . . I miss my home country every single day. Whether we live here in England for ten years or fifty, we will always miss our country because that's where our roots are.

However, these sylvan, peaceful memories of what is constructed as an idyllic childhood are not the whole story. Memory is also tied to important historical, political and personal struggles (Hua, 2005: 200). Whilst the earlier-arrived post-war migrants were settling in the UK, their homeland was experiencing massive political changes. Independence from Britain first placed Bangladesh as East Pakistan, but then a bloody war of renewed independence followed in 1971 to create the state of Bangladesh. Many of the older British Bangladeshis had powerful memories of those troubled years of violence and further partition. This is a small part of Kabir's long recollection about his early life:

I went to my village school and spent all my school years in Bangladesh. During the liberation war of 1971, I was a year 10 student and was preparing for the matriculation exam, similar to your GCSE exam here. When the war started, we witnessed the barbaric atrocities, me and my classmates. Friends were being chased by the Pakistani army and their Bangladeshi collaborators, and as we were relatively young males, we were eventually rounded up and captured, and tortured too. They looted and burned our village as well. Me and some of my friends managed to escape and cross the border; we had some training and went back to fight against them. I remember the terrifying death of one of my close friends.

Whatever profound political and socio-economic changes have happened over the past several decades, the British Bangladeshis still recite these memories, pleasant or otherwise, and are thereby encouraged to maintain strong transnational ties to their homeland. The ties are affective and symbolic, but also material, comprising remittances sent to support non-migrant family members, as well as physical visits to the key places of their remembered pasts. Indeed, the journeys are a reification of those memories. Especially when they are made on a regular basis, the visits are also being re-lived and re-made through the experiences of the present. In the next section, we examine these trips and the discourses surrounding them.

Visits 'home': generation and gender contrasts

The visit home is a diasporic journey of short-term duration which creates its own memoryscapes of places, events, kinship relations, social customs and cultural impressions. As Brah (1996: 183–184) points out, the experience of these trips varies intersectionally: here we focus especially on the generational and gendered aspects, given that among our research participants there is less variation across the other intersectional modalities of 'race', class and religion.

The central themes connected to most migrants' journeys to their homeland are articulated through the memories accumulated from such visits, which in turn reveal various admixtures of nostalgia, shared histories, and reinforced or changed identities (Marschall 2017: 4). On the whole, as one might expect, the first-generation migrants feel more strongly about their country and maintain firmer connections to it than the second generation. For the first generation, migration to the UK was the most significant event in their lives; hence, as we saw in the previous section, they preserve vivid memories of the land, people and environment where they spent their formative years. Meanwhile, the first generation actively transmits these images and memories of the homeland to their British-born children, encouraging them to visit the country of their grandparents, receive the hospitality always on offer, enjoy the food and warmth, and experience the homeland's 'way of life'. Through this continual process of forwarding the memories of the homeland from one generation to another, the second generation is 'trained' to think about their ancestors and to remember how to behave on visits to the homeland.

Timing and frequency of visits

Existing studies of transnational and diasporic communities acknowledge that migrants and their descendants maintain multiple connections, affiliations and relationships across borders, binding together and giving meaningful life to these diasporic spaces and transnational social fields (e.g. Brah, 1996; Glick Schiller, 2010; Levitt & Jaworsky, 2007). Among the familial, social, economic, political and cultural activities that migrants engage in across their transnational spaces, home trips are often mentioned, but rarely is systematic attention paid to their multiple nature, timing and frequency. The general impression, derived from studies in various global contexts, is that migrants visit their homelands, mainly their villages and towns of origin, around once a year for holidays (often coinciding with school holidays for family visits), and for special occasions such as weddings and religious festivals (see, e.g., Ali & Holden, 2006; Christou & King, 2014; Levitt, 2009; Mason, 2004; Stephenson, 2002; Vathi & King, 2011). Missing from these and other studies of visits is systematic detail on the temporalities and varied purposes of such visits.

What we know of the role of home journeys in sustaining the British Bangladeshi transnational community is accurately summed up by Zeitlyn (2015: 51):

> The visit is a big event in the lives of most British Bangladeshi families; they are the source of careful preparation, planning and imagining for many months to raise the considerable amounts of money necessary to pay for the flights, gifts for relatives and expenses of the visit . . . Visits to Bangladesh are a crucial meeting place for families . . . 'Being there' and 'being seen there', reconnecting with the people and places of their ancestral villages and bringing relatives and neighbours up to date with developments in the family are crucial elements of the visit . . . Visits can also be about being there at key

moments. Weddings, deaths, funerals and religious celebrations are all occasions where a visit might occur. Visits are arranged, where possible, to coincide with these events and in some cases the events are arranged with visits.

Whilst our findings support every aspect of Zeitlyn's account, we also find that the Bangladeshi transnational social field is more intense and interactive than is commonly understood. We found that migrants visit their home country surprisingly frequently and for a whole variety of reasons; some planned, but others, by force of circumstance, unplanned and arranged at short notice. Naturally, the nature and motivation of the visits vary from one individual and family to another. Generally, family trips with children are more planned and relatively infrequent, but individuals, couples and groups of friends travel more frequently and even spontaneously. The flight schedules between London and Bangladesh are virtually fully booked all year round, and our informants in Sylhet told us how their friends, relatives, co-villagers and hired drivers are frequently heading off to the airports to collect '*Londonis*'; British Bangladeshi visitors. The following interview exchange with Habib, a Sylhet-residing relative of a British Bangladeshi migrant family, provides typical insights:

Farid: On what occasions do they [migrants] visit Bangladesh? Is it just for special occasions?

Habib: Not always. Sometimes they come just for a visit, to meet their relatives, look after their houses, because sometimes they leave their houses locked up . . . and they come to check their condition . . . and to look after the things they have here and to solve any outstanding issues that arise in their absence.

Farid: Do they visit at any particular time of year?

Habib: What I have observed is that those who have kids going to school or college, they come during the school holiday time. But those who do not have these kinds of commitment come anytime. Sometimes, someone comes alone, depending on their need and the weather conditions here. For example, if they want to come just for a holiday, they try to avoid the rainy season and choose the winter time instead.

The weather, then, is a common criterion to consider for these visits. In other migration contexts, for example where migrants originate from Mediterranean countries, return visits take place in a warm, sunny, dry atmosphere of happy holiday relaxation, when the locals, too, are in festive mood. Examples include the cases of Greece, Cyprus, Turkey and Albania researched by the second author of this chapter (King *et al.*, 2011; King & Kılınç, 2014; Kılınç & King, Chapter 12 in this volume; Vathi & King, 2011). Unfortunately, the main British school holidays coincide with the uncomfortably hot and rainy period in Bangladesh. Whilst some second-generation children seemed oblivious to this, others were not. Zeitlyn (2012, 2015: 52–57), who interviewed young British Bangladeshi children about their homeland visits, found many complaining about the heat, flies, mosquitoes and smells. We did not interview young children, but we did ask the adult second generation to recall their travel to Bangladesh when they were children. And some first-generation interviewees spoke of their offspring's reactions to summer family trips. Falguni, a first-generation middle-aged mother interviewed in Sylhet whilst visiting with her teenage children, recalled their reactions on this and other visits over the years:

> My children don't like it here very much because . . . they get bitten by mosquitoes . . . they really suffer here, you can't imagine. If we could have the summer holiday in December instead . . . My children can't go out in this extreme weather to meet the relatives.

By contrast, second-generation Nazrul had fond and mischievous memories of his own childhood visits. Here he recalls with affection two particular incidents:

> Some of my best memories when growing up [were visits to] Bangladesh. You know, I remember, as a kid, I was smoking and my *mama* [maternal uncle] caught me and smacked the shit out of me [laughs] . . . I don't smoke now but, you know, some of my fondest memories.
>
> . . .
>
> When it's the monsoon season you have big *haors* [wetlands] . . . and I remember, once, we were going somewhere *noukay* [by boat] and it was raining and *eto batash* [very windy] so, what we did, we had an umbrella and turned it into a sail [laughter] . . . and the *nouka* [boat] was flying [laughs].

Although most visits are carefully planned, it is not uncommon for them to be arranged very quickly in response to an unexpected necessity, such as sickness, land/property matters or the need to accompany another person who cannot travel alone. For example, second-generation Johura had to squeeze time from her busy work schedule in London to take her elderly mother to Sylhet for an emergency visit:

> My mother, she is 70 now . . . she has difficulties, she is not able to travel independently . . . She needed a wheelchair at the airport, she also needed support on the journey, because she gets confused. It's a long journey and it can be quite exhausting for someone who is elderly. It's also quite an emotional experience [for her].

Likewise, Nazrul had to immediately board a plane for two successive trips in order to visit his father who had retired back to Bangladesh, suffered a stroke and then died.

> First he had a stroke, so as soon as he had the stroke I went there to visit him and then I came back . . . and then a couple of days later he passed away, and so I went back again.

Nazrul's father illustrates an emerging migration pattern – the 'retirement return' of the first generation – which, although not very widespread, affects the ongoing transnational family dynamics of care and visiting. Naturally, as retirees are of mature or advanced age, they require regular care and perhaps also medication, and this can imply regular visits to Sylhet for the adult second generation.

A final reason why visits are often made with virtually instantaneous timing is to resolve legal issues which have suddenly arisen. First-generation Kabir was interviewed initially in London, and we quoted from this narrative above. Then, several months later, he popped up in Sylhet during the second stage of the field-work. He had to return at a day's notice to sign papers relating to a land donation. Here is the full story:

> During our previous interview in London, I told you [speaking to Farid] that I had no plan to visit again this year. I had no wish to come. I even saw you off when you left for Bangladesh [to go on fieldwork there]. But, suddenly, some land issues arose. I had a shared piece of land not far from here, next to the road, which me and my cousin inherited from our grandparents . . . When the village elders were looking for land to build a new mosque, my cousin agreed to donate this piece of land. But he is not the sole owner; he only owns one-third of it. Yet he promised to donate it without seeking my per-mission. He then called me to inform me of this. I said to him: 'It's my land too. However, as you promised to donate it, I cannot insult you in front of them [the village elders]. So, how do you want to resolve this?' He said he would transfer his part-ownership of another piece of shared land to me in exchange, and I agreed to this. However, there is an urgent documentation process for all of this, and that is why I am here.

The relevance of generation and gender

Experiences and memories of visiting the (ancestral) home country vary consid-erably by gender and generation, even when these visits are *en famille*. Some of these differences are documented in the existing literature on British Bangladeshis. Gardner and Mand (2012) and Zeitlyn (2012, 2015: 52–61) provide insightful ethnographic observations on these family visits to Sylhet, focusing in their case especially on the children's perspective. We know from these and other studies that Bangladeshi society is very patriarchal and composed of patrilineal families. Compared to females, especially young females, males enjoy the relative freedom to go anywhere and do as they wish. Whilst most British Bangladeshi women travel to the homeland in the company of male relatives – husbands, fathers, family groups etc. – male migrants of any generation travel in the ways that they want or are deemed necessary – on their own, with family, siblings, cousins or in a group. British Bangladeshis with children tend to think carefully about when to take them, depending on the children's age and adaptability to the Bangladeshi 'home' envi-ronment. Too young, and they do not appreciate it and might get sick; much older, when they are teenagers, and they are likely to get bored and become rebellious.

Some aspects of the gendered experiences of young children visiting Sylhet are nicely captured in the fieldwork accounts of Zeitlyn (2012, 2015), although his participant observation evidence does not allow systematic, robust comparison. In one fieldwork vignette, described in both of his key publications, Zeitlyn (2012: 959–963; 2015: 58–61) observes the behaviour of two sisters, Nazrin (aged 6) and Shirin (11) as they visit the family farm with their parents and brothers, Rafique (9) and Tanvir (3). Whilst Rafique was able to join the local boys of the *bari* (the family homestead) and run around, play football, chase cows, climb trees and get muddy, Nazrin, who desperately wanted to join in (after all, she played football in England), was repeatedly hauled back by her 'minder' (her 16-year-old uncle) and consigned to the care of the *apa* (older sisters) who comforted her and oiled her hair. Shirin, on the threshold of adolescence, was even more carefully controlled, and not allowed to talk to men, only to the *apa* who were teaching her how to behave as a 'good' Bangladeshi girl. Meanwhile Tanvir, the youngest, was being spoilt by all the attention thrown at him and his behaviour deteriorated during the course of the visit.

As a 'model' of gendered sibling behaviour, this account of one family's visit to rural Sylhet is probably fairly accurate, and no doubt was chosen by Zeitlyn precisely because of this. Yet the same author also gives other examples which subvert, or at least nuance, the above vignette. Thus we hear from Ishrat (girl, aged 11) who particularly enjoyed the fun and games at her cousin's wedding ('It was fantastic . . . we had a cake fight') and the freedom of 'playing outside 24/7'. But we also get to know of the behaviour of Saiful (boy, age not given) who refused to play with the local boys his age and who complained bitterly about everything – the hard beds, the food, the toilets, the lack of TV and so on.

Insights from our own data on the gendered nature of adult visits reveal similarly mixed reactions. On the one hand, women migrants are grateful for the relief from the heavy burden of family and household chores and paid work that the holiday visit brings. They are able to relax in the sisterly company of the local women. On the other hand, visiting women, like the local women, are subject to limitations on their spatial movements. Nazrul reported the following interaction with his wife about their visits to Bangladesh, sparked off by the media attention given to Nadia Hussain, the British Bangladeshi winner of the popular British TV cookery competition 'The Great British Bake Off':

You know, I look at my wife's experience. Most Bangladeshi women that you talk to, about their experiences of [visiting] Bangladesh, they say it's never been good, for a number of reasons. You know, I was watching this, hmm . . . this Bangladeshi girl Nadia Hussain, the Great British Bake Off; my wife made me watch that programme the other night. And the one thing that she [Nadia Hussain] said that really stuck out, on the TV programme, was that, since she was very young, 'our father brought us kids to Bangladesh, every two years . . . But the only thing we ever saw was the village, we were never allowed out of our village'. And my wife said: 'there, you know, that's true, I had similar experiences'.

Similar patterns of gendered, but also highly variable, reactions are evidenced from parallel studies carried out on family visits to Pakistan by Bolognani (2007), Cressey (2006) and Mason (2004). Meanwhile, Rytter (2010) describes a play, 'A Sunbeam of Hope', written and performed by a Pakistani community group in Copenhagen, which is a satirical account of a family visit to Pakistan. The play employs exaggerated stereotypes of the different generations and genders, to the great amusement of the audience, made up of Pakistani migrants. Let us quote just one fragment of the play to demonstrate its combination of insight and humour. The two teenage children are introduced to their grandfather, whom they have never met before. The boy is dressed in a hip hop outfit and has bleached hair; the daughter is more modestly dressed; neither speak the local language. As the grandfather approaches his grandchildren, he moves to greet them in the traditional manner, putting his hands on their heads. The children misread his gesture and respond by giving the old man 'high fives'.

Our interview data, as stated earlier, is with the first generation and adult second generation. We have seen from examples given earlier that the first generation has stronger ties to the homeland than the subsequent generations. The first generation's visits to their country of origin are all about re-experiencing the 'place' of home, catching up with their relatives and friends, and maintaining their properties and inheritance in a changing environment. For the second generation, the home trips have a somewhat different set of meanings, and often different itineraries too. First, they consider travel to Bangladesh more as a holiday destination – but one they are semi-obliged to choose because of the strength of family connections there. This means that, whilst they make the obligatory visit to the ancestral village or town, they are also more likely to take in other sites on their holiday itinerary. Yet, wherever they go, they experience a new socio-cultural environment and a new way of life, a contrast to the one they were brought up in. They experience – as they relate in their interviews – a new culture, generous hospitality of local people, authentic food and refreshments, and what they regard as genuine human warmth.

This contrast in traditions of hospitality between Bangladesh and Britain (and even among British Bangladeshis in Britain) was something that struck many second-generation participants. British-born Abul recounted his impression of this contrast:

> To be honest, I love Bengali culture . . . especially the hospitality. For example, if you come to my home [in London] right now, I can offer you a cuppa, like a cup of tea and a biscuit, nothing else. Maybe I can offer you lunch, maybe; but it's not from my heart. I am not going to offer you to stay at my home overnight . . . But if you go to Bengali society, the houses there, they are going to offer you food, tea, staying overnight . . . like they care about you from the heart.

For the first generation, visits are more focused on their parental homes, but here too, the nature of visiting is changing. Some of the longer-established first generation now have two homes in Bangladesh, one in the ancestral village in the family compound, and another in Sylhet city or another big town. Visiting the village house and paying their respects to their relatives and the ancestors' graves becomes important for those who choose to mainly stay in their city home. Having done everything else, they take the opportunity to travel around to visit various tourist attractions. Two of these stand out in the narratives. One is going to Jaflong, a mountain resort area where the highlight is a boat trip to the water-fall. The other is Cox's Bazar, a southern coastal town close to the border with Myanmar, where they enjoy the long sandy beach, staying in nice hotels, fresh seafood, shopping and boat trips to the offshore islands.

Of tensions, property disputes and being a 'Moo-Aloo'

The generally positive memoryscapes of the homeland and visits there are nowadays being threatened by disputes around property ownership. Earlier we heard how Kabir got annoyed when his cousin donated some of their jointly owned land for a new mosque – a conflict that was quickly settled by trading some other shared-ownership land. But in other respects, these property disputes represent deeper structural cleavages in the long-term evolution of the Bangladeshi diasporic community in Britain. On the one hand, long-settled migrants in Britain have accumulated capital to invest in the home country, and in addition may have been bequeathed land by deceased relatives there. Many migrants, especially the first generation, have invested in businesses, purchased extra land and built 'nice' houses as a visible symbol of their material success. These houses are like 'anchors' in the homeland, used as a place to stay when visiting, and to be used as an inheritance for the second generation to maintain their ties to the homeland, and to pass them on to their children in turn. On the other hand, the home country has been through a fundamental political, social and economic transition, during which time the migrants have mostly been absent. They find that the country they once knew and loved, with its family solidarity, kinship ties and social attachments, has now changed.

The problems become manifest when migrants return to claim their inherited assets, when they want to sell property or when they want to purchase land and build new property. Others – the first generation – come back to Bangladesh to retire and so need to take back the care of their properties. Or the second generation wants to reclaim their inheritance after the death of their parents.

Most of the well-established Bangladeshi migrants in London have sent money to a Bangladeshi relative – typically a brother – to purchase land and properties for them. When the migrant returns to check, they find that the relative they gave the responsibility to make the purchase has put their name on the official registration documents too. Some relatives have gone even further, and substituted their name on the record of land owned by migrants, taking advantage of the latter's absence as well as the lax nature of updating the municipal records. In other cases, relatives have simply occupied the land/property of the absentee migrants and used them for their own benefit, or have even sold them on illegally to a third party. These are some of the problems that British Bangladeshis face when it comes to affirming or reclaiming the ownership of their assets.

The inevitable question arises: why not follow the proper legal process? There is no easy answer to that. The local people have better knowledge of the legal rules and how they can be manipulated and 'bent' to their advantage in an over-all system that is to some extent corrupt. They take advantage of the migrants' absence and use delaying tactics in subverting the legal procedures. Migrants do not generally have the time or resources to be physically present to sort things out. Migrant participants are aware of their disadvantaged status in dealing with the Bangladeshi bureaucracy, and that they are considered as 'Moo-Aloos', a local term which literally means 'sweet potato' but whose hidden meaning is that they are too simple and disconnected to understand how business is done nowadays in Bangladesh. Whilst the first generation, mostly poorly educated, struggles to understand the complicated land laws and legal jargon that is used to conduct busi-ness, the second generation, although better educated, are even further removed from the Bangladeshi reality and may even lack much knowledge of the Bengali language. Neither do they understand, or want to engage in, the techniques of bribery often required to 'get things done'.

The cultural construction of the Moo-Aloo is based on a combination of jealousy and admiration. Local people are very much aware that many of the British Bangladeshis who visit Sylhet – the *Londonis* – have acquired con-siderable wealth, at least by local standards. They have bought land and built large, status-enhancing houses in the villages. Visitors reinforce their sta-tus by distributing gifts to relatives and hosting festivals. We illustrate this lavish expenditure with an account from Abul, a second-generation British Bangladeshi who was about to embark on a three-week trip to Bangladesh. To give a bit more background, Abul is in his 20s and works in a computer store. His parents are now separated; they originate from different parts of eastern Bangladesh – his mother's family from Sylhet, his father from Brahmanbaria in south-eastern Bangladesh. His brother has 'returned' to Dhaka.

> I am buying lots of stuff, I spent nearly £7,000. For my brother I brought a Rolex, also iPhone . . . I am being introduced to two families . . . I have already sent two parcels by cargo and I am going to take 40kg of stuff with me . . . I have sent clothes, trainers, watches, headphones, biscuits, chocolate, that's all. Oh, and some cosmetics.

In addition, the retail and leisure landscape of Sylhet has been transformed on the basis of the tourism market fuelled by visiting British Bangladeshis. New shopping malls in Sylhet city and in tourist resorts cater to the cash-rich visi-tors, and hardly at all to the locals, with their tiny disposable incomes. Gardner and Mand (2012: 980) write that these malls are a reassuring sign of modernity for visiting migrant families, who in other spaces are disturbed by the squalor of rural life. A particular location mentioned by many of our participants, especially those visiting with children, is 'Dreamland', an amusement park on the outskirts of Sylhet city, again created mainly for the *Londoni* market. This funfair is part of the migrant-tourist-visitor experience for many families. Interestingly, it is detached not only from the reality of Sylheti rural life, but also from the participants' lives in London, where they do not visit expensive play parks on a regular basis.

Conclusion

In this chapter we have considered migration and visits 'home' as examples of the 'time-placeness' of mobility, infused with deep layers of meaning associated above all with memories of past times, places and experiences. The trajectories of the migrants' memories are both very long and very wide, encompassing many things, places, people and events. As many other authors have also pointed out (eg. Levitt & Waters, 2002), the depth and strength of the relationship with the homeland vary significantly between the two generations studied here, and indeed within the generations across different time-frames. Hence, for the first generation, memories of their childhood in Sylhet are very distant in time, if not in place, from their experiences of the homeland on recent visits. Likewise, for the second generation living in London, memories of childhood visits are different from those they make as adults, perhaps taking their own children, the third generation, with them. A key finding of the research is that these home-country visits are not confined to summer holiday trips or special occasions such as family weddings, but take place more frequently, more spontaneously, at any time of the year and for a wider variety of reasons.

Across a wider conceptual plane, our chapter has brought together notions of migration, mobility (notably visiting friends and relatives, VFR), tourism and memory in an innovative analysis of past and present times and social landscapes. The migratory system created by the particular history of Bangladeshi migration, in this case to East London, can be regarded as an 'ethnoscape' defined by ethnic ties between origin and destination (cf. Appadurai, 1990, 1996); as a 'transnational social field' characterised by more or less intense social and kinship relations stretched over this long-distance migration (Glick Schiller, 2005); and as a 'diasporic space' à la Brah (1996) in which a sense of diasporic identity is maintained both by the condition of absence and exile from the homeland and by regular visits back and forth. Our focus on East London and Sylhet supports the contention of Phillips and Reyes (2011: 9) that long-distance migration and transnational networks de-centre the nation-state as the primary locus of cultural meaning. Mobility decisions are increasingly referenced to transnational kinship networks, bringing 'significant changes in the cultural landscapes of belonging'.

Through our fieldwork and interview evidence, as well as detailed reference to cognate literature (notably Zeitlyn, 2012, 2015), we have documented the following memoryscapes of migration and visiting, each relating to a different time, age and migration:

- the first generation's memoryscapes of their early lives in rural Sylhet – these are bucolic images filled with positive nostalgia about school, playing in an amphibian landscape of ponds and fields, and friendly socialisation with other children and older villagers;
- the first generation's memories of more recent visits to their homeland – these are shaped by reconnections with family and friends, generating a positive image of being a 'successful' migrant, but also evolving tensions over land and property ownership;
- the memoryscapes and experiences of young second-generation children on their family visits to the homeland – here we find the most contrasting images between boys' and girls' behaviour and between happiness and discovery on the one hand, and boredom and complaints on the other;
- the second generation's more geographically diverse memoryscapes of such visits, which comprise not only the ancestral family home but also more touristic locations and experiences in Bangladesh – on the whole these are positive impressions of connecting to the Bengali culture of family hospitality and warmth.

Three issues suggest themselves for further research. The first picks up what we discussed in the previous subsection, namely the growing conflicts over property ownership and inheritances. This is a major concern for the harmonious evolution of the British Bangladeshi transnational community. Some migrants are sufficiently knowledgeable and flexible to cope with the legal wrangles. Others are struggling, depressed and losing hope, with obvious implications for their future relationship with the homeland. This key challenge for the future stands in contrast to the positive, even celebratory landscapes intoned above, but the combination of satisfaction and disillusionment is not unusual in studies of counter-diasporic mobilities (eg. Christou & King, 2014; Wessendorf, 2013). There is a role here for the home-country government to step in to help resolve the legal impasse by creating greater legal clarity and transparency and a more efficient local-level bureaucracy.

The second issue regards the possibility of permanent return migration. Thus far, rather few migrants have followed the example of Nazrul's father and moved back to the home country to retire; and even fewer second-generation Bangladeshis would consider a counter-diasporic move to the parental homeland for good. This is largely because the homeland offers far fewer employment and income opportunities, and has an inferior health and welfare system, when compared to the UK. It seems that Bangladesh is not yet at a stage where it is ready to follow the lead of other post-colonial migration countries, such as India or the ex-British colonies in the Caribbean, where return migration, including of the second generation, has been noted and documented (see, *inter alia*, Duval, 2004; Jain, 2010; Levitt & Waters, 2002; Potter, 2005; Potter *et al.*, 2005).

The final topic is based on the realisation that, within the transnational family and social space of an established migrant diaspora, VFR mobilties are potentially bi-directional. The very notion of VFR implies a reciprocity of the visits, so that both migrants and their non-migrant relatives and friends visit each other in both the homeland and the host country, switching roles as host and guest as they co-create the VFR transnational experience (Humbracht, 2015; Janta *et al.*, 2015; Wagner, 2015). Although the British Bangladeshi transnational social field is inherently unequal, particularly in respect of financial resources and access to tourist visas, visits in the 'other direction' are still happening, creating new and different memoryscapes, and these are now a focus of our ongoing research.

References

Adams, C. (1987). *Across seven seas and thirteen rivers: Life stories of pioneer Sylheti settlers in Britain.* London: Eastside Books.

Agnew, V., ed. (2005). *Diaspora, 'memory, and identity: A search for home.* Toronto: University of Toronto Press.

Ali, N. and Holden, A. (2006). Post-colonial Pakistani mobilities: The embodiment of the 'myth of return' in tourism. *Mobilities* 1(2), 217–242.

Anwar, M. (1979). *The myth of return: Pakistanis in Britain.* London: Heinemann.

Appadurai, A. (1990). Disjuncture and difference in the global cultural economy. *Theory, Culture and Society* 7(2), 295–310.

Appadurai, A. (1996). *Modernity at large: Cultural dimensions of globalization.* Minneapolis, MN: University of Minnesota Press.

Baldassar, L. (2001). *Visits home: Migration experiences between Italy an Australia.* Melbourne: Melbourne University Press.

Bolognani, M. (2007). The myth of return: Dismissal, survival or revival? A Bradford example of transnationalism as a political instrument. *Journal of Ethnic and Migration Studies* 33(1), 59–76.

Brah, A. (1996). *Cartographies of diaspora: Contesting identities.* London: Routledge.

Butalia, U. (2011). The persistence of memory. In: K.R. Phillips & G.M. Reyes, eds., *Global memoryscapes: Contesting remembrance in a transnational age.* Tuscaloosa, AL: University of Alabama Press, pp. 28–45.

Christou, A. & King, R. (2010). Imagining 'home': Diasporic landscapes of the Greek-German second generation. *Geoforum* 41(4), 638–646.

Christou, A. & King, R. (2014). *Counter-diaspora: The Greek second generation returns 'home'.* Cambridge, MA: Harvard University Press.

Cressey, G. (2006). *Diaspora youth and ancestral homeland: British Pakistani/Kashmiri youth visiting kin in Pakistan and Kashmir.* Leiden: Brill.

Duval, D.T. (2004). Linking return visits and return migration among Commonwealth East Caribbean migrants in Toronto. *Global Networks* 4(1), 51–67.

Gardner, K. (1995). *Global migrants, local lives: Migration and transformation in rural Bangladesh.* Oxford: Oxford University Press.

Gardner, K. (2002). *Age, narrative and migration: Life history and life course amongst Bengali elders in London.* Oxford: Berg.

Gardner, K. & Mand, K. (2012). 'My away is here': Place, emplacement and mobility amongst British Bengali children. *Journal of Ethnic and Migration Studies* 38(6), 969–986.

Glick Schiller, N. (2005). Transnational social fields and imperialism. *Anthropological Theory* 4(4), 439–461.

Glick Schiller, N. (2010). A global perspective on transnational migration: Theorising migration without methodological nationalism. In: R. Baubock & T. Faist, eds., *Diaspora and transnationalism: Concepts, theories and methods*. Amsterdam: Amsterdam University Press, pp. 109–130.

Hua, A. (2005). Diaspora and cultural memory. In: V. Agnew, ed., *Diaspora, memory, and identity: A search for home*. Toronto: University of Toronto Press, pp. 191–208.

Humbracht, M. (2015). Reimagining transnational relations: The embodied politics of visiting friends and relatives mobilities. *Population, Space and Place* 21(7), 640–653.

Jain, S. (2010). *For love and money: Second-generation Indian Americans in the Indian knowledge economy*. COMPAS Working Paper 10–76, University of Oxford, Oxford.

Janta, H., Cohen, S.A. & Williams, A.M. (2015). Visiting friends and relatives mobilities. *Population, Space and Place* 21(7), 585–598.

King, R. & Kılınç, N. (2014). Routes to roots: Second-generation Turks from Turkey 'return' to Turkey. *Nordic Journal of Migration Research* 4(3), 126–133.

King, R. & Lulle, A. (2015). Rhythmic island: Latvian migrants in Guernsey and their enfolded patterns of space-time mobility. *Population, Space and Place* 21(7), 599–611.

King, R. & Olsson, E., eds. (2014). Diasporic return. Special Issue, *Diaspora* 17(3), 255–384.

King, R., Christou, A. & Teerling, J. (2011). 'We took a bath with the chickens': Memories of childhood visits to the homeland by second-generation Greek and Greek Cypriot 'returnees'. *Global Networks* 11(1), 1–23.

King, R., Lulle, A., Mueller, D. & Vathi, Z. (2013). *Visiting friends and relatives and its links with international migration: A three-way comparison of migrants in the UK*. Willy Brandt Working Papers in International Migration and Ethnic Relations, 2013/1, Malmö University.

Levitt, P. (2009). Roots and routes: Understanding the lives of the second generation transnationally. *Journal of Ethnic and Migration Studies* 35(7), 1225–1242.

Levitt, P. & Jaworsky, B.N. (2007). Transnational migration studies: Past developments and future trends. *Annual Review of Sociology* 33, 129–156.

Levitt, P. & Waters, M.C., eds. (2002). *The changing face of home: The transnational lives of the second generation*. New York: Russell Sage.

Marschall, S. (2017). Tourism and memories of home: Introduction. In: S. Marschall, ed., *Tourism and memories of home: Migrants, displaced people, exiles and diasporic communities*. Bristol: Channel View Publications, pp. 1–31.

Mason, J. (2004). Managing kinship over long distances: The significance of 'the visit'. *Social Policy and Society* 3(4), 421–429.

Phillips, K.R. & Reyes, G.M., eds. (2011). *Global memoryscapes: Contesting remembrance in a transnational age*. Tuscaloosa, AL: University of Alabama Press.

Potter, R.B. (2005). 'Young, gifted and back': Second-generation transnational return migrants to the Caribbean. *Progress in Development Studies* 5(3), 213–236.

Potter, R.B., Conway, D. & Phillips, J., eds. (2005). *The experience of return migration: Caribbean perspectives*. Aldershot: Ashgate.

Rytter, M. (2010). 'A sunbeam of hope': Negotiations of identity and belonging among Pakistanis in Denmark. *Journal of Ethnic and Migration Studies* 36(4), 599–617.

Stephenson, M.L. (2002). Travelling to the ancestral homelands: The aspirations and experiences of a UK Caribbean community. *Current Issues in Tourism* 5(5), 378–425.

Tsuda, T., ed. (2009). *Diasporic homecomings: Ethnic return migration in comparative perspective*. Stanford, CA: Stanford University Press.

Vathi, Z. & King, R. (2011). Return visits of the young Albanian second generation in Europe: Contrasting themes and comparative host-country perspectives. *Mobilities* 6(4), 503–518.

Wagner, L. (2015). Shopping for diasporic belonging: Being 'local' and being 'mobile' as a VFR visitor in the ancestral homeland. *Population, Space and Place* 21(7), 654–668.

Wessendorf, S. (2013). *Second-generation transnationalism and roots migration: Cross-border lives*. Farnham: Ashgate.

Williams, A.M., Chaban, N. & Holland, M. (2011). The circular international migration of New Zealanders: Enfolded mobilities and relational places. *Mobilities* 6(2), 125–147.

Zeitlyn, B. (2012). Maintaining transnational social fields: The role of visits to Bangladesh for British Bangladeshi children. *Journal of Ethnic and Migration Studies* 38(6), 953–968.

Zeitlyn, B. (2015). *Transnational childhoods: British Bangladeshis, identities and social change*. London: Palgrave Macmillan.

12 Translocal narratives of memory, place and belonging

Second-generation Turkish-Germans' home-making upon 'return' to Turkey

Nilay Kılınç and Russell King

Introduction

In this chapter, we explore the relocation decisions and post-return lives of German-born second-generation Turkish migrants who have 'returned' to and settled in Antalya, a cosmopolitan tourist hub on the Mediterranean coast of Turkey. We examine how these individuals successfully (in most cases) re-make their sense of 'home' in this socially liberal tourist space. Antalya offers them the chance to 'be who they want to be' away from the discriminatory nature of German society, and detached from the strictures of both Turkish mainstream society and the ethnic-Turkish social spaces in Germany.

Our contribution speaks directly to the three keywords in the title of this book. It is about the *migration* of Turks to Germany and then the 'return' migration of their descendants back to Turkey. We put 'return' in inverted commas because the migrants are not in the true sense returning to the place of their birth or where they have lived before. However, in the eyes of the second-generation protagonists of this research, the move is usually seen as a return to the ethnic homeland (cf. Tsuda, 2003). Second, our analysis connects to *travel* in two distinct ways: the research participants have chosen to relocate in a very specific tourist centre in Turkey, and this relocation was often preceded by multiple holiday visits 'home' to Turkey whilst they were growing up in Germany. Finally, our empirical analysis builds on the narrative *memories* of participants' past lives in, and feelings about, multiple places and spaces – the industrial towns in Germany where they were born and grew up; various locations in their parental homeland which they visited on summer trips, including their parents' home towns and other places such as Istanbul or coastal resorts; and their more recent lives as resettled migrants in Antalya.

The phenomenon of second-generation 'return' migration provokes two initial theoretical reflections. The first is that this is a counter-intuitive form of migration – a violation of the push–pull set of factors that drove the original (i.e. first-generation) migrants to move from a poor country (Turkey) to a richer one (West Germany), where their labour could be both valorised as a vital contribution to rebuild the postwar economy, and seen as a personal vehicle for migrant self-improvement via stable work contracts and higher incomes. Why, then, would the second generation reverse the trajectory of their parents and migrate from a rich country to one which is still relatively underdeveloped, if not as impoverished as when their parents departed?

The second theoretical framework provides something of an explanation of the paradox just noted. This starts from the notion that the successful integration of the second generation (let alone the first generation) into German society is by no means assured. Mandel (1995) called the Turkish-German second generation 'non-citizens' of the country they were born in. As the largest immigrant minority in Germany (2.5 million according to Rittersberger-Tiliç, Çelik & Özen, 2013: 90), 'Muslim' Turks are subject to racism, discrimination and Islamophobia, despite Germany's claim to be a welcoming, multicultural society where substantial efforts have been made to 'integrate' Turks and other migrant-origin populations. By no means all of our research participants felt or experienced the discriminatory or xenophobic backlash against their presence in Germany. More common instead was the kind of identificatory ambiguity that is often characteristic of the migrant second generation. At a practical level, for second-generation Turkish-Germans, this ambiguity is related to a feeling of being somehow 'stuck' between the inward-looking space of Turkish family life in Germany, and the wider, more liberal, but not fully accessible social sphere of the host country. Whilst this combination can provide vibrant identity mixes which are seen as dualistic, transnational or cosmopolitan (Kaya, 2007; Vertovec, 1999), there can also be confusion, contestation and constant negotiation between different identity repertoires. This leads some members of the second generation to seek a fresh start in the ancestral homeland, where they can focus on improving themselves and their lives.

There is also a sense in which the very 'reverseness' of second-generation return – that is, the second generation returning not to the place of their birth and upbringing but to their parents' homeland and, once there, looking back to their own German birthland – creates challenges for the labelling of the directionality of migration. At the same time, this type of migration also introduces innovative perspectives on the phenomenon of transnationalism and on the contested nature of such terms as 'home', 'home-making' and 'homeland'. In an early intervention in this semantic debate, Gmelch (1992) wrote of the 'double passage' of Caribbean migrants 'abroad' and 'back home'. Research on second-generation return from various global contexts including Japan, Southern Italy and Greece reveals that the second generation's construction of the mythical homeland is often challenged once they have a longer-term lived experience upon return (Christou, 2006; Christou & King, 2014; Tsuda, 2003; Wessendorf 2007). Our own earlier research on second-generation Turkish-German relocation to Istanbul also revealed some elements of dissatisfaction – about the chaos and traffic in this mega-city, the lack of professionalism in the work sphere and patriarchal gender relations (Kılınç, 2014; King & Kılınç, 2014, 2016). In all these cases, a consistent theme was a strengthening of the 'backward gaze' to the birth country, and the intensification of a kind of 'reverse transnationalism' (King & Christou, 2011, 2014).

Another part of the paradox of this 'counter-diasporic' migration is played out in relation to how the second generation understands and experiences the complexly nuanced notions of 'home' and 'homeland'. The multi-locality of 'homeland' creates ambiguity for its meaning and significance, especially in regard to the second generation's ongoing processes of identity and belonging. The Turkish-German case certainly vindicates Levitt's (2009) argument that the second generation's emotional attachment to the ancestral homeland cannot be dismissed, since they have been brought up, in most cases, in 'transnational social fields' – that is to say, in

> households . . . in which people, goods, money, ideas and practices from [Turkey] circulate in and out on a regular basis; they are not only socialised into the rules and institutions of the country where they live, but also into those of the country where their families come from.
>
> (Levitt, 2009: 1226)

Furthermore, the multi-locality of the second generation's experiences of past, present and possible future homes/homelands are not restricted to the bi-locality of their prior residence in Germany (since their family may have moved whilst they were there) and their parental 'home-place' in Turkey (since their parents may originate from different places, and the return holiday visits may also have been to multiple places, including the resort area of Antalya). Our study of return/relocation to Antalya demonstrates that home is to be understood not simply as a physical entity (even if the physical environment of this place is a crucial pull factor) but its construction requires social interactions and emotional feelings which are developed over time. Only then can the participants in our research attach meaning to this place as 'home' and satisfy the brief but iconic definition of Rapport and Dawson (1998: 9): 'home is [the place] where one best knows oneself'.

In the next section of the chapter, we dig deeper into the conceptualisation of 'home' in the context of second-generation return, developing our discussion in two main directions: first, in relation to memory, diaspora and nostalgia, and second, through the optic of translocal geographies and positionalities. The following section briefly outlines the methods used for the field interviews and describes the singular character of the field-site of Antalya, including its appeal to tourists and second-generation 'returnees'. In the succeeding account of empirical findings from the thematic analysis of the interview narratives, we set out the four main rationales for 'return' articulated by the participants, each rationale or 'longing' corresponding to a somewhat different interpretation of memories and experiences of different translocal fields and positionalities. These rationales, which we analyse as narrative tropes, are longing for *tolerance*, feeling *competent*, searching for the *true self* and achieving a relaxed and enjoyable *lifestyle*. The conclusion highlights the novel significance of the results in the light of other studies of return migration and diasporic return.

Translocal geographies of memory, 'home' and 'return'

We build our conceptual framework for analysing second-generation 'return' and the concomitant search for a new 'home' in the ancestral homeland on the notion of *translocality* (Anthias, 2009; Brickell & Datta, 2011). Whilst not dismissing the overall power of transnationalism as a theoretical tool for framing international migrations at a (multi-)national level, our argument is that most of the daily activities and interactions of migrants, including the second generation, are not so much tied to the grand narratives of nations and diasporas, but expressed in a more grounded way at the local level and illustrate a more human-agency approach. This is true at both ends of the migratory system, sending and receiving, 'home' and 'away' – except that the very notions of 'home and away' are blurred and problematised in the case of second-generation 'return' dynamics.

For our participants, 'home' has multiple resonances – in the past, through the present and projected into the future. It is thus a processual concept; something which is sought, and ultimately 'found' and 'created' in Antalya. Participants' family history of migration and their own past and continuing engagement with mobility progressively reshapes their thoughts about where 'home' is. Hence memory and nostalgia are part of their ongoing construction of home, which takes place both as an element of their personal, individualistic lives and as part of the Turkish diaspora which is 'translocalised' between their place of residence in Germany and the family's geographical roots in certain places in Turkey. Here, we see a discontinuity between the now-standard postmodern theories of 'home' and 'belonging' as fluid, multiple and ongoing processes, especially in a migratory context (eg. Christou, 2006; Rapport & Dawson, 1998), and the aspirations of some members of the second generation who vocalise a longing for a 'home in the homeland' where they can experience a 'homely' feeling and 'true' belonging in the land of their ancestral roots (King & Kılınç, 2014; Wessendorf, 2007).

Boym (2011) has explored the linkages between nostalgia, memory and home and suggests three types of relationship, based on different fractions of the key word nostalgia – *nostos* (home) and *algia* (longing for). *Restorative* nostalgia focuses on the *nostos*, resurrecting a lost or left-behind home through reconstructing memories, rituals and material artefacts of the homeland; living, in a way, a kind of home which is 'frozen in time' by preserving customs, national identity, physical memorabilia and community traditions. The ways in which certain diasporas – including many Turkish families in Germany – cling to their rural and provincial traditions and recreate a kind of 'home away from home' are examples of this kind of nostalgia, focused on restoring the past – both time and place – in the present diasporic locality. *Reflective* nostalgia stresses the *algia* – the pain and longing – through the manner in which space is temporalised with fragments of memory, resulting either in a condition of constant homesickness, or embracing nostalgia as a romance in one's imagination. Finally, Boym argues that nostalgia is not always retrospective, i.e. backward-looking, but *prospective* as well, meaning that the past and the present form a partnership with a direct impact on future outcomes. Hence the prospective nostalgia of home is the proximity of 'two images – of home and abroad, past and present, dream and everyday life' (Boym 2011: 14).

Following this useful heuristic categorisation, we argue that the second-generation returnees engage in creative 'memory-work' by rationalising their needs in the present with their experiences in the past, some of which may be decidedly negative. Our, and others', research on the second generation's 'return' reveals that memory and nostalgia function not only in fashioning a conventional mythologised 'return' to 'home', but also appear as strong tools in difficult circumstances of dissatisfaction, alienation, exclusion and rupture (e.g. Christou & King 2014; Kılınç 2014). We label this creative, reflexive group of 'returnees' as 'memory entrepreneurs' who use their memories of multiple places and discourses as strategies to move forward, transforming their past frustrations and disappointments into a route to a 'better life', where they can create an improved livelihood for themselves in a 'new' place which they can nevertheless call 'home'.

The notion of 'memory entrepreneurship' is not entirely new. We find it briefly referenced by Olick and Robbins (1998: 128), where it is seen as a manipulation of the past for particular purposes, with links to the 'memory industry' of nostalgia. Our reference to the second generation as memory entrepreneurs is rather different and builds on recent notions of 'knowledge entrepreneurship' which focus on individuals' ability to recognise or construct opportunities to improve their knowledge in a particular area without necessarily prioritising financial profit (Frederick, O'Connor & Kuratko, 2015; Skrzeszewski, 2006). In this regard, the strategy of the second generation to relocate to Antalya is both a quest for a more fulfilling life and a project to acquire more knowledge about themselves. Their self-reflexive memories are a resource to compare and contrast their past lives and selves with their present lives and aspirations, which then shape their future decisions regarding place of settlement, career options and everyday lifestyle choices. Since the second generation have a dual frame of reference in terms of their social, cultural and symbolic capitals, they use their memories and nostalgia from both Germany and Turkey as reference points for self-realisation in their post-'return' lives. As the empirical findings will illustrate, their resettlement in Antalya is the outcome of a deeply reflexive process of memory-work wherein they 'processed' their desires and dislikes. They sought a place where they could fashion a new 'home' and avoid certain social scenarios, such as discrimination and intolerance.

What we have suggested above raises an important question. If we understand home as a 'movable feast' and not fixed in time and space, is it possible that 'you can make home anywhere' (cf. Rykwert, 1991: 54)? In the case of the second generation, it is apparent that home can be carried in the memory and (re-)built in a new place. However, when resettling in a new space – such as the Turkish parental homeland – not all locations are equally accessible and appealing, as second-generation individuals have different preferences, lifestyles, experiences and family and personal histories. Hence it is important to see how individuals use their memories and nostalgia in order to create a 'homely feeling' and even a 'new self' in a new place. Fashioning another home in a different, albeit somewhat familiar place also challenges memories and nostalgic feelings about places left behind and sets in motion new interactions with places of the past and present (Rubenstein, 2001).

Following Anthias (2008), we understand 'home' and 'self-identity' in a diasporic context through the lens of *translocational positionality*. This optic addresses issues of identity and home in terms of locations which are not fixed but are time- and context-dependent, and therefore involve shifts and contradictions. Anthias further explains that translocational positionality is the space at the intersection of agency – involving social positions as well as the meanings and practices attached – and structure, in which social positions and effects are merged. In this space, identities are embedded within power hierarchies constructed at both individual and collective levels. In the case of second-generation Turks who are born and raised in Germany, 'translocational space' is where the homeland is referenced affectively and materially on a daily basis (Levitt, 2009: 1231). This group's ongoing constructions of home and belonging are formulated in respect of their experiences in transnational, national and local spatial settings, and within social, economic and political structures.

In our analysis of narrative thematic findings, which follows the next section on methods, we look at the second generation's connections with places and spaces in their everyday lives. We explore what kind of strategies and interactions take place to create a feeling of 'home' in their new place of settlement, and how they use their translocal memories in these processes. The premise is that the Turkish-German second generation settled 'in place' in the southern coastal town of Antalya so they can remember and live with both countries and cultures in positive ways. Resettling in Antalya was very much related to the town's urban and cosmopolitan setting, with many German tourists and expat settlers; in this touristic, cosmopolitan space, the returnees can experience German, Turkish and 'global' culture. They live and work in a liberal environment where they feel that they can 'own' their lives. They purposely use their memories in order to retain a 'good life', taking lessons from their past experiences.

Research site, methods and sample characteristics

As we have already made clear, this research was undertaken in and around Antalya, a tourist city on the south coast of Turkey. In early 2014, 30 second-generation Turkish-Germans who had 'returned' to live and work in this area were interviewed by the first-named author, using a set of questions and discussion themes which had been developed by the second author in an earlier joint project on the relocation of second-generation Greek-Americans and Greek-Germans to Greece (see Christou & King, 2014; King & Christou, 2010).

Antalya and its hinterland have been transformed by tourism, capitalising on the region's rich natural and cultural attractions: a historic city centre, stunning surrounding scenery, a warm and sunny climate, and a coastal location with many attractive beaches. Once famed for its citrus orchards, remnants of these still survive in a verdant landscape bathed in a classic Mediterranean climate: hot in summer, yet tempered by sea breezes, and mild in winter thanks to its sheltered southerly aspect shielded by a steep mountain backdrop. Annual tourist numbers to Antalya have grown rapidly from 1.8 million in 1995 to 7.5 million in 2005 and 12 million in 2013. Germans, British, Russians and Dutch are the main tourist nationalities, alongside domestic tourists, some of the latter having bought or built second homes for summer holiday and weekend use. As well as this mix of tourists, the area has also become a major hub for attracting both Turkish migrant returnees and foreign, mainly German, settlers (Rittersberger-Tiliç, Çelik & Özen, 2013).

Research participants were contacted via several means: some initial personal contacts of the authors followed by snowball chains, websites of local institutions, and social media sites of Turkish-German returnees. The sample of participants was gender-balanced and mostly aged in their 30s and 40s at the time of interview, although the full age-range was 21 to 55. Equally important was the age at 'return', which varied between 16 and 41 years. Standard ethical procedures for this kind of interview-based fieldwork were followed, including securing informed consent for the interviews to be recorded. We use pseudonyms to preserve participants' anonymity, and we do not disclose the precise names or locations of businesses and residences. Following the participants' preferences, the interviews were mostly in Turkish, with some passages and phrases in German or English. The recorded narratives – most of which lasted an hour or more – were transcribed and simultaneously translated into English. NVivo was used to store and sort the narrative data, followed by thematic analysis.

The interviews took the form of loosely structured conversations, reflecting the informal settings in which they took place – in cafes, restaurants, outdoor leisure spaces or the homes of the participants. Nevertheless, an attempt was made to encourage the interviewees to relate a more or less chronological account of four main topics: the migration history of their parents; their own memories and experiences of growing up as part of a Turkish migrant family in Germany, including visits to the Turkish 'homeland'; their decision to independently 'return' to settle in Turkey, and specifically Antalya; and finally their experiences and feelings post-return.

The parents' migratory path from Turkey to Germany followed the standard 'guestworker into settlement' pattern of the 1960s and 1970s. Most originated from rural areas and small towns in the interior of Turkey and were recruited to work in German industry: hence they settled in the main industrial districts and large cities in Germany. Only two of the interviewees had parents who originated from Antalya. This pattern of geographical origins is intrinsic to our analysis, as we shall see further on in more detail.

The participants themselves had a range of educational backgrounds acquired in the German system, including a minority with tertiary-level qualifications. But also represented were those at the other end of the formal achievement spectrum: school and college drop-outs and others who had somehow 'gone off the rails'.

Especially for this latter group, 'escape' to Antalya proved to be a kind of salvation and 're-birth' in terms of their ongoing life trajectory.

After relocating to Antalya, our participants found either employment or business opportunities in activities related to the tourism sector. This finding was not a result of our opportunistic sampling strategy, but common knowledge in the area. The situation reflected, on the one hand, the dominance of tourism in the economy of the city and its surrounding satellite coastal resort towns; and on the other, the participants' wish to trade on their linguistic capital (bilingualism in Turkish and German, and usually good knowledge of English) in order to engage in the flexible labour market niches and businesses allied to tourism. Interviewees included the owners or managers of hotels, restaurants, cafes, shops and hairdressers, salespersons in shops and real-estate offices, and tourist guides and interpreters/translators. Figure 12.1 illustrates an example of a returnee-owned business.

In the empirically based account that follows, we privilege the narratives of four carefully selected informants in order to illustrate the key themes embedded

Figure 12.1 Jewellery shop in Antalya owned by a Turkish-German returnee. The slogan, in both German and Dutch, is funny: 'Genuine fake watches with warranty here!' It is also ironic in that the German word 'Getürkte' ('fake') is thought to have an etymology related to the Turks

Photo by Nilay Kılınç

in the interviews. We focus especially on memories of growing up in 'industrial' Germany, the decision and the circumstances of their relocation to Antalya, and their feelings of 'home' and 'belonging' in this new translocal but cosmopolitan tourist space.

The four case-studies discussed below are all, to varying extents, 'success stories' of individuals who have achieved positive changes in their lives in terms of career, self-development and general wellbeing by relocating to Antalya. It is important to stress that they were not specially selected by us on the criterion of 'success', but were broadly representative of those who were interviewed, all of whom were employed in the tourism sector. We only interviewed people who were working in this sector, so the sample reflects those who were 'out there' in the tourist economy and its easy-to-access spaces. Informal conversations, not included in the sample, were undertaken with a small number of Turkish-German returnees who were involved in dealing drugs and other illegal activities – we obviously cannot talk about success stories in their cases.

Memories of growing up in Germany and visiting the 'Turkish homeland'

The first stage in our empirical analysis of the narrative data examines what the participants recalled about their early lives growing up and living as younger adults in Germany. In particular, we highlight their often ambivalent and conflictual experiences of partaking in three socio-geographic spheres: their Turkish families, homes and ethnic community spaces in Germany; the wider host-country social space of school, work, media and leisure in Germany; and their holiday visits, usually *en famille*, to their parental homeland, where a different assemblage of Turkish spaces was experienced.

According to the narrative evidence, the second generation's 'Turkish' upbringing was mostly related to their family sphere: the bricks-and-mortar home where they spoke Turkish, ate 'Turkish' food, watched Turkish TV channels and – to varying degrees – celebrated Turkish national and religious holidays. Note that we selectively put 'Turkish' in inverted commas as this descriptor is wide, flexible and open to interpretation, especially as regards cuisine, customs, religious observance and strength of national identity, depending on which part of Turkey the first-generation migrants originated from. Hence the second generation grew up in a 'Turkish' household consisting of their parents' memories and nostalgic attachments to the village or town where they had spent their early lives. Keeping their traditions and sustaining a 'Turkish' way of life is active memory-work. Cooking Turkish food starts with remembering those recipes; speaking the language requires remembering and practising. In summary, keeping ties with the homeland whilst 'away' is all about remembering certain things and ignoring or forgetting others. It is, thus, a selective and perhaps idealised appropriation of the homeland ways, and becomes ever-more distant from it as time passes, not least because the society of the homeland origin-place is also in constant evolution.

The family-home space was very much in contact with the neighbourhood locale, and most of the participants mentioned that, at least initially, they did not live in areas heavily populated by other Turks, but mostly had German neighbours, getting a head start in speaking German, and learning how things are done by Germans. Most of the interviewees were nostalgic about their early childhood years; their memories were of being raised in a peaceful environment; discrimination and hostility were not part of their daily lives.

It was within the school setting that they first realised they were 'different', since they were part of a Turkish minority in classes that were predominantly made up of German 'locals', plus some other immigrant children from Italy, Greece, Spain and former Yugoslavia. When they built friendships with their German classmates, they had a chance to further encounter German households, and that was when they more concretely realised how things were done and lived differently between the two cultures. Within school, they took part in most if not all extra-curricular activities, joining sports teams, going on school trips, celebrating Christmas and Easter. Hence their early school years were spent within and across multiple cultural and ethnic spaces in which they were actively negotiating their 'Turkish' and 'German' sides.

However, their later school years were the time-space where the first tensions and conflicts arose, as they simultaneously hit their teenager years and became divisively channelled by the rigid streaming of the German secondary school system. The division of students into *Hauptschule, Realschule* and *Gymnasium* constituted a major change in their lives, as most Turkish pupils were directed to the *Hauptschule*, and less commonly to the *Realschule* – schools which prepared students for trades and vocations – rather than to the *Gymnasium*, geared more to the university cycle of higher education. Many participants recalled how the German teachers would consciously eliminate the *Gymnasium* option for Turkish students, thereby decreeing that they would do lower-skilled jobs in the future.

The educational division and discrimination was followed by a school environment which was not fulfilling for the Turkish second generation who were our research participants. They tended to socialise with other Turkish students who came from more traditional families living in the emerging Turkish enclaves of German towns and cities. These memories of grouping with other Turkish and immigrant students were mostly apparent in the men's narratives, as the Turkish families were much more protective towards their daughters. Outside of school, the main socialisation space of the Turkish and other immigrant youth was the youth centre, with its common room, TV, music, board games and pool. Some of the participants interviewed in Antalya had gotten into 'bad habits' at this stage of their lives, including membership of youth gangs, petty criminality, and drug use and selling. Those who were prosecuted and convicted were given the choice of deportation to reduce their imprisonment to half its original length. In our sample of 30, there are six deportation cases who had to 'return' to Turkey as they did not have German citizenship.

These memories of their later teenage years and beyond appear as a negative articulation of an identity crisis: not entirely belonging and being supported by their Turkish families and communities, and being pushed by the Germans to the periphery (Kaya, 2007). Hence the 'ghetto culture' of speaking *Kanak*, a hybrid, pidgin mix of Turkish, German and Americanised English, and performing a 'tough' masculinity appear as ways of building a protective wall against both of the dominant cultures in their lives. Despite the (self-)destructive nature of this hybrid youth culture, the second generation found in this lifestyle and behaviour a way to cope with their insecurities, to claim a form of belonging and power within the societal hierarchy, and to embrace to a certain degree their combined working-class and immigrant background.

At the same time as the second generation matured into adulthood, the attitude of German society towards its large, growing and diverse immigrant population (but always with the Turks stigmatised as the dominant 'other') significantly hardened, creating a widespread feeling of discrimination and marginalisation. This is well illustrated in the following interview extract from Burcak (female, aged 35):

> In Duisburg there were many immigrants. Over time the intolerance towards them increased incredibly! Our neighbourhood was mainly German, but you could feel that people in the town were not happy living next to foreigners. With the rise of Islamophobia, it became difficult for us to exist as Turks and Muslims; there was just too much polarisation . . . this was the case where we lived. A simple example: when we entered a shop, the sales assistant would always treat us in a condescending way. If I touched something, let's say I held up a jumper, they would immediately come over and put it in a neat way. But the German customers would try everything and leave a mess behind them, which was OK, it was acceptable because they were German. But everything we did was wrong and unacceptable . . . So yeah, this kind of stuff piled up over the years, and we wanted to return to Turkey.

These complex and fluctuating dynamics of childhood and youth socialisation and identity construction in German towns were punctuated by frequent holiday visits to Turkey, usually lasting several weeks in the summer. These childhood visits were the first direct experiences and memories of the ancestral homeland. The second generation observed that these visits had huge importance for their parents, who saved money over the entire year to make the trip and buy presents for family and close friends in Turkey. They also saw how certain symbolically valued Turkish products – principally food and artefacts – were brought back to Germany on the return trip. Most participants remembered these holiday visits positively, and nostalgically referred to reuniting with non-migrant family members, receiving love and care from them, exchanging gifts, and reacting enthusiastically to the warm and happy atmosphere – even if, at least until the 1990s, Turkey was still regarded as a 'backward' country.

These early semi-touristic visits to Turkey had special importance in two respects. The first is that the second generation realised that Turkish people in Turkey were different from the Turks they knew in Germany – many of the former were modern, educated and sophisticated. Especially in urban and touristic areas, they saw how middle-class people dressed and behaved. This created a more positive image of Turkey and Turkish people in their eyes, and was the first step in framing their subsequent decision to move there at a later stage. The second discovery was less positive: they found that, especially in the rural communities of their parents' origin, they were called *Almancı* – a derogative term meaning 'German' or, more precisely, 'Germanised' in a pretentious way. Therefore they realised that they were no longer seen as fully Turkish, and this created an obvious tension in the evolution of their self-identification.

If the memories of their social experiences in the villages and towns of the interior were mixed, all the participants mentioned that the times they spent having a 'real' holiday in the coastal resorts stayed as positive memories. They enjoyed the sun, sea, good Mediterranean food and relaxed atmosphere of these holidays with their families. They also discovered that their parents were less protective and controlling during these summer holidays, so the youngsters had more space and freedom to act and be the way they wanted. Even though they were aware that life in Turkey had its downsides and challenges, the holidays spent there created a nostalgic feeling of the ancestral homeland as a warm and pleasant place, where life was more easygoing compared to the highly organised and time-regulated pattern of life in Germany.

Narrating the 'return' through negotiations of self-identity in translocal fields

In an earlier phase of our research into second-generation 'return' to Turkey, based on interviews in Istanbul and nearby small towns, we found that family and social networks were key in shaping the relocation process (King & Kılınç, 2014). However, the Antalya participants' parents and relatives do not (except in two cases) live close by: they either continue to live in Germany or are located in the Turkish regions, villages and towns where they originally came from. What attracted the participants we interviewed for this later phase of research to settle in and near Antalya? Three main 'pull factors' emerged from the interview narratives, all of them mentioned briefly already. First, the physical setting was viewed as important – the beauty of the coastline and its backdrop of mountains, the agreeable climate, and the fact that this was an area they had positive memories of from childhood holidays. Second, participants emphasised that here was a region where they could sustain viable livelihoods as entrepreneurs or employees in the tourism sector. And third, there was the wider social setting – an easygoing environment where they were able to indulge their various 'alternative' lifestyle practices which would be frowned upon both in other parts of Turkey and by the Turkish community in Germany.

This last pull factor was the key aspect that lay behind our first of four narrative tropes: the longing for *tolerance* as a signifier shaping the imaginary of return. Part of this was related to their nostalgia towards a more tolerant society experienced in their early lives in Germany, and part was reflected in the disappearance of this tolerance, and its replacement by discrimination, later in their 'German lives' – as narrated by Burcak above. In addition to discrimination on the basis of ethno-national and religious criteria, intolerance towards other aspects of second-generation identity and behaviour may also play a role, such as pressure from their families and the Turkish ethnic community around them to 'conform'. Female participants, especially, mentioned problems related to marriage, or their wish to live independently, or as divorcees with children. These latter problems were still apparent in their lives when they returned to Turkey to live in their family villages and towns of origin – even, albeit to a lesser extent, in Istanbul (see King & Kılınç, 2014: 130, 132; 2016: 182). Hence their decision to settle in Antalya is related to the special character of this translocal space and their positionality within it. In this cosmopolitan tourist town with its international residents, expats and a constant throughput of tourists, they can maintain their translocal activities and embrace their hybrid identities and alternative lifestyles without being judged. Within the tourist economy, where all of the participants work in one capacity or another, their multicultural background and linguistic skills are highly appreciated. Because of the high number of German tourists and settlers in the area, they are able to speak German all day, and Turkish to the locals, as well as a Turkish-German mix with other friends and colleagues who are second-generation 'returnees', plus English on many occasions too.

The narrative extracts below are from Nejla, one of the oldest participants, aged 54 when she was interviewed in 2014. In fact, Nejla had been born in Turkey and then taken as a baby by her mother to join her father who was already working in Germany. Nejla's 'rebellion' had been her insistence on remaining single, despite pressures from her relatives to get married. She return-migrated to Turkey aged 26, finding work in the hotel industry in various locations before finally settling in Antalya in her early 30s. Here she is able to live her life as a mature, independent, single professional woman without anyone passing comment or bothering her – in fact, after more than 20 years in the place, she is well known and respected.

> I was working as a translator in the courts [in Germany], but those were the years when there were lots of problems with the Turks, and I was working in cases involving Turkish people. I got tired of all the negativity about the Turks. And Germans would not believe that I was Turkish, and that bothered me too. If I went to a bar with friends, German guys would ask me if I was Italian or Spanish, and when I told them I was Turkish, they would say things like 'oh, be careful – what if your father or brothers came here now and shot you?' And I would tell them that this is not always the case and there were lots of liberal Turks, but they would keep teasing me.
>
> . . .
>
> When I told my parents that I was moving to Turkey, my mother thought I could never adapt, and my father bet that I'd be back in Germany after one year. But I didn't see it that way. I came to Turkey and finally I was just 'Nejla', not 'Nejla the Turkish woman', as I was in Germany. In Germany . . . 'We are Turkish, we do not do that', my family would repeatedly say. Being Turkish meant living with many rules and taboos. In Antalya I can be free . . . everyone can be different, and this is accepted; there is no pressure to preserve our old values.

The first part of Nejla's narrative above highlights the intolerance and prejudice of German society towards the Turkish community and the stereotypes held. But she also talks, in the second paragraph, about the pressure coming from the Turkish family side. Having mainly German friends, being educated and having an active work-life in Germany, Nejla feels that her life outside the family-home space is seen as a threat to 'Turkish' values.

But when asked where she thinks she 'belongs' and where her 'home' is, Nejla finds it difficult to answer. Her ambiguous response reveals the complexity of these notions for the second generation whose translocal habitus has evolved in stages. Nevertheless, in conclusion Nejla stresses that Antalya is her 'hub', even though her immediate family still lives in Germany and her extended family lives in central Turkey.

> I have always felt that I was Turkish, and I am proud of that. But I am Turkish with a German mentality and manners. For instance, everybody thinks my flat [in an up-market district of Antalya] is so German – I like the German minimalism. And I have many German friends here, and my German is still better than my Turkish. When it comes to work ethics and organisation, I am German as well . . . But I would never go back to live in Germany. Despite the general problems in Turkey, Antalya is a high-spirited place to live. When my German friends visit me here, they are envious of my life . . . so active and fulfilling. This is a life they cannot imagine in their small German towns . . . Basically, Antalya is my hub, I am really happy here.

The second key narrative theme, related especially to the nostalgia of their early years in the German school system, and then their later feelings of educational devaluation, is the second generation's longing for *feeling competent*. They search for a space where they can realise their human and transcultural capital and understand how things work. In Turkey, and especially in Antalya, this can be achieved through access to career and investment opportunities in the tourism sector, largely on the basis of their excellent knowledge of the three main requisite languages – Turkish, German and English. Their language and other intercultural skills would not guarantee them a job in their parents' rural places of origin, and in big cities like Ankara, Istanbul and Izmir, because many well-educated locals have these skills as well, and the competition is harder. Hence the second generation relocates, either directly from Germany or, like Nejla, via intermediate stays elsewhere in Turkey, to Antalya, the tourism hub *par excellence* for German-speaking visitors and expats for the past 30 years. Speaking fluent German, understanding the German culture and ways of life, and being able to relate to customers at multiple levels were great advantages for the second generation in the retail sector and hospitality businesses. They could make a good living, aided by fairly low living costs compared to the major cities of Turkey. In short, they *felt competent* in Antalya.

Participant Altan (male, 37) is an excellent example of using the second generation's human and cultural capital acquired from their German upbringing and education, and from their holiday visits to Turkey. His is also one of the more dramatic stories of transformation from a troubled life in Germany to a materially and emotionally satisfying one in Antalya. The back-story is that he dropped out of *Gymnasium* in Stuttgart, finding he could make money dealing drugs. His damascene moment came at 19 when, visiting his parents' village, he realised he could turn over a new leaf and start a business in the tourism sector. He took a diploma in Turkey to become a tour guide, and today he runs a successful tourism agency in Antalya. The extract below is long, reflecting the twists and turns in Altan's life.

> I came to Turkey for a long holiday, to take a break from my destructive life in Germany . . . I must say it was tough to start with, the first year in my parents' village in Kayseri . . . everyone tried to rip me off. I was young and had lots of money from my illegal deals in Germany . . . they saw me as a typical *Almancı*, naïve . . . I thought I was cunning, a quick learner, but in Turkey I realised everyone was like that! . . . From Germany I was used to people keeping their promises. Even in the drugs world, we did business by the German rules: you are on time, your word is your bond. Here people say one thing, but do another. You cannot count on people, especially where money is concerned.
>
> So I knew I had to get out of Kayseri; I couldn't stand living in a village with such people. I needed a place where my German and English could earn me money, and hopefully clean money. Antalya was perfect for that. I think that there is nowhere quite like Antalya . . . I have travelled to so many places, experienced different cultures; Antalya is so relaxed and it is such a flexible place – people don't mind what you do, you can do whatever you want. It's also unique with its nature and climate. For me the most important thing was the opportunities. A guy like me who had no higher education could start from zero and come to where I am now . . . Especially when I first came here, people who could speak German fluently were like gold. There were thousands of German tourists here, but no qualified workers in the tourist sector, the locals didn't know any foreign languages. There was a huge demand for people like me . . .
>
> So I worked as a tourist guide. It's a great feeling when you can tell people about your country, its culture, nature, history, from ancient times . . . in the native language of the tourists. I am a certified tourist guide, so I can go anywhere in Turkey . . . I have worked with many different groups – for instance, leading a group of Orthodox priests, taking them to the old churches . . . I love showing the beautiful side of Turkey . . . Also my character, my personality, leaves a good impression on the tourists. They see a witty guy who is knowledgeable, they know the tour will be good and interesting. This is the ideal job for me!
>
> I like Antalya a lot. I meet many interesting people from all over the world and I tell them how we roll here! [laughing] When you earn well, life is cheap here. I am living now in a gated community with good

security . . . My house is 300 square metres and we have a huge pool. This standard of life is not possible anywhere else . . . with what I am paying for this luxurious place, I could barely rent a 100 square metre flat in Istanbul, and maybe a dog shed in Germany . . . Plus here, what I am eating has taste, not like plastic . . . In Europe, all the fruit and vegetables, even the meat, taste like plastic. Here, everything is organic. We have clean air and water, mountain and sea air: what can beat that? . . . My life here is great . . . I am doing a job that satisfies me . . . So I don't regret that I returned . . . I think it was a good decision to return.

Altan's narrative may be ego-centric and self-justifying, but it is a remarkable instance of an innately clever young man (he made it into the *Gymnasium*) going off the rails but making money, and then using his competences (his languages, witty personality and other 'soft skills') to reinvent himself as a tour guide and successful business owner in Antalya. Much of what he says is also about the final two narrative themes: searching for the *true self* and achieving a *relaxed and enjoyable life*.

Narratives about looking for the *true self* highlight 'return' as rehabilitation and reinvention of the self in a new place. Key themes voiced under this narrative heading are 'starting from a clean slate' and taking individual decisions without the intervention of the family. In towns and cities where they have family and kin, the second generation sees no room for discovering who they are and what they really want for themselves; they are 'expected' to follow certain paths in education, career and marriage. Many participants said they needed to find somewhere where they can 'start over again', be themselves and take their own decisions. Antalya appeared to them as a neutral, yet somewhat familiar (from holiday visits) space where most of the interviewees did not have roots or prior contacts. At the same time, moving to Antalya was also about celebrating their Turkish identity, albeit only to a certain extent, since the place has a strong 'German' influence too.

Several features of Antalya, most of them mentioned already, combine to make it an ideal place in Turkey to (try to) rediscover one's true self amidst the identificatory confusions of the second generation and rebelling against the pressures from family to follow a prescribed life-path. The natural beauty and calming qualities of the place were frequently held up as crucial to wellbeing and individual expression. Here, their lifestyle choices, such as having tattoos and body piercings, drinking alcohol and smoking marijuana, and exploring alternative belief systems were all tolerated and free from public or family condemnation.

To illustrate this theme, we look at the interview with Aziz (male, 36), which includes various phases of identity negotiations in different places. Aziz comes from a guestworker family originating from a small village in Sivas, central Turkey. Born and brought up in Stuttgart, his early social life outside the family home mainly involved German friends due to the long working hours of his parents. First, he presents the identity dilemma of the second-generation youth and the challenge of discovering 'who you really are':

We, the second generation, are the most problematic generation, in our relationship both with our parents and with Germany. There are reasons for this, of course . . . We had working-class parents who worked long hours. I barely saw my father at home, and when he was around, he was always too tired and grumpy. He never cuddled me, I never sat on his lap, he never read a book to me. He never told me: 'Son, I love you'. But I am not alone in this. Many of the second generation came from exactly this kind of home background. Parents who are working hard for a better future, but forgetting to give their children love.

When you grow up sort of alone, you have so many questions in your head like 'Who am I?' or 'What are we?' Sometimes you feel you belong to Germany but then someone annoys you or says something hostile because of your appearance and you become angry . . . It's because you make so much effort to fit in, but you are still taken for an outsider. This creates confusion and disappointment. Then you come home and your parents expect you to behave in certain ways as well . . . they put expectations on you, and then you try to fit into that . . .

In summary, you need to be many things, but that is not the actual challenge . . . the challenge, for your mental wellbeing, is to be one thing. I had a different mentality compared to my parents and the other Turkish people around me. And I was seen as different by German society . . . So you just feel lost.

Aziz presents these challenges as part of the reason why he, too, started using drugs. Caught in possession by the police at the Dutch border, he was deported back to Turkey as he did not hold a German passport. Further stages in his back-and-forth story proceed as follows:

When I was deported to Turkey, I lived in Istanbul for a while. I was working in the tourist area, in a shop selling carpets. Istanbul was like a new world to me, it was so lively, and I was quite happy with life there. I was serving tourists every day, I was earning well, Istanbul has a good nightlife and there was lots of entertainment. But my German girlfriend in Stuttgart wanted to get married and so I did that and returned to Germany . . . I wanted to work again, but no one hired me, so I worked on building sites. I missed my life in Istanbul. Life in Germany didn't satisfy me, it was a dull and small life. In Istanbul I was praised because I could speak German and English, I was spending my entire day in a historic place with international people. Istanbul was magical – the Bosphorus, the sunny weather, great food. And I had returned to Germany, to rainy days and a monotonous life where I am no more than a working-class labourer and criminal. Maybe that's why my marriage didn't last.

After six years in Stuttgart, Aziz returned to Istanbul to try to restart his previous 'good life' there. But for his second return, he realised he needed a calmer place to live and work.

When I came back to Istanbul, things felt different, more and more chaotic. My father was planning a trip to Antalya and invited me to help him . . . I walked around Kaleci (Old Town) and gazed at the port, the deep blue sea and the majestic mountains. I inhaled the sea air and immediately thought to myself, 'This is it!' Since then I have been living in Antalya.

Aziz's reason for choosing Antalya was related to the final narrative trope – looking for a *relaxed way of life* which was not available in Germany. The contrasts were set out by the participants in the following comparison. In Germany they were discouraged by low wages (or unemployment), high living costs, limited social life, gloomy weather and rising intolerance towards foreigners. In Turkey, where they had nostalgic memories of carefree summer holidays, the options were basically threefold, in their eyes. In their parents' villages and towns of origin, they have few chances to access good employment. The rural life is, in one sense, slower and more relaxing, but the tight community structure and conservative values are seen as stress factors. Those who returned and tried to build a life in the big cities, especially Istanbul, had problems, like Aziz did eventually, with the chaotic dynamics of urban life with dense traffic, air pollution and high living costs. The third, and favoured, option was Antalya, where the second generation found a place where they could earn a decent living, have a calmer and more relaxed pace of life, yet also participate in a lively cosmopolitan culture. The tourist economy, with its flexible working hours and in-built sociability, offered the chance to fashion a better work–life balance. Indeed, many of the participants used the word 'paradise' to describe Antalya. Furthermore, they saw it as a 'bubble' because it was shielded from the social and political realities of Turkey. We round off with further interview clips from Aziz.

I love Antalya: moving here was the best decision I ever made. It's a beautiful city, and Kaleci is like a city in itself. Everyone knows each other there; I feel safe; we are protected by the walls of the old city. Every day is fun: there are so many people to talk to, and then there are also all the tourists . . . I speak German every day and spend most of my time with German tourists. Everyone knows me here – mostly because of my dog. I walk around a lot and everyone knows me as 'the guy with the white dog'. It's totally relaxing here; you can walk for hours with great views in front of you.

I follow the German news every day . . . I am worried about the politics in Turkey, but in Antalya one feels away from all those problems. That's why there is no way I could live in a different place in Turkey. I have lots of tattoos, I don't follow any religion, I have a dog, and I am a single guy – all these things are accepted in Antalya. Here, people do not dig into my past or misjudge me for what I have done; I am no longer obliged to explain myself . . . When I moved to Antalya, I became more sure of what I like and what I don't like: I have understood, in a way, 'who I am'. Now Antalya is my home. Germany used to be my home, but not anymore.

Conclusion

In framing an explanation for why second-generation Turkish-Germans choose to 'return' to Turkey, and specifically to Antalya, we have drawn on a wide range of conceptual ideas, interfaced with empirical evidence from 30 in-depth interviews with research subjects who have made this counter-diasporic move. Whilst some of our analysis was based on a general thematic reading of the full set of interview narratives, we selected four returnees – Burcak, Nejla, Altan and Aziz – to illustrate in more detail the four key narrative tropes and to introduce a biographical element into our overall account.

We acknowledge that, at first sight, 'second-generation return' represents a somewhat paradoxical situation: why would the children of migrants go back to the country their parents left to escape poverty and unemployment? It has been the task of this chapter to resolve this apparent paradox through the voices of the 'returnees' themselves, as well as drawing attention to the fact that the Turkish-German case is by no means unique – the phenomenon has been analysed in several other migration contexts around the world, including other Southern European countries such as Greece (Christou & King, 2014), Cyprus (Teerling, 2014), Italy (Wessendorf, 2007) and Portugal (Sardinha, 2011), and further afield such as India (Jain, 2011) and the Caribbean (Phillips & Potter, 2009; Potter, 2005; Potter & Phillips, 2008). For all those cases, including Turkey, part of the explanation lies in the rapid development of the diasporic home country in the several decades since the original migrants left, thereby offering the second generation better opportunities than were available to their parents, especially in economic sectors (tourism, commerce etc.) and places (cities, tourist resorts) where their 'foreign' education and language skills can be capitalised upon. This takes us to another key part of our analysis: the singular character of Antalya as a cosmopolitan tourist space where second-generation returnees can not only find employment and business opportunities rather readily, but can also live the kind of lives they want – often 'independent' and 'alternative' lifestyles – without the judgemental sanctions of their families and the wider Turkish society.

This independence is key to the participants' own evaluation of their 'success'. Their proactive decisions to relocate not to their parents' home-places, or to the major metropolitan centres of Turkey, are directly linked to their desire to find what for them is a more fulfilling and autonomous lifestyle, free from prior ties and constraints, and thereby achieve self-development. We are aware of cases of tension and disillusionment within the overall phenomenon of second-generation 'return' to Turkey, but these are more common in other return destinations, as we have highlighted in other research (King & Kılınç 2014, 2016). Furthermore, even in cases of disappointment, the second generation are mostly limited in their mobility options, as the majority of the Antalya participants hold Turkish passports and, by residing in Turkey long-term, they have reduced rights to 're-return' to Germany or move elsewhere in the EU. Hence they have chosen the 'best option' available in Turkey – which they see as Antalya.

The constellation of theoretical and methodological concepts that we brought to bear on our research material comprised memory, including the sub-concept of memory entrepreneurship; nostalgia – not just as retrospective and backward-looking but also as prospective, towards the future; home and belonging – always contextual, relational and in flux; and the specificity of place and space encapsulated in the framework of translocal geography, and the shifting positionalities of our participants in the various translocal spaces that they occupied at various stages of their lives. Our deployment of memory entrepreneurship highlights the second generation's individualised agency in evaluating past, present and future circumstances and in reconciling memories of their earlier lives with the actualities of their new lives in Antalya in a context of self-realisation. Or, put differently, how the 'outer, social' self, and the 'inner' self, help to shape each other (Maton, 2008: 50).

The key pathway through this interlocking conceptual landscape was to focus on the way in which our research participants were able to fashion a new 'home' in Antalya. In the words of Hage (1997: 105), they were able to mobilise their nostalgic feelings, building on memories of previous visits, to 'guide home-building in the present' and to achieve the 'kind of homely feeling' that they sought. Hage's argument is important in that nostalgia should not be understood 'only in the past as "it was"' (Graham & Khosravi, 1997: 128), which entails a refusal to engage with the present, but rather a 'bittersweet feeling' – the creative memory-work of past experiences imagined from the standpoint of the present and projected into the future (Hage, 1997: 104–105).

Our study has been about a narrowly defined section of the migrant and diasporic population – second-generation 'returnees' – and about a single place – Antalya as the favoured tourist area where the participants' return ambitions can be successfully realised. Whilst we are confident in justifying our specific focus in terms of the light our participants have shed on important questions of home, belonging and identity, none of which are to be seen as fixed and static, we conclude by wondering if there are many other 'Antalyas' around the world, offering an 'escape to paradise' for those whose complex migration heritage and troubled personal lives need a space of rest and salvation.

References

Anthias, F. (2008). Thinking through the lens of translocational positionality: an inter-sectionality frame for understanding identity and belonging. *Translocations*, 4(1), 5–20.

Anthias, F. (2009). Translocational belonging, identity and generation: questions and problems in migration and ethnic studies. *Finnish Journal of Ethnicity and Migration*, 4(1), 6–15.

Boym, S. (2011). *The future of nostalgia*. New York: Basic Books.

Brickell, K. & Datta, K. eds. (2011). *Translocal geographies: space, place and community*. Farnham: Ashgate.

Christou, A. (2006). *Narratives of place, culture and identity: second-generation Greek-Americans return 'home'*. Amsterdam: Amsterdam University Press.

Christou, A. & King, R. (2014). *Counter-diaspora: the Greek second generation returns 'home'*. Cambridge, MA: Harvard University Press.

Frederick, H.H., O'Connor, A. & Kuratko, D.F. (2015). *Entrepreneurship: theory/ processes/practice*. Victoria: Cengage Learning.

Gmelch, G. (1992). *Double passage: the lives of Caribbean migrants abroad and back home*. Ann Arbor, MI: University of Michigan Press.

Graham, M. & Khosravi, S. (1997). Home is where you make it: repatriation and diaspora culture among Iranians in Sweden. *Journal of Refugee Studies*, 10(2), 115–133.

Hage, G. (1997). At home in the entails of the west: multiculturalism, 'ethnic food' and migrant home-building. In: H. Grace, G. Hage, L. Johnson, J. Langsworth & M. Symonds, eds., *Home/world: space, community and marginality in Sydney's West*. Annandale, NSW: Pluto Press, pp. 99–153.

Jain, S. (2011). The rights of 'return': ethnic identities in the workplace among second-generation Indian-American professionals in the parental homeland. *Journal of Ethnic and Migration Studies*, 37(9), 1313–1330.

Kaya, A. (2007). German-Turkish transnational space: a separate space of their own. *German Studies Review*, 30(3), 483–502.

Kılınç, N. (2014). *Second-generation Turkish-Germans 'return' home: gendered narratives of (re-)negotiated identities*. Sussex Centre for Migration Research, Working Paper 78, Brighton: University of Sussex.

King, R. & Christou, A. (2010). Cultural geographies of counter-diasporic migration: perspectives from the study of second-generation 'returnees' to Greece. *Population, Space and Place*, 15(2), 113–129.

King, R. & Christou, A. (2011). Of counter-diaspora and reverse transnationalism: 'return' mobilities to and from the ancestral homeland. *Mobilities*, 6(4), 451–466.

King, R. & Christou, A. (2014). Second-generation "return" to Greece: new dynamics of transnationalism and integration. *International Migration*, 52(6), 85–99.

King, R. & Kılınç, N. (2014). Routes to roots: second-generation Turks from Germany 'return' to Turkey. *Nordic Journal of Migration Research*, 4(3), 126–133.

King, R. & Kılınç, N. (2016). The counter-diasporic migration of Turkish-Germans to Turkey: gendered narratives of home and belonging. In: R. Nadler, Z. Kovacs, B. Glorius & T. Lang, eds., *Return migration and regional development in Europe*. Basingstoke: Palgrave Macmillan, pp. 167–192.

Levitt, P. (2009). Roots and routes: understanding the lives of the second generation transnationally. *Journal of Ethnic and Migration Studies*, 35(7), 1225–1242.

Mandel, R. (1995). Second-generation non-citizens: children of the Turkish migrant diaspora in Germany. In: S. Stephens, ed., *Children and the politics of culture*. Princeton, NJ: Princeton University Press, pp. 265–281.

Maton, K. (2008). Habitus. In: M. Grenfell, ed., *Pierre Bourdieu: key concepts*. London: Acumen, pp. 49–65.

Olick, J.K. & Robbins, J. (1998). Social memory studies: from 'collective memory' to the historical sociology of mnemonic practices. *Annual Review of Sociology*, 24, 105–140.

Phillips, J. & Potter, R.B. (2009). Quality of life issues and second-generation return migration: the case of 'Bajan-Brit' returnees. *Population, Space and Place*, 15(3), 239–252.

Potter, R.B. (2005). 'Young, gifted and back': second-generation transnational return migration to the Caribbean. *Progress in Development Studies*, 5(3), 213–236.

Potter, R.B. & Phillips, J. (2008). 'The past is still right here in the present': second-generation Bajan-Brit transnational migrants' views on issues relating to race, colour and class. *Society and Space*, 26(1), 123–145.

Rapport, N. & Dawson A., eds. (1998). *Migrants of identity: perceptions of home in a world of movement.* Oxford: Berg.

Rittersberger-Tiliç, Çelik, K. & Özen, Y. (2013). Return to Turkey. In: B. Tatjanan & A. Kreienbrink, eds., *Rückkehr und Reintegration: Typen und Strategien an den Beispielen Türkei, Georgien und Russische Föderation.* Bundesamt für Migrationsforschung. Beiträge zu Migration und Integration 4, Nürnberg, pp. 83–167.

Rubenstein, R. (2001). *Home matters: longing and belonging, nostalgia and mourning in women's fiction.* Berlin: Springer.

Rykwert, J. (1991). House and home. *Social Research,* 58(1), 51–62.

Sardinha, J. (2011). 'Returning' second-generation Portuguese-Canadians and Portuguese-French: motivations and senses of belonging. *Journal of Mediterranean Studies,* 20(2), 231–254.

Skrzeszewski, S. (2006). *The knowledge entrepreneur.* Lanham, MD: Scarecrow Press.

Teerling, J. (2014). *The 'return' of British-born Cypriots to Cyprus: a narrative ethnography.* Brighton: Sussex Academic Press.

Tsuda, T. (2003). *Strangers in the ethnic homeland: Japanese Brazilian return migration in transnational perspective.* New York: Columbia University Press.

Vertovec, S. (1999). Conceiving and researching transnationalism. *Ethnic and Racial Studies,* 22(2), 447–462.

Wessendorf, S. (2007). 'Roots migrants': transnationalism and 'return' among second-generation Italians in Switzerland. *Journal of Ethnic and Migration Studies,* 35(7), 1083–1102.

13 Conclusion

Sabine Marschall

This book has covered a wide range of mobility categories from voluntary, highly educated transnationals or 'elite' migrants to economic migrants and the forcibly displaced. It explored a large diversity of geographical contexts, from Greek diasporic communities in Brazil to German-Turkish returnees; multinational skilled migrants in Australia; Asian Indian immigrants in the United States; the diaspora of the formerly Portuguese enclave of Macau; Jewish American immigrants from Eastern Europe; a Jewish South African of Lithuanian extraction now living in the United Kingdom; British-Bangladeshi migrants; Armenian exiles in the United States; Turkish and Sikh immigrants in Australia; and American WWII veterans settled in France. The contributors of this book have balanced ethnographic vignettes of contemporary migrant societies with archival research providing historical accounts that reach back more than a century. They have probed the core concern of this volume – the intersection of memory, migration and travel – from multiple disciplinary angles and a myriad of conceptual approaches. Many conclusions might be drawn from the rich findings of their case studies, of which the following will present but a few.

While transnationalism remains an important theoretical frame for the case studies in this book, Kılınç and King's point made in Chapter 12, that more attention should be paid to 'translocality', the grounded and locally rooted experiences of people at both ends of the migratory system, implicitly defines this collection as a whole. The stories and verbatim testimony of memories presented in this book complement the grand narratives of nations and diaspora with micro-histories of large and small migrant communities, families and individuals whose multifarious experiences render more complex and sometimes contradict broad categories and theories developed in the literature. Recognizing this diversity and context-bound specificity contributes to nuancing our understanding of established concepts in the fields of travel and tourism, migration and diaspora studies.

Migration and forcible displacement, among the most topical global issues of the present moment, are not only dynamics with far-reaching political and socio-economic consequences, but also cultural processes, in which personal and collective memories play an important role (Baldassar, 1998). As mentioned in the Introduction, many researchers in the field of migration and diaspora studies, anthropology, geography, history and other disciplines have shown how memories of home and ancestral homelands are embedded and embodied in migrant culture and home-making practices, in food-ways, festivals, rituals, commemorations, music, material culture and much more. The chapters of this volume add valuable examples and insights to this scholarship, but their unique contribution lies in highlighting the role that travel and tourism play in enabling such memories and memory-based identity practices to unfold.

Memory, body and place

In the current age of globalization, static and bounded conceptualizations of place have been amended by an emphasis on the fluidity and dynamically changing character of locales as they intersect with the 'outside', the wider region or global sphere (Gustafson, 2001). Places, notably the home(land) of diasporic communities, are constructed and produced – not only materially and discursively, but also through memory, imagination and multisensory personal interaction, as the chapters in this volume illustrate. For first-generation migrants and exiles, the homeland and places associated with home are usually the most significant touchstones of memory and identity. Whether subsequent generations have grown up with a fierce sense of identification or detachment and alienation, the place of family origin remains a point of reference, a link with the family's geographical and cultural origins.

It is precisely the absence from home or the homeland and the inability to physically experience significant places and social relations there that shape migrants' emotional subjectivities and engender practices of remembrance. The ethnographic material presented in many of the chapters describes in detail and through personal testimony how memories attached to home and homeland culture – embedded in distinct places, social relations and multisensory intangible elements – are carried to new geographical contexts and social settings by migrants and refugees. This testimony adds to recent scholarly interest in the embodiment and emplacement of memory (e.g. Donohoe, 2014), the fact that every narrative about the past is located somewhere, and that memories based on personal experience are always embodied – an important distinction between first-generation memory and the postmemory of descendants.

Memories of home and cultural identity are crystallized, preserved and periodically activated through social and cultural performances, personal habits and idiosyncratic invented practices that allow migrants to 'feel' at home, imaginatively 'revisit' their remembered homeland and re-immerse themselves in its culture. The elaborate staging and communal celebration of cultural festivals, as described by Kostas in Chapter 4, or extended family weddings (Brettell in Chapter 3) as condensed assemblages of tangible and intangible elements – music, dance, food, dress, rituals, smells and material objects – evoke, preserve and transfer memories of home. The preparation and eating of home food; the wearing of special clothes; even the most ordinary routine home-making practices of migrants (Roberts in Chapter 2) engender physical, emotional and cognitive processes that can conjure up a deep sense of home and belonging.

Homeland as resource

What is most important about the wedding ceremonies of Asian Indians in Texas, argues Brettell in Chapter 3, is their bi-nationality, the fact that they are celebrated both in the host and home country. It is through the travelling of people and objects from one country to the other that identity, social status and belonging to both places are affirmed – for those who can afford it. A piece of home is always transported across when wedding guests and authentic material objects arrive from India and elsewhere in the diaspora, and home attachment is renewed when the wedding party travels to India to re-stage the celebration in accordance with the ritual requirements and social practices rooted in genuine home locations.

Similarly, for those who have the means, the home-making practices of skilled migrants in Australia, as Roberts illustrates, are enhanced by and to some extent dependent on occasional travel to the home country, where memories are refreshed and resources such as precious food items, clothes and home decorations are replenished. With the rise of mass tourism during the second half of the 20th century and particularly the advent of low-budget travel due to more recent technological and operational changes in the tourism industry, temporary return journeys home have become affordable and common even among economic migrants and relatively poor communities. Bangladeshi migrants in Britain (Miah and King in Chapter 11) embark on regular homeland visits to maintain kinship ties, attend to property matters and demonstrate their success abroad, but also to exchange gifts and stock up on supplies of cherished goods from home. First-generation Turkish migrants in Germany (Kılınç and King in Chapter 13) spent every annual vacation back in Turkey, visiting family in the home village and relaxing at the beach in Antalya. Childhood memories of these holidays in Turkey become part of the imaginary of the homeland for the second generation, some of whom in fact return-migrate to Turkey. They choose to settle not in their parental home village, but in Antalya, the fondly remembered place of touristic leisure and pleasure, which now provides them with employment and a source of livelihood precisely through tourism.

Hence, for the first generation, the homeland is an important place of emotional and material resources, which they can tap into through return visits of varying lengths and frequency. Migrant return travel is a font of personal emotional well-being; a cherished opportunity for immersion in valued social relations and cultural practices; a treat(ment) for nourishing the soul and reinforcing identity and belonging. In more pragmatic terms, visits to the old country are an opportunity to attend to expedient concerns, practical matters and material needs, such as procuring supplies for comfort and survival in the host-country context. Ironically, one may suspect that the more such products and memory props are available for consumption in the host-country setting, the more occasion for indulgence in remembrance and longing for home – which in turn may result in more desire for return travel. For the host-land-born second generation of migrants and even the 1.5 generation, those brought to the host country as children, the homeland visit fulfils other needs and carries different resonances.

Descendant 'return'

During the 19th and early 20th centuries, people who migrated in search of greener pastures rarely had the opportunity and means to revisit their old country. For those forcibly displaced, as the Armenians in Bertram's chapter (10), migration was definitely a one-way journey with no return. For many Jewish immigrants and refugees, as in the case of Mazel's parents (Chapter 7) and some cases featured in Czendze and Francisco's chapter (8), the notion of return was too painful to consider. However, the children born in the host country grow up and develop their own relationship with and perhaps curiosity about the place of parental origin. Being generally more mobile than the previous generation, the desire to travel there – with or without older members of the family – becomes part of the process of negotiating identity and belonging. Without knowing it, they have been prepared for this trip over the course of their lifetime – through their parents' memory work and exposure to collective memories and cultural practices within the community.

In the context of migration, memory, customs and home culture develop in peculiar ways: on the one hand, the circumstances and resources within the host environment force migrants to make strategic changes and creative adaptations, which sometimes lead to new interpretations of old memories and the emergence of innovative cultural practices and unique traditions. On the other hand, selectively remembered customs and collective memories tend to freeze, stagnate or mythologize in diaspora through lack of contact and opportunities of exchange with the homeland, itself constantly dynamic and culturally evolving. Ultimately, a widening gap can occur between the national cultural memory fostered within the home country and the transcultural memory born and bred in the diaspora.

This gap becomes evident when migrants and especially their descendants embark on homeland visits, where comparisons are drawn, differences observed and reflections induced. For first-generation migrants, the contrast between life experience in the host country and the familiarity of home evokes and sharpens memory, as Miah and King show for the British-based Bangladeshis (Chapter 11). For later generations, the first-time visit of the ancestral homeland permits a view of the diasporic community from the outside, or rather from the true centre, where the peculiar insularity of its cultural identity may be noted and myths about the home exposed. Much has been written about how such experiences affect the descendant travellers' personal sense of identity and belonging, but far less attention has been paid to how memories of these journeys are disseminated upon return and how the impressions and insights gained in the homeland are infused back into the diasporic cultural space.

Kostas' chapter (4) is a particularly good illustration of how the journey to Greece leads descendants of Greek migrants in Brasilia to re-discover the *panigiri* festival, a cornerstone of immigrant identity in the 'authentic' host-country context. The personal experience of the homeland's 'way of life' and its cultural expressions provides the second generation with a new understanding of Greek culture, affirming identity and instilling a commitment towards preserving customs, but also inspiring them to initiate change. Their newly created version of the *panigiri* re-interprets the festival as a cultural rather than religious event, hence attracting the younger immigrant generation. Opening up this previously exclusive expression of Greek cultural memory and diasporic identity to the affiliated Brazilian host population and even tourists moreover promotes the transformation of cultural into transcultural memory. The second generation's recognition of the commodification value of the community's most iconic cultural event is not least due to their discovery – on a touristic trip to Greece – that the *panigiri* is also a tourist attraction in the homeland.

For exilic descendants of the Armenian genocide, the visit of the lost ancestral homeland – the lived, visceral experience of the physical place and bodily interaction with the social, material and immaterial aspects of an environment that has been brought alive innumerable times through the memories of parents and the community – is perceived as a pilgrimage. Memories of these profoundly meaningful journeys are shared upon return and directly inspire others to travel. As Bertram shows in Chapter 10, the encounter of familiar food in these lands evokes memories and stirs deep emotions (more about that below), inspiring one group of descendants to compile and publish a cookbook. This book – targeted at the Armenian diaspora and interested sections of the wider public – is far more than a collection of recipes. It is about recording and sharing memories; preserving culinary heritage; promoting food and foodways as integral dimensions of cultural identity in diaspora – and not least, reclaiming identity.

One of the most significant changes in the development of migration and diaspora in the past few decades is that in the current age of globalization, transnationalism and high mobility, migrants no longer live with the same extent of isolation from the homeland that characterized earlier generations. Cultural gaps between homeland customs and interpretations developed in diaspora result more likely from new influences in the host-country context than lack of contact with the homeland. Partaking in family events, rituals and festivals with transnational dimensions and involving bi-directional travel between home and host-land, as exemplified by Brettell's case study (Chapter 3), provides not only first-generation migrants but also descendants embedded in the host-country culture with constant opportunities for comparison and synchronization.

In short, 'return' travel to the homeland, travel to diasporic communities elsewhere in the world and international touristic journeys more generally help descendants realize that the cultural memory and memory culture they have grown up with in the diaspora are multidimensional and multi-sited, dispersed along multiple routes and not exclusively tied to one geographic locality or nation state (Erll, 2011b).

Migrant associations

For migrants and exiles, the family is usually the primary source of support and site of upholding and transferring cultural beliefs, values and customs. Beyond the family and immediate community, several chapters in this book (notably Chapters 3, 4, 8 and 9) affirm the importance of migrant organizations and associations in connecting migrants with their old country, safeguarding homeland memory and tying together first and later generations in different historical and geographic contexts. Such associations play a practical, supportive role by assisting new immigrants with various administrative challenges and socio-economic needs, while symbolically linking them with home through community events and activities that promote socializing, reminiscing and maintaining cultural identity. The associations are also vehicles for drawing descendants into the immigrant community fold and entrench their absorption of traditions, customs and cultural identification patterns. In fact, as Pereira illustrates for the Macanese diaspora in Chapter 9, the associations – through their activities and membership admission criteria – contribute crucially to defining cultural identity ('Macaneseness').

Czendze and Francisco's chapter (8) on Jewish immigrants in the United States demonstrates how the interplay between the work of the associations and the return travel of immigrants influences the mental construction of home and even shifts notions of the true diasporic homeland. Transatlantic tourism to the old country in Eastern Europe entails documentation and verification of internalized images and strengthening of emotional ties. Upon returning to the States, the associations serve as an effective platform for the dissemination of travel narratives, photographs and films made by homeland visitors, increasing nostalgic attachment and myths about home and authentic Jewish life. Where travellers discover poverty, destruction and neglect or experience hostile encounters with the local population, disaffection and alienation seep in. Sharing their remembered impressions from these journeys sparks new impulses on the diasporic community's imaginary of home, even inducing stronger host-land attachment and confidence in identifying as Americans, while simultaneously intensifying their commitment to relief work and financial support.

Czendze and Francisco, Pereira, and Brettell demonstrate explicitly or implicitly how the work of these organizations becomes increasingly symbolic and mnemonic over time, their focus shifting from expedient community support to symbolic and commemorative initiatives. As a permanent return to the homeland is either impossible, illusory or undesirable, the associations facilitate remembrance, nostalgia and mythologizing of the old home. At the community level, migrant associations replicate and complement kinship networks as the social frame for remembrance and the semi-public staging of migrant home culture. A collective memory of the home country and the potentially traumatic experience of its loss emerges through migrant association-supported commemorative ventures such as community gatherings on anniversary dates, festivals and events, or the promotion of public monument initiatives. This opens up new dimensions and dynamics of expressing identity, belonging and feelings of togetherness that can temporarily bridge divisions within the community, as Brettell shows.

Several chapters illustrate how the migrant associations' symbolic and commemorative work inspires members of the first and later generations to visit the home country. Apart from lending direct logistical support to individuals who want to embark on return visits, some of the associations themselves organize group trips to the homeland or – as in the case of the Macanese – even liaise with state authorities to stage and sponsor ambitious diasporic homecoming events. Upon returning from such homeland visits, the association once again provides a platform for the communal sharing of memories – in personal gatherings or through newsletters and other media – thereby inspiring and encouraging others.

Today, the role of migrant associations is complemented and to some extent replaced by online networks and social media technology, which allow not only for a more efficient organization of practical and symbolic support, but also the creation of virtual diasporas that can be joined from anywhere in the world. Czendze and Francisco (Chapter 8) argue that such online networks, some specifically devoted to genealogy, others to preserving and identifying local Jewish heritage, influence memory and travel behaviour for their Jewish diaspora members. Digital media and tourism facilitate both connections in the virtual world and the actual travel to real places associated with, or discursively positioned as, home.

War

How migrants, displaced people and diasporas remember their homeland and relate to the notion of return depends much on the circumstances under which they left or lost their home. Political conflict and warfare have always been primary reasons for migration and displacement, whether people are directly affected by military violence (flight, expulsion) or forced to leave a country devastated by the aftermath of conflict. Two chapters (5 and 6) have engaged explicitly with war veterans and their descendants, but in several additional chapters the legacy of the First and Second World Wars and the Holocaust form salient backdrops for the memories and travel experiences of individuals and diasporic communities. Kostas' chapter moreover mentioned the salience of the Greek Civil War (and WWII) for the development of cultural and national identity within the Greek migrants' community in Brasilia.

As mentioned earlier, the trauma of the Armenian genocide during WWI and the impossibility of return are deeply ingrained in the collective memory of the Armenian exilic community in the United States (Bertram, Chapter 10). During temporary return visits to Anatolia, emotional descendants witness the destruction of their ancestral villages and the erasure of their material and symbolic heritage. In this context, the preparation and consumption of food – one of the most ordinary aspects of everyday life – takes on a political dimension. For the community in exile, food and foodways have always been mnemonic symbols of homeland and vehicles of imaginary return passed on through the generations. Diasporic Armenians in the US consolidated food-related conventions that some may consider quite generic to the wider region inhabited by diverse peoples into the notion of 'Armenian cuisine', which physically and symbolically nurtured the community in exile. Savouring such familiar food in the homeland, the place of diasporic origin now occupied by 'the enemy', causes ambivalent feelings of belonging and renewed outrage, as the enemy's perceived appropriation of ethnic foodways is seen as another strike at expunging the unique cultural footprint of the Armenians in Anatolia.

Focusing on the same general region, Cevic and Ploner's chapter (5) explores family war memories of veterans who previously fought on opposite sides at Gallipoli during the First World War, namely Turks and Sikhs (the latter as part of the ANZAC forces). Their descendants now belong to immigrant communities in Australia, where they face their own struggles for acceptance and belonging. The recourse to family memories of the war and the heroic fight of their (great-) grandfathers are brought into focus through annual ANZAC commemorations in Australia, often resulting in further family history research and sometimes actual travel to Gallipoli or other places in Turkey. The fact that a Sikh immigrant, for instance, whose own ancestors and ethnic community members were previously excluded from – or even humiliated in – ANZAC commemorative parades, would enthusiastically embrace the memory of Gallipoli shows how memories of the past can be creatively appropriated and turned into a resource for diasporic identity projects in the present.

Given the immense volume of literature on the subject of military service in France during the Second World War, Gordon's chapter (6), too, has drawn attention to a neglected and somewhat surprising dimension that contradicts many common perceptions held about this seminal historical time and place. Focusing similarly on servicemen who fought on opposite sides, he described how the sightseeing and touristic explorations by both German and Allied officers during their time in France were later fondly remembered – perhaps with increasing lapses of time even overshadowing some of the adverse memories more predictably associated with warfare. Some veterans revisited France and a few even migrated there after the war, often motivated by romantic interests and relationships that developed or matured in the context of these touristic experiences.

Such happy memories of wartime contrast fiercely with the experiences of Jewish refugees in the United States (Chapter 8) and those of Mazel's family described in Chapter 7. Where rising antisemitism and its culmination in the Holocaust during the Second World War forced families into exile, the relationship towards the place that was once home is problematized or compromised forever. For descendants, this relationship can be re-negotiated through 'return' visits. When Mazel travelled to Lithuania, where his parents were born and his parental grandparents had lived and been killed along with most of the local Jewish community, depressing feelings of sadness and outrage unexpectedly alternated with a strange sense of familiarity.

Postmemory and beyond

This leads us to Marianne Hirsch's concept of postmemory, discussed in several chapters of this book, which theorizes how the second generation, 'the generation after', 'remembers' the trauma of their parents and grandparents. Descendants have a sense of 'owning' family memories of pain and suffering, inherited from and deeply internalized through growing up in the midst of survivors. But post-memory, according to Hirsch (2008: 104), is also a question of 'guardianship', safeguarding and protecting a traumatic personal and generational past, with which descendants have a 'living connection' and which is at risk of passing into history.

As a direct descendant, Mazel identifies himself with the 'postmemory generation' and his autobiographical account powerfully illustrates – in content and tone – how he personally absorbed the pain and loss that his family suffered through the Holocaust. He has been exposed to shared family memories and photographs all his life and his need to understand and probe deeper led him to 'interview' his parents; yet he was surprised to feel an uncanny sense of 'homecoming' when visiting the town of his father's birth for the very first time. While the memory of the Holocaust has clearly overshadowed Mazel's life, reminding us of Hirsch's (2008, 2012) argument that overwhelming inherited memories can dominate the postmemory generation to the extent that their own life story is displaced, Mazel insists that Hirsch's definition of postmemory does not completely resonate with him. His mental landscape was more complexly shaped by the intertwining of the belated or inherited memories of his family's past and his own experience of witnessing and fighting the injustices of apartheid while growing up in South Africa. The second generation may be exposed to their own traumas, which are not directly comparable to those of their parents yet shape their consciousness and nuance their perspective. In some cases, the descendants' own trauma, forever reconstructed in the process of remembering, may affirm their postmemory as 'one trauma can recall, or reactivate, the effects of another' (Hirsch, 2008: 104).

Bertram (Chapter 10) is not sure whether the descendants of the Armenian genocide victims indeed share the memory and feel the anguish of their (grand) parents *as if it were their own*. Yet she certainly emphasizes the pain that these descendants feel when hearing the genocidal stories from their own family members and the anguish they experience as 'pilgrims' to the homeland, when they personally witness the occupied family homes and destroyed collective sites of Armenian culture. The postmemory of the second generation is qualitatively and temporally distinct from survivor memory, explains Hirsch (1996), as it is not mediated through recall of personal experience, but through projection, imagination and creative investment. The physical encounter of the village, its multisensory bodily experiences and most especially the savouring of familiar foods – dinner in the homeland – conjure up memories and fuel the imagination. These food encounters, argues Bertram, transport the mind into a home-centred dream state (Bachelard's reverie), which 'protects' the traveller from being overwhelmed by negative emotions.

Hirsch (2008: 10) sees postmemory as a structure of intergenerational transfer of traumatic experience and as a consequence of traumatic recall, which (unlike posttraumatic stress disorder) occurs at a generational remove. Her definition of postmemory always remains firmly tied to trauma, although not necessarily limited to the Holocaust. By drawing on recent research in the field of epigenetic memory, Gordon in Chapter 6 opens up the question of whether the concept of postmemory could be extended to also include the happy recollections of previous generations.

To my knowledge, no empirical research has yet been presented to sustain this proposition. In fact, one might suggest that the significance and utility of the postmemory concept would, on the contrary, benefit from further narrowing and sharpening of focus. I would argue that postmemory is not experienced by all descendants who have grown up in homes overshadowed by the traumatic memories of parents and grandparents, but what matters is the societal context – the social frames of memory, in Halbwachs' terms – which contextualizes and validates these memories outside the family. The specificities of the political and historical context that resulted in the trauma and – more importantly – the wider social and political post-conflict discourses around guilt and victimhood influence the younger generation's historical consciousness and might implant a sense of critical distance in their relationship to their family's memories. This is not to say that descendants do not deeply empathize with the suffering of their parents and grandparents or recognize the multifarious ways in which the legacy of trauma has affected their lives, but rather their sense of 'ownership' of these memories.

Ultimately, the discussion around postmemory could also be enriched by investigating more specifically the role that migration, displacement, exile and diaspora, as well as travel, play in postmemory, but such research must be left to another book.

Concluding remarks and future research

In conclusion, while the chapters in this volume have provided valuable empirical evidence and analytical insights about the interplay of memory, migration and travel, they have invariably opened up multiple avenues of further research. One of the most important – in my view – is the role of technology. Whether based on historical research or on ethnography in the contemporary world, the contributors to this book have demonstrated how the material and affective ties of migrants and exiles with their original homeland have always been crucially dependent on and determined by technological factors. Transportation options influence both personal mobility and the movement of goods, while information and communication technology determines the extent of staying in touch: the level of communicative contact and exchange with the place of origin. The rapid advancement of technology is likely to result in the further blurring of mobility categories and more research is needed to explore how these developments will affect the relationship with and even the mental construction of 'home'; the emotional attachment to places of origin and the mobile person's subjectivity and sense of identity.

Greater levels of mobility and technological progress impact the emergence and sustention of transnational and transcultural memory, carried back and forth by travelling people or transported physically or electronically in various media (Erll, 2011a). Importantly, these dynamics, and most especially advancements in digital communication technology, will affect not only collective, but also personal types of memory. The chapters in this book have often emphasized the sensory dimensions and embodied nature of memory, especially in the home-oriented place-making memory practices of the first generation or the physical (re-)encounter with the material and social world of the former or ancestral home(land). Future generations deeply anchored in the world of information technology – digital social media, virtual reality and especially emerging technology such as the 'internet of things' – may find entirely new ways of sustaining, experiencing and enhancing their relationship with the remembered home. Technological advances will not only influence individual remembrance practices and societal memory culture, but may even affect memory itself, perhaps rendering it altogether less embodied and more tied to sensory experiences and stimuli generated through technology rather than through visceral bodily experiences in the real world. This still sounds futuristic at the time of writing, but then we may consider how people a few decades ago would never have imagined the ways in which the migrants, exiles and travellers described in this book use technology for negotiating their sense of identity, home and belonging.

References

Baldassar, L. (1998). The Return Visit as Pilgrimage: Secular Redemption and Cultural Renewal in the Migration Process. In E. Richards & J. Templeton (eds), *The Australian Immigrant in the Twentieth Century*. Canberra: Australian National University, pp. 127–156.

Donohoe, J. (2014). *Remembering Places: A Phenomenological Study of the Relationship between Memory and Place*. Lanham, MD: Lexington Books.

Erll, A. (2011a). Travelling Memory. *Parallax*, 17(4), 4–18.

Erll, A. (2011b). *Memory in Culture*. London and New York: Palgrave.

Gustafson, P. (2001). Meanings of Place: Everyday Experience and Theoretical Conceptualizations. *Journal of Environmental Psychology*, 21(1), 5–16.

Hirsch, M. (1996). Past Lives: Postmemories in Exile. *Poetics Today*, 17(4), 659–686.

Hirsch, M. (2008). The Generation of Postmemory. *Poetics Today*, 29(1), 103–128.

Hirsch, M. (2012). *The Generation of Postmemory: Writing and Visual Culture after the Holocaust*. New York: Columbia University Press.

Index

adoption 21, 76
adoptive 13
affect 44, 133, 173, 224, 259, 265–266
affective 41, 44, 60, 64, 192–193, 195,
   197–198, 201, 206, 208, 220, 265
alienated 99
alienation 33, 238, 257
ancestors 11, 14, 16, 22, 82, 136, 160–161,
   164, 171–172, 181, 191, 196, 205, 221,
   227, 263
ancestry 164–165, 174, 181–182
artefact 23, 45–47, 145, 237, 244
authentic 53, 75, 82, 152–153, 205, 207,
   226, 258–259, 261
authenticity 49, 202, 212
autobiographical 8, 10, 88, 98, 106, 115,
   118, 126, 147, 193, 198,
   204, 264

bond 8, 28, 157, 214, 248
border 2, 6–9, 13–14, 18, 28, 33, 41, 103,
   113, 130, 172, 216–217, 221, 227, 250

child 33, 36–38, 110, 114, 159, 163, 201
childhood 9–10, 17, 21, 34–36, 38–39, 46,
   72, 77, 84, 89, 113, 150, 178, 192–193,
   195, 197, 199, 201–203, 209, 213, 215,
   218–220, 223, 229, 232–233,
   243–245, 258
children 6, 8–9, 12, 17, 29, 31, 48–50,
   54–55, 74–75, 77, 80, 82, 91, 95, 102,
   109, 113–114, 117, 119, 123, 126,
   131–132, 142, 145, 152, 156, 159, 162,
   189, 198, 201, 207–208, 213, 215,
   221–227, 229–231, 233, 243, 246, 250,
   252, 254, 258–259
citizen 32–33, 39, 48, 71, 85, 91, 110, 112,
   161, 204–205, 235, 254
citizenship 4, 26, 33, 41–44, 62, 92, 110,
   202, 215, 243

commemoration 3, 5–6, 23, 45, 47, 49, 51,
   53, 55–57, 59, 61, 63–65, 71, 85–90,
   92–94, 98–101, 112–113, 120, 122, 127,
   154, 160–161, 167, 192, 257, 263
cultural: cultural belonging 99; cultural
   change 21, 43, 84; cultural memory 5,
   15, 18, 22, 45, 47, 53–54, 56, 59–60, 66,
   81, 88, 106, 120, 126, 232, 260
curiosity 95, 107, 164, 182, 259

descendants 2, 9, 16, 77, 80, 82, 86, 101,
   115, 124, 136, 140–141, 155, 159–161,
   167–168, 171–172, 174, 183, 191–192,
   197, 200, 203, 217–218, 221, 257,
   259–265
destination 1–2, 12, 14, 24–25, 29, 36,
   59, 68, 82, 98, 108, 137, 176, 179, 181,
   229, 252
destruction 36, 107, 116, 148, 153–154,
   156, 163, 261–262
diaspora 2–11, 13–15, 17–23, 25, 59,
   64–66, 70, 75, 82, 84, 100, 102–103,
   120, 136, 143, 145–148, 158, 162–163,
   165–167, 169–189, 191–192, 198–202,
   205–206, 208, 210–212, 214, 217–218,
   230–232, 236–237, 254, 256,
   258–262, 265
diasporic: diasporic community 1–2, 6,
   15, 19–22, 46, 49, 67, 78, 82, 87, 100,
   102, 121–122, 160, 171, 177–178, 183,
   186–188, 221, 227, 232, 256–257,
   259–262; diasporic consciousness 4–5,
   7, 14, 165; diasporic identity 4–5, 7, 19,
   47, 159, 173, 229, 260, 263; diasporic
   memory 5, 14, 17–18, 192; diasporic
   tourist 11
difference 2, 6–7, 12, 44, 79–80, 99–100,
   109, 119, 141–142, 148,
   224, 231, 259
disaster 1, 5, 8, 144

displaced people 1, 9, 13, 17, 19–22, 102, 121–122, 186–188, 232, 262
displacement 1, 3, 5–6, 8–9, 21–23, 45, 59, 64, 89, 149, 256, 262, 265

emigrant 1, 11, 19–20
emigration 171–172
emotion 3, 26, 32, 36, 40–43, 46, 62–64, 81, 125–126, 133, 137, 142–143, 147, 153, 157, 193, 195, 203, 209, 211, 260, 264
evacuation 21
evacuee 1
excursion 58, 190
exile 1–2, 6, 10–11, 17–22, 41, 102, 109, 121–122, 146, 186–188, 191–193, 197–198, 201, 203, 208–209, 211, 229, 232, 256–257, 260, 262–263, 265–266
expatriate 1, 44, 109, 114–115, 117
expellee 1
exploration 15–16, 18, 21, 36, 43, 84, 104, 110, 213

familiar 1, 10, 12–14, 22, 24, 28, 31, 34, 37–38, 40, 48, 50, 53, 72–73, 84, 94, 111, 113, 144, 152, 179, 181, 185, 189, 191–193, 206, 210, 239, 249, 260, 262, 264
familiarity 12, 179, 197–198, 200–201, 217, 259, 263
fatherland 119
footsteps 77
foreigner 74, 111, 131, 198, 244, 251
forgetting 5, 87, 89, 102, 156, 242, 250

genealogical 20, 160, 163–164
generation: descendant generation 180, 193; first generation 67, 74, 77, 80–81, 213–214, 218, 221, 224, 226–230, 235, 258, 266; later generation 2, 9, 259, 261; second generation 17, 31, 53, 67, 70, 73, 75, 77–78, 82, 84, 99, 102, 117, 144, 167, 213, 215, 218, 221, 223–224, 226–232, 234–239, 242–244, 247, 249–254, 258–260, 263–264; third generation 11, 79, 96, 117, 154, 202, 229; younger generation 9, 14, 18, 68, 73, 76, 79, 82, 89, 180, 183, 265
generational 6, 16, 89, 96, 102, 119, 213, 215, 220, 264
gift 46, 50, 213, 221, 244, 258
global 1, 4, 7, 19, 21–24, 26, 33, 37, 41–44, 46, 54, 56, 59, 62–64, 84, 124,

146, 160–161, 163, 213, 216–217, 221, 231–232, 235, 239, 256–257
globalization 7, 11, 17, 77, 159, 231, 257
guest 1–2, 19, 29, 33, 39, 49–50, 52–53, 58, 74, 201, 231, 258
guide 13, 139, 241, 248–249, 253

habitus 247, 254
heritage 3, 11, 13, 15, 20, 22–23, 39, 41, 47, 53, 56, 60–61, 63, 72–73, 75, 77, 80–81, 83–84, 91, 94, 98–100, 103, 105, 136–137, 143–145, 155, 159–160, 162–163, 167, 175, 179–180, 182–183, 185–186, 188, 191–192, 203, 215, 253, 260, 262; cultural heritage 75, 80–81, 83–84, 100, 180; family heritage 99; heritage sites 136–137; heritage tourism 13, 20, 144, 188, 192; personal heritage 13, 23
historical 5, 11, 16, 22, 42, 73, 76, 82, 87–88, 90–91, 96–97, 101–102, 109, 118, 121, 141–142, 147, 156, 161, 164, 176, 210, 212, 214, 216, 220, 254, 261, 263, 265
holiday 6, 14, 17, 21, 27, 32, 54, 60, 78, 98, 199, 214, 221–223, 225–226, 229, 234, 236, 240, 242, 244–245, 248, 251, 258
Holocaust 5, 20, 105, 117, 120, 126–127, 129, 131–133, 137, 140–144, 153–157, 160, 163–166, 168–169, 210–212, 263–264, 266
homecoming 11, 14, 16, 19–22, 28, 86, 100, 126, 133–137, 143–144, 146, 170, 172–177, 184–188, 203, 232, 262, 264
homesick tourism 21, 167
homesickness 34, 106, 179, 237
hometown 16–17, 116, 129, 147–148, 150–155, 158–161, 163, 167
homing 44, 173
hospitality 202, 221, 226, 230, 247
host 1–2, 4–9, 12–15, 19–20, 39, 58, 67–68, 71, 80, 82, 84, 87, 92, 99, 156, 172, 176, 193, 195, 197, 199–200, 202, 208–209, 214, 231–232, 235, 242, 258–261
house 21, 35, 38–39, 63, 95, 138–140, 150, 156, 169–170, 189, 192–199, 202, 204, 207–211, 215, 219, 222, 226–228, 249, 255
hybridity 4, 7, 88

identification 1, 4–6, 17, 20, 23, 32–33, 80, 87, 100, 145, 245, 257, 261 identity: collective identity 7, 40, 59–60, 70, 157–158; diasporic identity 4–5, 7, 19, 47, 159, 173, 229, 260, 263; ethnic identity 7, 81, 159–160, 163, 254; group identity 3, 5; identity formation 100; national identity 39, 70, 75–77, 81, 85, 87, 89, 91, 237, 242, 262; touristic identity 12

imaginary 10, 75, 100–101, 104, 106–109, 116, 120, 245, 261–262

imagination 5, 10, 14, 25, 28, 30, 34–35, 94, 97, 112–113, 164–165, 216, 237, 257, 264

imagined community 5, 101

immigrants 1, 5–6, 8, 15–17, 19–21, 37, 45, 47–48, 50, 52–54, 56, 58–59, 61–62, 64, 66–85, 90–93, 99–100, 110–111, 117, 147–148, 151, 153, 157–160, 167–168, 187, 212–213, 244, 256, 259, 261

internet 160–161, 163, 266

itinerary 190, 226

kin 52, 64, 213, 218–219, 231, 249

kinship 22, 42, 205, 213–214, 220, 227, 229, 232, 258, 261

legacy 11, 16, 21–22, 93, 100, 124, 136–137, 154, 179, 192, 202, 262, 265

leisure 11, 13, 15, 27, 41–42, 118, 124, 228, 240, 242, 258

longing 11–12, 19, 21, 34, 36, 43, 73, 106, 137, 146–149, 153, 159, 167, 185, 193, 196, 212, 236–237, 245, 247, 255, 258

marketing 83

meaning 1, 8, 17, 19, 22, 31, 34, 36, 39, 59, 66–67, 71, 76–77, 84, 86, 89, 99, 101, 106, 117, 137, 158, 162, 169, 173, 193, 196, 210, 226, 228–229, 236–237, 239, 245, 266

media 7, 18, 79, 85, 88, 90, 94, 97, 101–103, 119, 121, 163–164, 216, 225, 240, 242, 262, 265–266

memento 52, 118

memoir 119, 149, 189, 192–193, 195, 211

memorial 56–60, 62, 86, 88–89, 92, 94, 97, 101–102, 104, 110, 124, 137, 144, 146–148, 153–155, 160, 163–164, 166, 169

memory: ancestral memory 19; autobiographical memory 8, 118, 126, 198; childhood memory 9, 17, 39, 258; collective memory 5–6, 14–15, 20, 25, 47, 70, 87, 107–108, 119–121, 142,

147–148, 154, 158–159, 162–163, 165, 167, 254, 256, 259, 261–262; cultural memory 5, 15, 18, 22, 45, 47, 53–54, 56, 59–60, 66, 81, 88, 106, 120, 126, 232, 260; diasporic memory 5, 14, 17–18, 192; distorted memory 217; embodied memory 21, 42, 60, 75, 81, 217; emotional memory 31, 152; episodic memory 8, 106, 115; false memory 132–133, 143; forgotten memory 217; genetic memory 14; group memory 7; happy memory 105, 263; individual memory 59, 108–109, 113, 147; memory culture 260, 266; memory gaze 174; memory sites 13; personal memory 3, 8, 13, 21, 43, 52, 84, 119–120, 173, 176, 181, 185; prosthetic memory 97, 101–102; re-memory 9, 23, 134–135, 142, 145; shared memory 6, 60, 87; social memory 5, 8, 66, 81–82, 107, 254; traumatic memory 16, 136, 157, 265

migrant 1–4, 6–34, 39, 42–43, 46, 59–60, 62–66, 68–69, 71, 74, 76, 81–83, 86–92, 94–95, 99, 101–102, 104, 117–119, 121–122, 142, 170–172, 174–177, 179–181, 184, 186–188, 214–222, 224–232, 234–235, 237, 240, 242, 244, 252, 254–262, 265–266

minority 5, 85, 87–88, 90, 92, 94, 100, 171, 235, 240, 243

mnemonic 9, 16, 75, 88, 254, 261–262

mobility 2–3, 7–11, 13, 17–18, 21–29, 31–34, 36, 40–43, 61–64, 71, 84, 103, 147, 157, 173, 213–214, 218, 229–233, 237, 252, 254, 256, 260, 265

mother country 17

motivation 3, 11, 13, 25, 35, 76, 78, 99, 110, 161, 222, 255

motive 92, 136

museum 3, 83, 88, 127, 134, 136, 144–145, 160–161

myth 3, 5, 10, 22, 30, 85, 90, 94, 103, 149, 152, 166, 215, 231, 259, 261

mythical 10, 85, 87, 89, 93, 235

narrative 9–10, 16, 19, 24–25, 29–30, 34, 36, 38–40, 52, 67, 86–96, 98, 100–101, 110, 113, 122, 126–127, 134, 136, 144, 161, 164–166, 174, 176, 178, 180, 184–186, 202, 206, 219, 224, 227, 231, 234–237, 239–243, 245–247, 249, 251–257, 261

nation 1–2, 4, 18, 32–33, 58, 60, 64, 80, 88,
101, 155, 171, 202, 229, 237, 256, 260
national 3, 15–16, 18, 23–26, 28, 33,
39–40, 47, 54–56, 59–61, 70–77, 79,
81–82, 85, 87–94, 96–98, 100–103, 110,
121, 134, 143, 148, 164, 186, 192, 214,
216, 237, 239, 242, 246, 262, 266
nationality 85, 91, 171, 177, 180, 240, 258
native 42, 46, 52, 112, 114, 147–152,
192–193, 197–198, 209–210, 248
nostalgia 5, 8–10, 12, 15, 19, 34, 36, 43,
60, 73, 77, 121, 123, 146–149, 157, 164,
166, 173, 177, 184, 186, 192, 197, 200,
208, 212, 214, 221, 230, 236–239, 245,
247, 253, 255, 261
nostalgic 3, 73, 75, 84, 87, 105–106,
136–137, 148, 150, 152–153, 159, 173,
185, 195, 197, 201, 213, 219, 239,
242–243, 245, 251, 253, 261

origin 2, 4–5, 8–9, 11, 13, 16, 22, 24–25,
29, 32–33, 36, 47, 53, 56, 59–60, 66,
68, 70, 73–78, 81–83, 95, 101, 140,
148–149, 152–153, 155, 170–174, 179,
181, 183–184, 193, 214–215, 218, 221,
226, 229, 235, 240, 242, 245–247, 251,
257, 259, 262, 265
outsider 12, 30, 39, 42, 98, 250

perception 2–3, 6, 13, 74–76, 81–82, 89,
100, 102, 107, 163, 180, 183, 185, 212,
255, 263
performativity 8, 75, 210
personhood 46
photograph 8, 20, 51, 57, 96, 105, 122,
126, 134–135, 144, 151, 160–161,
189–190, 194, 203, 261, 264
pilgrim 20, 90, 109, 143, 162, 189–193,
197–200, 202–205, 207–211, 264
pilgrimage 12, 21, 23, 47, 59, 61, 88, 90,
97, 102, 136, 143, 178, 189–190, 192,
197–199, 201, 211–212, 218,
260, 266
place: place of birth 32; place of origin 2,
8, 16, 60, 70, 73–74, 78, 149, 155, 170,
172, 179, 181, 183–184, 214, 265; place
of residence 15, 237
policy 4, 32, 84, 91, 136, 140, 232

refugee 1–2, 8–10, 13, 21–22, 27, 31–33,
46, 63, 84, 89, 102, 160, 172, 192, 198,
254, 257, 259, 263
remnant 240
resettlement 1, 10, 88, 238

return: imaginary return 10, 262;
impossibility of return 262; migrant
return 3–4, 9, 12–13, 227, 258; myth
of return 215, 231; permanent return
9, 82, 230, 261; provisional return 2,
9–10; return journey 4, 9, 17, 26, 30,
258; return tourism 50; return travel
12, 16, 59, 218, 258, 261; return trip 3,
10, 69, 244; return visit 2–3, 9, 11–13,
18–19, 29, 84, 106, 217, 222, 231–232,
258, 262, 266; returnee 10, 17, 21,
66, 83–84, 232, 236, 238–242, 246,
252–254, 256
reunion 7, 11, 14, 20, 22, 160–162, 179
revisit 2, 16, 217, 257, 259
roots: roots tourism 3, 9, 11, 16, 137, 143;
search for roots 159

sacred 8, 12, 89, 102, 153
self: former self 40; Self and Other 22, 30;
self-actualization 11; sense of self 3, 30,
43, 88
senses 34, 42–44, 60–61, 202, 255
sensory 34, 36–40, 44, 47, 50,
60–61, 266
shopping 12, 23, 116, 227–228, 233
sightseeing 14, 104, 263
sojourner 1, 189, 198
souvenir 11–12, 23, 105, 118, 124
spiritual 1, 4, 35, 68, 119, 146, 192, 196,
201, 210
subjectivity 26, 30, 69, 265
survivor 9, 105, 117, 124, 127, 132–133,
154–155, 157, 161, 189, 191, 197,
201–203, 207, 264

technology 6, 48, 103, 216, 262, 265–266
testimony 67, 78, 154–155, 178, 182, 186,
256–257
tour operator 11
tourist gaze 107, 116, 119, 124
trace 10–11, 24, 89, 108, 121, 132, 161,
192, 196, 204, 208
tradition 8, 14, 45–46, 49, 52–53, 60, 63,
68, 70–72, 74–77, 80–81, 85–86, 88–90,
100, 157, 159, 167, 180, 184, 226, 237,
242, 259, 261
traditional 12, 24, 27, 29, 38, 50, 53,
55, 57, 60, 66, 68, 71–72, 75, 77–78,
97, 146, 148, 152, 157–158, 178,
226, 243
transnationalism 6–7, 17, 19–24, 26, 36,
42, 47, 62–64, 168, 231–233, 235, 237,
254–256, 260

transport 56, 69, 176, 264
trauma 5, 9–10, 17, 20, 87, 103, 105, 116, 119–120, 122, 124, 127, 129, 132, 146, 153, 164–165, 262–265
travel: travel account 98–99, 191; travel agent 168; travel experience 16, 20, 76, 262; travel narrative 261
travelogue 191

uprooting 42

victim 2, 4–5, 90, 132, 137–138, 141, 154, 160
violence 60, 92, 141, 144, 155, 187, 220

yearning 19, 186

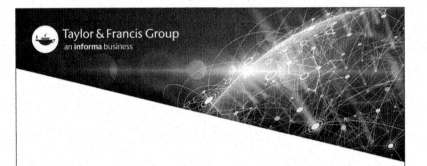